African Politics and Society

A MOSAIC IN TRANSFORMATION

Peter J. Schraeder

LOYOLA UNIVERSITY CHICAGO

BEDFORD / ST. MARTIN'S
Boston • New York

For Bedford/St. Martin's

Political Science Editor: James R. Headley
Senior Editor, Publishing Services: Douglas Bell
Production Supervisor: Cheryl Mamaril
Project Management: Stratford Publishing Services, Inc.
Text Design: Stratford Publishing Services, Inc.
Cover Illustration: Elizabeth Wolf
Composition: Stratford Publishing Services, Inc.
Printing and Binding: Haddon Craftsman, an R. R. Donnelley & Sons Company

President: Charles H. Christensen
Editorial Director: Joan E. Feinberg
Director of Editing, Design, and Production: Marcia Cohen
Manager, Publishing Services: Emily Berleth

Library of Congress Catalog Card Number: 99-62329

Manufactured in the United States of America.

5 4 3 2 1 0
f e d c b a

For information, write: Bedford/St. Martin's, 75 Arlington Street, Boston, MA 02116
(617-426-7440)

ISBN: 0-312-07603-7 (paperback)
      0-312-21947-4 (hardcover)

Published and distributed outside North America by:
MACMILLAN PRESS LTD
Houndmills, Basingstoke, Hampshire RG21 6XS and London.
Companies and representatives throughout the world.

ISBN: 0-333-80271-3

A catalog record for this book is available from the British Library.

Acknowledgments

Chapter-Opener Photo Credits *Chapter 1:* Courtesy of the South African Embassy, Washington, D.C.; *Chapter 2:* Courtesy of Northwestern University Archives; *Chapter 3:* Express Newspapers/Archive Photos; *Chapter 4:* AP Photo/Jean-Marc Bouju; *Chapter 5:* Courtesy of Keith June/produced by Marianne Scanlon; *Chapter 6:* Reuters/Corinne Dufka/Archive Photos; *Chapter 7:* Courtesy of Leonardo A. Villalón; *Chapter 8:* Courtesy of Catherine Anne Scanlon/produced by Marianne Scanlon; *Chapter 9:* Reuters/Bryan Snyder/Archive Photos; *Chapter 10:* Courtesy of Keith June/produced by Marianne Scanlon; *Chapter 11:* Courtesy of Keith June/produced by Marianne Scanlon; *Chapter 12:* Reuters/Corinne Dufka/Archive Photos; *Chapter 13:* Courtesy of the African/African-American Summit Office, Phoenix, Arizona/produced by Marianne Scanlon; *Chapter 14:* Reuters/Rick Wilking/Archive Photos.

TO CATHERINE ANNE

You Complete Me

PREFACE

FROM THE MOMENT I stepped off the plane in Mogadishu, Somalia, during the summer of 1985, I knew that my decision to make the study of African politics and society a lifelong endeavor was the right one. A gentle breeze from the Indian Ocean broke the heat of the moonlit evening and the sounds of passengers returning to their families and friends filled the night. A Somali oral poet sang beautiful, mesmerizing chants as he stepped onto the tarmac, rejoicing in his return home. The poet expressed a joy and excitement that I especially felt, as this was my first visit to a continent that was the focus of my studies. In the months that followed, I too began to feel at home, having been welcomed into the lives and families of Somali friends and colleagues. I reveled in learning Somali politics and culture, bargaining with street vendors and market women, sipping Somali spiced tea with village elders, interviewing members of the Somali government, and exploring the vast reaches of the countryside. Somalia had become a new home for me — an experience that would repeat itself often in the next fourteen years as I lived, worked, and traveled in more than half of Africa's fifty-three countries.

In each place that I have lived and worked, I have learned lessons that are reflected in this book. In Senegal, West Africa, I had the privilege of teaching for two years at Cheikh Anta Diop University, one of Africa's oldest institutions of higher learning, named after the famed Senegalese historian. A highlight of this period was one of several visits to Gorée Island — the transshipment point for thousands of slaves destined for the Americas — with Keith June, a very close African-American friend who came to Senegal to better understand the African diaspora. This visit, and our extended, nightly discussions with my Senegalese friends, most notably the family of Professor Elhadj Mbodj and his brother Bathie, personalized the destructive impact of the slave trade, as well as its creation of an equally indelible cultural link between Africa and the United States. Indeed, this experience reinforced my belief that any contemporary understanding of African politics and society by necessity had to draw upon the past.

Working in Southern Africa offered similar lessons of the importance of history. In the case of Zimbabwe, a visit to the massive stone enclosures known as Great Zimbabwe offered testament to the rise and decline of hundreds, if not thousands, of sophisticated African empires and political systems that pre-dated the arrival of the colonial powers. Great Zimbabwe's importance as a political icon for nationalist movements is clearly demonstrated by the deci-sion of Zimbabwean leaders to adopt Zimbabwe as the name of their country. In the case of South Africa, one only has to visit the former prison cell of President Nelson Mandela on Robben Island to appreciate the resilience of this African nationalist spirit and its ability to transform the colonial legacy.

The greatest lessons, however, are ultimately taught by people and not places. My interviews with members of Botswana's legislature offered com-pelling views on the future of democratic consolidation, derived from their participation in Africa's longest-running democracy. Research meetings with members of the Council for the Development of Social Science Research in Africa (CODESRIA), the largest pan-African research institute located in Dakar, Senegal, introduced me to the exciting research projects and networks that are being advanced throughout the African continent. Evenings of discus-sions with Burkinabé, who regularly went to the cinema in Ouagadougou, Burkina Faso — the site of the world-renowned, biannual Pan-African Film Festival (FESPACO) — taught me the nuances of the politics of African cin-ema. Even the art of travel itself has offered impressive opportunities to learn. While traveling from Dar es Salaam, Tanzania, to Lusaka, Zambia, on the Tanzanian-Zambian (TANZAM) railroad, for example, an invitation to share food with Zambian railroad workers returning home for vacation turned into a fascinating all-night discussion about the prospects of regional integration. The stories and lives of these and other African citizens serve as the corner-stone of my understanding of continuity and change in African politics and society. It is through their lives and works that I seek to introduce the reader to the fascinating worlds of the African continent.

About This Volume

This book represents the first comprehensive, solely authored textbook to examine continuity and change in African politics and society from the precolo-nial era to the present, with particular focus on the post–Cold War era (1989–present). Each chapter stands alone, allowing the reader to select those topics that are of the greatest interest. For example, those who do not wish to focus on theory can skip Part II ("Rival Theoretical Perspectives") and begin with any of the topics described in Parts III through VI. Each chapter emphasizes the major themes of a topic through illustrative case studies. The range of case studies includes countries from all regions and colonial traditions of the African conti-nent. Each chapter concludes with a list of readings for further exploration and research. Boxed elements highlight fundamental issues of importance.

The book is divided into six major parts. Part I is comprised of an intro-ductory chapter that sets out the major themes of the book. This chapter also introduces the reader to a wide variety of resources to carry out research on Africa, including the addresses of the most extensive Web sites devoted to African politics and society and a list of the most noteworthy African studies journals. An appendix provides a country-by-country list of 128 introductory volumes, bibliographies, and historical dictionaries for undertaking library-based research on individual African countries.

Part II explores the general evolution of two rival theoretical perspectives that have competed in their quest to explain African politics and society. The liberal tradition (Chapter 2) envisions the development of free-market democracies on the African continent similar to those found in Western democracies. The critical tradition (Chapter 3) offers important critiques of the prevailing liberal model of development and, in its most extreme form, emphasizes that true development will only occur in the aftermath of revolutionary struggle and the creation of socialist regimes throughout the continent. Each chapter concludes with a discussion of theoretical developments in the post–Cold War era.

The thematic focus of Part III is the historical context of African politics and society and its importance in a comprehensive understanding of contemporary Africa. Chapter 3 explores the rich mosaic of political and economic systems that existed during the precolonial independence era (prior to 1884). Chapter 4 outlines the political and economic impacts of the colonial era (1884–1951), including an extended discussion of the slave trade. Finally, Chapter 5 discusses the rise of African nationalism and the emergence of the contemporary independence era (1951–present). Together these three chapters provide the basis for assessing continuity and change in African politics and society from the precolonial era to the present.

Part IV focuses on the sociocultural context of contemporary trends on the African continent. This section begins (Chapter 7) with a discussion of two concepts — ethnicity and class — that have served as the basis of often competing interpretations. Although each concept is capable of explaining one piece of the African puzzle, neither alone is capable of explaining society or politics as a whole. Chapter 8 examines how three major ideologies — capitalism, socialism, and Marxism — have competed for influence in the development strategies of African leaders during the contemporary independence era. We examine whether the different ideological pathways have led to greater or lesser development performance, or if all African ideologies have performed equally well during the contemporary independence era. This section concludes (Chapter 9) with an analysis of the political themes of the African novel, a form of African literature that increasingly is recognized by social scientists as a unique means of gaining insights into African politics and society.

Part V is devoted to explaining continuity and change in governance throughout the African continent. This discussion begins (Chapter 10) with a discussion of the evolving relationships between African states and civil societies. An important theme of this chapter is that the state-society relationship serves as an important foundation of a comprehensive understanding of African politics and society. Chapter 11 explores the nature and impacts of one state actor — African militaries — through an analysis of military coups d'état and the rise and decline of military governance during the contemporary independence era. Special attention is paid to understanding the prospects for demilitarization and transitions to civilian rule. Finally, Chapter 12 explores the African continent's highly diverse experiments in democracy, ranging from the single-party regimes of the 1960s to the multiparty regimes associated with the so-called third wave of democratization at the end of the twentieth century.

The last section of the book is devoted to the foreign relations of the African continent during the contemporary independence era. Chapter 13 begins with an analysis of the various actors involved in the formulation and implementation of African foreign policies. The remainder of the chapter examines the development of the "pan-African ideal" of African political and economic cooperation, as witnessed by the efforts of the Organization of African Unity (OAU) and a variety of projects in regional economic integration. Finally, Chapter 14 explores Africa's relationships with a host of international actors, most notably the United States, France, the International Monetary Fund (IMF), and the United Nations. A special focus is placed on understanding the evolution of Great Power competition in Africa, from the ideologically based Cold War (1947–89) to the economically motivated Cold Peace of the 1990s and beyond.

Acknowledgments

Several individuals and institutions provided invaluable support during the process of writing this book. First and foremost, an intellectual debt is due Mark W. DeLancey, who continues to share his excitement for all things African with his colleagues and students at the University of South Carolina. Thanks to Mark's grant-writing acumen, I was able to take part in a linkage project in Somalia and begin my own lifelong journey in the field of African studies. Although fourteen years have passed since I last took a graduate course with Mark, he and others who know him will recognize much of his thinking in this book.

This book has also greatly benefited from the intellectual exchanges with my own students at Loyola University Chicago during the last ten years. It is through the trial and error of teaching this course to literally hundreds of undergraduate and graduate students that I have been able to hone my arguments and focus on those topics of greatest importance. During this period, I have had the privilege of working with several highly motivated graduate assistants who contributed to the completion of this book, including Brian Endless, David Jesuit, Jonathan Riggs, Bruce Taylor, and Patrick Van Inwegan. I particularly wish to thank Mara Naselli, a graduate assistant whose interest in Africa led her to contribute countless hours of her substantial research and editing skills to honing the final version of this book. Without her aid and cheerful demeanor, this book never would have been finished on time.

Colleagues too numerous to mention read varying portions of the book at different stages of development. Each offered a unique perspective that was ultimately woven into the final fabric. Patrick Boyle and Robert Mayer, two colleagues at Loyola University Chicago, provided thoughtful critiques of several chapters and the daily encouragement necessary for such a long-term project. Claude Ake (Centre for the Advancement of the Social Sciences, Port Harcourt, Nigeria), Daniel Compagnon (Université des Antilles et de la Guyane, French Guadeloupe), Guy Martin (University of Virginia), and Crawford Young (University of Wisconsin at Madison) offered valuable critiques on both the project outline and a variety of chapters in the earlier stages of this project. Claude Ake's tragic death in a plane crash in 1996 robbed the African continent of one of its greatest thinkers. Several of his ideas are memorialized in Chapter 3. I am particularly indebted to John F. Clark (Florida International University), Siba Grovogui (Johns Hopkins University), James Jude Hentz (Virginia Military Institute), Gilbert Khadiagala (SAIS, Johns Hopkins University), Assis Malaquias (St. Lawrence University), and Amy Patterson (Elmhurst College), who read the manuscript in its entirety and offered invaluable suggestions for revision. Each of these scholars will recognize their intellectual contributions to this book.

Several institutions also made generous contributions during the writing process. Loyola University Chicago provided a generous paid leave of absence and much-appreciated summer grants and research assistance. I am particularly indebted to Ron Tabata, a designer with Loyola University's Center for Instructional Design (LUCID), who went beyond the call of duty in preparing the maps and figures that constitute an integral part of this book. I am also extremely grateful to those institutions, most notably the U.S. Information Agency (USIA) and the Council for the International Exchange of Scholars (CIES), that facilitated my involvement as a Fulbright Lecturer in Dakar, Senegal, during the 1994–95 and 1995–96 academic years. It is largely due to my two-year Fulbright experience that I was able to reflect on the changes in African politics and society associated with the end of the Cold War and integrate knowledge from extensive field experience in francophone West Africa. As I have often noted to Ellen Berelson and her counterparts throughout USIA and CIES, I cherish the Fulbright program as the most innovative and effective tool of U.S. foreign policy.

I especially would like to thank the editorial and production staff at Bedford/St. Martin's. James R. Headley, political science editor, demonstrated patience, insight, and good cheer as this project wound its way to fruition. His predecessors, Don Reisman and Beth Gillett, also offered critical support at earlier stages of this project. Doug Bell, the production editor, skillfully guided my book through the production process. Linda DeMasi and the staff at

Stratford Publishing Services, as well as Jennifer Campbell, my copyeditor, expertly polished and transformed my manuscript into a book.

Last but not least, my family and friends have provided constant encouragement during the writing process. As I recognized long before I was initiated to the concept of clan politics during my initial fieldwork in Somalia, one's extended families are the key to success in any endeavor. Toward this end, I wish to thank Bill and Helen, Bill and Laura, Tom and Jorja, Jason and Tammy, Jerry, Paul, Phillip, Tricia and all other members of the extended Schraeder clan, and especially my newborn son, Maximilian Edward Schraeder. I also wish to thank my wife's family, the Scanlons, particularly Patrick and Marianne, John and Julie, Susan and Mike, Elizabeth and Scott, Margaret, Emmie, Abbie, Jack, Patrick, and Katy. As many of you will note as you read this book, Marianne's artful eye is responsible for the production of several photographs. Her artful wit was equally valuable during the writing process.

My greatest sustenance, however, remains my wife, Catherine Anne, to whom this book is dedicated. We met as a result of the Fulbright program, she leaving for Bangladesh and I for Senegal. When my Fulbright grant was renewed for a second year, Catherine Anne joined me in West Africa, and we were subsequently married on the Island of Zanzibar. Together we have witnessed and experienced many of the events recorded in this book, and she has spent innumerable nights reading and critiquing successive drafts of every chapter. As a result, this book is as much Catherine Anne's as it is mine.

I alone, however, take full responsibility for the substantive arguments put forth in these pages; readers are asked to point any criticisms squarely in my direction. Please email all comments to <pschrae@luc.edu>.

Peter J. Schraeder

CONTENTS

PART II   RIVAL THEORETICAL PERSPECTIVES

PART III   HISTORICAL CONTEXT

Chapter 5 Political and Economic Impacts of Colonialism (1884–1951)   *87*

Chapter 6 Nationalism and the Emergence of the Contemporary Independence Era (1951–Present)   *116*

PART IV   SOCIOCULTURAL ENVIRONMENT

Chapter 7 Ethnicity and Class   *137*

Chapter 8 Ideology and the Politics of Development   *168*

PART V   CONTINUITY AND CHANGE IN GOVERNANCE

Chapter 14 Africa in World Politics   *317*

ILLUSTRATIONS, TABLES, AND BOXES

List of Maps

List of Figures

List of Tables

List of Boxes

ABOUT THE AUTHOR

PETER J. SCHRAEDER received his doctorate in international studies from the University of South Carolina, after completing undergraduate work in French language and politics at the Sorbonne and international studies at Bradley University. He is currently an associate professor in the department of political science at Loyola University Chicago where he also teaches as part of the interdisciplinary black world studies and international studies programs. A specialist of African politics and international relations, Schraeder has lived, worked, or traveled in more than half of the fifty-three countries that comprise the African continent. In addition to teaching at Cheikh Anta Diop University in Senegal (1994–96) as part of the prestigious Fulbright scholar exchange program, Schraeder has held visiting appointments at Somali National University (1985), the African Studies Program at Northwestern University (1989–90), the Harare (Zimbabwe) branch of the French Institute of African Research (1996), and the Faculty of Law and Economics at the University of French Guadeloupe (1999). Schraeder's research has been published in such diverse scholarly journals as *African Affairs, The Journal of Modern African Studies, The Journal of Politics, Middle East Journal, Politique Africaine,* and *World Politics.* He is the author of *United States Foreign Policy toward Africa: Incrementalism, Crisis, and Change* (1994) and the editor of *Intervention in the 1980s: U.S. Foreign Policy in the Third World* (1988) and *Intervention into the 1990s: U.S. Foreign Policy in the Third World* (1992). Forthcoming books include *United States Intervention Abroad: The New Millennium* and *Exporting Democracy? Rhetoric versus Reality in the International Pursuit of Democratization.* Schraeder's tenure (1998–99) as president of the International Studies Association/Midwest (ISA/Midwest) is complemented by active involvement in a wide variety of professional organizations, most notably the African Studies Association (ASA) and the International Studies Association (ISA).

Understanding the African Renaissance

Nelson Mandela, first president of South Africa (1994–1999), after that country's historic transition to a multiracial, multiethnic, and multiparty democracy in 1994.

THE AFRICAN CONTINENT is in the midst of a renaissance of monumental proportions. The 1994 inauguration of Nelson Mandela as South Africa's first democratically elected president symbolized the successful efforts of thousands of African pro-democracy groups to instill democratic practices throughout the African continent. Mandela's willingness to embrace his former captors of nearly twenty-eight years to construct a new South Africa embodied the vision of a new generation of African leaders — a generation committed to creating multiracial and multiethnic societies based on an ethic of tolerance, the protection of universal human rights, and the rule of law. African policymakers, technocrats, and private entrepreneurs are also at the forefront of restructuring once-moribund African economies to unleash the African entrepreneurial spirit. As a result, once-dismal projections of Africa's inability to feed itself are being replaced by increasingly positive projections of rising food production. The **African renaissance**[1] is perhaps best captured by the flourishing of newspapers, radio and television, and literature that is accompanying the progressive decline of state-sponsored censorship. A new generation of African reporters, writers, and scholars remains firmly committed to protecting and strengthening the democratic achievements of the last decade of the twentieth century. As a result, the dawn of the new millennium constitutes an exciting period of change and opportunity for all those interested in the future evolution of the African continent and its peoples.

Approaching the Study of African Politics and Society

Several themes guide our analysis of the nature and evolution of Africa's social, economic, and political renaissance in the chapters that follow.

African Continent Is a Rich Mosaic of Diversity

First and foremost, the African continent is a rich mosaic of tremendously diverse countries and peoples (see Map 1.1). Encompassing a landmass three times larger than the continental United States, Africa is comprised of fifty-three sovereign countries that range in size from the microstate of Djibouti (approximately the size of Massachusetts) to the continental giant of Sudan (approximately the size of Western Europe). The populations of African countries are equally diverse in both size and ethnicity. Whereas the Seychelles have a population of less than 100,000 Seychellois of mixed African, South Asian, and European descent, Nigeria leads the continent with over 100 million citizens divided among nearly 250 ethnic groups. Economically, oil-rich Libya boasts a gross national product (GNP) per capita of over $5,000, whereas economically impoverished Mozambique struggles to recover from decades of civil war with a GNP per capita of less than $100. The political dimension of this African mosaic is also diverse. Proclaiming adherence to the major political ideologies of the twentieth century, African leaders have variously employed capitalism, Marxism, socialism, and Islamic revivalism as the bases

MAP 1.1 Contemporary Africa

for creating a wide variety of political regimes, including monarchies, military dictatorships, Islamic republics, and liberal democracies.

Necessity of a Continental Perspective

A second theme of this book is that a complete understanding of African politics and society requires a continental perspective inclusive of both North Africa (often referred to as **Saharan Africa**) and the four regions (East Africa, Central Africa, West Africa, and Southern Africa) typically referred to as **Sub-Saharan Africa.** Classic studies often focus exclusively on Sub-Saharan Africa due to the belief that several dimensions of North African politics and society, most notably the greater influence of Arab culture and Islam, combine to make that region unique and therefore noncomparable to neighboring regions in the south. Although specific geographical regions, countries, and even regions within countries may embody varying degrees of uniqueness, this book nonetheless seeks to examine the continental trends that transcend individual regions and therefore provide us with a comprehensive understanding of African politics and society. For example, one by necessity must focus on both Saharan and Sub-Saharan Africa in order to understand the rise and decline of the trans-Saharan trade network during the precolonial and colonial eras, as well as the subsequent impact of this trend on contemporary African politics and society. Similarly, any comprehensive understanding of the rise of African nationalism and the emergence of the contemporary independence era must necessarily begin with that region — North Africa — which witnessed the first wave of nationalism and independence during the 1950s. In short, a comprehensive understanding of African politics and society requires the bridging of the gap that historically has separated studies of Saharan and Sub-Saharan Africa.

To Understand the Present, One Must Understand the Past

A third theme of this book is that any comprehensive understanding of contemporary African politics and society must draw upon Africa's past. The evolution of African history can be divided into three broad historical periods:

1. **Precolonial Independence Era (prior to 1884)**: A rich and varied political history of the rise and fall of hundreds, if not thousands, of independent African political systems.
2. **Colonial Era (1884–1951)**: The period of direct European colonial rule in which the vast majority of previously independent African political systems were replaced by colonial states controlled by Belgium, Britain, France, Germany, Italy, Portugal, and Spain. The Berlin Conference of 1884, a gathering primarily attended by the European Great Powers that consecrated the creation of formal empires in Africa, marks the beginning of this period.
3. **Contemporary Independence Era (1951–present)**: A new era of political independence, marked by the end of colonialism and the emergence of the fifty-three countries that currently comprise the African continent. This period began symbolically with Libya's independence in 1951 and continues to the present.

The primary focus of this book is the politics and society of the contemporary independence era. However, to fully understand the antecedents of these contemporary issues, Part III, "Historical Context," is devoted to exploring the politics and economics of the precolonial independence era (Chapter 4), the political and economic impacts of colonialism (Chapter 5), and the decolonization process that led to the emergence of the contemporary independence era (Chapter 6). These historical chapters enable the reader to assess the broad historical sweep of continuity and change in African politics and society and the degree to which the past influences the present.

The **dependency-decolonization debate** over the degree to which the colonial era still influences contemporary African politics and society testifies to the significance of understanding the past. According to scholars belonging to the **dependency school of thought,** the granting of legal independence that began in the 1950s did little to alter the constraining web of economic, political, military, and cultural ties that continued to bind African countries to the former colonial powers (see Chapter 3).[2] This conceptualization of African politics — often referred to as **neocolonialism** — is especially prominent in writings about the relationship between France and its former colonies, primarily due to policies designed to maintain what French policymakers refer to as their *chasse gardée* (an exclusive hunting ground) in francophone Africa. Even in those former colonies where the European power was either too weak (e.g., Spain) or uninterested (e.g., Britain) to preserve privileged ties, the rise of the Cold War and superpower intervention ensured the gradual replacement of European neocolonial relationships with a new set of ties dominated by Moscow and Washington. According to this perspective, direct colonial rule has been replaced by a series of neocolonial relationships that perpetuates external domination of African politics and society.

Scholars of the **decolonization school of thought** argue instead that legal independence was but the first step of an evolutionary process permitting African leaders to assume greater control over their respective political and social systems.[3] According to this perspective, although external influences were extremely powerful in the immediate postindependence era, layer upon layer of this foreign control is slowly being "peeled away" with the passage of time. While carefully underscoring that individual African countries can follow different pathways, proponents of the decolonization school argue that the most common pattern of political self-realization begins with legal independence, followed by efforts to assure national sovereignty in the military, economic, and cultural realms. "In this view, each layer of colonial influence is supported by the others, and as each is removed, it uncovers and exposes the next underlying one, rendering it vulnerable, untenable, and unnecessary," explains I. William Zartman, one of the most prominent proponents of the decolonization school. "Thus, there is a natural progression to the removal of colonial influence: its speed can be varied by policy and effort, but the direction and evolution are inherent in the process and become extremely difficult to reverse."[4] Although the dependency-decolonization debate is far from being resolved, the year 2018 will mark a symbolic turning point as the contemporary independence era (1951–2018) will have then lasted as long as the colonial era (1884–1951).

Influential Impact of the International System

A fourth theme of the chapters that follow is that changes in the international system have significantly influenced African politics and society. From the middle of the fifteenth to the end of the nineteenth centuries, the international community's acceptance of slavery as a legitimate form of commerce had a devastating impact on the African continent. It has been estimated that the European and Arab slave trades together were responsible for the forced

BOX 1.1

RESEARCHING AFRICA I: AFRICA ON THE INTERNET

The following four categories of electronic addresses provide useful starting points for carrying out research related to Africa on the internet.

Places to Start (wide range of information)

African Studies WWW (U. Penn)
http://www.sas.upenn.edu/African_Studies/AS.html

Harvard Africa Studies — Useful Links
http://www.fas.harvard.edu/cafrica/

Berkeley-Stanford Joint Center for African Studies
http://www-portfolio.stanford.edu/103667

African Studies Internet Resources — Columbia
http://www.columbia.edu/cu/libraries/indiv/area/Africa/

Northwestern University
http://www.nwu.edu/african-studies/

Contemporary News Updates

African News Online
http://www.africanews.org/index.html

Electronic News on Africa (Columbia University)
http://www.columbia.edu/cu/libraries/indiv/area/Africa/ejournals.html

Washington Post — Africa Regional Page
http://www.washingtonpost.com/wp-srv/inatl/africa.htm

New York Times
http://www.nyt.com

Title VI (U.S. government-funded) African Resource Centers

Boston University
http://www.bu.edu/afr/

Central Connecticut State University
http://www.ccsu.ctstateu.edu/afstudy

Columbia University
http://www.columbia.edu/cu/libraries/indiv/area/Africa/

Howard University
http://www.howard.edu/

Indiana University — Bloomington
http://www.indiana.edu/~afrist/

Lincoln University
http://aux.lincoln.edu/departments/poli-sci/

Tuskegee University
http://www.tusk.edu/

Michigan State University
http://www.h-net.msu.edu/~africa/

Ohio State University and Ohio University
http://www.ohiou.edu/ (Ohio University) or
http://www.acs.ohio-state.edu/ (Ohio State)

Stanford University
http://www-portfolio.stanford.edu/103667

University of California — Berkeley and Stanford University
http://www-portfolio.stanford.edu/103667

University of California — Los Angeles
http://www.isop.ucla.edu/jscasc/

University of Florida — Gainesville
http://www.clas.ufl.edu/africa

University of Illinois — Champaign/Urbana
http://wsi.cso.uiuc.edu/CAS/

University of Kansas
http://www.ukans.edu/~afs/

University of Pennsylvania with Bryn Mawr, Haverford and Swarthmore
Colleges
http://www.sas.upenn.edu/African_Studies/AS.html

University of Wisconsin-Madison
http://polyglot./lss.wisc.edu/afrst/asphome.html

Yale University
http://www.yale.edu/ycpo/ycps/A-D/afamstFM.html

Non-United States–Based Resource Centers

African Studies Centre (Afrika-Studiecentrum) (Leiden, The Netherlands)
http://www.fsw.leidenuniv.nl/www/w3_asc/

Center for African Area Studies, Kyoto University (Japan)
http://www.africa.kyoto-u.ac.jp/

Center for Afrikastudier (Copenhagen, Denmark)
http://www.teol.ku.dk/cas/default.htm

Centre d'Etude d'Afrique Noire (CEAN) (Bordeaux, France)
http://www.cean.u-bordeaux.fr/

Institut für Afrika-Studien (Bayreuth, Germany)
http://endjinn.soas.ac.uk/AEGIS/bayreuth.html

International African Institute (IAI) (London, United Kingdom)
http://www.oneworld.org/iai/info.htm

Nordic Africa Institute (Uppsala, Sweden)
http://www.nai.uu.se/indexeng.html

Peacelink for Africa (Rome, Italy)
http://www.peacelink.it/afrinews.html

School of Oriental and African Studies (SOAS), University of London (London, United Kingdom)
http://endjinn.soas.ac.uk/CAS/home.html

For further reading, see Roger Pfister, *Internet for Africanists and Others Interested in Africa: An Introduction to the Internet and a Comprehensive Compilation of Relevant Addresses* (Bern: Swiss Society of African Studies; Basel: Basier Afrika Bibliographien, 1996).

removal and enslavement of more than thirty million Africans (see Chapter 5). This international norm was finally rejected during the nineteenth century, only to be replaced by the legitimization of Europe's occupation of Africa and the creation and expansion of European empires.

Three watershed events significantly influenced the international balance of power and the evolution of African politics and society during the twentieth century. First, the extended global conflict of World War II heralded the decline of Europe as the most powerful region of the world, as well as the rise of the United States and the former Soviet Union as the unparalleled superpowers of the twentieth century. Africa's direct involvement in the war began with fascist Italy's invasion and occupation of Ethiopia in 1935. The war weakened the European empires to such a degree that the first wave of decolonization began during the 1950s. Subsequent waves of decolonization ensured that, except in the case of Spain's continued control over two small coastal enclaves (Ceuta and Melilla) in Morocco, African independence from direct colonial rule was largely complete by the end of the twentieth century (see Chapter 6).

Another watershed event of the twentieth century was the outbreak of the Cold War (1947–89).[5] An important outcome of this ideological struggle was the emergence of the African continent as a battlefield for proxy wars between the United States and the former Soviet Union. During the 1960s, for example, the White House ordered a series of covert campaigns in the Democratic Republic of the Congo (Congo-Kinshasa; formerly Zaire) that not only led to the assassination of Prime Minister Patrice Lumumba (denounced in Washington as a "Castro or worse"), but also ensured the rise to power in 1965 of a pro-West military strongman, Mobutu Sese Seko.[6] The Cold War also fostered the longevity of numerous African dictators who were courted by the superpowers with lavish offers of economic and military aid in exchange for loyalty. In the case of Congo-Kinshasa, the United States provided Mobutu's military dictatorship with approximately $1.5 billion in economic and military aid during a period of more than twenty-five years. As long as Mobutu was willing to pursue Washington's anticommunist agenda throughout Africa, U.S. policymakers overlooked his regime's authoritarian character and severe violations of human rights.[7]

The third watershed event of the twentieth century was the end of the Cold War in 1989. The collapse of single-party regimes throughout Eastern Europe and the former Soviet Union powerfully influenced African pro-democracy activists and sparked a wave of democratic transitions in all regions of the African continent (see Chapter 11). Much to their dismay, authoritarian leaders could no longer successfully ally themselves ideologically with one of the superpowers in exchange for protection against opposition movements. The Soviet Union had ceased to exist, and a new Russian regime preoccupied with domestic economic restructuring had largely withdrawn from African politics. Also, the United States began to downplay anticommunist political-military relationships in favor of promoting trade and economic investment. The Clinton administration's refusal in 1997 to prevent the pro–United States Mobutu from being overthrown by a popular guerrilla movement, led by Laurent-Désiré Kabila, exemplified this new international order (see Chapter 14). Although Mobutu's downfall was primarily determined by the emergence of organized domestic opposition to his increasingly corrupt regime, the inaction of the Clinton administration would have been unthinkable prior to the end of the Cold War. Indeed, presidents from John F. Kennedy to George Bush had supported a series of military interventions designed to keep Mobutu in power and prevent the emergence of new leadership that presumably might have been more sympathetic to the foreign policy interests of the former Soviet Union and its allies.

Central Importance of the Domestic Dimension

A fifth theme of this book is the central importance of African domestic actors in any understanding of continuity and change in African politics and society. The international environment may provide the context within which decisions are made, but one must not overlook the impacts of individual African leaders, citizens, and social movements. The reader will be introduced to a variety of Africans in the following chapters: the leaders and citizens of the political systems of the precolonial independence era; the armed resistance movements of African kingdoms and ethnic groups that challenged the imposition of colonial rule; the nationalist movements that led their countries to independence beginning in the 1950s; the military officers who illegally took power in coups d'état and established military dictatorships; the civilian politicians who have led democratization movements intent upon replacing

BOX 1.2

RESEARCHING AFRICA II: AFRICAN STUDIES JOURNALS

The study of African politics and society has prompted the publication of a wide variety of academic journals and yearbooks. The following list is designed to serve as a starting point for carrying out research. Dates in parentheses mark the first year of publication.

African Studies Association Journals (with political content)

African Studies Association (United States): *African Studies Review* (1957)

Canadian Association of African Studies: *Canadian Journal of African Studies/Revue Canadienne des Études Africaines* (1967)

Nordic Association of African Studies: *Nordic Journal of African Studies* (1992)

Royal African Society and the African Studies Association of the United Kingdom: *African Affairs* (1901)

Swiss Society of African Studies: *Genève-Afrique. Journal of the Geneva Institute of Development Studies and the Swiss Society of African Studies* (1962)

Other Journals on African Politics

Africa: Journal of the International African Institute/Revue de l'Institut Africain International (1928)

Africa Quarterly (1961)

Africa Today (1954)

The African Review: A Journal of African Politics, Development and International Affairs (1971)

Afrique et Développement/Africa Development (1976)

Asian and African Studies (1965)

Indian Journal of African Studies (1988)

Issue: A Journal of Opinion (1970)

Journal of African Policy Studies (1995)

Journal of Asian and African Studies (1966)

Journal of Contemporary African Studies (1981)

The Journal of Modern African Studies (1963)

Journal of Southern African Studies (1974)

The Maghreb Review: A Bi-Monthly Journal on North African Affairs (1976)

Northeast African Studies (1979)

Review of African Political Economy (1974)

TransAfrica Forum (1982)

Ufahamu: Journal of the African Activist Association (1970)

Journals of Related Disciplines

African Archaeological Review (1983)

African Economic History (1972)

African Journal of International and Comparative Law/Revue Africaine de Droit International et Comparé (1989)
African Literature Today (1968)
African Urban Quarterly (1986)
African Urban Studies (1978)
The International Journal of African Historical Studies (1968)
Journal of African Civilization (1968)
Journal of African Economies (1992)
The Journal of African History (1960)
Journal of African Languages and Linguistics (1979)
Journal of African Law (1957)
Journal of Religion in Africa (1967)
Research in African Literatures (1970)

Leading Non-English-Language Journals

Africa. Rivista Trimestrale di Studi e Documentazione dell'Istituto Italiano per l'Africa e l'Oriente (Italian: 1946)
Afrika Spectrum (German: 1966)
Afrique Contemporaine (French: 1962)
Estudios Africanos (Spanish: 1985)
Politique Africaine (French: 1980)
Revista Internacional de Estudos Africanos (Portuguese: 1985)

Current Events Summaries

Africa Analysis (1986)
Africa Confidential (1960)
Africa Research Bulletin: Political Series (1964)

Annuals and Yearbooks

Africa Contemporary Record: Annual Survey and Documents (1970)
Africa South of the Sahara (1971)
New African Yearbook (1982)

Journals for Bibliographical Searches

The African Book Publishing Record (1975)
A Current Bibliography on African Affairs (1963)
International African Bibliography (1971)

---

authoritarian regimes with democratic forms of governance; African writers and filmmakers who have spoken out against abuses of human rights; and presidents and other national leaders who manage the foreign relations of their countries. In short, a true understanding of African politics and society must include the Africans themselves.

Balancing Afro-Pessimism and Afro-Optimism

A final theme is the necessity of seeking balance in our understanding of African politics and society. It is widely recognized, for example, that the U.S. media — the primary source of Africa-related knowledge for the vast majority of the U.S. population — provide at best an incomplete, and at worst a highly stereotypical, image of African politics and society. News editors interested in "what will sell" most often cover the sensational events, such as famines, military coups d'état, civil wars, and ethnic conflicts, that neatly fit the preconceived notions of their audiences.[8] This incomplete understanding of Africa has contributed to the rise of **Afro-pessimism**: the belief that, in the extreme, Africans are incapable of reversing what is perceived as the African continent's eventual slide toward poverty and anarchy.[9]

One need not err on the side of **Afro-optimism**, that is, the belief that all is well, to recognize the imperative of achieving a more balanced understanding of African politics and society.[10] For every famine there exists an agricultural "success story" such as Botswana, where forward-thinking leadership has made that country a net exporter of foodstuffs. For every military coup d'état there exists a transition to civilian rule, such as in Benin, where nineteen years of military dictatorship (1972–91) have been replaced by democracy (1991–present). For every civil war there exists a case of conflict resolution as in Mozambique, where a peace accord signed in 1992 ended nearly thirty years of guerrilla warfare. For every ethnic conflict there exists a well-meaning attempt to create multiethnic cooperation, such as South Africa's democratization under the leadership of Nelson Mandela. These issues and others are examined in the chapters that follow.

Key Terms

African renaissance
Saharan Africa
Sub-Saharan Africa
Precolonial Independence Era
   (prior to 1884)
Colonial Era (1884–1951)
Contemporary Independence Era
   (1951–present)

dependency-decolonization debate
dependency school of thought
neocolonialism
decolonization school of thought
Afro-pessimism
Afro-optimism

For Further Research

The following books constitute excellent starting points for researching individual African countries. Three series are represented, each of which embodies specific strengths. The *World Bibliographical Series* (WBS), published by Clio Press, offers the most extensive, up-to-date, annotated bibliographies of sources relevant to each country. Each volume also includes an introductory overview essay and an extensive index. The *African Historical Dictionaries* (AHD) series, published by Scarecrow Press, constitutes mini-encyclopedias of a country's historical figures, places, terms, and events. Each volume also includes an introductory overview essay and a comprehensive bibliography. Finally, the *Nations of the Modern World* (NMW) and *Nations of Contemporary Africa* (NCA) series, published by Westview Press, offer the best up-to-date descriptive overviews. Each volume contains separate chapters discussing history, economics, politics, international relations, and other relevant topics.

Algeria

Lawless, Richard I. (1995). *Algeria* (WBS, vol. 19).

Naylor, Phillip Chiviges, and Alf Andrew Heggoy (1994). *Historical Dictionary of Algeria* (AHD, no. 66, 2nd ed.) (1st ed., 1981, no. 28, by Heggoy).

Angola

Black, Richard (1992). *Angola* (WBS, vol. 151).

Broadhead, Susan H. (1992). *Historical Dictionary of Angola* (AHD, no. 52, 2nd ed.) (1st ed., 1980, no. 26, by Phyllis Martin).

Tvendten, Inge (1997). *Angola: Struggle for Peace and Reconstruction* (NMW).

Benin

Decalo, Samuel (1995). *Historical Dictionary of Benin* (AHD, no. 61, 3rd ed.) (2nd ed., 1987, no. 7, by Decalo; 1st ed., 1976, no. 7, by Decalo).

Botswana

Parson, Jack (1984). *Botswana: Liberal Democracy and the Labor Reserve in Southern Africa* (NCA).

Ramsay, Jeff, Barry Morton, and Fred Morton (1996). *Historical Dictionary of Botswana* (AHD, no. 70, 3rd ed.) (2nd ed., 1989, no. 44, by Morton, Andrew Murray, and Ramsay; 1st ed., 1975, no. 5, by Richard P. Stevens).

Wiseman, John A. (1992). *Botswana* (WBS, vol. 150).

Burkina Faso

Decalo, Samuel (1994). *Burkina Faso* (WBS, vol. 169).

Englebert, Pierre (1996). *Burkina Faso: Unsteady Statehood in West Africa* (NCW).

McFarland, Daniel Miles (1978). *Historical Dictionary of Upper Volta* (AHD, no. 14).

Burundi

Daniels, Morna (1992). *Burundi* (WBS, vol. 145).

Eggers, Ellen K. (1997). *Historical Dictionary of Burundi* (AHD, no. 73, 2nd ed.) (1st ed., 1976, no. 8, by Warren Weinstein).

Cameroon

DeLancey, Mark W. (1989). *Cameroon: Dependence and Independence* (NCA).

DeLancey, Mark W., and Peter J. Schraeder (1986), *Cameroon* (WBS, vol. 63).

DeLancey, Mark W., and H. Mbella Mokeba (1990). *Historical Dictionary of Cameroon* (AHD, no. 48, 2nd ed.) (1st ed., 1974, no. 1, by Victor T. LeVine).

Cape Verde

Lobban, Richard, and Marlene Lopes (1995). *Historical Dictionary of Republic of Cape Verde* (AHD, no. 62, 3rd ed.) (2nd ed., 1988, no. 42, by Lobban and Marilyn Halter; 1st ed., 1979, no. 22, by Lobban and Halter).

Lobban, Richard A., Jr. (1995). *Cape Verde: Crioulo Colony to Independent Nation* (NMW).

Shaw, Caroline S. (1991). *Cape Verde* (WBS, vol. 123).

Central African Republic

Kalck, Pierre (translated by Thomas O'Toole) (1992). *Historical Dictionary of The Central African Republic* (AHD, no. 51, 2nd ed.) (1st ed., 1980, no. 27, by Kalck).

Kalck, Pierre (1993). *Central African Republic* (WBS, no. 152).

O'Toole, Thomas (1986). *Central African Republic: The Continent's Hidden Heart* (NCW).

Chad

Azevedo, Mario J., and Emmanuel U. Nnadozie (1997). *Chad: A Nation in Search of Its Future* (NMW).

Decalo, Samuel (1987). *Historical Dictionary of Chad* (AHD, no. 13).

Joffe, George, and Valerie Day-Viaud (1995). *Chad* (WBS, vol. 177).

Comoro Islands

Newitt, M. D. D. (1984). *Comoro Islands: Struggle against Dependency in the Indian Ocean* (NCA).

Ottenheimer, Martin, and Harriet Ottenheimer (1994). *Historical Dictionary of Comoro Islands* (AHD, no. 59).

Congo-Brazzaville

Decalo, Samuel, Virginia Thompson, and Richard Adloff (1996). *Historical Dictionary of Congo* (AHD, no. 69, 3rd ed.) (2nd ed., 1984, no. 2, by Thompson and Adloff; 1st ed., 1974, no. 2, by Thompson and Adloff).

Fegley, Randall (1993). *Congo* (WBS, vol. 162).

Côte d'Ivoire

Mundt, Robert J. (1995). *Historical Dictionary of Côte d'Ivoire (The Ivory Coast)* (AHD, no. 41).

Democratic Republic Of Congo (Congo-Kinshasa)

Bobb, F. Scott (1988). *Historical Dictionary of Zaire* (AHD, no. 43).

Williams, Dawn Bastian, Robert W. Lesh, and Andrea L. Stamm (1995). *Zaire* (WBS, vol. 176).

Leslie, Winsome J. (1993). *Zaire: Continuity and Political Change in an Oppressive State* (NCA).

Djibouti

Schraeder, Peter J. (1991). *Djibouti* (WBS, vol. 118).

Egypt

Goldschmidt, Jr., Arthur (1994). *Historical Dictionary of Egypt* (AHD, no. 67, 2nd ed.) (1st ed., 1984, no. 36, by Joan Wucher King).

Makar, Ragai N. (1988). *Egypt* (WBS, vol. 86).

Equatorial Guinea

Liniger-Goumaz, Max (1988). *Historical Dictionary of Equatorial Guinea* (AHD, no. 21, 2nd ed.) (1st ed., 1979, no. 21, by Max Liniger-Goumaz).

Sundiata, I. K. (1990). *Equatorial Guinea: Colonialism, State Terror and the Search for Stability* (NCA).

Eritrea

Prouty, Chris, and Eugene Rosenfeld (1994). *Historical Dictionary of Ethiopia and Eritrea* (AHD, no. 56, 2nd ed.) (1st ed., 1981, no. 32, by Prouty and Rosenfeld).

Ethiopia

Prouty, Chris, and Eugene Rosenfeld (1994). *Historical Dictionary of Ethiopia and Eritrea* (AHD, no. 56, 2nd ed.) (1st ed., 1981, no. 32, by Prouty and Rosenfeld).

Wubneh, Mulatu (1987). *Ethiopia: Transition and Development in the Horn of Africa* (NCA).

Gabon

Barnes, James Franklin (1992). *Gabon: Beyond the Colonial Legacy* (NCA).

Gardinier, David E. (1992). *Gabon* (WBS, vol. 149).

Gardinier, David E. (1994). *Historical Dictionary of Gabon* (AHD, no. 58, 2nd ed.) (1st ed., 1981, no. 30, by Gardinier).

The Gambia

Gailey, Harry A. (1987). *Historical Dictionary of The Gambia* (AHD, no. 4, 2nd ed.) (1st ed., 1975, no. 4, by Gailey).

Gamble, David P. (1988). *The Gambia* (WBS, vol. 91).

Ghana

Myers, Robert A. (1991). *Ghana* (WBS, vol. 124).

Owusu-Ansah, David, and Daniel Miles McFarland (1995). *Historical Dictionary of Ghana* (AHD, no. 63, 2nd ed.) (1st ed., 1985, no. 39, by Daniel Miles McFarland).

Pellow, Deborah (1986). *Ghana: Coping with Uncertainty* (NCA).

Guinea

Binns, Margaret (1996). *Guinea* (WBS, vol. 191).

O'Toole, Thomas, and Ibrahima Bah-Lalya (1995). *Historical Dictionary of Guinea* (AHD, no. 16, 3rd ed.; 2nd ed., 1987, no. 16, by O'Toole; 1st ed., 1978, no. 16, by O'Toole).

Guinea-Bissau

Forest, Joshua (1992). *Guinea-Bissau: Power, Conflict and Renewal in a West African Nation* (NCA).

Galli, Rosemary (1990). *Guinea-Bissau* (WBS, vol. 121).

Lobban, Richard, and Peter Mendy (1996). *Historical Dictionary of the Republic of Guinea-Bissau* (AHD, no. 22, 3rd ed.) (2nd ed., 1988, no. 22, by Lobban and Joshua Forrest; 1st ed., 1979, no. 22, by Lobban).

Kenya

Collison, Robert L. (1996). *Kenya* (WBS, vol. 25).

Miller, Norman N. (1993). *Kenya: The Quest for Prosperity* (NCA, 2nd ed.) (1st ed., 1984, by Miller).

Ogot, Bethwell A. (1981). *Historical Dictionary of Kenya* (AHD, no. 29).

Lesotho

Bardhill, John E. (1985). *Lesotho: Dilemmas of Dependence in Southern Africa* (NCA).

Haliburton, Gordon (1977). *Historical Dictionary of Lesotho* (AHD, no. 10).

Willet, Shelagh, and David Ambrise (1996). *Lesotho* (WBS, vol. 3).

Liberia

Dunn, D. Elwood, and Svend E. Holsoe (1985). *Historical Dictionary of Liberia* (AHD, no. 38).

Dunn, D. Elwood (1995). *Liberia* (WBS, vol. 157).

Libya

Lawless, Richard I. (1987). *Libya* (WBS, vol. 79).

St. John, Ronald Bruce (1991). *Historical Dictionary of Libya* (AHD, no. 33).

Madagascar

Bradt, Hilary (1993). *Madagascar* (WBS, vol. 165).

Covell, Maureen (1995). *Historical Dictionary of Madagascar* (AHD, no. 50).

Malawi

Crosby, Cynthia A. (1993). *Historical Dictionary of Malawi* (AHD, no. 54, 2nd ed.) (1st ed., 1980, no. 25, by Cynthia A. Crosby).

Decalo, Samuel (1995). *Malawi* (WBS, vol. 8, rev. ed.).

Maldives

Reynolds, Christopher H. B. (1993). *Maldives* (WBS, vol. 158).

Mali

Imperato, Pascal James (1996). *Historical Dictionary of Mali* (AHD, no. 11, 3rd ed.) (2nd ed., 1986, no. 11, by Imperato; 1st ed., 1977, no. 11, by Imperato).

Imperato, Pascal James (1989). *Mali: A Search for Direction* (NCA).

Mauritania

Calderini, Simonetta, Delia Cortese, and James L. A. Webb, Jr. (1992). *Mauritania* (WBS, vol. 141).

Pazzanita, Anthony G. (1996). *Historical Dictionary of Mauritania* (AHD, no. 68, 2nd ed.) (1st ed., 1981, no. 31, by Alfred G. Gerteiny).

Mauritius

Bennett, Pramila Ramgulam (1992). *Mauritius* (WBS, vol. 140).

Bowman, Larry W. (1991). *Mauritius: Democracy and Development in the Indian Ocean* (NCA).

Selvon, Sydney (1991). *Historical Dictionary of Mauritius* (AHD, no. 49, 2nd ed.) (1st ed., 1982, no. 34, by Lindsay Rivière).

Morocco

Findlay, Anne M., and Allan M. Findlay (1995). *Morocco* (WBS, vol. 47, rev. ed.).

Park, Thomas K. (1996). *Historical Dictionary of Morocco* (AHD, no. 71, 2nd ed.) (1st ed., 1980, no. 24, by William Spencer).

Mozambique

Azevedo, Mario (1991). *Historical Dictionary of Mozambique* (AHD, no. 47).

Darch, Colin (1987). *Mozambique* (WBS, vol. 78).

Isaacman, Allen F. (1983). *Mozambique: From Colonialism to Revolution, 1900–1982* (NCA).

Namibia

Grotpeter, John J. (1994). *Historical Dictionary of Namibia* (AHD, no. 57).

Schoeman, Stanley, and Elna Schoeman (1997). *Namibia* (WBS, vol. 53).

Sparks, Donald L., and December Green (1992). *Namibia: The Nation After Independence* (NCA).

Niger

Charlick, Robert B. (1991). *Niger: Personal Rule and Survival in the Sahel* (NCA).

Decalo, Samuel (1997). *Historical Dictionary of Niger* (AHD, no. 20, 3rd ed.) (2nd ed., 1989, no. 20, by Decalo; 1st ed., 1979, no. 20, by Decalo).

Zamponi, Lynda F. (1994). *Niger* (WBS, vol. 164).

Nigeria

Myers, Robert A. (1989). *Nigeria* (WBS, vol. 100).

Oyewole, Anthony (1997). *Historical Dictionary of Nigeria* (AHS, no. 40, 2nd ed.) (1st ed., 1987, no. 40, by Oyewole).

Wright, Stephen (forthcoming 1999). *Nigeria: Struggle for Stability and Status* (NMW).

Rwanda

Dorsey, Learthen (1994). *Historical Dictionary of Rwanda* (AHD, no. 60).

Fegley, Randall (1993). *Rwanda* (WBS, vol. 154).

Sao Tome and Principe

Hodges, Tony (1988). *Sao Tome and Principe: From Plantation Colony to Microstate* (NCA).

Senegal

Clark, Andrew F., and Lucie Colvin Phillips (1994). *Historical Dictionary of Senegal* (AHD, no. 65, 2nd ed.) (1st ed., 1981, no. 23, by Lucie G. Colvin).

Dilley, Roy, and Jerry Eades (1994). *Senegal* (WBS, vol. 166).

Gellar, Sheldon (1995). *Senegal: An African Nation between Islam and the West* (NMW, 2nd ed.) (1st ed, 1982, by Gellar).

Seychelles

Bennett, George, with Pramila Ramgulam Bennett (1993). *Seychelles* (WBS, vol. 153).

Franda, Marcus F. (1982). *The Seychelles: Unquiet Islands* (NCA).

Sierra Leone

Binns, Margaret, and Tony Binns (1992). *Sierra Leone* (WBS, vol. 148).

Foray, Cyril Patrick (1977). *Historical Dictionary of Sierra Leone* (AHD, no. 12).

Somalia

Castagno, Margaret F. (1975). *Historical Dictionary of Somalia* (AHD, no. 6).

DeLancey, Mark W., Sheila L. Elliott, December Green, Kenneth J. Menkhaus, Mohammad Haji Moqtar, and Peter J. Schraeder (1988). *Somalia* (WBS, vol. 92).

Laitin, David D., and Said Samatar (1987). *Somalia: Nation in Search of a State* (NCA).

South Africa

Davis, Geoffrey V. (1994). *South Africa* (WBS, vol. 7, rev. ed.).

Saul, John, and Patrick Bond (1998). *South Africa: Apartheid and After* (NMW).

Saunders, Christopher (1983). *Historical Dictionary of South Africa* (AHD, no. 37).

Sudan

Daly, M. W. (1992). *Sudan* (WBS, vol. 40).

Fluehr-Lobban, Carolyn, Richard A. Lobban, Jr., and John Obert Voll (1992). *Historical Dictionary of the Sudan* (AHD, no. 53, 2nd ed.) (1st ed., 1978, no. 17, by John Voll).

Swaziland

Booth, Alan R. (1983). *Swaziland: Tradition and Change in a Southern African Kingdom* (NCA).

Grotpeter, John J. (1975). *Historical Dictionary of Swaziland* (AHD, no. 3).

Nyeko, Balam (1994). *Swaziland* (WBS, vol. 24, rev. ed.).

Tanzania

Darch, Colin (1996). *Tanzania* (WBS, vol. 54).

Ofcansky, Thomas P., and Rodger Yeager (1997). *Historical Dictionary of Tanzania* (AHD, no. 72, 2nd ed.) (1st ed., 1978, no. 15, by Laura S. Kurtz).

Yeager, Rodger (1991). *Tanzania: An African Experiment* (NCA 2nd ed.) (1st ed., 1982, by Rodger Young).

Togo

Decalo, Samuel (1996). *Historical Dictionary of Togo* (AHD, no. 9, 3rd ed.) (2nd ed., 1987, no. 9, by Decalo; 1st ed., 1976, no. 9, by Decalo).
Decalo, Samuel (1995). *Togo* (WBS, vol. 178).

Tunisia

Findlay, Allan M., Anne M. Findlay, and Richard I. Lawless (1982). *Tunisia* (WBS, vol. 33).
Perkins, Kenneth J. (1989). *Historical Dictionary of Tunisia* (AHD, no. 45).

Uganda

Collison, Robert L. (1981). *Uganda* (WBS, vol. 11).
Ofcansky, Thomas P. (1995). *Uganda: Tarnished Pearl of Africa* (NMW).
Pirouet, M. Louise (1995). *Historical Dictionary of Uganda* (AHD, no. 64).

Zambia

Bliss, Anne M., and J. A. Rigg (1984). *Zambia* (WBS, vol. 51).
Burdette, Marcia M. (1988). *Zambia: Between Two Worlds* (NCA).
Grotpeter, John J. (1979). *Historical Dictionary of Zambia* (AHD, no. 19).

Zimbabwe

Potts, Deborah (1993). *Zimbabwe* (WBS, vol. 4, rev. ed.).
Rasmussen, R. Kent, and Steven L. Rubert (1990). *Historical Dictionary of Zimbabwe* (AHD, no. 46, 2nd ed.) (1st ed., 1979, no. 18, by Rasmussen).
Sylvester, Christine McNabb (1991). *Zimbabwe: The Terrain of Contradictory Development* (NCA).

For Further Reading

Alden, Patricia, David Lloyd, and Ahmed I. Samatar, eds. *African Studies and the Undergraduate Curriculum*. Boulder: Lynne Rienner, 1994.
Aryeetey-Attoh, Samuel, ed. *Geography of Sub-Saharan Africa*. Upper Saddle River: Prentice-Hall, 1997.
Azevedo, Mario, ed. *Africana Studies: A Survey of Africa and the African Diaspora*. Durham: Carolina Academic, 1993.
Bastian, Misty L., and Jane L. Parpart, eds. *Great Ideas for Teaching about Africa*. Boulder: Lynne Rienner, 1999.
Bates, Robert H., V. Y. Mudimbe, and Jean O'Barr, eds. *Africa and the Disciplines: The Contributions of Research in Africa to the Social Sciences and Humanities*. Chicago: University of Chicago Press, 1993.
Cook, Chris, and David Killingray. *African Political Facts since 1945* (2nd ed.). New York: Facts on File, 1991.

Danaher, Kevin. *Beyond Safaris: A Guide to Building People-to-People Ties with Africa.* Trenton: Africa World, 1991.

DeLancey, Mark W., ed. *Handbook of Political Science Research on Sub-Saharan Africa: Trends from the 1960s to the 1990s.* Westport: Greenwood, 1992.

Gordon, April A., and Donald L. Gordon, eds. *Understanding Contemporary Africa* (2nd ed.). Boulder: Lynne Rienner, 1996.

Guyer, Jane I. *African Studies in the United States: A Perspective.* Atlanta: African Studies Association, 1996.

Neve, Herbert T., ed. *Homeward Journey: Readings in African Studies.* Trenton: Africa World, 1994.

Pfister, Roger. *Internet for Africanists and Others Interested in Africa: An Introduction to the Internet and a Comprehensive Compilation of Relevant Addresses.* Bern: Swiss Society of African Studies; Basel: Basier Afrika Bibliographien, 1996.

Schmidt, Nancy J. "Africana Resources for Undergraduates: A Bibliographic Essay." In Phyllis M. Martin and Patrick O'Meara, eds., *Africa* (3rd ed.). Bloomington: Indiana University Press, 1995.

Witherell, Julian W., ed. *Africana Resources and Collections: Three Decades of Development and Achievement; A Festschrift in Honor of Hans Panofsky.* Metuchen: Scarecrow, 1992.

Zell, Hans M., and Cecile Lomer, eds. *The African Studies Companion: A Resource Guide and Directory.* London: Hans Zell, 1997.

Notes

1. For a more detailed discussion of this term, see Peter Vale and Sipho Maseko, "South Africa and the African Renaissance," *International Affairs* 74, no, 2 (1998):271–88.
2. For a discussion, see Timothy M. Shaw and Catherine M. Newbury, "Dependence or Interdependence: Africa in the Global Political Economy," in Mark W. DeLancey, ed., *Aspects of International Relations in Africa* (Bloomington: Indiana University Press, 1979), pp. 39–89.
3. For example, see I. William Zartman, "Europe and Africa: Decolonization or Dependency?" *Foreign Affairs* 54 (1976):325–43.
4. *Ibid.*, pp. 326–27.
5. See Peter J. Schraeder, *United States Foreign Policy toward Africa: Incrementalism, Crisis and Change* (Cambridge: Cambridge University Press, 1994).
6. *Ibid.*, Chapter 3, esp. pp. 53–80.
7. *Ibid.*
8. For example, see Beverly G. Hawk, ed., *Africa's Media Image* (New York: Praeger, 1992). See also a special 1994 issue (vol. 22, no. 1) of *Issue: A Journal of Opinion* devoted to exploring the media's portrayal of Africa.

9. For an example of this extreme view, see Robert D. Kaplan, "The Coming Anarchy," *The Atlantic Monthly* 273, no. 2 (1994):44–76. See also Goran Hyden, "African Studies in the Mid-1990s: Between Afro-Pessimism and Americo-Skepticism," *African Studies Review* 39, no. 2 (1996):1–17.

10. For one optimistic account, see Karl Maier, *Into the House of the Ancestors: Inside the New Africa* (New York: John Wiley and Sons, 1998).

2

Study of Africa
within the Liberal Tradition

Melville J. Herskovits, first president of the African Studies Association (ASA) and founder of the Program of African Studies (PAS) at Northwestern University.

THE STUDY OF AFRICAN politics and society has been dominated by a **liberal tradition** that envisions the development of free-market democracies on the African continent similar to those found in the Western democracies of Canada, Europe, Japan, and the United States.[1] In the 1950s, liberal scholars assumed that African countries, as well as developing countries in other regions of the Third World such as Asia, Latin America, and the Middle East, would advance along the same path of political and economic development already traveled by their Western counterparts. Subsequent decades clearly demonstrated, however, that political and economic development can proceed along many different paths, each strewn with different obstacles and dead ends. The dramatic changes associated with the end of the Cold War, most notably the spread of pro-democracy movements throughout the African continent, have reinvigorated research within the liberal tradition, which continues to point to the Western democratic tradition as the model to be emulated by African leaders. This chapter highlights the general evolution of the major themes and scholarly concerns of the liberal tradition, from the 1950s to the present.

Predominance of Modernization Theory (1950s–Early 1960s)

In 1955, David E. Apter captured the sentiments of an entire generation of Africanist scholars within the liberal tradition when he underscored the "tremendous sense of excitement" associated with carrying out field research in the soon-to-be-independent African country of Ghana.[2] For Apter and his contemporaries, the African continent represented an intellectual challenge which, similar to that faced by the Western explorers of the 18th and 19th centuries, offered the possibility of making discoveries that could ensure both fame and fortune within their given academic disciplines. Unlike the earlier explorers, however, the scholars of the 1950s carried with them an intellectual blueprint for understanding the development of Africa that became known as **modernization theory**.

Building upon the disciplines of economics, psychology, sociology, and political science, modernization theory was promoted by Africanists within the liberal tradition as the key to the development of the African continent. The economic dimension of modernization theory draws upon the theories of economists such as Walt W. Rostow. In his widely cited book, *The Stages of Economic Growth: A Non-Communist Manifesto* (1960), Rostow argues that all countries evolve through the same "stages of growth" as leaders seek to transform "backward" agriculturally based societies into modern industrial economies.[3] Drawing upon the experience of the Western industrialized countries, modernization theorists argued that African countries were at the starting point of a process that would mechanize agriculture and industrialize major urban areas. According to these theorists, the growth rate of a country's gross national product (GNP) constitutes one of the best measures of the modernization process.

The social dimension of modernization theory draws upon advances within the fields of psychology and sociology, by such noted scholars as Max Weber and Talcott Parsons. Of particular concern to researchers interested in the social aspect of the modernization equation is the process by which individuals replaced their "traditional" (often pejoratively described as "primitive") ways of thinking in favor of a more "modern" outlook on life. The modernization approach assumes that ethnic divisions in African countries (which were perceived as hindrances to development) would fade away as modernizing societies became "melting pots" similar to the experience of the United States and the other Western countries. Several factors were thought to contribute to the creation of a modern society: urbanization, where individuals moved from the rural areas to the towns and cities; exposure to various forms of mass media (especially newspapers and radio); formal education at the high school and university levels; and occupational experiences, such as working in "modern" factories.[4]

The political dimension of modernization theory draws upon classic theories of democratic pluralism within the field of political science.[5] Scholars believed that the key to political development was a rapidly growing electorate both willing and able to participate in the political process. A growth in political participation was expected to foster the growth and specialization of government agencies, as African leaders responded to the legitimate demands of their respective populations. In short, the sum total of the economic, social, and political components of modernization theory is the firm belief that the newly independent African countries were on a path leading to the creation of industrialized, modern, and pluralist democracies.

One approach of modernization theory that became popular during the 1950s was **structural-functionalism**. As outlined in the landmark work, *Politics of the Developing Areas* (1960), edited by Gabriel A. Almond and James S. Coleman, the structural-functionalist approach assumes that all political systems perform similar "functions," despite the fact that these functions may be performed by different "structures." The function of "interest articulation," in which a political leader or official defines and acts upon popular interests, for example, may be performed by an *elected* Senator in the U.S. political system or by the *Ogaz*, a *hereditary* prince, in the Somali political system.[6] Although the two systems in which the leaders operate are significantly different, both the Senator and the *Ogaz* perform the same political function for their respective political systems.[7]

The structural-functionalist approach represented the desire of scholars within the liberal tradition to promote a **value-neutral** (bias-free) **scientific framework** for comparing any political system, regardless of its culture or history. As demonstrated by the Almond and Coleman volume, however, structural-functionalism and the modernization literature in general were based on several assumptions. For example, Almond and Coleman assume that ethnic attachments hinder development, and industrialization is regarded as the ideal end of a modern economy. In the political realm the assumptions of modernization theory are especially clear. Those familiar with the U.S. political system have noted that Almond and Coleman's neat division of governmental functions into three separate categories (rule-making, rule application, and rule adjudication) bears a remarkable resemblance to the U.S. Constitution's classic separation of powers between the three major branches of government (congressional, executive, and judicial).[8] Indeed, the core assumption of the structural-functionalist approach is that all African political systems will eventually evolve into stable multiparty democracies, patterned after the United States and the other Western countries.

The optimistic belief that modernization theory could serve as a blueprint for African development during the 1950s and the 1960s directly resulted from a unique convergence of several historical trends. First, the extended global conflict of World War II heralded the success and desirability of liberal democracy. Not only had the United States led the Allies in defeating Nazi Germany and Imperial Japan, occupation by the Allied forces had contributed to the nurturing of democratic forms of government in both defeated countries. Second, this optimism was reinforced by an equally firm belief within the scholarly community that technological advancements in the West would lead to the resolution of problems historically associated with industrial societies, such as poverty and unemployment. As a result, scholars began to focus on transferring their knowledge and technical expertise to the newly emerging independent countries of the developing South. Third, the dramatic pace of decolonization that began in Africa during the 1950s made the African continent a region of particular interest to U.S. scholars within a variety of disciplines, most notably political science. A fourth trend — the emergence of Cold War conflict between the United States and the former Soviet Union — added ideological urgency to the perceived necessity of promoting economic, social, and political modernization in Africa. In sharp contrast to their counterparts of the 1990s, scholars during the 1950s and the 1960s were much more willing to accept the Cold War rationales of the U.S. government and worked with its various agencies to ensure the defeat of communism on the African continent. Finally, a widely shared belief in "American exceptionalism" — the view that the United States was uniquely qualified to lead the world — led U.S. scholars to conclude that their models of development would be both relevant and easily applied to an African context.[9]

Rise of Modernization Revisionism (Late 1960s)

The first major set of critiques of the modernization approach to African politics emerged from within the liberal tradition during the late 1960s. Rather than seeking to completely discredit their predecessors within the discipline, critics sought to revise what they perceived as significant but rectifiable flaws within an otherwise sound approach. The body of scholarship produced by this generation of Africanists became known as **modernization revisionism**.[10]

The first major revisionist critique calls into question the tendency of earlier scholars to portray the modernization process as a "zero-sum" game, in which "advances" toward certain levels of modernity within an African political and social system are inevitably accompanied by an equal "decline" in that system's traditional culture. According to this logic, a 20 percent advance in modern institutions, for example, would be accompanied by a 20 percent decline in traditional institutions. Revisionist scholars argue instead that traditional institutions often adapt to, and coexist with, modern institutions. As a result, a society conceivably could assume many modern characteristics at the same time that it retained or even enhanced various aspects of its traditional culture.

In the case of northern Nigeria, C. S. Whitaker, Jr. demonstrates in *The Politics of Tradition: Continuity and Change in Northern Nigeria 1946–1966* (1970) how the creation and expansion of modern political institutions, such as the national parliament, cabinet system, and political parties, both during and after Nigeria's independence from British colonial rule, was accompanied by the strengthening of the political roles played by traditional Muslim leaders known as *emirs*.[11] Political leaders associated with the Northern Peoples' Congress (NPC), a modern postindependence political institution that might have undermined the traditional leaders, instead sustained and cultivated the power and influence of the traditional *emirs*. "Far from modern institutions having simply driven out traditional ones," explains Whitaker, "elements of the institutions of each type or origin *coalesced* to form a workable system of power and authority."[12]

A second major revisionist critique disputes the assumption of earlier scholars that traditional attitudes and institutions are inherently irrational and therefore hinder the modernization process. Modernization revisionists instead underscored the importance of building upon traditional cultures and values to promote development in the newly independent African countries. According to the modernization revisionists, disregarding the importance of such traditional characteristics as ethnic affiliations and beliefs constitutes a formula for disaster.

According to Whitaker's study of northern Nigeria, the importance of traditional values within the modernization process was clearly illustrated by the role of political parties within regional elections during the 1960s. "A principal function of any 'modern' political party operating under a system of representative government on a foundation of mass suffrage is to mobilize the mass electorate for the exercise of choice at the ballot box," explains Whitaker in a summary of the modernization imperative of creating a multiparty political system. "A cardinal aspect of this function is communication with the electorate: the formulation and articulation of issues and interests which will stimulate

BOX 2.1
AFRICAN STUDIES ASSOCIATION (ASA)

The **African Studies Association** (ASA) is the largest nonprofit organization that fosters the exchange of information and ideas among scholars, practitioners, and government officials interested in the study of Africa. The organization was officially launched at a conference held in New York City, March 22–24, 1957, that was attended by thirty-five individuals. Melville J. Herskovits, who in 1945 founded the Program of African Studies at Northwestern University — the first such program of its kind in the United States — was elected the ASA's first president, and in so doing reinforced his reputation as one of the pioneers of the American study of African politics and society (see the opening photo of this chapter). More than four decades later, the ASA counts more than 2,500 individuals among its formal membership, with more than 1,000 participants taking part in its annual meeting devoted to Africa. The association publishes a quarterly scholarly journal, *African Studies Review,* of the most recent Africana research, as well as *Issue: A Journal of Opinion,* a journal designed to debate contemporary issues.

Despite an interdisciplinary and cross-national approach to the study of Africa, the ASA has not been without controversy. The organization's first, and perhaps most significant, internal conflict occurred October 15–18, 1969, when ASA's Black Caucus staged a series of protests at the twelfth annual meeting held in Montreal, Canada. At issue in this dispute were the demands of African-American scholars of Africa to have a larger say in the governance of the organization. The meetings were disrupted when the association refused to accede to the demand that 50 percent of ASA's Board of Directors should be African-American scholars. The often heated and acerbic debates that followed, in both the plenary session and a variety of African studies journals, created a rift that has yet to be completely healed. One important result of African-American concerns over who controlled the collection and dissemination of Africana knowledge was the birth of the **African Heritage Studies Association** (AHSA), a rival African studies association targeted primarily toward the African-American scholarly community. The AHSA was launched on June 29, 1969.

Subsequent debates within the ASA have also taken on an ideological tone. Some conservative Africanists claim they have been marginalized in the field of African studies. In a spirited debate published in the eighteenth volume of *Issue: A Journal of Opinion,* L. H. Gann, a self-proclaimed conservative Africanist, critiqued what he perceived as a liberal bias in the study of Africa. One contemporary issue severely criticized by Gann and other conservative Africanists was the 1993 decision of the ASA and other regional studies associations (most notably the Latin American Studies Association) to officially oppose the National Security Education Program (NSEP): a language studies program funded through the U.S. Defense Department, in which student grantees would sign a contract agreeing to work in some capacity for a national security agency of the U.S. government after completing their study and research abroad. One attempt to counterbalance the perceived liberal bias of the ASA was the creation of the **American African Affairs Association** (AAAA), a scholarly association of conservative Africanists.

Discussion drawn from David Robinson, "The African Studies Association at Age 35," *African Studies Review* 37, no. 2 (1994):1–12; Cyprian Lamar Rowe, "Crisis in African Studies: The Birth of the African Heritage Studies Association," *Black Academy Review* 1, no. 3 (1970):3–10; and L. H. Gann, "The Struggle for African Area Studies: A View from Wisconsin — A Response," *Issue: A Journal of Opinion* 18, no. 1 (1989):51–53; as well as the responses to Gann's article in the next issue.

the attention, sympathy and support of as many of that electorate as possible."[13] However, in sharp contrast to what the modernization theorists originally had predicted, the NPC party successfully performed the "mobilization" function of the political system by appealing to such traditional values as the "religious duty to obey and protect hereditary leaders."[14] In many cases, those politicians shortsighted enough to wholeheartedly embrace modernization theory and ignore the importance of appealing to traditional values were vanquished by their competitors.

A third major revisionist critique questions the assumption that modernization constitutes a **unilinear** (one-way) process in which traditional characteristics such as ethnic affiliations ultimately would erode over time, replaced by more modern forms of affiliation (e.g., professional or community-based organizations). Revisionist scholars argue instead that ethnicity and other forms of ordering traditional societies (such as clan and caste) often are revitalized and strengthened by the modernization process. In some instances, the modernization process even fostered the creation of an ethnic self-consciousness or group identity where none before had existed. For example, at the beginning of the twentieth century, the Igbo ethnic group constituted a "classical segmented political system" in which approximately two hundred separate Igbo villages and communities shared a common language, culture, and beliefs, but lacked common governance or any sense of nationhood (see Chapter 4).[15] By the late 1960s, however, the growth of Igbo nationalism contributed to the secession of the Igbo-inhabited southeastern province of Nigeria, an act that led to a civil war (1967–70) from which the Nigerian federal government emerged victorious.

The creation of an ethnic group identity among the Igbo was especially relevant to the revisionist critique of modernization theory because the Igbos had often been characterized by foreign observers as one of the most modern of Nigeria's ethnic groups. The highly egalitarian nature of Igbo political culture, which places great emphasis on seeking status through individual achievement rather than personal connections, was seen to embody the positive elements of a modern political culture. Indeed, the Igbo appeared to constitute a textbook example of a modernizing people. Moving to the urban areas in search of higher education and economic advancement, Igbos eventually began to dominate "white collar" positions within education, journalism, business, and politics. They were also responsible for the formation of the National Council of Nigerian Citizens (NCNC), the first political party with a truly countrywide program. Unlike the more parochial, ethnically based parties, the NCNC mobilized popular support that transcended individual ethnic groups. In short, if one would have asked a modernization theorist during the 1950s which of Nigeria's ethnic groups was most likely to secede based on the "parochial" principle of ethnic identity, the Igbo ethnic group of southeastern Nigeria would not have been at the top of the list.

Despite their willingness to criticize modernization theory, the modernization revisionists simply seek to revise the shortcomings of what is still considered to be an otherwise sound approach for understanding political and socioeconomic change in Africa. In fact, both modernization theorists and their revisionist counterparts share many optimistic assumptions about the development process. Among the most important of these assumptions are the desirability of a rapidly expanding electorate willing and able to take part in the political process; the mutually reinforcing nature of rising levels of participation and the promotion of equality and stability within developing societies; a perception of protests and violence as the "exceptions" rather than the norm of politics; and the emergence of multiparty democratic political systems as the natural outcome of the modernization process.

Concern with Stability and the "Politics of Order" (Late 1960s–Early 1970s)

Several trends during the 1960s contributed to the rise of a more pessimistic genre of scholarship that for the first time called into question the optimistic assumptions held by modernization theorists and revisionists.[16] The most important of these trends was the dramatic rise in violence and instability in the newly independent nation-states of Africa. In addition to the spread of guerrilla insurgencies, secessionist movements, civil wars, and assassinations for political gain, African militaries increasingly were taking power away from civilian leaders in military coups d'état. Prior to 1963, there were only two successful military coups: the Sudan in 1956 and the Democratic Republic of the Congo (Congo-Kinshasa) in 1960. From this point forward, however, an explosion of military involvement in the policymaking process began. From 1956 to 1985, there were a total of 131 coups (60 successful and 71 unsuccessful). This violent trend was a far cry from the peaceful, democratic transfers of power expected by modernization theorists and their revisionist counterparts.

The changing demands of U.S. foreign policy in the 1960s also heavily influenced the rise of pessimism toward the modernization process in Africa.

The intensification of the Cold War during this period led the administration of John F. Kennedy and its successors to formulate counterinsurgency doctrines, designed to defeat what were perceived as communist-inspired guerrilla insurgencies in the Third World. Counterinsurgency was a key justification of the growing U.S. military involvement in Vietnam and emphasized the "containment" of communism by means which often ran counter to the optimistic ideals of modernization theory. When the normative goal of modernization theory — the creation of democratic political systems — clashed with anticommunist national security interests, U.S. leaders often supported national security efforts even when it meant creating alliances with unsavory, undemocratic leaders in Africa and other portions of the Third World.[17] In short, anticommunist, authoritarian African leaders curried U.S. favor because they helped carry out containment policies that curtailed communist expansion.

The changes in U.S. domestic politics during the 1960s also contributed to the rise of a more pessimistic view of the modernization process in Africa. In addition to being concerned with instability abroad, U.S. policymakers were troubled by growing levels of protest and violence at home. Policymakers were especially troubled by the potential for violence associated with the civil rights movement and growing protests against U.S. military involvement in the Vietnam War. As a result, slogans of "law and order" became the focal points of presidential campaigns carried out by Barry Goldwater in 1964 and Richard M. Nixon in 1968. Moreover, these slogans were reinforced — again, counter to the optimistic ideals of modernization theorists — often by violent government responses to public demonstrations, ranging from the attacks on political protestors by riot police at the 1968 Democratic convention in Chicago, Illinois, to the killings by National Guardsmen of seven antiwar protestors at Kent State University in 1970.

The net result of these three trends was a shift in the modernization literature from the optimistic belief in **political development** to a more pessimistic expectation of **political decay** (conflict and chaos) in the newly independent African countries.[18] In a landmark work that captured this shift and altered the debate within academic and political circles, Samuel P. Huntington in *Political Order in Changing Societies* (1968) argues that rather than contributing to democracy and stability, the modernization process fosters political instability within the developing world, often with dire consequences for U.S. foreign policy.[19] According to Huntington and his contemporaries, democracy is neither a natural nor a direct end result of modernization. Rather, states attempting to modernize are faced with six major **crises of development**, which, if not solved, could lead to the downfall of regimes and the spread of political decay:

- **crisis of identity:** creating a common nationalist outlook among ethnically, linguistically, and religiously diverse peoples;
- **crisis of legitimacy:** building a national consensus on the legitimate exercise of authority;

- **crisis of participation:** guiding rising public demands for inclusion in the political decision-making process;
- **crisis of penetration:** creating an effective government presence throughout the territory;
- **crisis of distribution:** balancing public demands for goods and services with the government's responsibility to provide public goods such as economic growth;
- **crisis of integration:** creating harmonious relationships among the society's many groups and interests competing for access to and control of the political decision-making process.[20]

According to Huntington and his contemporaries, the solution to these crises is **institutionalization:** the creation of strong government structures able to ensure political stability and order throughout society. "The most important political distinction among countries," explains Huntington, "concerns not their *form* of government but their *degree* of government."[21] In sharp contrast to the optimistic impulse of modernization theorists and revisionists to favor rapidly expanding levels of popular political participation, Huntington and his contemporaries argue that the process of institutionalization had to be the top priority of African leaders. According to this interpretation of African politics and society, African leaders were to dramatically limit the levels of popular political participation in the name of ensuring stability and order.

BOX 2.2

SHOULD RESEARCHERS WORK WITH THE U.S. GOVERNMENT?

A much-debated question within the field of African studies is the extent to which scholars should work with U.S. government agencies in the formulation and implementation of U.S. foreign policy toward Africa. The African Studies Center at Michigan State University addressed this question in 1990 by sending out an extensive survey questionnaire to 2,592 U.S. Africanists "with an ongoing interest in the study of Africa" (23 percent responded to the questionnaire).

The figures contained in Table 2.1 offer two important insights. First, the type of government agency involved significantly affects whether an Africanist will cooperate with the U.S. government. Africanists are overwhelmingly wary of becoming involved with military and intelligence institutions, including the Central Intelligence Agency (CIA), the Defense Intelligence Agency (DIA), and colleges and universities that fall under the umbrella of the U.S. Defense Department (e.g., The Defense University). Africanists are still wary of but increasingly likely to become associated with institutions that focus on the political or diplomatic aspects of national security, such as the Department of State and the United States Information Agency (USIA). The greatest level of acceptance is accorded to government institutions that: (1) promote scholarly research independent of direct government control (e.g., the National Science Foundation [NSF]); (2) primarily focus on the socioeconomic development of the African continent (e.g., the United States Agency for International Development [USAID]); and (3) freely and openly debate the outlines of policy with direct public input (e.g., the U.S. Congress).

TABLE 2.1

Should Researchers Work with the U.S. Government?
(percent of scholars who responded "yes" to specific institutions)*

	Conduct Sponsored Research In Africa	Conduct Sponsored Research in U.S.	Deliver Lecture or Testify	Attend Workshop or Hearing	Offer Informal Advice
CIA or DIA	8	10	27	34	31
The Defense University	12	13	38	42	38
Department of State	47	49	81	85	84
U.S. Information Agency (USIA)	50	48	75	80	79
U.S. Congress	66	69	86	88	88
U.S. AID	71	67	84	89	87
National Science Foundation (NSF)	78	75	82	86	82

* Responses were to the following statement: "If invited in the future, I would participate in the following Africa policy activities listed below."

The nature of involvement with government institutions also significantly affects whether an Africanist will cooperate with the U.S. government. Most Africanists would refuse to undertake research related to Africa that was directly sponsored by military or intelligence agencies. However, a significantly higher number of Africanists nonetheless would be willing to deliver a lecture or offer informal advice to officials working within these agencies. Indeed, Africanists across the board are more willing to engage in occasional contacts than pursue extended research relationships with all government agencies.

The willingness to lecture and offer advice is further substantiated by the strong belief of 79 percent of Africanists that they have "an obligation" to use their regional knowledge "to participate actively in the formation of U.S. policy toward Africa." The question therefore is not so much one of whether Africanists should work with the U.S. government, but with what institutions and in what capacity.

Discussion drawn from Michael Bratton, Reinhard Heinisch, and David S. Wiley, "How Africanists View U.S. Policy: Results of a Survey," *Issue: A Journal of Opinion* 19, no. 2 (1991):14–31.

The primary institutions that scholars of order focus upon as crucial to maintaining stability include African militaries, bureaucracies inherited from colonial rule, and, most important, political parties. In fact, despite the fact that he remains strongly opposed to communism, Huntington especially admired the Leninist model of creating a "vanguard" single party, such as once existed in the former Soviet Union and the other former communist countries of the Eastern bloc. "They may not provide liberty," explains Huntington, "but they do provide authority; they do create governments that govern."[22] The appeal of these single-party political systems thus lay not in their ideology (communism), but rather in their ability to set the agenda for development, to serve as vehicles for mobilizing scarce resources, and to control what are perceived as the "destabilizing" influences of growing popular political participation.

In *Creating Political Order: The Party-States of West Africa* (1966), Aristide R. Zolberg offers an early example of the political order approach within an African context.[23] As is evident from the title, Zolberg perceives the single-party system as providing the primary prerequisite — order — for the successful modernization of African societies. Although he cautions that such a political system is neither "genuinely democratic" nor able to ensure the "immediate and revolutionary change in the human condition," he nonetheless argues that strong single parties "might help relieve the heavy burdens of imitation and self-doubt with which Africans have been saddled too long and might enable them to regain confidence in their ability to rule themselves."[24] "That, ultimately," he concludes in the last sentence of the book, "is the only soil in which democracy has been known to grow."[25] As we will discuss in Chapter 12, the so-called **politics of order** was firmly embraced by the vast majority of African leaders who oversaw the creation and maintenance of single-party regimes from the 1950s to the 1980s.

Demands for Policy Relevance and Public Policy Research (Mid-1970s–1980s)

The liberal tradition of studying African politics and society experienced yet another major transformation that began in the mid-1970s and continued throughout the 1980s. During this period, scholars sought to make their research agendas more **policy relevant** in response to critiques that their "grand theories" were so abstract as to be of little use for solving the day-to-day policy problems faced by African policymakers. For example, an African prime minister trained in the United States may have wondered about the relevance of modernization theory as he attempted to resolve a national labor strike. In short, scholars within the liberal tradition were being called upon by policymakers to move beyond grand theorizing in favor of research focusing on the everyday management problems faced by African policymakers.

The response to demands for policy relevance resulted in the popularity of two broad streams of **public policy research** that draw upon the disciplines of economics and political science.[26] The first stream of research, the **political-economy approach**, is based on the assumption that politics and economics are so inextricably intertwined that previous attempts at examining each discipline in isolation offered solutions that did not apply to "real-world" conditions. An integral aspect of this approach is the adoption of **rational-choice models** from the discipline of economics. These models assume that individuals are "rational" (logical) and make their decisions based on a "cost-benefit analysis" of the trade-offs between a variety of possible outcomes. The political component of this approach emphasizes the necessity of understanding the variety of policy choices available to individual policymakers and groups within society, as they bargain for an outcome that they (rationally) perceive as being in their best interests.

In *Markets and States in Tropical Africa: The Political Basis of Agricultural Policies* (1981), Robert H. Bates clearly falls within the political-economy tradition.[27] The primary purpose of the book is to explain why food production declined in Africa during the initial decades of the contemporary independence era, thereby contributing to recurring cycles of famine and starvation. The critical starting point of Bates's analysis is the assumption that individuals make choices based on a rational analysis of their self-interests. As a result, the answer to the question posed at the beginning of his book — "Why should reasonable men adopt public policies that have harmful consequences for the societies they govern?" — is found in the political calculations made by African policymakers.[28]

The second stream of public policy research focuses on **public policy analysis**: the assessment of the "outputs" (end results) of government policies and programs. Public policy analysis is devoted to exploring the various strategies available to policymakers for solving the variety of economic, social, and political problems associated with the development process. This "problem-solving" approach is very action oriented: it is used to analyze the choices available to policymakers and then determine which of those choices is most appropriate for development.

Donald Rothchild and Robert L. Curry, Jr., in *Scarcity, Choice, and Public Policy in Middle Africa* (1979), clearly fall within the tradition of public policy analysis.[29] First, the mere fact that these two authors collaborated — Rothchild is a political scientist and Curry is an economist — clearly underscores their commitment to a political-economy approach. Second, the authors assume that rational government policies are the result of cost-benefit considerations made by African policymakers. The most important aspect of the book is its emphasis on adopting a "problem-solving approach" to aid African policymakers in overcoming the "constraints" imposed by such factors as economic scarcity, environmental degradation, and inherited colonial institutions. In short, Rothchild and Curry argue that African leaders have the ability to make "choices" from a variety of "strategies," each of which entails different trade-offs depending on the nature of policy goals selected by that leadership.

The Rothchild and Curry book is also significant in that it addresses one of the major criticisms advanced by dependency theorists and other scholars associated with the "critical tradition" of African politics and society (see Chapter 3). As discussed in the following chapter, dependency theorists argue that the liberal tradition focuses too heavily on the internal (domestic) sources of development problems in Africa. They believe that the primary emphasis should be placed on the external (international) constraints faced by these countries. Rothchild and Curry respond to this critique by adding two new "crises of development" to the six crises outlined by the theorists of order:

- **crisis of national survival**: ensuring the survival of the territorial integrity of the country as originally constituted at independence;
- **crisis of foreign control**: securing economic, social, and political freedom from external control.

The recognition of the importance of international factors in Rothchild and Curry's book clearly demonstrates the rising influence of certain elements of the critical tradition within the thinking of liberal theorists during the 1970s and the 1980s, though both schools of thought remained strongly divided throughout this period.

A final element in the shift toward public policy research during the 1970s and the 1980s was a growing emphasis on the importance of the "African state": the formal institutions of power within African political systems, including but not limited to the presidency, judiciary, government bureaucracies, national legislature, and military forces (see Chapter 10). More precisely, scholars increasingly focused on the relationship of the state to both domestic groups (such as African elites and ethnic groups) and international groups (such as foreign elites and international organizations). An excellent example of this trend is a jointly edited volume by Donald Rothchild and Victor A. Olorunsola, *State versus Ethnic Claims: African Policy Dilemmas* (1983), which explores the evolving relationship between weak African states and increasingly vocal ethnic groups who feel disenfranchised from the political process.[30] By the end of the 1980s, the state had become the focal point of liberal Africanists seeking to understand the successes and failures of over three decades of African independence from colonial rule.

New Directions in the Post–Cold War Era (Late 1980s–Present)

The end of the Cold War marked the emergence of a new era that both continues and changes the Africa-related liberal scholarship that was produced from the 1950s to the early 1980s. One of the most important changes associated with this new era is that the ideological assumptions of the Cold War — anticommunism and containment of the Soviet Union — no longer influence scholarship as they did during the modernization era of the 1950s and the 1960s. The end of the Cold War reinforced the historical tendency of foreign scholars and academic institutions to neglect the African continent in favor of other regions of perceived greater interest, most notably Europe, Asia, and the Middle East. This trend is perhaps best demonstrated by the U.S. federal government's declining commitment of financial resources to African studies programs and basic research devoted to Africa, as well as the decision of several private foundations, such as the Social Science Research Council (SSRC), to end their specialized programs devoted to Africa.[31]

A second change associated with the end of the Cold War is renewed scholarly interest in the emergence and consolidation of multiparty democracy in Africa (see Chapter 12). Reminiscent of the optimism expressed by modernization theorists during the 1950s and the 1960s, the liberal tradition at the end of the 1980s was reinvigorated by the emergence of pro-democracy movements that fostered dozens of experiments in multiparty democracy throughout the African continent. An initial euphoria surrounded what some scholars optimistically referred to as the "rebirth of political freedom" throughout Africa,[32] making transitions to democracy the most studied topic in the field of African studies during the 1990s.[33] The best example of this trend is Michael Bratton and Nicolas van de Walle's *Democratic Experiments in Africa: Regime Transition in Comparative Perspective* (1997), which offers the first comprehensive analysis of all the democratic transitions that took place between 1989 and 1994.[34] Although contemporary scholars from the liberal tradition no longer assume (as did their predecessors of the 1950s and the 1960s) that the consolidation of African democracies will be either easy or automatically assured, they nonetheless point to the Western democratic tradition as the model to be emulated by African leaders.

A third component of liberal scholarship in the post–Cold War era is a renewed interest in the concept of ethnicity as crucial to an informed understanding of African politics and society (see Chapter 7). This scholarly focus is fueled by the tremendous upsurge in ethnic competition and conflict throughout the African continent. The implications of this growing trend are mixed. One view, derivative of modernization theory, optimistically argues that ethnic problems can be resolved by creative solutions, such as federal arrangements that recognize the importance of ethnic diversity but maintain the territorial boundaries of the nation-state as formalized by the contemporary independence era. As explained by Donald Rothchild in *Managing Ethnic Conflict in Africa: Pressures and Incentives for Cooperation* (1997), "third party" mediators particularly can be highly effective in facilitating the resolution of ethnic conflicts, which are not inevitable in the post–Cold War world.[35]

Another view, which stems from the "politics of order" branch of the liberal tradition, perceives the growth of ethnic and other wider cultural tensions as inevitable in the wake of the Cold War, now that international relations are no longer dominated by the two superpowers. This scholarly tradition is best captured in the widely debated book by Samuel P. Huntington, *The Clash of Civilizations and the Remaking of World Order* (1996), which essentially argues that cultural clashes between Western civilization and those of other regions of the world will serve as the defining characteristic of the twenty-first century.[36] Although Huntington dismisses the importance of African culture in his book, he and other scholars representative of this tradition are more inclined to favor the classic emphasis on stability and order to ensure the continued territorial integrity of African countries in the face of ethnic conflict.

A fourth issue of liberal scholarship in the emerging post–Cold War era revolves around the merits of decentralized-versus-centralized power in African countries. In sharp contrast to the proponents of stability, who argued during the 1960s and 1970s for the centralization of power in order to overcome crises of development, scholars during the 1990s increasingly began weighing the benefits of decentralized power. An excellent example of this is an edited volume by James Wunsch and Dele Oluwu, *The Failure of the Centralized State: Institutions and Self-Governance in Africa* (1990).[37] Clearly derivative of the democratic assumptions of the modernization theorists and their revisionist counterparts, as well as the public policy focus of the 1970s and the 1980s, scholars such as Wunsch and Oluwu maintain that the decentralization of authority away from central governments, in favor of greater power to local bodies (such as city or local state governments), is the key to overcoming ethnic conflict. These scholars argue that decentralized political arrangements constitute the best means for ensuring the success of true participatory democracies, in which local needs are the basis for government policies and programs of development.

A final trend in liberal scholarship revolves around the concept of "civil society": the vast array of voluntary associations throughout society, such as political parties, labor unions, student organizations, and religious groups, that seeks access to state power (see Chapter 10). Whereas African leaders consistently co-opted and repressed civil groups, effectively silencing people's demands on the state from the 1950s to the 1980s, the end of the Cold War marked the resurgence of vibrant and vocal civil societies intent on opening up the political space within their respective countries. The wide variety of debates over the nature and future implications of this trend is nicely captured in *Civil Society and the State in Africa* (1994), jointly edited by John W. Harbeson, Donald Rothchild, and Naomi Chazan.[38] According to these scholars, civil society constitutes the "missing key" to sustained political reform throughout the African continent.[39]

Together these five sets of scholarly developments demonstrate the continued vitality of the liberal tradition of African politics and society at the beginning of the twenty-first century. Far from achieving agreement on the specifics of which liberal theories are most relevant to the socioeconomic and political-military challenges confronting African policymakers, the liberal tradition embodies a rich diversity of competing ideas, theories, and policy prescriptions.

Vigorous intellectual debate and disagreement will surely continue over the prospects of democratization, the inevitability of ethnic cooperation and conflict, the relative merits of centralized versus decentralized forms of government, and the strength and importance of civil society. These differences notwithstanding, proponents of the liberal tradition remain bound together by their common belief in the Western democratic tradition as the model to be emulated by African leaders.

Key Terms

liberal tradition
modernization theory
structural-functionalism
value-neutral scientific framework
modernization revisionism
African Studies Association (ASA)
African Heritage Studies Association
   (AHSA)
American African Affairs Association
   (AAAA)
unilinear
political development
political decay
crises of development
crisis of identity

crisis of legitimacy
crisis of participation
crisis of penetration
crisis of distribution
crisis of integration
institutionalization
politics of order
policy relevant
public policy research
political-economy approach
rational-choice models
public policy analysis
crisis of national survival
crisis of foreign control

For Further Reading

Almond, Gabriel A., and James S. Coleman, eds. *Politics of the Developing Areas*. Princeton: Princeton University Press, 1960.

Apter, David E., and Carl G. Rosberg, eds. *Political Development and the New Realism in Sub-Saharan Africa*. Charlottesville: University Press of Virginia, 1994.

Bratton, Michael, and Nicolas van de Walle. *Democratic Experiments in Africa: Regime Transition in Comparative Perspective*. Cambridge: Cambridge University Press, 1997.

Coleman, James S. (edited by Richard L. Sklar). *Nationalism and Development in Africa: Selected Essays*. Berkeley: University of California Press, 1994.

Coleman, James S., and C. R. D. Halisi. "American Political Science and Tropical Africa: Universalism vs. Relativism." *African Studies Review* 26, nos. 3–4 (1983):25–62.

Harbeson, John W., Donald Rothchild, and Naomi Chazan, eds. *Civil Society and the State in Africa*. Boulder: Lynne Rienner, 1994.

Khadiagala, Gilbert M. "Reflections on Development Theory and Political Practice in Africa." *A Current Bibliography on African Affairs* 22, no. 4 (1990):343–70.

Kilson, Martin. "African Political Change and the Modernization Process." *Journal of Modern African Studies* 1, no. 14 (1963):425–44.

Menkhaus, Kenneth J. "Political and Social Change." In Mark W. DeLancey, ed., *Handbook of Political Science Research on Sub-Saharan Africa: Trends from the 1960s to the 1990s*. Westport: Greenwood, 1992 (pp. 9–40).

O'Brien, Donal Cruise. "Modernization, Order, and the Erosion of a Democratic Ideal: American Political Science 1960–70." *Journal of Development Studies* 8, no. 2 (1972):351–78.

Packenham, Robert. *Liberal America and the Third World: Political Development Ideas in Foreign Aid and Social Science*. Princeton: Princeton University Press, 1973.

Rothchild, Donald. *Managing Ethnic Conflict in Africa: Pressures and Incentives for Cooperation*. Washington: Brookings Institution, 1997.

Staniland, Martin. *American Intellectuals and African Nationalists, 1955–1970*. New Haven: Yale University Press, 1991.

Wunsch, James S. "Development Administration in Africa: 1960–1990." In Mark W. DeLancey, ed., *Handbook of Political Science Research on Sub-Saharan Africa: Trends from the 1960s to the 1990s*. Westport: Greenwood, 1992 (pp. 41–72).

Wunsch, James, and Dele Olumu, eds. *The Failure of the Centralized State: Institutions and Self-Governance in Africa*. Boulder: Westview, 1990.

Notes

1. For an overview of the liberal tradition within the field of comparative politics, see Richard A. Higgott, *Political Development Theory: The Contemporary Debate* (London: Croom Helm, 1983). For a general overview within an African context, see Gilbert M. Khadiagala, "Reflections on Development Theory and Political Practice in Africa," *A Current Bibliography on African Affairs* 22, no. 4 (1990):343–70.

2. See David E. Apter, *The Gold Coast in Transition* (Princeton: Princeton University Press, 1955). After Ghana's independence in 1957, the title was changed to *Ghana in Transition*. The quotation is taken from the second revised edition (Princeton: Princeton University Press, 1972), p. xxiii.

3. Walt W. Rostow, *The Stages of Economic Growth: A Non-Communist Manifesto* (Cambridge: Cambridge University Press, 1960).

4. See, for example, Daniel Lerner, *The Passing of Traditional Society: Modernizing the Middle East* (New York: The Free Press, 1958); and Alex Inkeles and David H. Smith, *Becoming Modern: Individual Change in Six Developing Countries* (Cambridge: Cambridge University Press, 1974).

5. For example, see A. F. K. Organski, *The Stages of Political Development* (New York: Knopf, 1965).

6. Gabriel A. Almond and James S. Coleman, eds., *Politics of the Developing Areas* (Princeton: Princeton University Press, 1960). For a more extensive analysis of structural functionalism, see Gabriel A. Almond and G. Bingham Powell, Jr., *System, Process, and Policy: Comparative Politics* (Boston: Little, Brown, 1978).

7. Among the other political functions said to be performed by all political systems are political socialization and recruitment, interest aggregation, and political communication.

8. See, for example, Vicky Randall and Robin Theobold, *Political Change and Underdevelopment: A Critical Introduction to Third World Politics*, 2nd ed. (Durham: Duke University Press, 1998), p. 28.

9. See Robert A. Packenham, *Liberal America and the Third World: Political Development Ideas in Foreign Aid and Social Science* (Princeton: Princeton University Press, 1973). See also Irene L. Grendzier, *Managing Political Change: Social Scientists and the Third World* (Boulder: Westview, 1985).

10. This term was originally coined by Samuel P. Huntington, "The Change to Change," *Comparative Politics*, 3, no. 3 (1971):283–32. For general overviews of this theme, see Joseph Gusfield, "Tradition and Modernity: Misplaced Polarities in the Study of Social Change," *American Journal of Sociology* 72 (1967):351–62; and Reinhard Bendix, "Tradition and Modernity Reconsidered," *Studies in Comparative Society and History* 9, no. 3 (1967):292–346; and Randall and Theobold, *Political Change and Underdevelopment*, ch. 2.

11. C. S. Whitaker, Jr., *The Politics of Tradition: Continuity and Change in Northern Nigeria 1946–1966* (Princeton: Princeton University Press, 1970).

12. *Ibid.*, p. 460 (emphasis added).

13. *Ibid.*, p. 464.

14. *Ibid.*

15. See Paul Anber, "Modernization and Political Disintegration: Nigeria and the Igbos," *Journal of Modern African Studies* 5, no. 2 (1967):163–79.

16. For the analysis that formed the basis of this discussion, see Donal Cruise O'Brien, "Modernization, Order, and the Erosion of a Democratic Ideal: American Political Science 1960–70," *Journal of Development Studies* 8, no. 2 (1972):351–78. See also Mark Kesselman, "Order or Movement? The Literature of Political Development as Ideology," *World Politics* 26, no. 1 (1973):139–54.

17. For a discussion of these and other themes related to U.S. intervention in the Third World, see Peter J. Schraeder, ed., *Intervention into the 1990s: U.S. Foreign Policy in the Third World* (Boulder: Lynne Rienner, 1992).

18. See Samuel P. Huntington, "Political Order and Political Decay," *World Politics* 17, no. 3 (1965):386–430.

19. Samuel P. Huntington, *Political Order in Changing Societies* (New Haven: Yale University Press, 1968).

20. See Leonard Binder et al., *Crises and Sequences in Political Development* (Princeton: Princeton University Press, 1971).

21. Huntington, *Political Order in Changing Societies*, p. 7 (emphasis added).

22. *Ibid.*, p. 8.

23. Aristide R. Zolberg, *Creating Political Order: The Party-States of West Africa* (Chicago: Rand McNally). See also his earlier study, *One-Party Government in the Ivory Coast* (Princeton: Princeton University Press, 1964, rev. ed., 1969).

24. Zolberg, *Creating Political Order,* p. 161.

25. *Ibid.*

26. For a discussion of this trend, see Higgott, *Political Development Theory,* pp. 21–42.

27. Robert H. Bates, *Markets and States in Tropical Africa: The Political Basis of Agricultural Policies* (Berkeley: University of California Press, 1981). See also his earlier work, *Rural Responses to Industrialization: A Study of Village Zambia* (New Haven: Yale University Press, 1976).

28. *Ibid.*, p. 132.

29. Donald Rothchild and Robert L. Curry, Jr., *Scarcity, Choice, and Public Policy in Middle Africa* (Berkeley: University of California Press, 1979).

30. Donald Rothchild and Victor A. Olorunsola, eds., *State versus Ethnic Claims: African Policy Dilemmas* (Boulder: Westview, 1983). See also Donald Rothchild and Naomi Chazan, eds., *The Precarious Balance: State and Society in Africa* (Boulder: Westview, 1988).

31. Jane I. Guyer, *African Studies in the United States: A Perspective* (Atlanta: African Studies Association, 1996).

32. See Richard Joseph, "Africa: The Rebirth of Political Freedom," *Journal of Democracy* 2, no. 3 (1991):11–24.

33. For an introduction to this vast literature, see Rob Buijtenhuijs and Céline Thiriot, *Democratization in Sub-Saharan Africa, 1992–1995: An Overview of the Literature* (Leiden: The Netherlands African Studies Centre, 1995).

34. Michael Bratton and Nicolas van de Walle, *Democratic Experiments in Africa: Regime Transition in Comparative Perspective* (Cambridge: Cambridge University Press, 1997).

35. Donald Rothchild, *Managing Ethnic Conflict in Africa: Pressures and Incentives for Cooperation* (Washington: Brookings Institution, 1997). See also Harvey Glickman, ed., *Ethnic Conflict and Democratization in Africa* (Atlanta: African Studies Association, 1995).

36. Samuel P. Huntington, *The Clash of Civilizations and the Remaking of World Order* (New York: Simon & Schuster, 1996).

37. James Wunsch and Dele Oluwu, eds., *The Failure of the Centralized State: Institutions and Self-Governance in Africa* (Boulder: Westview, 1990).

38. John W. Harbeson, Donald Rothchild, and Naomi Chazan, eds., *Civil Society and the State in Africa* (Boulder: Lynne Rienner, 1994).

39. *Ibid.*, p. 1.

3

Study of Africa within the Critical Tradition

Kwame Nkrumah (1909–1972), one of the most noteworthy politician-scholars of the contemporary independence era, served as the first president of Ghana and wrote several widely acclaimed books within the critical tradition.

THE STUDY OF AFRICAN politics and society has been enriched by a **critical tradition** that significantly questions the prevailing liberal model of political and socioeconomic development.[1] In its most extreme form, this scholarly tradition emphasizes that the achievement of true development will only occur in the aftermath of revolutionary struggles and in the creation of socialist regimes throughout the African continent. Unlike proponents of the liberal tradition, who sought to emulate the political and economic systems of the northern industrialized democracies of Canada, Europe, Japan, and the United States, critical scholars instead sought inspiration from a variety of socialist countries, including Cuba, North Korea, the People's Republic of China (PRC), the Soviet Union, Eastern Germany, and the other communist regimes of Eastern Europe. The fall of the Berlin Wall, the decline of single-party Marxist regimes, and the fragmentation of the former Soviet Union into several independent and noncommunist countries triggered an intellectual crisis within the critical tradition. Although the vast majority of scholars associated with the critical tradition continue to embrace some variant of the socialist ideal, the declining popularity of socialist and especially Marxist ideals among a new generation of African policymakers has prompted a significant reexamination of critical thought. The primary purpose of this chapter is to highlight the general evolution of the major themes and scholarly concerns of the critical tradition from the 1950s to the present.

Classical Marxism (Nineteenth Century) as Precursor to Contemporary Critical Thought

Karl Marx (1818–1883) was a German scholar whose writings served as the inspiration for more than a century of scholarship highly critical of the liberal tradition, as well as the ideological basis for seven decades of communist rule in the former Soviet Union.[2] Writing during the nineteenth century, Marx was surrounded by a variety of social ills that accompanied the expansion of free market capitalism known as the **industrial revolution**, the process whereby the countries of Europe were transformed from agriculturally based rural societies into industrially based urban societies. In the case of Manchester, England, the first of hundreds of industrialized cities, urban squalor accompanied a major growth in population — from 25,000 in 1772 to 455,000 in 1851. In addition to lacking amenities often taken for granted in the West during the latter portion of the twentieth century, such as proper sewage and garbage disposal systems, cities like Manchester were often drab places in which buildings and people alike were blackened with the heavy soot from the coal used to run factories.[3] The absence of strict child labor laws and other forms of government regulation of the workplace meant that it was not uncommon to find children of six years of age working in unsafe factory conditions, and people of all ages working fourteen-hour days with no health care benefits or sick leave. In short, Marx lived during an era in which the spread of free market capitalism appeared to foster new forms of human exploitation.

Marx argues that all societies can be divided into classes, which are bound together in a relationship of exploitation (see Chapter 7).[4] Within capitalist society, a dominant bourgeoisie (property-owning) class exploits the work of the proletariat (working) class. Marx was particularly concerned with the ability of a rising bourgeoisie to expropriate the property of the petty bourgeoisie within capitalist societies.[5] This process results in a growing class of propertyless workers (the proletariat), who are forced to either accept poor jobs and unsafe working conditions or starve. Most important, once propertyless, workers are caught in a vicious cycle in which their labor serves to create more property and wealth for the bourgeoisie. In essence, workers become trapped in a miserable existence akin to slavery. But this condition is not permanent, Marx claims, for it can be overcome through proletarian revolution.

Marx argues that a revolutionary situation emerges when advances in technological, scientific, and other forms of material development (the **forces of production**) outgrow an outmoded system of ownership of property among classes (the **relations of production**) such that the dominant class finds it increasingly difficult to maintain control over the rest of society through its traditional means.[6] Since no "civilized" society ever forfeits its material level of development, the net result of the growing contradiction between the forces of production and the relations of production is a heightened class struggle in which the ruling class is eventually overthrown. According to Marx, such revolutionary events are part of a general historical trend in which all societies are moving along the same path of development.[7] In the *Manifesto of the Communist Party* (1848), for example, Marx suggests that all societies have to pass through ancient, feudal, and capitalist **modes of production** (the combination of the forces and the relations of production) on the path to achieving what he perceives as the inevitable and desirable final stage of revolutionary development: a socialist (communist) society in which the proletariat reigns supreme.

It is important to note, however, that the majority of Marx's writings focus on the unfolding of revolutionary development in the industrializing countries of Europe; he pays little attention to the various regions of the southern hemisphere, including Africa. In fact, Marx held a highly negative view of what he referred to as "Asiatic" (non-Western) societies.[8] Similar to the viewpoint adhered to by the modernization theorists described in Chapter 2, Marx suggests that non-Western societies were stagnant, backward, and led by barbarians and despots. This negative perception was reinforced by a firm belief that these same societies, unlike those of Europe, lacked the ability to move *independently* through the various stages of historical revolutionary development on the path to socialism.[9]

Since Marx perceived that most Third World societies were incapable of achieving social change on their own, he concluded that the spread of colonialism was a "brutal but necessary" stage in their historical development.[10] This stage was "brutal" in the sense that the Western powers often adopted barbaric methods to defeat peoples unwilling to submit themselves to foreign rule, and "necessary" in the sense that colonial rule facilitated the introduction of capitalism — the preliminary stage to socialism — into "backward" areas around the globe. These arguments are clearly portrayed in Marx's description of British colonial rule in India, where he worked as a foreign correspondent for the *New York Daily Tribune:* "England, it is true, in causing a social revolution in Hindustan, was actuated only by the vilest interests, and was stupid in her manner of enforcing them," explains Marx in an article written June 25, 1853. "But that is not the question," he continues, "whatever may have been the crimes of England she was the unconscious tool of history in bringing about the revolution."[11] In a later article, "The Future Results of British Rule in India," Marx underscores the importance of colonialism in destroying backward societies and in making them conducive to the promotion of capitalist forms of development: "England has to fulfill a double mission in India," he explains, "one destructive, the other regenerating — the annihilation of old Asiatic society and the laying of the material foundations of Western society in Asia."[12]

Similar to the perspective held by the modernization theorists described in Chapter 2, a strong belief in the "developmental" nature of capitalism is at the center of Marx's early writings about the impact of European colonialism in the Third World. Marx was particularly impressed by the ability of the European powers to transplant "modern" (capitalist) types of industry, such as factories and transportation networks, to the southern hemisphere, thereby providing a spark that would ignite the modernization process. In India, for example, Marx describes the construction of British-designed railroads as critical to the colony's future development: "The railway system will therefore become, in India, truly the forerunner of modern industry."[13] Unlike the expectations of modernization theorists, however, Marx argues that colonialism and the implementation of capitalism are developmental, in that they constitute a necessary stage in the advancement toward socialist revolution in the southern hemisphere. Despite the fact that Marx recognized the terrible costs associated with the spread of capitalism under the guise of colonialism, he argued that they were costs worth paying if the result was the creation of a socialist society.[14]

Dependency Theory and the "Development of Underdevelopment" Thesis (Late 1960s–Early 1970s)

A body of literature known as **dependency theory** became the first critical perspective to gain acceptance within the African scholarly community during the contemporary independence era. Emerging as a major alternative to liberal theories of development during the late 1960s and the early 1970s, dependency theory originated among Latin American specialists such as André Gunder Frank,[15] who criticized liberal and critical theorists alike for being too "Western-centric" in their analyses. In fact, even Marx is criticized by dependency theorists as a European who portrayed non-Western peoples in a negative light and who was primarily concerned with the fate of Europe.[16]

Dependency theorists were particularly concerned with understanding why, despite the optimistic projections of modernization theory, the regions of the southern hemisphere were suffering from economic stagnation, dictatorial leaders, and political instability and unrest. Whereas liberal theorists had argued that *internal* shortcomings, such as misguided economic policies and poor leadership, were at the center of the southern hemisphere's problems, dependency theorists argued that *external* constraints, most notably the domination of the developing countries by the industrialized powers of Western Europe and North America, were responsible for the majority of economic and political misery in the southern hemisphere.

Dependency theorists argue that international relations between capitalist countries and underdeveloped areas are inherently exploitative, and that the international capitalist system is the primary cause of this exploitation. In *How Europe Underdeveloped Africa* (1972), Walter Rodney argues that, prior to the spread of international capitalism by the end of the sixteenth century, Africa was developing both politically and economically, as were most regions of the non-European world.[17] Yet as foreign encroachment by Europe, culminating in direct colonial rule, increasingly led to Africa's inclusion within the global capitalist system, all forms of independent development on the continent were extinguished. Instead, European domination led to the **development of underdevelopment**: the gradual impoverishment of the African continent as previous African development was "blunted, halted, and turned back."[18]

The "development of underdevelopment" thesis catagorizes all countries as either **metropoles** (the centers of economic and political power) or **satellites** (those areas controlled and exploited by the metropoles). In the case of the French empire, France served as the metropole and its colonies (e.g., Senegal, Côte d'Ivoire, and Algeria, among others) constituted the satellites. According to the dependency theorists, the maintenance of this highly unequal international structure was made possible by African **compradors** (political and economic elites) who knowingly or not served as the cultural, economic, military, or political agents of the European colonialists. According to dependency theorists, this relationship did not change once African countries achieved independence from European colonial rule beginning in the 1950s, but rather is reinforced by **neocolonial** leaders who are more interested in maintaining ties with foreign powers than contributing to the true development of their own countries.

For dependency theorists, the twin outcomes of development of the northern industrialized countries and underdevelopment of countries in the southern hemisphere are inextricably linked. Indeed, the early dependency theorists came to the conclusion that the exploitation of Africa was critical to the development of advanced industrial capitalism in Europe. "It would be extremely simple-minded to say that colonialism in Africa or anywhere else *caused*

Europe to develop its science and technology," explains Rodney. "However," he concludes, "it would be entirely accurate to say that the colonization of Africa and other parts of the world formed an indispensable link in a chain of events which made possible the technological transformation of the base of European capitalism."[19]

Dependency theorists argue that the **extraction of surplus** is the basic process that led to the development of the European metropoles and the underdevelopment of the African satellites during both the colonial and independence eras. In the case of European investment in Africa, for example, dependency theorists argue that the net result, especially during the colonial era, was an outflow of capital that benefited Europe at the expense of Africa. As will be discussed in Chapter 5, European administration of the colonial territories ensured that substandard wages could be paid to African workers and that, little, if any, profits were reinvested in the colonies in the form of social services designed to benefit Africans. Most profits were instead repatriated back to the European metropoles where they contributed to the material well-being of Europeans. "In this sense," concludes Rodney, "the colonies were the generators of the capital rather than the countries into which foreign capital was plowed."[20]

The "development of underdevelopment" thesis serves as the defining difference between the classical Marxist and dependency schools of thought. Although Rodney draws much of his vocabulary and inspiration from Marx's writings, he accepts the basic argument of traditional dependency theorists that colonialism led to the stagnation and underdevelopment of the African continent. This differs from the classical Marxian interpretation of colonialism as leading to the industrial development of non-Western societies in preparation for their transition to socialism. Some scholars attempted to show that the later writings of Marx, particularly his analysis of economic stagnation in Ireland, offered a precursor to the development of underdevelopment thesis.[21] However, classical Marxists and dependency theorists remained divided during the early 1970s over whether capitalism contributed to the development or underdevelopment of African societies.

"Circulationist" Revisions of Dependency Theory (1970s)

During the 1970s, a group of scholars referred to as **circulationists** revised dependency theory and offered a more sophisticated analysis of the development of underdevelopment thesis.[22] Drawing on the writings of Arghiri Emmanuel, *Unequal Exchange: A Study of the Imperialism of Trade* (1972), these scholars focus on the exploitative nature of international trade relationships that benefit the northern industrialized countries at the expense of the various regions of the southern hemisphere.[23]

BOX 3.1

ASSOCIATION OF CONCERNED AFRICA SCHOLARS (ACAS)

The Association of Concerned Africa Scholars (ACAS) was formed in 1977 by a group of Africanists who believe that academics should be effective **political activists** in addition to excellent teachers and researchers. The primary purpose of this group is to maintain a communication and action network between scholars interested in promoting a "progressive" set of U.S. foreign policies toward Africa. Eight sets of principles have historically guided ACAS activities:

- opposition to apartheid, racial and class domination, and minority rule;
- support for efforts by African states to end their economic dependency;
- recognition of the right of African nations to political autonomy and to their own forms of social and economic organization;
- support for democratic governments, genuine popular participation, and the right to form political parties;
- commitment to the protection of human rights;
- support for colleagues in Africa who face political repression;
- greater equity in North/South economic relations;
- economic and technical support for African peoples to help them deal with the pressing needs and crises of the continent.

The ACAS Executive Committee and Board of Directors are comprised of distinguished Africanists who pursue the ACAS political agenda through the funding of a Political Action Committee, a lobbying office in Washington, D.C., and the publication of a trimestrial newsletter, the *ACAS Bulletin*. For further information, send an email to <acas@prairienet.org> or contact the ACAS homepage at <http://www.prairienet.org/acas/>.

Immanuel Wallerstein, founder of the Fernand Braudel Center for the Study of the World System at the State University of New York, Binghamton, has contributed greatly to the sophistication of dependency theory and is recognized as the leading scholar within the circulationist tradition. In *The Capitalist World-Economy* (1979),[24] as well as a massive three-volume work, *The Modern World System* (1974, 1980, 1989),[25] Wallerstein makes his first contribution to the sophistication of dependency theory: a detailed historical analysis of the rise of what he refers to as the **capitalist world economy**, an exploitative worldwide capitalist system controlled by the major industrial powers. This system is marked by alternating periods of economic expansion and contraction (i.e., economic decline) of the world economy in which **core countries** (metropoles) emerge and **peripheral countries** (satellites) grow more impoverished. According to this view, the creation of European empires in Africa at the end of the nineteenth century — the "scramble for Africa" described in Chapter 5 — was the direct result of a contraction in the capitalist world economy from 1873 to 1897.[26]

Wallerstein's second contribution to dependency theory is a more concise analysis of the possibility for development and social change within the regions of the southern hemisphere. Unlike Marxists who argued that revolution would lead to a higher stage of political and economic development, but more in keeping with the development of underdevelopment thesis, Wallerstein argues that true social change can only occur when the entire capitalist world economy has been overthrown. Any attempt at social change by one country within the current confines of the capitalist world economy, according to this analysis, is ultimately destined to fail. In the case of the Soviet Union, a country once admired by many critical theorists as capable of leading revolutionary change in Africa, the circulationists argue that the socialist ideals of the Russian revolution of 1917 were doomed from the start, due to its isolation within an extremely hostile capitalist world economy dominated by the United States. The eventual overthrow of communism and the fragmentation of the country in 1991 confirmed this view. According to Wallerstein, meaningful development for Africa will only occur once the capitalist world economy has been overthrown by worldwide revolution and replaced by a world economy based on socialist principles.

Wallerstein's most important contribution to dependency theory is a more sophisticated understanding of the metropolis-satellite (core-periphery) model of the world economy originally proposed by André Gunder Frank. Disagreeing with what he perceived as an overly simplistic view of a world in which countries are either extremely powerful (the core) or in the process of being marginalized (the periphery), Wallerstein pointed out the existence of a third tier of countries, the **semi-periphery**, that is neither very powerful nor completely impoverished.[27] These semi-peripheral countries constitute rising regional powers that are economically and politically powerful in their immediate regions and have aspirations to someday join the core in its control of the capitalist world system. The semi-peripheral countries are further distinguished in that they are both exploited by the core and exploiters of the periphery. For example, whereas the semi-peripheral power of Nigeria is perceived as being exploited by the core country of Great Britain (the former colonial power), it nonetheless exploits peripheral powers within the West African region, such as Benin, with which it has strong political and economic ties. Other major African powers that are considered semi-peripheral states include Côte d'Ivoire and Senegal in West Africa; Libya and Egypt in North Africa; Kenya in East Africa; the Democratic Republic of the Congo (Congo-Kinshasa) in Central Africa; and South Africa in Southern Africa.[28]

Wallerstein argues that the existence of the semi-periphery is the primary reason why the capitalist world economy has not yet been overthrown in favor of a socialist world economy. In order for revolution to occur, the world system must become polarized between the few richest countries and the vast majority burdened by high levels of urban poverty, mass unemployment, and, subsequently, rising social unrest. This process, according to Wallerstein, began during the worldwide expansion of the capitalist world economy at the beginning of the fifteenth century, and continues to unfold as Africa becomes increasingly marginalized at the beginning of the twenty-first century. The semi-periphery delays the process of polarization by undermining the creation of a unified front against the core. These countries instead perceive themselves as economically and politically better off than the peripheral countries, and thus either intentionally or unintentionally serve as the agents of the core by seeking to strengthen their standing within an otherwise exploitative system. It is important to remember, however, that the semi-periphery is only perceived as a temporary palliative to an aging, increasingly dysfunctional capitalist world economy that eventually will polarize and result in world revolution.

Emergence of Neo-Marxist Forms of Scholarship (Late 1970s–1980s)

Scholars drawing upon classical Marxism also criticized the dependency approach of the 1970s, and contributed to a rising debate that questioned several aspects of the world systems approach of the circulationists. Similar to the evolution of scholarship within the liberal tradition during this same period, these scholars criticized their predecessors for promoting grand theories that were so abstract as to be of little use to **political activists,** who were interested in promoting socioeconomic change within their respective countries. Dependency and world systems theories were of little use to socialist African leaders who sought practical solutions to guide their countries toward socialist alternatives. A Marxist union leader might similarly wonder how abstract theories that ignore the problems of cooperation and conflict between classes within African societies could be applied to seek changes in labor laws and the working conditions of factory workers. The **neo-Marxist school** addressed these practical problems and dominated the critical tradition of African politics and society from the late 1970s to the late 1980s.[29]

The work of Samir Amin, an Egyptian scholar, is recognized as serving as an intellectual bridge between the dependency/circulationist and neo-Marxist traditions.[30] In one of his most-cited works, *Neo-Colonialism in West Africa* (1973), Amin demonstrates his intellectual attachment to the dependency and circulationist approaches by arguing that the development of West Africa has been "blocked" by the region's incorporation into an inherently unequal capitalist world economy, and that this state of affairs has been reinforced by neo-colonial West African leaders during the contemporary independence era.[31] Amin documents how Senegal's economy was structured around the production of virtually nothing but groundnuts (peanuts) during nearly a century of

French colonial rule. As discussed in Chapter 5, this agricultural specialization provided the French with inexpensive heating oil, which is derivative of ground-nuts, and hampered the economic development of Senegal. The largely groundnut-oriented economy was maintained even after independence, due to the shared interests of French investors and political elites who sought to maintain priv-ileged ties with the country, as well as Senegalese leaders who depended on profits from this sector to maintain power. The net result of this "outwardly-directed" development strategy, according to Amin, has been a permanent cri-sis of public finances, tight dependence on foreign technical assistance, and an increasing balance of payments deficit. Rather than generating an "internal dynamism" geared toward the domestic needs of the Senegalese population, this path has resulted in the Senegalese economy being highly dependent on foreign interests and investment.[32] Amin thus declares that the "groundnut econ-omy, far from contributing to Senegal's development, is making possible the plunder of its economy and its continuation in a state of underdevelopment."[33]

However, Amin sets the tone for a series of neo-Marxist critiques by "part-ing company" with the dependency and circulationist approaches in two major areas.[34] In the case of dependency theory, Amin suggests that one can-not assume that the "extraction of surplus" from the peripheral areas of the southern hemisphere was necessary for the development of the northern indus-trialized countries, because, he argues, development of individual countries and/or regions can occur independently. Although colonial exploitation of African colonies aided development in the northern industrialized countries, the wealth of northern countries was not contingent upon exploitation. As demonstrated in the title of another of his most recently translated books, *Delinking: Towards a Polycentric World* (1990), Amin argues instead that African countries can pursue **autocentric** (self-reliant) **development** by attempt-ing to withdraw in various degrees from the capitalist world economy.[35] As a result, Amin rejects the simplistic development of underdevelopment thesis in favor of a more nuanced view that accounts for a variety of developmental processes and outcomes.

Amin also departs from the circulationist tradition by rejecting the notion that only one mode of production — the capitalist world economy — exclu-sively exists within the international system.[36] The tremendous number of differ-ences both between and within African economies suggests that it is far too simplistic to try and include them all within the broad category of the capitalist mode of production. The international system is instead comprised of both capi-talist and noncapitalist economies that coexist within geographical regions (e.g., West Africa), individual countries (e.g., Senegal), and even subnational regions of individual countries (e.g., the southern Casamance region of Senegal).

The emerging neo-Marxist school of thought that drew inspiration from Amin contributed to the reformulation of critical thought in at least four major areas. First, neo-Marxist scholars such as Claude Ake reject the "devel-opment of underdevelopment" thesis (see Box 3.2). Although Ake agrees with

BOX 3.2

SOCIAL SCIENCE AS IMPERIALISM?

The creation and rapid expansion of African universities from the 1950s to the 1990s has been accompanied by the growth of African social sciences programs that embody academic agendas significantly different from those shared by their counterparts at Western universities. In the case of Nigeria, which maintains one of the largest university systems on the African continent, scholars have noted the evolution of a distinct brand of political science scholarship that is uniquely Nigerian in nature.

Professor Claude Ake, whose life was tragically cut short in a plane crash in Nigeria on November 7, 1996, remains one of the most noted Nigerian scholars from the critical tradition. Born in Nigeria, Ake received a Ph.D. in Political Science from Columbia University in New York, and served as the president of the Nigerian Political Science Association and the Council for the Development of Social Science Research in Africa (CODESRIA). In 1992, he founded and became the director of the Centre for Advanced Social Science (CASS) in Port Harcourt, Nigeria. A steadfast critic of Nigeria's military dictatorships, Ake was also at the forefront of academic debates concerning the proper place of Western scholarship within Nigerian institutions of higher learning.

One of Ake's most provocative books, *Social Science as Imperialism: The Theory of Political Development* (1982), assesses the impact of Western social science on its related disciplines in Africa. Ake severely criticizes what he labels the academic "imperialism" of Western social scientists, who have dominated international debates over the proper path of development for African countries. Ake's critique of Western social science is threefold: (1) "it foists, or at any rate attempts to foist on the developing countries, capitalist values, capitalist institutions, and capitalist development"; (2) "it focuses social science analysis on the question of how to make the developing countries more like the West"; and (3) "it propagates mystifications, and modes of thought and action which serve the interests of capitalism and imperialism" (p. xiii).

In order to overcome this intellectual imperialism, Ake underscores the necessity of promoting a more Africa-centric and socialist-oriented academic tradition that builds upon African heritages and serves African interests. Ake argues that African social scientists should commit themselves to research that will facilitate the radical transformation of African governments from the essentially Western-oriented, elite-based model originally handed down from the departing colonial powers, to one which fosters "mass" interests and development needs, particularly within the neglected rural areas of most African countries.

For further discussion see Ufot B. Inamete, "The Profile and Development of Political Science in Nigeria," *International Studies Notes* 15, no. 3 (1990):85–90; and Yolamu Borongo, ed., *Political Science in Africa: A Critical Review* (London: Zed, 1983).

his dependency/circulationist colleagues that capitalism is inherently exploitative, he nonetheless disagrees that the worldwide expansion of capitalism has
had a permanent regressive effect on Africa. Similar to its portrayal in classical
Marxism, the spread of capitalism to Africa is instead viewed by Ake and
many other neo-Marxist scholars as one "developmental" stage in an overall
movement toward socialism.

A second important contribution of the neo-Marxist literature is the recognition that individual African countries can achieve **dependent development**
within the capitalist world system. Semi-peripheral countries have experienced
rising levels of industrial output, mechanization of agriculture, and urbanization. It is the combination of these factors which, according to classical Marxism, promotes the emergence of an urban proletariat capable of leading class
struggle and revolution in the pursuit of socialism.

The third and most important contribution of neo-Marxist scholars is the
application of class analysis to explain the historical evolution of African politics and society. Neo-Marxist scholars have underscored the necessity of moving beyond unwieldy, abstract notions of core, semi-peripheral, and peripheral
countries in favor of analyzing cooperation and conflict among the variety of
class groupings that comprise individual African countries. This approach is
most notable in the analysis of the evolution and impact of African ruling
classes. As already noted, both the dependency theorists and the circulationists
tend to dismiss the importance of African elites as independent actors, suggest-
ing instead that they are always wittingly or unwittingly serving the interests of
foreign powers. This results in a mechanistic understanding of political change
that completely disregards the power actually wielded by African ruling classes.

The neo-Marxist scholars have sought to correct this shortcoming not only
by classifying and analyzing various types of African ruling classes, ranging
from the so-called bureaucratic bourgeoisie (civil service and government
employees) to the commercial bourgeoisie (top executives of major business
enterprises), but also by examining the goals and impacts of other classes
within African societies, such as the petty bourgeoisie (individuals involved in
smaller trading activities), the proletariat (urban-based, wage-earning, working class), and the rural peasantry (see Chapter 7). One of the most noted
works within this genre is Irving Leonard Markovitz's *Power and Class in
Africa: An Introduction to Change and Conflict in African Politics* (1977),
which adopts the concept of class to analyze the historical evolution of African
politics and society, including an extremely detailed discussion of the impact of
colonialism on traditional African class structures.[37] Markovitz is particularly
concerned with the impact of the ruling class within African societies, or what
he refers to as the bureaucratic bourgeoisie: the "combined ruling group con-
sisting of the top political leaders and bureaucrats, the traditional rulers and
their descendants, the leading members of the liberal professions, the rising
business bourgeoisie, and top members of the military and police forces."[38]

Similar to developments within the liberal tradition during the 1970s and the 1980s, a final contribution of the neo-Marxist tradition was a growing emphasis on the role of the "state," particularly in terms of its relationship to powerful international and domestic classes (see Chapter 10). According to the dependency theorists, the state serves the same function as a hinge on a door: just as the hinge allows for the door to open so that individuals may enter into a room, the state facilitates the penetration and control of African societies by external powers.[39] It is precisely for this reason, for example, that the dependency theorists often dismiss African elites as neocolonial leaders who knowingly or unknowingly open the door to foreign interests to the detriment of their respective societies.

The neo-Marxist scholars disagree sharply with the "hinge" conceptualization of the state. They argue instead that the ruling class of the state can cooperate with the dominant economic classes of society to pursue capitalist development that runs counter to the interests of foreign powers. For example, despite the fact that one of the most noted early works by Colin Leys, *Underdevelopment in Kenya: The Political Economy of Colonialism* (1974), clearly falls within the dependency tradition, his later analysis has incorporated several of the critiques of the neo-Marxist tradition.[40] One of the most prominent critical scholars of Kenyan politics, Leys argues that Kenya's ruling classes and dominant economic classes combined forces to achieve a form of capitalist development that favors the Kenyan bourgeoisie at the expense of external economic interests.

Evolving debates within the neo-Marxist tradition are grappling over whether the African state is merely reflective of the interests of the dominant socioeconomic class of a particular African country (the orthodox Marxist interpretation), or whether the ruling class of the state itself can be independent of, and carry out policies counter to, that powerful domestic economic class. One of the most notable contributions to this debate has been offered by Richard L. Sklar, who argues that "class relations, at bottom, are determined by relations of power, not production."[41] This brief quote highlights Sklar's belief that the ruling classes of the African state must not be perceived as mere reflections of that society's economic system, nor as mere puppets of its dominant economic class. Rather, it is important to focus on the *political* basis of competition between classes within African societies, and recognize that a wide range of possibilities exists, in terms of class domination and control. For example, whereas in one case the dominant economic class of a society may control the actions of the ruling class of the state, the reverse may also be true depending on the power relationship between the two classes. In short, Sklar argues that one cannot automatically assume that one class or coalition of class groupings will always dominate other internal or even international class groupings. One must instead examine the potentially different political realities of class relationships in individual case studies.

New Directions in the Post–Cold War Era (Late 1980s–Present)

The end of the Cold War signified the beginning of a new era for critical scholarship devoted to understanding African politics and society. The decline of communism in Eastern Europe and the former Soviet Union removed an ideological beacon of hope for a variety of African Marxists seeking socioeconomic development independent of the capitalist path. Ideological allies on the African continent, such as Marxist regimes in Ethiopia and Angola, suddenly found themselves cut adrift by new leaders in Eastern Europe and Russia who were desperately seeking to cultivate cooperative relationships with the West. Even African students were not immune. After the reunification of East and West Germany, for example, thousands of African students from a variety of socialist and Marxist countries studying in East Germany were informed that their scholarships and visas had been terminated, and were told to return to their countries of origin. As poignantly stated by Timothy M. Shaw, one of the most prolific scholars within the critical tradition, these events ushered in a "profound period of revisionism" as the "revolutionary, nationalist scenario" anticipated by African radicals at the end of World War II gave way to an extreme "pessimism" at the beginning of the 1990s.[42]

A second trend associated with the end of the Cold War is a resurgence of debate over preferred forms of democracy. The downfall of communist regimes in Eastern Europe and the former Soviet Union — the intellectual heartland of single-party rule — reinforced the growing tendency of critical scholars to question the viability of single-party political systems in Africa. However, some critical scholars question the so-called third wave of democratization and the role of foreign powers in promoting multiparty democracy as a form of neocolonialism that is contributing to the **recolonization** of the African continent. According to Claude Ake, the adoption of multiparty political systems in many cases has fostered the **democratization of disempowerment**: a process whereby multiparty elections allow for the rotation of self-interested elites of different parties, while the vast majority of the population remains disempowered from the political system.[43] As Ake poignantly argues in *Democracy and Development in Africa* (1996), the critical aspect of true democracy is not multiparty elections but the assurance of "popular" (mass) participation within African political systems.[44] It is precisely for this reason that scholars from the critical tradition have placed a renewed focus on understanding the role of social movements in the struggle for democracy, as witnessed by the publication of an edited volume by Mahmood Mamdani and Ernest Wamba-dia-Wamba, *African Studies in Social Movements and Democracy* (1995), that brings together scholars from throughout the African continent.[45]

A third element of change associated with the end of Cold War is a growing focus on the power and influence wielded by international financial institutions, most notably the International Monetary Fund (IMF) and the World Bank. Although critical scholars, such as Fantu Cheru, in *The Silent Revolution in Africa: Debt, Development and Democracy* (1989), focused on the "imperialist" influence wielded by these organizations during the 1980s, this attention intensified in the 1990s when the former Soviet Union — the only significant alternative source of development assistance outside of the Western world — ceased to exist. In essence, the decline and fragmentation of the Soviet Union immensely strengthened the international financial monopoly of the Western powers that basically control institutions such as the IMF and the World Bank. This left African leaders with little bargaining leverage when Western offers of foreign assistance and loans were accompanied by increasingly strident demands for the significant restructuring of their domestic economies (see Chapter 14). As aptly argued by Thandika Mkandawire and Adebayo Olukoshi, *Between Liberalisation and Oppression: The Politics of Structural Adjustment in Africa* (1995), the foreign imposition of what are commonly referred to as "structural adjustment programs" (SAPs) often runs counter to the legitimate needs of social forces, and therefore corrupts true efforts at creating responsive democracy in most African countries (see Chapter 14).[46]

Finally, the end of the Cold War solidified the thinking of an **African nationalist school of thought** within the critical tradition.[47] This school of thought, also called the **Dar school**, originally grew out of a core group of African scholars based at the University of Dar es Salaam in Tanzania, that founded the African Association of Political Science (AAPS) in 1973. These scholars argue that the critical tradition's classic focus on the negative impacts of the international economic system and domestic economic classes must be complemented by a growing recognition of the substantial political power and autonomy enjoyed by the African state.[48] Specifically, scholarship must reflect the indigenous power of African political institutions and actors in their relationships with domestic and international economic actors. An important practical element of this school of thought is the conscious attempt to promote Africa-focused scholarship that builds upon African research networks and the interests of African scholars. The present-day embodiment of the Dar school is the Council for the Development of Social Science Research in Africa (CODESRIA), the leading African social science research institute based in Dakar, Senegal.[49] CODESRIA sponsors a wide array of research activities, including the creation of research networks within individual African countries, the sponsorship of workshops at CODESRIA headquarters that are attended by a new generation of scholars from throughout the African continent, and a publishing house that provides one of the most important outlets for critical scholarship written by African scholars.

CODESRIA and other like-minded African research institutes have emerged as the leaders of efforts to reinvigorate the critical tradition at the beginning of the twenty-first century. The declining popularity of socialist and especially Marxist ideals among a new generation of African policymakers has prompted a significant reexamination of critical thought. As is the case with their liberal counterparts (see Chapter 2), critical scholars are far from achieving agreement as to which of their theories are most relevant for the socioeconomic and political-military challenges confronting African policymakers. They nonetheless remain bound together by their common belief in the need to confront the often disastrous social and economic costs associated with liberal models of development. They are particularly united in their opposition to what they perceive as rising foreign involvement in African economies and political systems, most notably the West's attempt to impose liberal models of development, in the form of support for SAPs and multiparty political systems.

Key Terms

critical tradition
industrial revolution
forces of production
relations of production
modes of production
dependency theory
development of underdevelopment
metropoles
satellites
compradors
neocolonial
extraction of surplus
circulationists

capitalist world economy
core countries
peripheral countries
semi-periphery
political activists
neo-Marxist school
autocentric development
dependent development
recolonization
democratization of disempowerment
African nationalist school of thought
Dar school

For Further Reading

Ake, Claude. *Democracy and Development in Africa*. Washington: Brookings Institution, 1996.

Ake, Claude. *Social Science as Imperialism: The Theory of Political Development*. Ibadan: Ibadan University Press, 1982.

Amin, Samir. *Delinking: Towards a Polycentric World*. London: Zed, 1990.

Avineri, Shlomo. *Karl Marx on Colonialism and Modernization: His Dispatches and Other Writings on China, India, Mexico, the Middle East and North Africa*. Garden City: Doubleday, 1968.

Barongo, Yolamu, ed. *Political Science in Africa: A Critical Review*. London: Zed, 1983.

Cheru, Fantu. *The Silent Revolution in Africa: Debt, Development and Democracy*. London: Zed, 1989.

Fatton, Jr., Robert. *Predatory Rule: State and Civil Society in Africa*. Boulder: Lynne Rienner, 1992.

Markovitz, Irving Leonard. *Power and Class in Africa: An Introduction to Change and Conflict in African Politics*. Englewood Cliffs: Prentice-Hall, 1977.

Mkandawire, Thandika. "The Social Sciences in Africa: Breaking Local Barriers and Negotiating International Presence. The Bashorun M. K. O. Abiola Distinguished Lecture Presented to the 1996 African Studies Association Annual Meeting," *African Studies Review* 40, no. 2 (1997):15–36.

Nzongola-Ntalaja. *Revolution and Counter-Revolution in Africa: Essays in Contemporary Politics*. London: Zed, 1989.

Packenham, Robert A. *The Dependency Movement: Scholarship and Politics in Development Studies*. Cambridge: Harvard University Press, 1992.

Rodney, Walter. *How Europe Underdeveloped Africa*. Washington: Howard University Press, 1982, rev. ed.

Shaw, Timothy M. "Reformism, Revisionism, and Radicalism in African Political Economy during the 1990s." *The Journal of Modern African Studies* 29, no. 2 (1991):191–212.

Shaw, Timothy M. *Towards a Political Economy for Africa: The Dialectics of Dependence*. New York: St. Martin's, 1985.

Sklar, Richard L. "Social Class and Political Action in Africa: The Bourgeoisie and the Proletariat." In David E. Apter and Carl G. Rosberg, eds., *Political Development and the New Realism in Sub-Saharan Africa*. Charlottesville: University Press of Virginia, 1994 (pp. 117–44).

Notes

1. For an overview of the critical tradition within the field of comparative politics, see Richard A. Higgott, *Political Development Theory: The Contemporary Debate* (London: Croom Helm, 1983).

2. For an overview, see Ronald H. Chilcote, *Theories of Comparative Politics: The Search for a Paradigm* (Boulder: Westview, 1981), pp. 81–135.

3. For a brief discussion, see R. R. Palmer and Joel Colton, *A History of the Modern World* (New York: Alfred Knopf, 1984), pp. 427–33. See also Pauline Gregg, *Modern Britain: A Social and Economic History since 1760* (New York: Pegasus, 1967).

4. For discussion, see Karl Marx, *Manifesto of the Communist Party* (1848), as reproduced in Robert C. Tucker, ed., *The Marx-Engels Reader* (New York: W. W. Norton, 1978), pp. 469–500.

5. See Karl Marx, *Capital,* vol. 1 (1867), chs. 26–32, as reproduced in *ibid.*, pp. 431–38.

6. For a discussion of the various versions of Marx's theory of revolution, see Claudio Katz, *From Feudalism to Capitalism: Marxian Theories of Class Struggle and Social Change* (New York: Greenwood, 1989).

7. For an analysis of how Marx himself began to question the universal nature of his theory, see Teodor Shanin, ed., *Late Marx and the Russian Road* (New York: Monthly Review, 1983).

8. For an overview of his writings devoted to the Third World, see Shlomo Avineri, *Karl Marx on Colonialism and Modernization: His Dispatches and Other Writings on China, India, Mexico, the Middle East and North Africa* (New York: Doubleday, 1968).

9. *Ibid.*, p. 11.

10. *Ibid.*, p. 12.

11. See "The British Rule in India," reproduced in *ibid,* pp. 83–89.

12. August 8, 1953. Reproduced in *ibid.*, pp. 125–31.

13. *Ibid.*, p. 129.

14. For a summary of the debates over this issue, see Stephen Katz, "The Problems of Europocentrism and Evolutionism in Marx's Writings on Colonialism," *Political Studies* 38 (1990):672–86.

15. See, for example, Frank's *Capitalism and Underdevelopment in Latin America: Historical Studies of Chile and Brazil* (New York: Monthly Review, 1967).

16. For discussion, see Katz, "The Problems of Europocentrism," pp. 672–86.

17. Walter Rodney, *How Europe Underdeveloped Africa* (Washington: Howard University Press, 1982)(rev. ed., with a postscript by A. M. Babu).

18. *Ibid.*, p. 224.

19. *Ibid.*, p. 174.

20. *Ibid.*, p. 212.

21. See, for example, K. Mohri, "Marx and Underdevelopment," *Monthly Review* 30, no. 11 (1979):32–42.

22. See Higgott, *Political Development Theory,* pp. 58–62.

23. Arghiri Emmanuel, *Unequal Exchange: A Study of the Imperialism of Trade* (London: New Left, 1976). See also Christopher Chase-Dunn, *Global Formation: Structures of the World Economy* (Oxford: Basil Blackwell, 1989); and Michael Barratt-Brown, *Fair Trade: Reform and Realities in the International Trading System* (London: Zed, 1993).

24. Immanuel Wallerstein, *The Capitalist World-Economy* (Cambridge: Cambridge University Press, 1979)

25. The subtitles of each of these volumes (published by Academic Press, New York) are: (vol. 1) *Capitalist Agriculture and the Origins of the European World-Economy in the Sixteenth Century*; (vol. 2) *Mercantilism and the Consolidation of the European World-Economy, 1600–1750* (1980); and (vol. 3) *The Second Era of Great Expansion of the Capitalist World-Economy, 1730–1840's* (1989).

26. See Immanuel Wallerstein, "The Three Stages of African Involvement in the World Economy," in Peter C. W. Gutkind and Immanuel Wallerstein, eds., *The Political Economy of Contemporary Africa* (Beverly Hills: Sage, 1976), p. 39.

27. For discussion, see Immanuel Wallerstein, "Dependence in an Interdependent World: The Limited Possibilities of Transformation Within the Capitalist-World Economy," *African Studies Review* 17, no. 1 (1974):1–26.
28. See, for example, Karen A. Mingst, "The Ivory Coast at the Semi-Periphery of the World-Economy," *International Studies Quarterly* 32 (1988):259–74.
29. For a critique of this literature, see Otwin Marenin, "Resolving Epistemological Contradictions in Marxist African Studies," *The Journal of Modern African Studies* 27, no. 4 (1989):641–69.
30. See Higgott, *Political Development Theory*, pp. 60–61.
31. Samir Amin, *Neo-Colonialism in West Africa* (New York: Monthly Review, 1973). Translated from the French by Francis McDonagh. Originally published as *L'Afrique de l'Ouest est Bloquée* (Paris: Les Éditions de Minuit, 1971).
32. *Ibid.*, p. 270.
33. *Ibid.*, p. 11.
34. Higgott, *Political Development Theory*, p. 61.
35. Samir Amin, *Delinking: Towards a Polycentric World* (London: Zed, 1990). Translated from the French by Michael Wolfers. Originally published as *La Déconnexion* (Paris: Éditions La Découverte, 1985).
36. See Samir Amin, *Unequal Development: An Essay on the Social Formations of Peripheral Capitalism* (New York: Monthly Review, 1976), pp. 293–386. Translated from the French by Brian Pearce. Originally appeared as *Le Développement Inégal* (Paris: Les Éditions de Minuit, 1973).
37. Irving Leonard Markovitz, *Power and Class in Africa: An Introduction to Change and Conflict in African Politics* (Englewood Cliffs: Prentice-Hall, 1977).
38. Irving Leonard Markovitz, ed., *Studies in Power and Class in Africa* (New York: Oxford University Press, 1987), p. 8.
39. See, for example, Hamza Alavi, "The State in Post-Colonial Societies: Pakistan and Bangladesh," *New Left Review* 74 (1972):59–81. The metaphor is taken from Higgott, *Political Development Theory*, p. 67.
40. Colin Leys, *Underdevelopment in Kenya: The Political Economy of Colonialism* (London: Heinemann, 1974). For examples of his later work, see "The 'Over-Developed' Post-Colonial State: A Re-evaluation," *Review of African Political Economy* 5 (1976):39–48; and "Underdevelopment and Dependency: Critical Notes," *Journal of Contemporary Asia* 7, no. 1 (1977): 92–107.
41. Richard L. Sklar, "The Nature of Class Domination in Africa," *The Journal of Modern African Studies* 17, no. 4 (1978):536.
42. Timothy M. Shaw, "Reformism, Revisionism, and Radicalism in African Political Economy during the 1990s," *The Journal of Modern African Studies* 29, no. 2 (1991):192.
43. Claude Ake, "The Democratization of Disempowerment." Paper presented at a conference on democratization sponsored by the Transnational Institute, Cologne, Germany, November 13, 1993.

44. Claude Ake, *Democracy and Development in Africa* (Washington: Brookings Institution, 1996).

45. Mahmood Mamdani and Ernest Wamba-dia-Wamba, eds., *African Studies in Social Movements and Democracy* (Dakar: CODESRIA, 1995).

46. Thandika Mkandawire and Adebayo Olukoshi, eds., *Between Liberalisation and Oppression: The Politics of Structural Adjustment in Africa* (Dakar: CODESRIA, 1995).

47. See Naomi Chazan et al., *Politics and Society in Contemporary Africa* (Boulder: Lynne Rienner, 1992), p. 20. Chazan et al. perceive this school of thought as a synthesis of the liberal and critical traditions, whereas this essay emphasizes their influence within the critical tradition. I thank Guy Martin for drawing my attention to this distinction.

48. Among the African scholars who fall within this grouping are Claude Ake (Nigeria); Peter Anyang' Nyong'o (Kenya); Michael Chege (Kenya); Fantu Cheru (Ethiopia); Mahmoud Mamdani (Uganda); Ibbo Mandaza (Zimbabwe); Guy Martin (Mali); Dan Wadada Nabudere (Uganda); Bade Onimode (Nigeria); Issa Shivji (Tanzania); and Yashpal Tandon (Uganda).

49. For an examination of this theme by a former director of CODESRIA, see Thandika Mkandawire, "The Social Sciences in Africa: Breaking Local Barriers and Negotiating International Presence. The Bashorun M. K. O. Abiola Distinguished Lecture Presented to the 1996 African Studies Association Annual Meeting," *African Studies Review* 40, no. 2 (1997):15–36.

4

Politics and Economics of the Precolonial Independence Era (Prior to 1884)

King Otumfuo Opoku Ware II (1910–1999) surrounded by his subjects and sitting on the "Golden Stool" — one of the highest symbols of royalty within the Asante empire and among the Asante people of present-day Ghana.

THE AFRICAN CONTINENT is the **cradle of humankind**. Archaeological find-ings have confirmed the emergence of modern *Homo sapiens* along the East African coast as early as 150,000 to 100,000 years ago.[1] Interestingly enough, Western missionaries, soldiers of fortune, entrepreneurs, and colonial adminis-trators dismissed such a possibility as heresy as late as the 1950s. An important corollary to this Eurocentric view was the denunciation of African civilizations as "primitive," "backward," and therefore "inferior" to the "superior" civiliza-tions of Western Europe.[2] Nothing, however, could be further from the truth. The history of the precolonial independence era, the period that officially ended with the imposition of direct colonial rule in 1884–85, is rich with examples of political and economic sophistication. Although some of these political systems degenerated into authoritarianism and economic stagnation, others embodied the full blossoming of democratic practices and economic expansion. The vast majority of political systems fell between these two ex-tremes. A clear understanding of Africa's multifaceted past is an essential build-ing block in understanding the challenges confronted by African leaders as they lead their countries into the twenty-first century.

Diversity of Segmented Political Systems

A rich mosaic of political systems existed during the precolonial independence era. One of the most difficult forms of African political organization for West-erners to understand is what anthropologists refer to as a **segmented political system**. The term "segmented" refers to a decentralized system marked by the diffusion of political power. Segmented political systems lacked a centralized state and a recognized political authority capable of enforcing a preferred set of policies throughout a territory. Though political authority was diffuse, many communities were still nations, in that the members of the community often shared the same language, customs, and cultural history. The nation sim-ply lacked a central political authority to which the members of that society owed allegiance. In short, a segmented system constituted a nation without a state. According to the work of Christian P. Potholm, there are five specific types of segmented political systems (see Figure 4.1).[3]

Band Organization

The most decentralized type of segmented political system in precolonial Africa was the **band organization**.[4] Sharing the same language, customs, and cultural history, the population was divided into small **hunter-gatherer groups** that ranged in size from several dozen people during times of plenty, to ten to twelve individuals during periods of economic hardship. The hunter-gatherer groups were principally comprised of members of an extended family and did not have any form of centralized political authority. Even political authority at the level of the band was neither formally structured nor permanently embod-

Band Organization

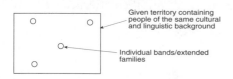

Classical Segmented System

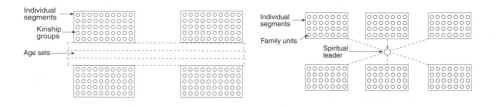

Universalistic Segmented System

Ritually Stratified Segmented System

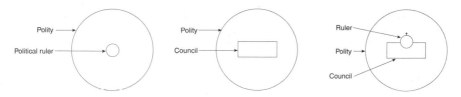

Autonomous Village System (City-State System)

FIGURE 4.1   Diversity of Segmented Political Systems

Source: Christian P. Potholm, *The Theory and Practice of African Politics* (Englewood Cliffs, N.J.: Prentice-Hall, 1979), pp. 13–19.

ied in one person. Decisions were the result of a face-to-face decision-making process in which all adult males took part.

The band organization was the dominant form of political organization approximately 30,000 years ago but is increasingly rare in Africa today. One of the most notable examples was the San people, who currently make up a very small portion of the populations of Namibia and Botswana.[5] This hunter-gatherer people is often derogatorily referred to in the West as the "Bushmen" of Southern Africa. The Tswana of Botswana also denigrate the San as *Basarwa:* "people from the sticks." The San became better known in the West as a result of their depiction in a popular movie, *The Gods Must Be Crazy,* and their unique use of a "click" language that is spoken through a series of clicks formed by moving the tongue against the teeth and palate. According to recent estimates, less than one thousand San maintain their traditional hunter-gatherer lifestyles in the Kalahari desert.

Classical Segmented System

The second type of decentralized political authority was the **classical segmented system**.[6] This system differed from the band organization principally in terms of the size and scope of the distinctive groups which comprised the common nation. Individual groups based on kinship, often referred to as "clans," could number in the tens or hundreds of thousands and were capable of tracing their common lineage back thousands of years to a specific founding member. The size of the clan ensured that more formal forms of leadership, often a group of leaders or a committee of elders, emerged to manage clan affairs, although no central authority ever evolved. Classical segmented systems typically fostered competition and conflict between extended clan families, especially in nomadic environments when drought and famine diminished already scarce water and food resources.

The Somali ethnic group constituted an excellent example of the classical segmented system.[7] The approximately 6 million Somalis who inhabited the Horn of Africa spoke the same language (Somali), adhered to the same religion (Islam), and shared a common cultural past, but were divided according to at least six major clan families: Daarood, Dir, Hawiye, Isaaq, Digil, and Rahanweyn. These clan families were subdivided into smaller units that assumed responsibility for organizing social, economic, and political activities. The smallest group, known as the *reer* (nomadic hamlet), ranged in size from five to fifty individual Somali families, and the largest, the clan, often included thousands or tens of thousands of members. The cornerstone of Somali political life was clan adherence to this maxim: "There are no permanent clan friends or enemies, only permanent clan self-interests." The precolonial history of Somali politics is therefore best described by the rise and fall of clan alliances in the absence of any central government, resulting in alternating periods of peaceful competition and clan warfare (see Box 4.1).

BOX 4.1

REGULATING CONFLICT IN SEGMENTARY SOCIETIES: THE ISSA *XEER*

Many people mistakenly assume that the lack of a centralized state or political authority in segmented societies fostered unending and unresolvable conflicts during the precolonial independence era. Nothing could be further from the truth. Among the Somalis of the Horn of Africa, an extremely complex system of conflict resolution was based on the payment of *dia* (literally, "blood payments"). In the extreme case of homicide, for example, the clan of the offending member was required to pay *dia* to the deceased member's clan or risk retaliatory action. The nomadic-pastoral tradition of the Somalis ensured that *dia* was normally paid in livestock. The amount paid to the injured party was based on tradition and decided by the elders of the parties to the conflict.

The Issa clan of the Somalis maintained one of the strictest and most detailed forms of *dia*, known as the Issa *xeer*. According to a renowned Djiboutian scholar, Ali Moussa Iye, the *xeer* served as the base of Issa pastoral democracy and resembled Jean-Jacques Rousseau's notion of the "social contract." The *xeer* clearly outlined the exact compensations to be paid to victims, and included specific livestock "exchange rates" depending on the type of animal to be used in payment (see Tables 4.1 and 4.2). The *xeer* not only played an important role in preventing conflict within and between clans, but also served as an important peace-making device once conflict broke out.

TABLE 4.1

Compensation for Permanent Injuries to Men

Body Part	Affected Portion of Body Part	Compensation (number of camels)
Right Leg	Entire	15.0
	Foot	5.0
	Tibia (Shinbone)	5.0
	Thigh	5.0
Left Leg	Entire	16.0
	Foot	5.0
	Tibia (Shinbone)	5.0
	Thigh	5.0
Right Ear	Entire	1.0
Left Ear	Entire	1.0
Teeth	1 Upper Incisor	2.5
	1 Lower Incisor	2.5
	1 Upper Canine	1.5
	1 Lower Canine	1.0
	2 Upper Premolars	2.5
	2 Lower Premolars	2.5
	1 Molar	1.0
Collarbone	Entire	1.0
Back	Permanent Injury Not Affecting Procreation	50.0
	Spinal Cord Injury Affecting Procreation	100.0
Right Arm	Entire	15.0

Body Part	Affected Portion of Body Part	Compensation (number of camels)
Left Arm	Entire	16.0
	Hand	5.0
	Forearm	5.0
Right Eye	Injured Pupil	14.0
	Punctured Pupil	15.0
Left Eye	Injured Pupil	15.0
	Punctured Pupil	16.0

TABLE 4.2

Exchange Rates for Compensation (in livestock)

Type of Livestock	Age	Equivalent (in lambs)
LARGE LIVESTOCK		
Male Camel	1 year	3.0
	2 years	6.0
	3 years	9.0
	4 years +	14.0
Female Camel	1 year	3.0
	2 years	6.0
	3 years	9.0
	4 years +	12.0
Cow	1–4 years	6.0
Bull	1–4 years	4.0
SMALL LIVESTOCK		
Goat	Adult	0.5
Sheep	1 year	1.0
	3 years +	2.0
OTHER DOMESTICATED ANIMALS		
Female Donkey	Adult	6.0
Male Donkey	Adult	4.0
Female Horse	Adult	30.0
Male Horse	Adult	72.0
Mule	Adult	4.0

Tables and discussion adapted from Ali Moussa Iye, *Le Verdict de l'Arbre: Le Xeer Issa; Étude d'une Démocratie Pastorale* (Dubai: the author, no date), p. 176. See also Paolo Contini, "The Evolution of Blood-Money for Homicide in Somalia," *Journal of African Law* 15, no. 1 (1971):77–84.

Universalistic Segmented System

The **universalistic segmented system** constituted a slightly more centralized version of the classical segmented system.[8] Despite the continued lack of any central authority, the members of various clan families were more closely unified by the existence of "age-sets": a status within the nation that transcended clan affiliation and was based on the period within which an individual was born. Age-set status applied regardless of the clan into which one was born, and allowed for a more systematic organization of the social, economic, and political affairs of the nation as a whole. In an age-set system based on five-year blocks of time, for example, a new age-set was created every five years. Everyone born during that period would constitute a member of the group. These age-sets predetermined an individual's assumption of various responsibilities within society, ranging from militarily defending the nation through the attainment of warrior status, or entering the ranks of senior political leader or senior elder. The underlying assumption of the age-set system was that different groups of individuals are better suited for specific tasks at different points in their lives.

The Maasai ethnic group was one of the most renowned examples of a universalistic segmented system.[9] Revered for their military and hunting prowess and distinguished by their deep red garments and ocher-colored hair, the Maasai today number approximately 300,000 and straddle the Kenyan-Tanzanian border. The precolonial clans of the Maasai were joined together by a complex age-set system for males that began when a young Maasai was circumcised between the ages of thirteen and seventeen. From that point forward, the age-set determined when the newest elite group of *moran* (warrior-recruits) would become junior warriors and subsequently graduate into the rank of senior warriors in the prestigious *eunoto* (graduation) ceremony. The *moran* period lasted approximately seven years. This period of a young Maasai's life was rivaled in importance only by his eventual assumption of senior elder status.

Ritually Stratified Segmented System

The **ritually stratified segmented system** constituted a variation of its classical counterpart in that otherwise independent clans were unified in the spiritual realm by a commonly revered spiritual or religious leader.[10] It is important to note that such a leader served primarily as a symbol of national unity, with duties usually restricted to presiding over religious ceremonies. He wielded very little, if any, political power, and was incapable of forcing recalcitrant clans or subclans into adopting a specific course of action. The religious and spiritual leaders often used their possession of sacred objects as the means for achieving and maintaining their special status within society.

The Shilluk people of Sudan were representative of a ritually stratified segmented system.[11] The symbolic head of the Shilluk nation was the *reth* (divine king). The *reth* served as the embodiment of the spirit of *Nyikang*, a mythical savior who conquered a new homeland for his people that was subsequently divided among the various Shilluk clans. The *reth* enjoyed no formal authority over the various Shilluk clans. He was a ritual leader who, in the words of the anthropologist, E. E. Evans-Pritchard, "reigned but did not govern."[12] The *reth* was responsible for guarding the "sacred spears" of *Nyikang* and making animal sacrifices to seek rain during drought and to celebrate victories in wartime. Although the sacred nature of his position ensured that the *reth* enjoyed significant powers of persuasion, he nonetheless lacked the formal political power necessary to impose his will on highly independent clans.

Autonomous Village System

As demonstrated in the previous four examples, most segmented societies were largely nomadic or seminomadic; their peoples followed **transhumance** patterns, in which the pursuit of food, water, and grazing lands for livestock were predetermined by seasonal changes in weather patterns. In the **autonomous village system**, however, urbanized groups sometimes ranging in the thousands and tens of thousands served as the cornerstones of local political organization.[13] Despite sharing the same language and culture, the populations of these highly autonomous villages were not unified by a central political authority or a centralized state. In some cases, these urban areas constituted virtual **city-states**, similar to the Italian city-state system of the Renaissance era. As opposed to its autonomous village counterpart, the population of the city-state was not always ethnically homogeneous. Most important, individual city-states enjoyed varying forms of centralized rule, ranging from despotic rulers to more democratic city councils. All of these varied forms of the city-state system belong under the broad category of segmented political system, due to the fact that the city-states as a whole were not controlled by a central authority.

The most renowned example of an African city-state system existed along the Swahili coast of East Africa. At the beginning of the fifteenth century, a vast network of Swahili city-states dotted the coastline from Mogadishu, the capital of Somalia, to the southern city of Kilwa Kisiwani in present-day Tanzania.[14] A flourishing Indian Ocean trade network in slaves, gold, and spices fueled the rise of these city-states, and particularly favored the geographically well-situated islands of Zanzibar, Pemba, and the Lamu Archipelago. The golden age of this system, roughly the first half of the fifteenth century, witnessed rising economic and political competition between city-states that had never succumbed to centralized political rule. These city-states nonetheless shared a greater Swahili culture that enjoyed a common religion (Islam) and language (Kiswahili), as well as a social system dominated by an elite of Arab and Persian descent.

Diversity of Centralized Political Systems

The diversity of segmented political systems was complemented by an equally rich number of **centralized political systems**. This type of political system corresponds to what Westerners consider to be the "normal" form of political organization: a political authority controls a centralized state that is capable of uniformly applying policies throughout a given territory, and the inhabitants of this political system owe their allegiance to the state. This broad category of political system encompasses what Westerners commonly refer to as the **nation-state**. In its purest form, the nation-state consists of one central authority (the state) and one ethnic group (the nation). In practice, however, most centralized political systems of the precolonial independence era were multiethnic in character although one ethnic group often dominated. Drawing upon Christian P. Potholm's work, one can distinguish three specific types of centralized political systems (see Figure 4.2).

Pyramidal Monarchy

A common form of centralized political system was the **pyramidal monarchy**.[15] Unlike its segmented counterparts, the pyramidal monarchy had a centralized authority, in control of a centralized state and capable of enforcing its

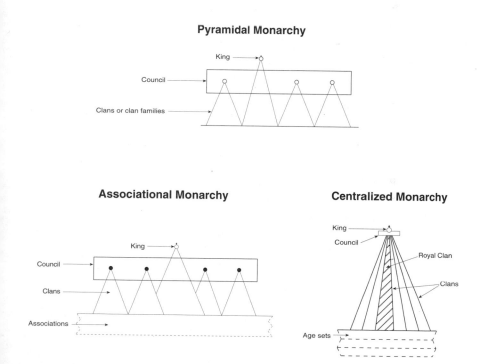

FIGURE 4.2   Diversity of Centralized Political Systems

Source: Christian P. Potholm, *The Theory and Practice of African Politics* (Englewood Cliffs, N.J.: Prentice-Hall, 1979), pp. 20–22.

will throughout the nation. The system was nonetheless pyramidal in that the king, despite his position at the top of the political pyramid, did not wield absolute control over his kingdom. Instead, the political culture of the pyramidal monarchy dictated that nonroyal clans and other ethnic groups enjoyed various degrees of autonomy from central government control, most notably in terms of their ability to raise their own taxes. The pyramidal monarchy therefore embodied a federal form of government similar to that of the United States, in which federal power is counterbalanced by the existence of fifty autonomous states. Most important, the political powers of the kingdom's subgroups were usually formalized through the creation of some type of royal council, which included leaders from the nonroyal clans and other ethnic groups. The royal council often served as an important source of countervailing power, similar to the U.S. model of "checks-and-balances" between the executive and legislative branches of government.

The Oyo empire of the Yoruba people of present-day Nigeria reached its height during the eighteenth century and is one of the best-documented examples of a pyramidal monarchy.[16] The original Oyo kingdom and its spiritual city of Ile Ife served as the cornerstones of an empire that ruled over a variety of other Yoruba kingdoms, as well as a variety of neighboring political systems controlled by non-Yoruba ethnic groups. The empire was headed by a sacred leader (the Alafin) drawn from the royal lineage of Yoruba kings (obas), and a royal council (the Oyo Mesi) also known as the Council of Seven Notables: a reference to the heads of the seven most important nonroyal lineages. An interesting set of checks-and-balances existed between these two bodies of government. The Alafin enjoyed several formal powers, such as the appointment of provincial governors and the ability to declare war, in addition to an equally important set of informal powers such as public persuasion, which grew out of the sacred nature of his office. The Oyo Mesi likewise enjoyed numerous formal powers: the selection of the Alafin's successor from a list provided by the royal clan in the case of death or incapacitation; control over the process for choosing the *Bashorun*, the supreme Yoruba military leader who was drawn from the ranks of the royal council; and, most important, the ability to impeach the Alafin should he stray too far from the accepted norms of Yoruba culture. As a result, a "delicate balance of power" existed between the two branches of government that fostered the maintenance of a relatively democratic society.[17]

Associational Monarchy

The second type of centralized political system was the **associational monarchy**.[18] The associational monarchy was similar to its pyramidal counterpart in all respects, most notably in terms of maintaining a federal system in which nonroyal clans and other ethnic groups enjoyed a certain measure of autonomy from the central authority. The unique aspect of the associational monarchy was the existence of "associational" groups that transcended individual clan or ethnic attachments. These groups served as intermediaries between local villages and the central authorities, and were often responsible for important duties, such as the collection of taxes within the political system. An important outcome of the existence of these associational groups was the further integration of the political system. Membership was highly prized as it provided opportunity to make contacts beyond one's own clan or ethnic group in the pursuit of economic or political gain.

The Mende people of Sierra Leone provides an interesting example of an associational monarchy.[19] A unique aspect of this political system was the widespread adherence to **secret societies**, known as the Poro society for men and the Sande society for women. Members were sworn to secrecy concerning the rites of passage. These societies transcended individual clan groups within Mende society and served both social and political functions. The most important social goal was the promotion of "socially acceptable behavior — womanly character and virtue, codes of male honor, or rules of public conduct on which there was common agreement as the ethical foundations for a healthy society."[20] Political functions of the secret societies ranged from wielding influence over central authorities on policy matters, to grooming eventual leaders with strong ties to the Poro and Sande societies.

Centralized Monarchy

The **centralized monarchy** was potentially the most authoritarian of the centralized political systems.[21] The most influential figure of what is also referred to as a **hierarchical political system** was a king to whom all within society were required to pledge their direct allegiance. The royal council, if one existed, was comprised of representatives directly chosen by the king, and was less likely to serve as a check on royal power than was the case in the pyramidal or associational monarchies. The political system was based on a very strong central authority that allowed little, if any, autonomy for nonroyal clans or other ethnic groups. These groups were unified by an age-set system that was completely loyal to the king. Other ethnic groups were readily absorbed into the political system when neighboring territories were conquered. The basis of citizenship was neither clan nor ethnic ties, but an individual's willingness to swear complete loyalty to the king.

The Zulu empire under the leadership of Shaka Zulu at the beginning of the nineteenth century is one of the most famous centralized monarchies.[22] The reign of Shaka is widely renowned for his creation of a militaristic Zulu empire that expanded its authority by conquering neighboring peoples and absorbing their warriors into the national army. Those warriors refusing to pledge direct allegiance to Shaka's rule were put to death on the battlefield. The national army was designed around a series of military-oriented age-sets, and successfully used military innovations such as *assegais* (short spears) on the battlefield. A standing national army and a militaristic ethic fostered a sense of unity that was strongly tied to Shaka's personal rule. As a result, the royal council and the heads of nonroyal clans constituted mere figureheads in a system that revolved around the Zulu king. Shaka's roughly ten-year reign was cut short in 1928 when he was assassinated by his half-brother, Dingane. **Regicide**, the murder of the king, was a common form of succession in highly centralized and authoritarian political systems, such as the Zulu empire under Shaka.

Regional Diplomatic Practices

Both the segmented and centralized political systems maintained an impressive array of foreign relations within their respective regions. Although diplomatic practices tended to be more formal when conducted by centralized monarchies, decentralized political systems nonetheless were faced with the same challenges of maintaining peaceful relationships with neighboring ethnic groups. When such efforts failed, or were met with confrontation, wars inevitably broke out and required a diplomatic response, regardless of whether handled by clan elders within a classical segmented system or the reigning monarch of a centralized monarchy.

Robert S. Smith's analysis of warfare and diplomacy in West Africa during the precolonial independence era clearly demonstrates the existence of sophisticated diplomatic practices that in many respects were similar to the practices of the second half of the twentieth century.[23] First, the dispatch of diplomats to neighboring political systems was extremely common. Often referred to as "messengers," "linguists," or "heralds," these individuals sometimes lived as resident diplomats in neighboring political systems. Unlike contemporary diplomats who work in elaborate embassies that may employ hundreds of workers, the resident diplomats usually served as the sole representatives of their peoples.

African diplomats also carried diplomatic credentials or "badges of office." Whereas all present-day diplomats carry special diplomatic passports, their precolonial African counterparts carried a variety of culturally significant credentials that included canes, staffs, whistles, fans, batons, and swords. Representatives of the Asante kingdom of present-day Ghana carried a diplomatic staff. The staff was topped by the figure of a hand holding an egg. This image was designed to "convey the warning that neither the king nor his representative should press a matter too hard nor treat it too lightly."[24] Regardless of culture or the time period in which they lived, few, if any, diplomats would question the diplomatic message portrayed by the Asante staff's image.

A third similarity with current diplomatic practices was the observance of diplomatic protocol and etiquette. For example, it was not uncommon for African diplomats to enjoy diplomatic immunity: freedom from political harassment or persecution by local authorities. This practice was also an extension of the traditional African custom of warmly welcoming strangers in their midst. Another example of diplomatic protocol and etiquette was the tendency of African kings "to converse only indirectly with their visitors and subjects."[25] What was often intended as a sign of respect and courtesy inevitably ensured a prominent role for diplomatic intermediaries, especially those who were knowledgeable about foreign languages and practices.

A final example of diplomacy that resonates with the contemporary era revolves around the "deliberate" and "tortuous" pace of diplomatic negotiations.[26] The extensive use of public flattery and gift giving, most notably intricately woven cloths, were integral aspects of such negotiations. One custom, still popular in West Africa, is the tradition of beginning or ending negotiations with the mutual breaking and eating of kola nuts. Available throughout West Africa, the kola nut is a stimulant and allows discussants to stay awake during extended periods of negotiations that sometimes last throughout the night. The kola nut, a symbol of West African hospitality, is broken into an equivalent number of pieces and shared among the participants attending the meeting.

The diplomatic network established by the Oyo empire during the eighteenth century offers important insights into the diplomatic practices of the precolonial independence era. The core of the empire consisted of the spiritual center of Ile Ife and the original Oyo kingdom led by the Alafin and the Oyo Mesi. The remainder of the empire was established by the Alafin and other political leaders as a series of concentric circles, in which those closest to the center were most closely tied to and dependent on the political favor of the Alafin; conversely, the further one ventured from Oyo and Ile Ife, the greater the independence of the local political leaders.

Four concentric circles of power roughly captured the diplomatic relations of the Oyo empire. The first circle consisted of Yoruba kingdoms, which owed direct allegiance to the Alafin due to the sharing of direct blood ties. These kingdoms were usually directly administered by Oyo. The second circle also consisted of Yoruba kingdoms whose leaders recognized the authority of the Alafin. The lack of direct blood ties, however, ensured that the leaders of these kingdoms enjoyed some degree of political autonomy from the center. A third circle was comprised of **suzerain kingdoms** that, although not inhabited by the Yoruba people, recognized the authority of the Alafin as the most influential leader within the region. A final circle consisted of largely independent political systems, such as the Nupe in the northeast, over which the Alafin had little or no influence.

The empire's citizens were divided into two basic categories: free and unfree. Free citizens were individuals who, depending on their clan or ethnicity, were more or less influential in the affairs of the empire. The most influential free subjects were members of the royal clan, followed by individuals of Yoruba descent, and finally non-Yoruba ethnic groups. Unfree subjects included individuals who voluntarily submitted themselves or another member of their family to *iwofa* status: a temporary form of indentured servitude similar to that practiced in the American colonies during the eighteenth century. Once the debt that required *iwofa* status was repaid, the individual became a free person. The Oyo empire also included large numbers of slaves, often taken from enemy kingdoms that were defeated during wartime, who were "usually employed as farm laborers or servants in households, as bodyguards to the chiefs and as long-distance traders *(alajapa)*."[27]

The administration of the Oyo empire was based on indirect rule. The Alafin exercised his authority by accrediting resident officials known as *agele* (also referred to as *asoju oba* — "the eyes of the king"), who in turn were supervised by royal messengers known as the *ilari*. These resident officials were responsible for overseeing the **tribute** to be paid by subordinate towns and kingdoms in recognition of their submission to the empire. For example, in 1748 the king of the Abomey kingdom agreed to pay a yearly tribute of "forty men, forty women, forty guns, and forty loads of cowries and corals" after the defeat of his kingdom's forces in a series of military engagements with the Oyo.[28] The Alafin also exchanged gifts with the leaders of friendly neighboring kingdoms, who were not under the control of the Oyo empire. In these cases the provision of tribute represented a relationship of mutual respect.

The successful expansion of the Oyo empire promoted a vigorous "guns-or-butter" debate: should the empire's resources be devoted to military preparation for further expansion, or should leaders concentrate on the economic development of those territories already conquered? From 1754 to 1774, the Alafin emerged as a voice of moderation, advocating for economic consolidation. The Bashorun (Secretary of Defense), however, promoted further military expansionism.[29] This period was marked by a severe power struggle between the office of the Alafin and the Bashorun, which ultimately favored the rise to power of an authoritarian Bashorun — at the expense of the traditionally powerful and prestigious Alafin. The upsetting of this delicate balance between the office of the Alafin and the Oyo Mesi (royal council) signified the beginning of the decline of the Oyo empire, and its ultimate replacement by what became known as the Ibadan empire.

The evolution of the "guns-or-butter" debate within the Oyo empire has two important implications for understanding the regional diplomatic practices of African empires. First, warfare served as an important dimension of foreign relations. Unlike current international norms that make wars exceptional events, the norms of the precolonial independence era ensured that warfare was more frequent and understood by African leaders as a legitimate tool of foreign policy. During the eighteenth century, for example, the leaders of the Oyo empire pursued war as an "annual or bi-annual exercise."[30] War was undertaken to satisfy both political and economic goals. The classic political rationales for launching attacks against neighbors ranged from placing more territory under the direct administration of the empire, to demonstrating the military capabilities of the empire to other kingdoms and outside powers. Economic factors also played an important role in military calculations. A successful military campaign increased control over external markets to which goods could be sold, raised the levels of tribute to be received from newly subjugated kingdoms, and ensured that greater numbers of slaves could be put to work within the empire and sold to outside powers.

At the heart of territorial expansion, however, was the maintenance of a dynamic political center that was capable of marshalling economic and military forces. In the case of the Oyo empire, the rules and regulations surrounding the selection of a new Alafin constituted an elaborate system of checks-and-balances that fostered political dynamism. When an Alafin died or was deposed, the elders of the royal lineage made up a list of potential replacements. The prospects had to be of royal lineage, born to a free woman and not a slave, and without physical blemish. The Oyo Mesi then chose the new Alafin from the royal list. The royal council had an obvious interest in curtailing the future Alafin's power by selecting a candidate who would best adhere to the constitutional conventions of the kingdom and who did not have too commanding of a personality, and therefore would not usurp or overshadow the power of the Oyo Mesi. The delicate balance maintained by this selection process had a tremendous impact on diplomacy within the empire. As previously mentioned, the disruption of this delicate balance in the mid-eighteenth century served as an important factor in the eventual decline of the Oyo empire.

Economic Diversity and Trade

Economic diversity was an important hallmark of the precolonial independence era. Three major types of economies existed. The first and earliest form of economic practice revolved around the continual search for food and water in the hunter-gatherer societies, such as the aforementioned San people of Namibia and Botswana. The activities of these groups ranged from foraging for fruits and edible roots to hunting for wild animals. The success of these very mobile groups depended on a sophisticated understanding of the relationship between the environment and food sources. The hunter-gatherer had to understand how the changing seasons affected not only the migration patterns of hunted animals, but the availability of specific types of fruits or edible roots in different regions. Once the dominant form of economic organization, the hunter-gatherer societies experienced a sharp decline by the middle of the nineteenth century as civilizations increasingly became based on the domestication of animals and/or the cultivation of crops.

A second form of economic system, **pastoral nomadism**, was based on the domestication and ownership of animals, most notably camels, cattle, sheep, and goats. The pastoral nomadic societies relied upon their herds as their primary source of nutrition. Like hunter-gatherers, they were highly mobile due to necessity. The constant search for food and water to nourish their animals often led to a particular animal serving as the centerpiece of their social status and customs. Interestingly enough, Western scholars historically perceived pastoral nomadism as a highly irrational way of living, in which the nomad contended with extremely harsh environmental conditions simply to achieve basic, subsistence-level needs. This stereotypical image of nomadic irrationality and obscurantism is clearly incorrect. As argued by I. M. Lewis, a noted observer of pastoral societies, the pastoral tradition in reality constituted a rational response to changing, and often deteriorating, environmental and economic conditions within marginal societies. The successful pastoralist required an "impressive knowledge of the faunal resources of his environment and his adjustment of herd movements to secure the best grazing and watering conditions which [were] accessible to him."[31]

An excellent example of a pastoral society was the Somalis of the Horn of Africa. Somali pastoralists shared a common nomadic tradition that placed great value on livestock, virtues of bravery and individualism, adherence to the Islamic faith, and an oral tradition that held singers and poets in high esteem. The camel was the mainstay of the economy, and a man's wealth was judged by the number of camels he owned.[32] The male camel was the primary means of transport, carrying the Somali *geer* (pastoral home) and goods for local and long-distance trade, and was also sometimes used for riding purposes. The female camel was the source of milk, one of the primary sources of nutrition for Somali nomads, and especially honored for her reproductive capacity. Other animals, such as cattle and goats, were also raised as important sources of milk and meat. It was the meat of the camel, however, that was the prized element of any Somali meal or family celebration.

The third and most prevalent form of economic practice during the precolonial independence era revolved around the cultivation of food crops. Agriculturally based societies depended on sedentary farmers who tilled the land season after season within a specific region. Sometimes pastoralism and agricultural practices were combined within a single economy known as **agropastoralism**. Under such an arrangement, some of the farmers who tended crops during the growing season would move with the society's herds during the dry season. By the nineteenth century, however, agriculturally based economies represented the dominant form of economic organization. Many farmers typically practiced the **slash-and-burn technique**, due to the generally poor quality of African soils and the wide availability of land.[33] According to this technique, a patch of land was cleared by burning and seeds were planted in the mounds of fertile ashes. When the soil became less productive after two or three years, a new area of land was cleared through fire and the process would begin again.

The degree to which a particular precolonial political system could depend on the cultivation of food crops by sedentary farmers significantly influenced a society's prospects for economic growth and political expansion. In the case of the Oyo empire, a strong agricultural base capable of yielding agricultural surpluses allowed for the creation of large armies, including highly trained cavalry units. Self-sufficiency in food also ensured that soldiers were not dependent on pillaging local communities in order to sustain themselves on the

BOX 4.2
GREAT ZIMBABWE

The awe-inspiring complex of stone walls and buildings known as the Great Zimbabwe is one of the most magnificent archaeological sites in southern Africa. The centerpiece of this site is the "Great Enclosure": a circular area, approximately 255 meters in circumference, in which walls up to five meters in thickness rise to heights approaching eleven meters. The stone bricks were cut by hand and fitted together without mortar to create Africa's oldest and most impressive stone structure, which dates back to the thirteenth century.

The term Zimbabwe is derivative of one of two words from the Shona language, *dzimba dza mabwe* (houses of stone) or *dzimba woye* (venerated houses), and serves as the proud name of the present-day country of Zimbabwe that emerged from white-minority rule in 1980. Interestingly enough, colonists and the white leadership of Rhodesia, the precursor to independent Zimbabwe, refused to recognize the possibility that an ancient African culture was responsible for building the stone structures at the Great Zimbabwe. Some even went to great pains to suggest that builders from non-African civilizations, such as the Phoenicians or the ancient Greeks, were actually responsible for the stone structures.

An increasingly rich array of archaeological and historical evidence clearly shows that the Great Zimbabwe was the center of a thriving Shona empire that lasted over two hundred years. The domestic economy was based on agriculture and cattle raising. A vigorous coastal trade in gold from mines in Leopard's Kopje, near the present-day Zimbabwean city of Bulawayo, was at the heart of the empire. The royal leadership of the Great Zimbabwe is thought to have controlled a vast territory where the ruins of approximately 150 smaller stone enclosures may be found. At its height, the Great Zimbabwe is believed to have housed approximately 11,000 people.

Historians are still in disagreement as to what led to the decline of the Shona empire in the mid-fifteenth century and the subsequent abandonment of the Great Zimbabwe site. Some argue that the move was forced by the depletion of local resources by a rapidly increasing population. Others argue that the true culprit was the loss of control over the gold trade, which led to economic impoverishment. Regardless of the reasons for its ultimate decline, the Great Zimbabwe monument serves as a testament to the ingenuity and prosperity of political systems during the precolonial independence era.

Discussion drawn from Peter S. Garlake, *Great Zimbabwe* (London: Thames and Hudson, 1973). See also S. I. G. Mudenge, *A Political History of Munhumutapa c. 1400–1902* (Harare: Zimbabwe Publishing House, 1988).

battlefield. Food was actually carried into the field, with some armies capable of sending their troops with up to three weeks of provisions. In the case of the Oyo empire, surpluses allowed Yoruba soldiers to carry a combination of "parched beans and a special kind of hard bread made of beans and maize flour."[34]

Surpluses were also critical to leaders intent upon practicing a vigorous form of regional diplomacy and trade. One broad type of trading pattern that developed is best described as **subsistence-oriented trade**.[35] This form of trade primarily, though not exclusively, revolved around the exchange of foodstuffs and other agricultural products. An impressive example of a subsistence-oriented trade network was maintained by the Tonga people of present-day Zambia. In addition to trading a variety of foodstuffs among themselves, the Tonga exchanged at least thirty different goods with ten neighboring ethnic groups over distances up to three hundred miles.[36] The cornerstone of this largely regional trade was the import of various iron implements such as hoes and spear blades in exchange for Tonga salt, a highly valuable commodity for food preservation. Although the Tonga were familiar with the procedures for creating iron implements, iron ore deposits were nonexistent in Tonga territory and therefore hindered the rise of a local iron-making industry.[37] Aside from a reliance on imported iron implements, the Tonga trade system remained largely focused on the subsistence economy. This tendency was clearly demonstrated by the seasonal nature of Tonga trade. Rather than promoting a permanent trading economy in which goods were constantly imported and traded, the Tonga system was highly seasonal in that it largely took place during the postharvest dry season.[38]

A second general type of trading pattern that existed during the precolonial independence era was **market-oriented trade**, which differed from subsistence trade in that luxury goods were often traded over long distances.[39] Permanent marketplaces and professionals who both created and responded to local demands for various types of goods and services were the cornerstones of this economic system. These trading practices at times tremendously affected the social and economic norms of a given society. As a result, market-oriented trade played a very important role in the rise and decline of local political systems.

One of the largest and best-researched market-oriented trading systems was the **trans-Saharan trade network**.[40] As early as 1000 B.C.E., the diverse political systems of West Africa were trading with North African kingdoms that shipped goods to and from the Middle East and Europe. Unlike current Western images of the Sahara desert as a desolate, inhospitable, and unpenetrable barrier, for traders of the era the region was perceived as an ocean which, like the seven seas, could be crossed relatively easily with the proper preparations and vessels. As a result, the trans-Saharan network included a variety of "ports of call" that developed into flourishing cities and allowed caravans of camels and traders to replenish supplies. Trans-Saharan trade not only was flourishing by the middle of the nineteenth century, but its financial value had exceeded estimates for all comparable periods prior to and including the so-called "golden age" of the network during the sixteenth century.

The types of goods capable of being transported along the trans-Saharan trade network were limited by two factors.[41] The journey across the Sahara desert usually lasted between seventy and ninety days, with the caravans averaging thirty to forty-five kilometers per day. Perishable items, such as foodstuffs, were clearly unsuitable for such a long journey. A second limiting factor involved the weight of the products shipped. Despite the fact that caravans of two thousand camels could carry upwards of three hundred tons of goods, including supplies to be consumed during the trip, merchandise nonetheless needed to have a "high value/low weight" ratio.[42] Freight charges alone often inflated the final cost of goods by 100–150 percent. Prices were further inflated if goods were lost, stolen, or exchanged for other services. The most profitable caravans therefore carried highly precious cargoes that weighed very little.

One category of merchandise, **state necessities**, was often essential to the pursuit of political power.[43] The state necessities sent northward included gold and slaves. Gold served as an important currency in Europe and the Middle East, and slaves served as soldiers or a form of cheap labor (see Chapter 5). The state necessities sent southward included cowry shells and weapons, most notably guns and swords. The cowry shells served as an important form of currency in West Africa, and weapons were sought to enhance both the defensive and the offensive capabilities of political systems. The trans-Saharan network also specialized in the trade of **luxury goods**.[44] The northern-bound luxury goods included ivory, leather goods, and ostrich feathers, as well as easily preserved foodstuffs, such as pepper and kola nuts. The southern-bound goods included cloths, copper, glassware, and decorative beads.

The vast economic reach of the trans-Saharan network contributed to the rise of four types of trading centers (see Map 4.1).[45] A series of **southern terminals** existed at the southern fringes of the Sahara desert, where northern-bound goods were packed onto camel caravans, and southern-bound goods were unpacked for distribution among the political systems of West Africa. A number of **desert oases** served as important rest areas for weary travelers, where water and food supplies could be replenished. On the northern fringes of the desert could be found the **northern terminals**. These cities served as the unpacking areas for northern-bound goods and the packing areas for southern-bound goods. Guides, provisions, guards, and camels were generally hired at both the northern and the southern terminals. Finally, a series of **northern coastal cities** oversaw the shipping of goods to and from Europe and the Middle East. A typical caravan might have begun in the southern terminal of Timbuktu, followed by an extended stop in the desert oasis of Ghat prior to arriving in the northern terminal of Ghadames. After the goods were unloaded

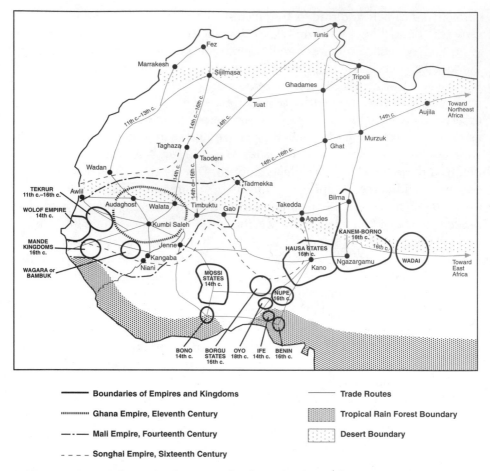

MAP 4.1   Trans-Saharan Trade Network (Eleventh–Sixteenth Centuries)

Source: Map based on Michael Kwamena-Poh et al., *Africa History in Maps* (Essex: Longman, 1987), p. 11.

from the caravan, they eventually would make their way to the coastal city of Tripoli for transport across the Mediterranean to the Middle East.

The trans-Saharan network constituted but one example of flourishing African trade that gradually integrated various regional economies into highly sophisticated trading relationships. Political systems of both the segmented and centralized varieties played important roles in these trading networks. Although much regional variation obviously existed, the African continent by the middle of the nineteenth century was creating the basis for integrated, sustainable development. This development built upon African political and economic strengths, and provided the basis for international relationships spanning the globe.

Key Terms

cradle of humankind

segmented political system

band organization

hunter-gatherer groups

classical segmented system

universalistic segmented system

ritually stratified segmented system

transhumance

autonomous village system

city-states

centralized political systems

nation-state

pyramidal monarchy

associational monarchy

secret societies

centralized monarchy

hierarchical political system

regicide

suzerain kingdoms

tribute

pastoral nomadism

agro-pastoralism

slash-and-burn technique

subsistence-oriented trade

market-oriented trade

trans-Saharan trade network

state necessities

luxury goods

southern terminals

desert oases

northern terminals

northern coastal cities

For Further Reading

Adjaye, Joseph K. *Diplomacy and Diplomats in Nineteenth Century Asante.* Trenton: Africa World, 1996.

Austen, Ralph. *Africa in Economic History: Internal Development and External Dependency.* London: James Currey, 1987.

Cambridge History of Africa (8 vols.). Cambridge: Cambridge University Press, 1975–82.

Connah, Graham. *African Civilizations: Precolonial Cities and States in Tropical Africa: An Archaeological Perspective.* Cambridge: Cambridge University Press, 1987.

Connah, Graham, ed. *Transformations in Africa: Essays in Africa's Later Past.* New York: Cassell and Continuum, 1998.

Davidson, Basil. *Africa in History: Themes and Outlines* (rev. ed.). New York: Collier Books and Macmillan, 1991.

Diop, Cheikh Anta. *Precolonial Black Africa: A Comparative Study of the Political and Social Systems of Europe and Black Africa, from Antiquity to the Formation of Modern States.* Trenton: Africa World, 1987.

General History of Africa (8 vols.). Berkeley: University of California Press; Oxford: Heinemann; Paris: UNESCO, 1981–93.

July, Robert W. *A History of the African People* (4th ed.). Prospect Heights: Waveland, 1994.

Kwamena-Poh, Michael, et al. *African History in Maps.* Burnt Mill, Harlow (Essex), England: Longman, 1982.

Lipschutz, Mark R., and R. Kent Rasmussen. *Dictionary of African Historical Biography* (2nd ed.). Los Angeles: University of California Press, 1989.

Newman, James L. *The Peopling of Africa: A Geographical Interpretation.* New Haven: Yale University Press, 1995.

Shillington, Kevin. *History of Africa.* New York: St Martin's, 1989.

Smith, Robert S. *Warfare and Diplomacy in Pre-Colonial West Africa* (2nd ed.). Madison: The University of Wisconsin Press, 1976.

Zeleza, Tiyambe. *A Modern Economic History of Africa. Volume 1. The Nineteenth Century.* Dakar, Senegal: CODESRIA, 1993.

Notes

1. This interpretation is based on anthropological digs ranging from Klasies River Mouth and Border Cave in South Africa to Omo in Ethiopia. See James L. Newman, *The Peopling of Africa: A Geographic Interpretation* (New Haven: Yale University Press, 1995), pp. 11–21. See also Christopher Stringer and Robin McKie, *African Exodus: The Origins of Modern Humanity* (New York: John Macrae/Holt, 1997).

2. The continuing prevalence of this Eurocentric bias is clearly demonstrated in Samuel P. Huntington, *The Clash of Civilizations and the Remaking of World Order* (New York: Simon & Schuster, 1996).

3. Christian P. Potholm, *The Theory and Practice of African Politics* (Englewood Cliffs: Prentice-Hall, 1979), pp. 11–24.

4. *Ibid,* pp. 12–14.

5. For example, see Elizabeth Marshall Thomas, *The Harmless People* (Capetown: Africa South Paperbacks, David Phillip, 1988). See also Alan Barnard, *Hunters and Herders of Southern Africa: A Comparative Ethnography of the Khoisan Peoples* (Cambridge: Cambridge University Press, 1992).

6. See Potholm, *The Theory and Practice,* pp. 14–15.

7. For an introduction, see Hussein Adam, *From Tyranny to Anarchy, toward Reconstruction: Rethinking the Somali Political Experience* (Washington: U.S. Institute for Peace, forthcoming 1999). See also the classic analysis by I. M. Lewis, *A Pastoral Democracy* (London: Oxford University Press, 1961).

8. See Potholm, *The Theory and Practice,* pp. 15–17.

9. See Cheryl Bentsen, *Maasai Days* (New York: Doubleday, 1989). See also Thomas Spear and Richard Waller, *Being Maasai: Ethnicity and Identity in East Africa* (London: James Currey, 1993).

10. See Potholm, *The Theory and Practice,* p. 17.

11. See E. E. Evans-Pritchard, *Essays in Social Anthropology* (London: Faber and Faber, 1962), pp. 66–86. See also Evans-Pritchard, *The Divine Kingship of the Shilluk of the Nilotic Sudan* (Cambridge: Cambridge University Press, 1948).

12. *Ibid.,* p. 74.

13. See Potholm, *The Theory and Practice,* pp. 18–19.

14. See John Middleton, *The World of the Swahili: An African Mercantile Civilization* (New Haven: Yale University Press, 1992).

15. See Potholm, *The Theory and Practice,* pp. 19–21.

16. See Robert Smith, *Kingdoms of the Yoruba,* 3rd ed. (Madison: University of Wisconsin Press, 1988).

17. *Ibid.,* p. 92.

18. See Potholm, *The Theory and Practice,* pp. 21–22.

19. See Kenneth Little, *The Mende People of Sierra Leone: A West African People in Transition,* rev. ed. (Oxford: Alden, 1967).

20. Robert W. July, *A History of the African People,* 4th ed. (Prospect Heights: Waveland, 1992), p. 98.

21. See Potholm, *The Theory and Practice,* pp. 22–24.

22. See E. A. Ritter, *Shaka Zulu: The Biography of the Founder of the Zulu Nation* (New York: Penguin, 1978).

23. The following analysis of diplomatic trends draws heavily upon Robert S. Smith. *Warfare and Diplomacy in Pre-Colonial West Africa,* 2nd ed. (Madison: University of Wisconsin Press, 1976), pp. 7–27. See also Joseph K. Adjaye, *Diplomats and Diplomacy in 19th Century Asante* (Trenton: Africa World, 1996).

24. *Ibid.,* p. 12.

25. *Ibid.,* p. 14.

26. *Ibid.,* p. 16.

27. Smith, *Kingdoms of the Yoruba,* p. 96.

28. *Ibid.,* p. 36.

29. *Ibid.,* p. 38.

30. For discussion, see J. F. Ade Ajayi and Robert Smith, *Yoruba Warfare in the Nineteenth Century,* 2nd ed. (Cambridge: Cambridge University Press, 1971).

31. I. M. Lewis, "The Dynamics of Nomadism: Prospects for Sedentarization and Social Change," in Theodore Monod, ed., *Pastoralism in Tropical Africa* (London: Oxford University Press, 1975), p. 429.

32. For an overview, see Axmed Cali Abokor, *The Camel in Somali Oral Traditions* (Uppsala: Scandinavian Institute of African Studies, 1987).

33. For a discussion of other farming techniques, see Tiyambe Zeleza, *A Modern Economic History of Africa. Volume 1: The Nineteenth Century* (Dakar: CODESRIA, 1993), pp. 86–92.

34. Smith, *Warfare & Diplomacy,* p. 59.

35. Richard Gray and David Birmingham, "Some Economic and Political Consequences of Trade in Central and Eastern Africa in the Pre-Colonial Period," in Gray and Birmingham, eds., *Pre-Colonial African Trade: Essays on Trade in Central and Eastern Africa before 1900* (London: Oxford University Press, 1970), p. 3.

36. *Ibid.,* p. 5.

37. Kenneth P. Vickery, *Black and White in Southern Zambia: The Tonga Plateau Economy and British Imperialism, 1890–1939* (New York: Greenwood, 1986), p. 27.

38. Gray and Birmingham, "Some Economic and Political Consequences," p. 6.

39. *Ibid.,* p. 3.

40. See Anthony G. Hopkins, *An Economic History of West Africa* (New York: Columbia University Press, 1973). The following account is drawn largely from this work.
41. *Ibid.*, p. 81.
42. See Ralph Austen, *Africa in Economic History: Internal Development and External Dependency* (London: James Currey, 1987), pp. 31–40, 273–74. It has been recorded that caravans carrying salt across "only a portion of the Sahara" could number between six thousand and twelve thousand camels.
43. Hopkins, *An Economic History of West Africa*, p. 81.
44. *Ibid.*
45. *Ibid.*, p. 85.

5

Political and Economic Impacts of Colonialism (1884–1951)

Silhouette of Keith June, an African American, standing in the Gate of Tears at the House of Slaves on Gorée Island (Senegal) — the final departure point for thousands of Africans who were loaded onto waiting ships and ultimately transported to a life of slavery in the Western Hemisphere.

IN OCTOBER 1884, the European colonial powers were invited to a conference in Berlin by German Chancellor Otto von Bismarck. The United States also attended as an observer nation, and its representative, John A. Kasson, signed the Berlin Convention, which formally ended the Berlin Conference in 1885. The Berlin Conference was designed to dampen escalating imperial conflict in Africa by officially demarcating the boundaries between existing European possessions. The conference also set in motion efforts to fully occupy those portions of the continent that remained independent, a process that was largely completed by the beginning of World War I. What became known as the **scramble for Africa** consecrated the creation of formal European empires and spheres of interest throughout Africa. Except for the unique cases of Ethiopia and Liberia, independent Africa ceased to exist, and African politics and society were controlled from the capital cities of seven European powers: Belgium, Britain, France, Germany, Italy, Portugal, and Spain. Disregarding the wishes of African leaders and their peoples, the European powers and their northern allies had permanently transformed African politics and society. Indeed, a firm grasp of the impacts of colonial rule is essential to understanding the challenges confronted by African leaders as they lead their countries into the twenty-first century.

Early Contacts with Europe and the Arab World

The scramble for Africa was preceded by a gradual process of European expansion into Africa over a period of roughly 450 years. Beginning in 1434, Portuguese explorers under the leadership of Prince Henry the Navigator began sailing the West African coastline. Prince Henry was followed by Vasco de Gama, whose famous voyage of 1497–99 extended Portugal's reach around the Cape of Good Hope into the Indian Ocean. The overriding economic purpose of Portuguese exploration was to circumvent Arab traders who controlled Portugal's overland access to the gold trade of West Africa and the silk and spice trades of Asia. Other goals included the spread of Christianity and the enhancement of Portuguese political-military power.[1]

The steady advance of Portuguese explorers marked the beginning of what is commonly referred to in the West as the **age of exploration**: the charting and mapping of lands previously unknown to European powers, prior to the ultimate imposition of colonial rule, including in Africa. The Portuguese were neither the sole nor the most powerful European empire to compete for global influence. From Prince Henry's initial voyages to the beginning of the Berlin Conference in 1884, the world witnessed the rise and decline of three **hegemonic powers**: Portugal (sixteenth century), the Netherlands (seventeenth century), and Great Britain (eighteenth and nineteenth centuries). A hegemonic power is a country whose global reach and overwhelming economic and military prowess allows its leaders to create and enforce the rules of the international system. During the twentieth century, for example, the United States emerged as the unparalleled hegemonic power.

One of the most devastating aspects of the increasingly Eurocentric world by the end of the fifteenth century was the perception of slavery as a legitimate and necessary tool of political-military and economic expansion. There were four major trade networks that specialized in the export of African slaves to different geographical regions: (1) the **Atlantic slave trade**, which primarily shipped slaves to the Western Hemisphere (North and South America, and the Caribbean); (2) the **trans-Saharan slave trade**, which principally sold slaves to the Mediterranean coastal regions; the **Red Sea slave trade**, which primarily sent slaves to the Middle East and South Asia; and (4) the **Swahili coast slave trade**, which focused on the Indian Ocean islands and South and Southeast Asia.

The Atlantic slave trade, also referred to as the **European slave trade**, began during the fifteenth century and was dominated by the European powers. Slaves were principally sought as cheap labor to work the colonial plantations of the Western Hemisphere that produced a variety of products, such as sugar, tobacco, and cotton, for export to Europe.[2] The trans-Saharan, Red Sea, and Swahili coast trade networks are usually jointly referred to as the **Islamic slave trade**. This network was dominated by the Islamic world, which began exporting slaves in "significant quantities" beginning in the ninth century.[3] Female slaves were sought to serve as concubines and servants, and males were inducted into imperial armies and worked on plantations.

One of the earliest recorded incidents of North American involvement in the European slave trade occurred in 1619, when a Dutch ship unloaded twenty African slaves in the British North American colonies. From this inauspicious beginning, the colonies eventually became part of a worldwide slave-trading network, the legacy of which, nearly four centuries later, would be over thirty million African-American citizens, roughly 12 percent of the U.S. population. The colonies comprising the future United States nonetheless constituted only a small portion (4.5 percent) of the European slave trade. The vast majority of the slaves were sent to work on plantations in South America (49 percent) and the Caribbean (42 percent), with relatively minor numbers sent to Central America (2 percent) and Europe (2 percent).[4]

The number and destinations of Africans sold into slavery have fostered a tremendous debate, what one scholar has referred to as the "numbers game," with important implications for understanding the historical evolution of African politics and society.[5] Although precise numbers are impossible to obtain, and all estimates should be greeted with a certain degree of wariness, some tentative conclusions can be discerned from recent estimates of the global slave trade of Africans (see Table 5.1).

The two most reputable estimates of the European slave trade suggest that between 11.7 and 15.4 million Africans were unwillingly uprooted from Africa

TABLE 5.1

Estimates of the Global Slave Trade (number of Africans)

Time Period	Slave Network				
	Atlantic: Estimate I	Atlantic: Estimate II	Trans-Saharan	Swahili Coast	Red Sea
801– 900	—	—	344,800	229,900	114,900
901–1100	—	—	2,000,000	459,800	229,900
1101–1450	—	—	2,143,700	804,600	402,300
Subtotal (800–1450)	—	—	4,488,500	1,494,300	747,100
1451–1600	367,000	442,400	879,300	344,800	172,400
1601–1700	1,868,000	2,158,100	816,100	229,900	114,900
1701–1800	6,133,000	8,792,600	821,800	229,900	229,900
1801–1900	3,330,000	4,000,600	1,385,100	862,100	1,063,200
Subtotal (1451–1900)	11,698,000	15,393,700	3,902,300	1,666,700	1,580,400
Total	11,698,000	15,393,700	8,390,800	3,161,000	2,327,500

Sources: Atlantic (Estimate I) figures are drawn from Paul E. Lovejoy, "The Volume of the Atlantic Slave Trade: A Synthesis," *Journal of African History* 23 (1982): 478. Atlantic (Estimate II) figures are derived from J. E. Inikori, "Africa in World History: The Export Slave Trade from Africa and the Emergence of the Atlantic Economic Order," in B. A. Ogot, ed., *General History of Africa. Volume 5. Africa from the Sixteenth to the Eighteenth Century* (Paris: UNESCO, 1992), p. 82. The figures assume a 13 percent death rate and a 40 percent overall increase by period. The Trans-Saharan, Swahili Coast, and Red Sea figures are derived from Ralph A. Austin, "The Trans-Saharan Slave Trade: A Tentative Census," in Henery A. Gemery and Jan S. Hogendorn, eds., *The Uncommon Market: Essays in the Economic History of the Atlantic Slave Trade* (New York: Academic Press, 1979), pp. 66, 68. The figures assume a 13 percent death rate.

and shipped across the Atlantic Ocean, from the middle of the fifteenth century to the end of the nineteenth century.[6] The height of this trade occurred during the eighteenth century, when 6.1 to 8.8 million Africans were sold into slavery. Not all of the slaves arrived at their intended destinations. Analyses of often meticulously kept ship logs suggest that at least 13 percent of the slaves did not survive the voyage across the Atlantic, most often due to severe dehydration and dysentery.[7] The tragic implication of this figure is that between 1.5 and 2 million Africans died in transit.

The Islamic slave trade lasted at least 750 years longer than its European counterpart, and was responsible for the forced displacement of nearly 14 million Africans.[8] The total number of slaves transported along the European slave network was either slightly higher (by 11 percent) or slightly lower (by 16 percent) than those traded within the combined Islamic network (based on the general range of estimates for the European slave trade contained in Table 5.1). If one also assumes that approximately 13 percent did not reach their destination alive, especially for those slaves who were forced to march across the Sahara desert on foot, at least 1.8 million Africans perished in transit. Again, dehydration and dysentery were the primary culprits of slave deaths. The cumulative volume and death rate of the European and Islamic slave trades therefore were roughly similar.

The European slave trade nonetheless exceeded Islamic trade in terms of geographical scope and intensity. The European network was nearly world-wide and included a system of **triangular trade** that linked Europe and Africa with the Western Hemisphere. The triangle refers to the three major routes that ships followed in the pursuit of economic profit (Europe-Africa, Africa–Western Hemisphere, and Western Hemisphere–Europe). Whereas ships bound for Africa from Europe usually carried a variety of manufactured products, and those bound for the Western Hemisphere from Africa carried slaves, the Europe-bound ships from the Western Hemisphere transported the output of colonial plantations, most notably rum, tobacco, sugar, and cotton.

The European slave trade also lasted a shorter period of time (roughly 450 years), but managed to transport much larger numbers of slaves. From 1451 to 1900, the number of slaves traded by the European network exceeded that of the Islamic network by 64 percent to 115 percent. Equally important, the yearly average of slaves traded within the Arab network (9,310) clearly exceeded that of Europe (2,447–2,949) from 1451 to 1600, whereas the seventeenth century witnessed a dramatic reverse. Beginning in 1601, the yearly average of slaves traded within the European network had risen to between 18,680 and 21,581. The average for the Islamic slave trade during this same period had only risen to 11,609. The European slave trade therefore not only surpassed that of the Islamic world during the seventeenth century, but it increasingly dominated the Islamic slave trade, as the European powers expanded their political-military and economic control over Arab and African countries alike during the nineteenth century.

A notable turning point in rising European global influence was Great Britain's decision in 1807 to make the slave trade illegal for British citizens. As the hegemonic power of the nineteenth century, Great Britain subsequently sought to enforce its antislavery vision throughout the international system. In the case of the United States, British actions led to rising diplomatic tensions despite the fact that the U.S. Congress had abolished the slave trade in 1808. Tensions emerged over Washington's unwillingness to allow Great Britain to stop and board ships carrying the American flag which were suspected of smuggling slaves. (It is estimated that at least 54,000 slaves were smuggled illegally into the U.S. between 1808 and 1861.)[9] Having fought a revolutionary war of independence against British colonialism, followed by the humiliating burning of Washington, D.C., by invading British troops during the War of 1812, neither the White House nor the U.S. Congress was willing to cooperate with Great Britain on the slavery issue. Active U.S. support for Britain's hegemonic vision only came about after President Abraham Lincoln announced the Emancipation Proclamation in 1862 as part of the North's political-military strategy to win the Civil War against the South. By the end of the nineteenth century, the majority of the world's nations perceived the slave trade as illegitimate.

Great Britain's active opposition to the slave trade was not primarily driven by an enlightened vision of humankind that understood the West's domination of nonwhite peoples outside of Europe to be repugnant. The economic imperatives associated with the rise and spread of the **industrial revolution** had simply made it more profitable for Great Britain and the other European powers to engage in legitimate trade with the African continent, as opposed to the illegitimate trade in human beings. The transformation that took place from the end of the eighteenth century to the end of the nineteenth century entailed the gradual replacement of the slave trade with the purchase of primary products grown on African plantations. Indigenous to the region, the palm tree and the peanut served as critical sources of oil that lubricated the machines of Europe's industrial revolution and served as the base of a variety of European manufactured products, such as soap, candles, and butter. Cotton served as another important primary product whose production expanded in leaps and bounds to satisfy the textile mills of Europe. European manufacturers also perceived the African continent as the target for sales of manufactured goods. Simply put, the European industrialists thought: "Why destroy African markets by exporting slaves to plantations in the Western Hemisphere when we can better profit from trade with Africans who work their plantations in closer proximity to Europe?"

The shift to legitimate commerce throughout the nineteenth century was accompanied by the arrival of steadily rising numbers of official and nonofficial Europeans in Africa. The official Europeans were government civil servants who transformed early slave ports into administrative enclaves. In many cases, such as the Island of Gorée off the coast of Senegal, these enclaves changed hands as European powers rose and declined in influence (see Box 5.1). The enclaves primarily served as diplomatic outposts. The activities of local European officials ranged from the management of trade relations and coordination of naval visits to dealing with the unexpected problems confronted by their citizens. In most cases, the enclave was the centerpiece of an emerging **informal empire**: political-military and economic domination without the formal occupation and control usually associated with the establishment of a centralized government over a given territory.

The most important pressures for further European expansion were found among the nonofficial Europeans. In the economic realm, private traders and entrepreneurs interested in gaining greater profits relentlessly pressed their home governments to extend the political-military reach of the enclaves into

BOX 5.1
ISLAND OF GORÉE AND THE ATLANTIC SLAVE TRADE

One of the most moving experiences for visitors to Senegal is a visit to Gorée, a small island approximately two miles off the coast of the nation's capital of Dakar, that once served as a major slave depot in West Africa. The island's first contact with Europe occurred in 1444 with the arrival of the Portuguese explorer Dinis Dias. The Portuguese named the island *Ilha de Palma* (Isle of Palms) and constructed a chapel in 1481, although they never occupied the island on a permanent basis.

The island's strategic location made it one of the focal points of Great Power competition from the seventeenth to the nineteenth centuries. The Dutch seized the island in 1627, renamed it *Goede Reede* (Good Harbor), and established the first permanent settlement. French domination, beginning in 1677 and lasting until Senegal's independence in 1960, was punctuated by brief periods of British occupation of the island (1693, 1758–63, 1779–83, 1800–17).

A visit to the *Maison des Esclaves* (House of Slaves), originally built in 1776 and refurbished as a historical site in 1990, offers a stark reminder of the primary reason Europeans were interested in Gorée: the highly lucrative slave trade. The world-renowned curator, Joseph N'Diaye, leads daily visitors past the weighing rooms, a series of dark holding rooms, and underground cells where tens of thousands of slaves were held prior to being shipped to the Western Hemisphere. The slaves were kept in the most atrocious of conditions, perhaps only exceeded by the cruelty of being chained below decks in the long ocean voyage across the Atlantic.

Upon entering the courtyard the visitor is first struck by a beautiful double-crescent staircase that surrounds both sides of a darkened central hallway. Immediately above the squalid slave quarters on the first floor were the living quarters of the Europeans who ran the slave house. It is difficult to imagine how human beings could bear to live above the tears and wails of other human beings separated from their families and held like animals.

The second vision encountered by the visitor is the brilliance of sunlight and blue ocean that emerges from an open passage at the end of the darkened central hallway (see the photo at the beginning of this chapter). The visitor's sensibilities are once again shocked when told that this doorway is nicknamed the "*Porte des Larmes*" (the Gate of Tears), a reference to the fact that it served as the gate of departure for African slaves as they were loaded onto waiting ships. The Island of Gorée and the House of Slaves are currently recognized as internationally protected historical sites by the UN Educational, Scientific, and Cultural Organization (UNESCO).

Discussion based on interview and guided tour with curator Joseph N'Diaye. See also IFAN, *Gorée: The Island and the Historical Museum* (Dakar: IFAN, 1993).

the interior. The European traders were especially interested in cutting out the African traders who controlled European access to the sources of lucrative trade beyond the coastal regions. Demands for political-military expansion were also supported by the numerous missionary societies, such as the London Missionary Society, that established themselves on the African continent. Renowned for establishing missionary outposts initially far beyond the political-military reach of their respective governments, missionaries demanding government protection during periods of civil unrest not surprisingly received a sympathetic hearing both at home and in the imperial enclaves.

The most noted group of nonofficial Europeans was the explorers. Despite their preposterous claims to have "discovered" indigenous peoples, the explorers nonetheless charted territories that were previously unknown to European governments. They also captured the imaginations of their respective peoples by publishing detailed accounts of their travels and "discoveries." One such individual was Captain Sir Richard Francis Burton (1821–90), a British subject who spoke at least twenty-nine languages and who wrote over forty books about his travels. "Burton was the paradigm of the scholar-adventurer," explains one of his many biographers, "a man who towered above others physically and intellectually, a soldier, scientist, explorer, and writer who for much of his life also engaged in that most romantic of careers, undercover agent."[10]

Imposition of Direct Colonial Rule

Burton's exploits both epitomized and fueled the **imperial mindset**[11] of nineteenth century Europe that accepted the necessity of promoting **direct colonial rule** throughout Africa. Racist and self-serving rationales, such as Britain's portrayal of its efforts as the "white man's burden" and France's pronouncement of its *"mission civilisatrice"* (civilizing mission), were offered to justify European domination over peoples deemed "backward," "ignorant," "uncivilized," "barbaric," "savage," and "godless heathens."

Two important turning points in this process were King Leopold II's declaration in 1884 that the entire Congo basin (present-day Democratic Republic of the Congo [Congo-Kinshasa], Burundi, and Rwanda) constituted the private property of the Belgian crown, and German Chancellor Bismarck's decision during that same year to declare protectorates over Togoland (Togo), Kamerun (Cameroon) and South-West Africa (Namibia). The decisions of these two leaders sparked the intensification of European efforts to occupy and declare ownership over those portions of Africa that remained independent. European leaders perceived themselves as locked in an imperial race to acquire territories, in order to prevent the balance of power from tipping too heavily in favor of their perceived rivals; hence the characterization of this historical period as the "scramble for Africa."[12]

The "rules" of the **international colonial regime** were simple and straightforward: to obtain ownership of a given territory that would be recognized as legally binding within the European nation-state system, the colonial power had to prove **effective occupation** by obtaining treaties signed by local African leaders. This pattern differed from that of an earlier age in which ownership was based on **discovery** (i.e., an explorer lands upon a territory previously unknown to the European world and claims ownership for his respective country). The reason for the shift was that much of Africa was already charted and therefore "known" to the various European colonial powers.

The treaties signed with local leaders were dubious at best, in essence serving only to validate claims among the various European powers. For example, many Europeans filed treaties signed by local inhabitants who were not in positions of authority, or who in any case were not allowed by local custom to sign away lands. Even when the proper local officials signed the treaties, the fact that they were written in a foreign language often meant that their true intent (i.e., European domination and ownership of local lands) was misunderstood or misrepresented. Often an African leader signed in good faith a paper described as representing a treaty of mutual respect and friendship, only to be faced in the future with the arrival of occupying forces determined to impose foreign rule.

The physical occupation of the African continent by the colonial powers was often met with political and even armed resistance from African kingdoms and ethnic groups. In the case of the Asante empire, Asante troops first clashed with the British colonial army in 1823. In fact, they fought a series of battles (1826, 1874, 1896) that ultimately delayed the final subjugation of the Asante to British colonial rule until 1900.[13] In battle the Asante, driven by the desire to avoid foreign occupation, were empowered by a disciplined warrior tradition that had served the kingdom well prior to the arrival of the European colonial powers. The Asante military abided by the motto: *Fere ne owuo efenim owuo* (If it is a matter of choosing between disgrace and death then I should choose death).[14] "Guided by this principle," explains F. K. Finn, a former member of the Ghanaian parliament, "an Asante military leader would normally commit suicide rather than fall into enemy hands."[15]

Several factors nonetheless ensured that armed resistance among the Asante and other ethnic groups opposed to European colonialism would ultimately be unsuccessful.[16] First, the European colonial powers, regardless of their conflicts on the European continent, were united in their quest to militarily occupy the African continent. Second, the European armies enjoyed technological superiority in the field of armaments. The Gatling gun, the precursor to present-day machine guns, was used to devastating effect against numerically superior African armies. Finally, the Europeans were able to exploit regional rivalries as part of a conscious policy of **divide-and-conquer**. In short, European subjugation of a particular African kingdom was often advanced by seeking the short-term aid of that kingdom's traditional African competitor within the region.

Except for the unique cases of Ethiopia and Liberia, the net result of the scramble for Africa was the imposition of foreign colonial rule and the end of

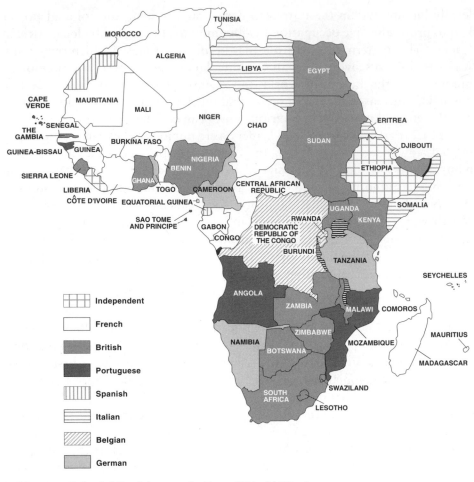

**MAP 5.1   Colonial Partition on the Eve of World War I
(with contemporary country names)**

the precolonial independence era. By the beginning of World War I, the African continent found itself divided into a series of seven colonial empires varying in size, shape, and geographical distribution (see Map 5.1). France and Britain maintained the most extensive colonial empires, with France dividing its territories into four major administrative regions: *Afrique Occidentale Française* (AOF — French West Africa); *Afrique Equatoriale Française* (AEF — French Equatorial Africa); the *maghreb* (Algeria, Morocco, and Tunisia); and *Départements d'Outre Mer-Territoires d'Outre-Mer* (DOM-TOM — Overseas Departments and Territories), including Mayotte and Réunion. The British empire in particular was constructed along a north-south axis as part of an unrealized British dream to construct a Cape-Cairo railroad linking South Africa with Egypt, and also included significant holdings in West Africa, most notably Nigeria and Ghana.

Belgium and Portugal led the **second-tier empires** that were relatively smaller than the French and the British. Belgium and Portugal were largely restricted to two neighboring regions — Central Africa for Belgium and Southern Africa for Portugal, although Portugal also ruled Guinea-Bissau in West Africa and the island territories of Cape Verde and Sao Tomé and Principe. Germany was stripped of its geographically widespread colonies following defeat in World War I.[17] In an experiment at the launching of the League of Nations, the forerunner to the United Nations, each German colony was temporarily transferred to another colonial power as a **mandate territory** pending transition to self-rule.[18] In the case of Italy, defeat in World War II ensured the loss of colonial holdings in Libya and Eritrea. The previously fascist Italian government was nonetheless "rewarded" for its final role in contributing to an Allied victory in World War II with permission to oversee a UN-mandated **trusteeship** of Italian Somaliland during the 1950s.[19] Spain maintained the smallest of the European empires, including control over the Moroccan coastal territories of Ceuta and Melilla.[20]

Each of the four major colonial empires that survived the ravages of World War II offered variations of colonial governance that nonetheless were highly similar in nature. British colonialism took on two specific forms. In those territories such as Rhodesia (Zimbabwe), in which a significant white population had permanently settled and was administering the domestic affairs of the colony, British policymakers envisioned granting some form of independent status to the state within the British Commonwealth of Nations, following the models of Australia and New Zealand. Throughout the remainder of Africa, British colonialism was based on the concept of **indirect rule**. This concept was popularized by Lord Lugard, perhaps the most renowned of British colonial administrators, who ultimately conceived of British colonialism as leading to independence under black majority-ruled governments.[21] Building upon the assumption that it was neither possible nor desirable to transform Africans into English citizens, British colonial administrators sought to rule indirectly through existing traditional leaders. As a result, British colonial administrators not only kept in place, but in many cases strengthened, a myriad of traditional forms of leadership within their colonies.[22]

French colonialism was based on a highly centralized form of **direct rule** in which each colony was divided according to administrative subdivisions. French officials directly administered the highest levels, and Africans considered loyal to France were appointed to administer the lower levels. The French model of colonialism was the most far-reaching in that it was based on a policy of **assimilation**.[23] According to this concept, all African subjects could theoretically achieve the status of full-fledged French citizens if they fully embraced French culture, and in so doing fulfilled a variety of requirements, including achieving fluency in the French language, converting to Christianity, obtaining at least a high school education, and becoming a property owner. Several Africans, such as Léopold Sédar Senghor, the first President of Senegal, fully embraced this policy to achieve the status of *évolué* (literally, an evolved or civilized person) and lead prestigious political careers both prior to and after the independence of their countries from colonial rule (see Chapter 6). In reality, the policy of assimilation was at best limited to a very small portion of the African elite who often found themselves caught between two worlds, one African and one French, in which their French compatriots would never truly accept them as equal citizens.

The Belgian and Portuguese colonial models were similar to the French in their desire to create a class of *évolués* (*assimilados* in Portuguese) that had adopted the major cultural traditions of Belgium and Portugal, respectively. Unlike their French counterparts, neither the Belgian *évolués* nor the Portuguese *assimilados* were ever envisioned to wield political power, whether in the form of political inclusion (as in an expanded French Republic) or ultimate independence (as envisioned under the British model). The Belgians deemed their approach "scientific colonialism" in an effort to put the best public face on what in reality was an extremely despotic form of governance designed to promote Belgian economic interests.[24] The Portuguese were less concerned with such rationales, particularly after the 1928 emergence of a military dictatorship headed by Antonio de Oliveira Salazar. Similar to the British, the Salazar dictatorship supported the migration of Portuguese settler communities capable of administering the colonies on a permanent basis.[25]

Political Impacts of Colonialism

Although in terms of world history the period of direct colonial rule was relatively short in duration (1884–1951) for the vast majority of African nations, it nonetheless transformed the domestic and international politics of the African continent. Despite the varied nature of Europe's experiments in colonial rule, it is possible to distinguish several cross-national political trends applicable to the African continent as a whole.

Application of the European Nation-State System to Africa

The most far-reaching political impact of colonialism was the imposition of the European nation-state system onto the extremely rich and varied African political systems that existed during the precolonial independence era. The origins of the nation-state system lie in the 1648 Treaty of Westphalia, which ended the Thirty Years' War (1618–48) in Europe. The treaty marked the beginning of the nation-state system, in which sovereign political entities independent of any outside authorities exercised control over peoples residing in separate territories with officially marked boundaries. When this system was grafted onto Africa, sovereignty remained in the hands of the occupying colonial powers. The application of this system to Africa therefore entailed the subdivision of the entire continent into separate colonies with clearly defined boundaries and centralized political authorities. With few exceptions, the boundaries of these colonial political units became the basis for the contemporary political map of Africa (see Chapter 6).

The imposition of the European nation-state system created a series of artificial states that, unlike their counterparts in Europe, did not evolve gradually according to the wishes of local African peoples. They instead were constructed by European authorities with little concern for local socioeconomic or political-military conditions. Indeed, a favorite account of Africanists is the image of two European leaders resolving a colonial territorial dispute by standing over a map and drawing a new line with a ruler! As a result, the artificially created colonial territories bore little resemblance to the classic definition of a nation-state — one people or ethnic group (the nation) ruled by a legitimate centralized authority (the state).

Division of African Nations among Several States

The second most important political impact of colonialism was the division of African ethnic groups among numerous colonial states. The division of the Somali people of the Horn of Africa is a notable example. Previously united by a common culture but lacking a centralized authority, this classically segmented political system (see Chapter 4) was ultimately subjugated and divided among four imperial powers: Britain, France, Italy, and an independent Ethiopia (see Map 5.2). The northwestern portion of the Somali nation became part of a French colony, *Le Territoire Français des Afars et des Issas* (French Territory of the Afars and the Issas), which achieved independence in 1977 as the Republic of Djibouti. The western Ogaden region was annexed by the Ethiopian empire and remains a province of the present-day Ethiopian state. The southeastern portion of the Somali nation became part of the British colony (and subsequent independent state) of Kenya. Two final portions, the British Somaliland Protectorate and Italian Somaliland, became part of the British and Italian colonial empires. These two portions achieved independence and formed a federation in 1961 that became known as the Republic of Somaliland.

The primary long-term problem associated with the division of one people among many states is the potential emergence of **irredentism**: the political desire of nationalists to reunite their separated peoples in one unified nation-state.[26] In the case of Somalia, irredentism emerged as the cornerstone of a Somali nationalist movement during the 1950s, which called for a redrawing of inherited colonial boundaries in the Horn of Africa. Symbolized by the five-pointed star emblazoned on the national flag of the Republic of Somalia, this irredentist quest envisioned the reunification of all five Somali territories within one pan-Somali state. The Republic of Somalia already included two of these territories (British Somaliland and Italian Somaliland), and therefore sought the "return" of Ethiopia's Ogaden region, the Somali portion of Djibouti, and the Northern Frontier District of Kenya.[27]

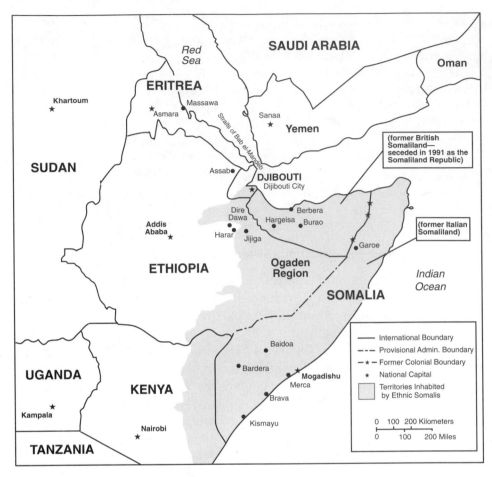

MAP 5.2   Partition of the Somali Nation

Somali leaders of the irredentist movement opted to seek reunification by force of arms. As a result, Somali leaders funded guerrilla insurgencies in Djibouti, Ethiopia, and Kenya during the 1960s, which led to the further deterioration of relations between the Republic of Somalia and its neighbors. The Republic of Somalia and Ethiopia also fought a war (1977–78) over the Ogaden region, which became internationalized due to the superpower involvement of the United States and the former Soviet Union, as well as their respective allies (most notably Saudi Arabia and Cuba).[28] Regardless of whether one is sympathetic to past Somali demands to redraw the inherited colonial boundaries of the Horn of Africa, or ultimately accepts the extreme methods of military force employed, there is no question that the roots of these conflicts are at least partially the result of illogically drawn European colonial boundaries.

Incorporation of Several African Nations into One State

The third most important impact of European colonialism was the incorporation of previously separate and highly diverse African peoples within one colonial state. Britain's creation of Nigeria illustrates this colonial practice and its consequences (see Map 5.3). Nigeria is comprised of over 250 different ethnic groups. Three major ethnic groups comprise roughly 66 percent of the total population and primarily reside in three geographical regions: the Igbo in the southeast; the Yoruba in the southwest; and the Hausa/Fulani in the north.[29]

A number of practical challenges are associated with the creation and maintenance of such a nation-state. For example, how does one communicate effectively across the entire territory? The British imposed English as the national language of administration, but only a minority of the population was fluent in the language at the time of independence. As a result, after independence a series of Nigerian governments included Igbo, Yoruba, and Hausa as official languages of administration, and recognized the importance of adopting less widely spoken languages in local education. Indeed, thirteen additional "state" languages are each spoken by more than 500,000 people, and another fifty-four "local" languages are each spoken by at least 100,000 people.[30] The practical challenges and financial costs associated with such a multilingual effort are enormous: Should all government documents be published in the four major languages or expanded to include the thirteen state languages or the fifty-four local languages? What language should be used for political debate in the National Assembly? Does television and radio broadcasting need to be transmitted in different languages? What should be the language of the nation's armed forces? Are some languages in actuality favored over others, providing an unfair advantage to a particular linguistic group?

In the case of Nigeria, religious diversity also posed a problem for the sociopolitical unity of the state. Although numerous Nigerian ethnic groups adhered to a variety of traditional religions, the Hausa/Fulani had converted to Islam and the Yoruba had converted to Christianity. Over the course of colonial rule, social and political identity became fragmented by the imposition of "Nigeria" — a concept which initially meant nothing to the diverse ethnic members of the new colonial state. How would individuals describe themselves over time? Am I British? Am I Nigerian? Am I Igbo? Or am I some combination of all or some of these identities?

The most notable challenge associated with the creation of these artificial colonial states was the potential clash between highly diverse political cultures. In the case of Nigeria, the extremely hierarchical political culture of the Hausa/Fulani dramatically clashed with the equally strong egalitarian political culture of the Igbo. The Hausa/Fulani political culture demanded complete deference of its subjects to the proclamations of the *emir* (king), whereas the Igbo political culture considered it the citizen's duty to publicly challenge and

MAP 5.3   Nigerian Mosaic

criticize the errors of his leaders. A Hausa/Fulani subject was expected to bow face down, his nose touching the ground, as a sign of his deference. An Igbo would never bow. The political ramifications of these differences, especially when one multiplies them by the over 250 ethnic groups that comprise Nigeria, were enormous even under the best of circumstances. The worst-case scenario emerged on May 30, 1967, when the Igbo formally seceded from Nigeria and created an independent Igbo country known as Biafra. A brutal three-year civil war followed (1967–70) in which an ultimately victorious Nigerian military government, led by Lieutenant Colonel Yakabu Gowon, undertook a devastating policy of starvation designed to bring the secessionist Igbos to their knees (see Chapter 7).

Destruction of Traditional Checks-and-Balances

A fourth political impact of colonialism was the dismantling of the traditional **checks-and-balances** that regulated political systems during the precolonial independence era. Whereas traditional leaders answered to the political norms and customs of their individual societies and/or ethnic groups during the precolonial independence era, the creation of the colonial state meant that the ultimate source of power became the European colonial administrator. In most cases, the European administrators would appoint only those Africans who pledged unswerving allegiance to the colonial power. Even under the British model of indirect rule, highly popular traditional rulers who were kept in power by British colonial administrators often saw their traditional power base deteriorate. Tensions frequently arose when the demands of British colonialism ran counter to the interests of the local population, and the local ruler had to choose between siding with his people and risking removal from office, or siding with the colonial authorities and maintaining favor with the Europeans. In many cases, even authoritarian African leaders could count on remaining in power as long as they served the interests of the European colonial power.

Authoritarian Political Legacy

A final political impact of colonialism, closely associated with the destruction of traditional checks-and-balances, was an authoritarian legacy that permeated all aspects of political life. In a normally functioning democracy, the relationship between the nation and the state is based on legitimacy. The primary objective of the colonial nation-state, however, was to achieve and maintain European domination. This authoritarian model of state-society relations became known as **Bula Matari** (he who breaks all rocks). As explained by Crawford Young, this title was bestowed on the famous explorer, Henry Stanley, after he successfully forced a caravan of African porters to dismantle and hand carry several steamships up the Congo river. In the context of state-society relations, Bula Matari embodied the vision of a state "which crushes all resistance."[31]

A coercive apparatus of police and military forces was therefore created in every colony with the intention of ensuring local compliance with colonial rules and regulations. Success was achieved through a conscious policy of **divide-and-rule**. Drawing upon the multiethnic and sometimes multiracial nature of their empires, the European powers would station troops from other ethnic or racial groups within a given colony. In the case of the famous French colonial force, *Les Tirailleurs Sénégalais* (The Senegalese Soldiers), colonial administrators sought to avoid the stationing of troops within their colony of origin, and certainly avoided the stationing of those troops among their ethnic group of birth.[32] The British were renowned for stationing troops from South Asia in their African colonies. The cornerstone of this practice was the expectation that troops with little or no ethnic attachment to the subjugated population

BOX 5.2

LIBERIA: SOLE AMERICAN COLONY?

The closest the United States ever came to becoming a colonial power in Africa revolved around its historically close "special relationship" with Liberia: a country founded in 1822 by freed American slaves who in 1847 declared their independence as a sovereign nation-state. The capital, Monrovia, was named after James Monroe, the fifth U.S. president. Thanks to its American patronage, Liberia, like Ethiopia, avoided occupation during the so-called scramble for Africa and was one of the founding members of the League of Nations and the United Nations.

The degree to which Liberia constituted a U.S. colony is open to interpretation. Unlike the European colonies, Liberia was neither the creation of, nor ultimately governed by, officials of the U.S. government. Liberia was instead founded by a private interest, the American Colonization Society, and the U.S. government consistently sidestepped international pressures to declare formal responsibility for the colony, which became independent twenty-five years after its founding and sixty-one years prior to the beginning of the Conference of Berlin (1884–85). Liberia's independence was not even officially recognized by the U.S. government until 1862, the year in which President Abraham Lincoln signed the Emancipation Proclamation freeing U.S. slaves in the Confederate States, as part of Northern military strategy in the U.S. Civil War.

A case can also be made for the existence of a *de facto* (as opposed to a *de jure*) American colony. According to this interpretation, the U.S. government wielded a significant degree of influence over Liberian leaders, ultimately serving as the guarantor of Liberia's independence when confronted with European aggression. In what served as the first and perhaps most notable event in a series of displays of "gunboat diplomacy," a U.S. naval officer, Lieutenant Robert F. Stockton, acquired the rights to the first lands permanently settled by freed American slaves by threatening local chiefs at gunpoint. Stockton's successors not only periodically provided military support to local efforts to expand the colony, but served notice that threats to Liberia's sovereignty would not be tolerated. J. Gus Liebenow, a specialist of Liberian politics, notes that the mere presence of an American commission of inquiry in 1909 "prevented both England and France from taking over the country as a protectorate as a result of Liberia's defaulting on the repayment of a series of European loans."

All observers are nonetheless in agreement that the United States was inextricably tied to the creation of Liberia, due to the simple reality that the country was principally founded by former slaves and a variety of other individuals of African descent, most notably slaves liberated from antislaving U.S. warships plying the West Africa coast. Although numbering less than 25,000, these resettled slaves evolved into a cohesive elite group, the so-called Americo-

Liberians, that perceived themselves as both different from and superior to the local African populations. The Americo-Liberian elite, comprising approximately 5 percent of Liberia's population, established a highly authoritarian form of government in which 95 percent of the population enjoyed few if any political rights. The "political paradox" of what became an Americo-Liberian dynasty lasting 133 years, explains Liebenow, was the "systematic denial of liberty" to the local population by "those who — on the basis of skin color alone — had been denied the rights and privileges of full participation in American society." In short, the oppressed became the oppressors with the tacit acceptance of the U.S. government.

The Americo-Liberian dynasty came to an end in 1980 when Master Sergeant Samuel K. Doe took power in a military coup d'état. Although many Liberians rejoiced at the overthrow of the hated Americo-Liberian elite, with many claiming that 1980 was truly the year of independence for the Liberian people, the Doe regime was equally uninterested in promoting democracy and created a highly authoritarian regime. President Doe was himself executed by opposition guerrilla forces in 1990, an event that heralded the collapse of the Liberian state and the unleashing of a brutal civil war. On July 19, 1997, Charles Taylor, the guerrilla leader whose forces executed Doe and bore the brunt of the fighting during the Liberian civil war, was elected president.

Discussion drawn from J. Gus Liebenow, *Liberia: The Quest for Democracy* (Bloomington: Indiana University Press, 1987).

---

would have few reservations about taking military action against that population. The same divide-and-rule logic was employed when creating local police forces.

The coercive nature of colonial police and military forces contributed to the creation of an authoritarian environment that carried over into the contemporary independence era. As will be discussed in Chapter 10, the first generation of African elites, who were trained within this colonial system and who led their countries to independence beginning in the 1950s, tended to create single-party political systems that banned political dissent. As further discussed in Chapter 11, this authoritarian trend was matched by an explosion of military coups d'état in the 1960s that replaced civilian regimes with a variety of military forms of governance.

Economic Impacts of Colonialism

The period of direct colonial rule also permanently altered the domestic and international economic relations of the African continent. Once again drawing upon the varied nature of Europe's colonial experiments, it is possible to distinguish several cross-national economic trends applicable to the African continent as a whole.

Creation of Closed Economic Systems

Leaders historically have sought to strengthen their economic power and increase the diversity of products available to their peoples by trading with their neighbors. Neighboring peoples often share similar cultural and historical characteristics that facilitate economic interaction, as well as geographical proximity, which makes them logical partners for economic cooperation. It is precisely for this reason that regional trading blocs, such as the European Union, the North American Free Trade Association, and the Southern Africa Development Community (SADC), have proliferated in specific geographical regions throughout the second half of the twentieth century (see Chapter 13). As already discussed, the same economic logic fueled burgeoning regional trade and economic cooperation throughout Africa during the precolonial independence era, as witnessed by the growth of the trans-Saharan trade network.

In the aftermath of the imposition of direct colonial rule, colonial administrators oversaw the destruction of regional economic ties through the transformation of individual colonies into **closed economic systems**. Colonial administrators sought to ensure that all economic interaction within a given empire took place exclusively between the European colonial power and its individual colonies. In the case of the German colony of Togoland, German colonial administrators strove to eliminate cross-border trade with the neighboring British colony of the Gold Coast (Ghana) and the neighboring French colonies of Dahomey (Benin) and Upper Volta (Burkina Faso), and instead fostered strong exclusive economic ties with Germany.

An important element of the closed economic model was the government's granting of trade monopolies to **chartered companies** that often assumed complete responsibility for overseeing the socioeconomic and political-military transformation of the colony, at least until a "proper" state structure could be developed by colonial administrators. In Germany's East African colony of Tanganyika, the German government granted complete sovereignty to the *Deutsch-Ostafrikanische Gesellschaft* (German East Africa Company) headed by Carl Peters, one of the most fervent proponents of German colonialism.[33]

The most important impact of these closed trading systems was that all regional trade, except that which took place within individual empires, was virtually destroyed — as illustrated by the decline of the trans-Saharan trade network. Regional trade that once crisscrossed the Sahara desert was gradually replaced, during the latter quarter of the nineteenth century, by externally oriented economies' shipping of products from the interior to the coastal regions, for eventual transshipment to Europe and other outposts of the global European empires. As a result, the once vibrant outposts of the Sahara desert, such as the fabled city of Timbuktu, which were built upon regional trade and economic development, entered a period of serious socioeconomic decline as their function as trade posts gradually disappeared. Indeed, one could associate emerging notions of the Sahara desert as a barrier to regional trade and investment with the gradual destruction of the trans-Saharan trade network at the end of the nineteenth century.[34]

Creation of Export-Oriented, Mono-Crop or Mono-Mineral Economies

The second economic impact of colonialism was the transformation of individual colonies into export-oriented economies that, in the extreme, produced one primary product desired by the European colonial power. These so-called **mono-crop** or **mono-mineral economies** were designed to serve as convenient and cheap sources of raw materials for European industry. Once developed, the colonies were also expected to serve as markets for the sale of manufactured goods produced in Europe and other regions of the widely scattered European empires.

One example of the promotion of a mono-crop colonial economy was French efforts during the nineteenth century to expand the cultivation of peanuts in Senegal. Peanuts, the oil of which was used for a variety of cooking and industrial purposes in Africa and Europe, historically had been grown on a limited scale in Senegal even prior to the imposition of direct colonial rule. The dramatic surge in peanut production that took place under the auspices of the colonial state resulted from an alliance between French colonial administrators and local Muslim religious leaders *(marabouts)*, both of whom jointly recognized the financial profits to be gained from making Senegal a center for peanut production within the French colonial empire.

The willingness of local *marabouts* to promote peanut production through the mobilization of their disciples *(taalibe)* achieved remarkable results. From 1885 to the eve of World War I, annual peanut production increased seven-fold, from 45,000 to 300,000 metric tons.[35] On the eve of independence from colonial rule in 1960, roughly two-thirds of Senegal's rural population was involved in peanut production, and the peanut crop accounted for at least two-thirds of the total value of all Senegalese exports.[36] As aptly noted by Sheldon Gellar, the prosperity of Senegal's colonial economy became "inextricably linked" to peanut production.[37]

The promotion of these mono-crop or mono-mineral colonial economies during the colonial era entailed serious costs for the local African populations, and significantly hindered the long-term economic development of the African continent. Two trends in particular demonstrate that the peanut economy nurtured under French colonialism constituted at best a mixed blessing for Senegal's socioeconomic development.[38] First, an economy geared toward the production of a primary product is vulnerable to the unreliability of international prices paid for that product. The economic history of the second half of the twentieth century clearly demonstrates that the prices for primary products fluctuate dramatically, and in general have gradually declined relative to the costs of manufactured products. As a result, something as simple as estimating government revenues from taxes in order to ensure a variety of government services becomes extremely difficult, if not impossible. How can a government, dependent on revenues from one product, maintain its domestic and international financial commitments if a significant portion of the crop is decimated by poor weather? Moreover, how does the government respond when, as in the case of Senegal, the peanut production that formed the basis for its colonial economy suffers a sharp decrease in international demand due to its replacement by a cheaper and more effective substitute, in this case, petroleum oil from the Middle East?

A second important point revolves around the negative relationship between the promotion of primary products and food production. Specifically, the creation of mono-crop and mono-mineral colonial economies was directly associated with a dramatic decline in the production of traditional foodstuffs. This agricultural shortcoming carried over into the contemporary independence era as levels of food production declined relative to the needs of growing populations, contributing to malnutrition and chronic famine conditions in various regions. One troubling consequence of this trend is that Africa was the only region of the world that suffered from a per capita decline in food production from the 1960s to the 1980s.

Evolution of Perverse Infrastructural Development

A third economic impact of colonialism was the perverse development of infrastructure, such as railroads and telecommunications, critical to economic development. An analysis of the railroad sector offers some telling insights (see Map 5.4). The colonial railroads were designed to haul primary products to the coast for eventual export to Europe and other geographical regions of the European empires. For example, the construction of the French colonial railroad linking Bamako, Mali, with Dakar, Senegal, the subject of a famous novel written by the Senegalese novelist Sembène Ousmane, was designed specifically to effectively transport peanut production.[39]

The export-oriented nature of these railroads is significant for two reasons. First, the design of these transportation systems inevitably hindered regional development. If the primary purpose of the colonial railroads had been the promotion of regional development, one could envision a different configuration in West Africa that would have crisscrossed the Sahara desert, or at minimum would have followed east-west trajectories across the northern and southern edges of the desert. In the case of the United States, for example, one of the most notable achievements of the nineteenth century was the linking of the east and west coasts by a single railway line that subsequently served as the basis for internal economic growth and development. In the case of West Africa, however, a series of railroads designed with little consideration of its impact on regional development simply links the interior with the coastal regions. Dreams of linking these railroads, even if the financial resources were available, are unlikely to be realized in the near future due to the fact that each railway line was often built using a different rail gauge.

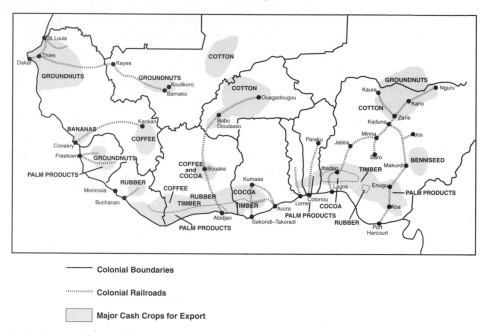

MAP 5.4   Railroads in Colonial West Africa (1930s)

Source: Map based on Michael Kwamena-Poh et al., *Africa History in Maps* (Essex: Longman, 1987), p. 61.

The export-oriented railroad systems also fostered the growth of other perverse forms of infrastructural development. For example, the primary reason why Bamako became the capital of Mali was its strategic location at the end of Dakar-Bamako railway line. Indeed, the importance of the railroad as one of the cornerstones of the colonial economy ensured that roads, telephone lines, and smaller towns and cities would eventually be built along the main railway line.

The perverse infrastructural demands of the colonial economy contributed to the uneven development of the African colonies, prompting some colonial observers to speak of the creation of **dual economies**: the first revolving around a European-induced cash economy and the second revolving around African subsistence farming. In the case of Senegal, Gellar suggests that the colonial economy could be divided into at least three sectors: (1) a *"modern," essentially European sector* principally based in the capital, Dakar, and other major urban areas where European colonial administrators and an emerging African elite would manage the major import-export houses and colonial banks; (2) a *cash-crop sector* principally located in the peanut-producing plantations and associated areas, such as mining towns along the railway line, where African farmers and workers could obtain cash employment; and (3) a predominantly *subsistence sector* where foodstuffs would be grown for local consumption.[40] The inherent inequality between these various sectors posed a significant challenge to leaders of the contemporary independence era who were intent on promoting broadly shared economic development.

Authoritarian Legacy of the State

The final economic impact of colonialism was an authoritarian legacy that permeated all aspects of economic life. The most nefarious side of this legacy was the institution of forced labor to ensure that sufficient numbers of farmers and workers were available to meet the needs of the colonial economy, such as tending plantation crops, working at the mines, and constructing roads and railroads. In the case of the British colony of Ghana, the meticulously kept records of the Transport Department document that it was not uncommon at the beginning of the twentieth century for Africans to be forced to work as "carriers" of boxes or bundles in areas where other forms of transport were either impracticable due to the tsetse fly or simply unavailable. The records document that these carriers were forced to work during a twelve-month period in which they averaged approximately four hundred miles a month. As a result, many carriers became incapacitated when their uncovered feet became "almost completely worn through."[41] The most shocking element of this report, explained Claude Ake, a Nigerian scholar, was how the British colonial authorities resolved this "technical" problem: henceforth the feet of the carriers were to be tarred![42]

Britain abolished forced labor in its colonies in 1923, but retained another less intrusive — yet nonetheless authoritarian — element of the colonial economy: **marketing boards**. This colonial economic institution, adopted in varying forms by all colonial powers, maintained monopolistic control over the buying and selling of primary products in each colony. Each year the board would determine a set price to be paid to farmers for a specific amount of an individual product. Lacking alternatives, the farmers had no choice but to sell their goods through the colonial marketing board. The most egregious injustice of this economic relationship was the marketing board practice of purchasing products at prices well below that of the international market. In turn, the marketing board would then sell the product at a handsome profit for the colonial authority.[43]

In the British colony of Nigeria, four marketing boards maintained monopoly rights over the production and marketing of four primary export crops: the Nigerian Cocoa Marketing Board, the Nigerian Palm Produce Marketing Board, the Nigerian Groundnut Marketing Board, and the Nigerian Cotton Marketing Board. These four marketing boards were "so profitable" to the colonial state that they were transformed into four regional marketing boards with responsibility for all primary products produced within their respective zones.[44] The importance of these boards to the financial success of the colonial state, at the expense of African producers, is illuminated by the enormous profits obtained. The British colonial state in Nigeria made a 733 percent profit on peanuts and a 559 percent profit on palm oil, of which little or none was passed along to the African producers.

Although the most coercive elements of the colonial economy, such as forced labor, were eventually abolished, the coercive role of the state in the economic arena carried over into the contemporary independence era. During the first three decades of this era, the majority of African policymakers oversaw the strengthening of state involvement in the economy. As will be discussed more extensively in Chapter 10, an important element of state economic involvement was the creation and rapid expansion of government-owned or government-controlled corporations (known as "parastatals") in all sectors of the economy, especially telecommunications, energy, and transportation. The often corrupt and inefficient nature of these corporations contributed in the 1980s to what is now commonly referred to as the "crisis of the African state": the increasing inability of the independent successor of the colonial state to respond to the day-to-day needs of African populations. The scope and impact of the political and economic legacies of the colonial state remains an issue of paramount importance at the beginning of the twenty-first century.[45]

Key Terms

scramble for Africa

age of exploration

hegemonic powers

Atlantic slave trade

trans-Saharan slave trade

Red Sea slave trade

Swahili coast slave trade

European slave trade

Islamic slave trade

triangular trade

industrial revolution

informal empire

imperial mindset

direct colonial rule

international colonial regime

effective occupation

discovery

divide-and-conquer

second-tier empires

mandate territory

trusteeship

indirect rule

direct rule

assimilation

irredentism

checks-and-balances

Bula Matari

divide-and-rule

closed economic systems

chartered companies

mono-crop economies

mono-mineral economies

dual economies

marketing boards

For Further Reading

Boahen, A. Adu. *African Perspectives on Colonialism*. Baltimore: Johns Hopkins University Press, 1987.

Boahen, A. Adu, ed. *General History of Africa* (vol. 7), *Africa under Colonial Domination 1880–1935*. Berkeley: University of California Press; Oxford: Heinemann; Paris: UNESCO, 1985.

Echenberg, Myron. *Colonial Conscripts: The Tirailleurs Sénégalais in French West Africa, 1857–1960*. Portsmouth: Heinemann, 1991.

Farwell, Bryon. *The Great War in Africa 1914–1918*. New York: W. W. Norton, 1986.

Freund, Bill. *The Making of Contemporary Africa: Development of African Society since 1800* (2nd ed.). Boulder: Lynne Rienner, 1998.

Inikori, Joseph E., and Stanley L. Engerman, eds. *The Atlantic Slave Trade: Effects on Economies, Societies, and Peoples in Africa, the Americas, and Europe*. Durham: Duke University Press, 1992.

Mamdani, Mahmood. *Citizen and Subject: Contemporary Africa and the Legacy of Late Colonialism*. Princeton: Princeton University Press, 1996.

Mudimbe, V. Y. *The Idea of Africa*. Bloomington: Indiana University Press, 1994.

Oliver, Roland, and Anthony Atmore. *Africa since 1800* (4th ed.). Cambridge: Cambridge University Press, 1994.

Packenham, Thomas. *The Scramble for Africa: The White Man's Conquest of the Dark Continent from 1876 to 1912*. New York: Random House, 1991.

Roberts, Andrew, ed. *The Colonial Moment in Africa: Essays on the Movement of Minds and Materials, 1900–1940*. Cambridge: Cambridge University Press, 1990.

Robinson, Ronald, and John Gallagher (with Alice Denny). *Africa and the Victorians: The Climax of Imperialism*. Garden City: Anchor, 1968.

Thomas, Hugh. *The Slave Trade: The Story of the Atlantic Slave Trade: 1440–1870*. New York: Simon & Schuster, 1997.

Wesseling, H. L. *Divide and Rule: The Partition of Africa, 1880–1914*. Westport: Praeger, 1996.

Young, Crawford. *The African Colonial State in Comparative Perspective*. New Haven: Yale University Press, 1994.

Notes

1. See M. Kwamena-Poh et al., *African History in Maps* (London: Longman, 1987), pp. 12–13.
2. See Joseph E. Inikori and Stanley L. Engerman, eds., *The Atlantic Slave Trade: Effects on Economies, Societies, and Peoples in Africa, the Americas, and Europe* (Durham: Duke University Press, 1992).
3. J. E. Inikori, "Africa in World History: The Export Slave Trade from Africa and the Emergence of the Atlantic Economic Order," in B. A. Ogot, ed., *General History of Africa. Volume 5. Africa from the Sixteenth to the Eighteenth Century* (Paris: UNESCO, 1992), p. 74.
4. See Philip D. Curtin, *The Atlantic Slave Trade: A Census* (Madison: University of Wisconsin Press, 1969), pp. 88–89.

5. Curtin, *The Atlantic Slave Trade,* p. 3. See also David Henige, "Measuring the Immeasurable: The Atlantic Slave Trade, West African Population and the Pyrrhonian Critic," *Journal of African History* 27 (1986):295–313.

6. See Paul E. Lovejoy, "The Volume of the Atlantic Slave Trade: Synthesis," *Journal of African History* 23 (1982):478; and Inikori, "Africa in World History."

7. See Kenneth F. Kiple and Brian T. Higgins, "Mortality Caused by Dehydration during the Middle Passage," in Inikori and Engerman, eds., *The Atlantic Slave Trade,* pp. 321–38.

8. See Ralph A. Austin, "The Trans-Saharan Slave Trade: A Tentative Census," in Henry A. Gemery and Jan S. Hogendorn, eds., *The Uncommon Market: Essays in the Economic History of the Atlantic Slave Trade* (New York: Academic, 1979), pp. 23–76.

9. See Peter Duignan and L. H. Gann, *The United States and Africa: A History* (Cambridge: Cambridge University Press, 1984).

10. Edward Rice, *Captain Sir Richard Francis Burton: The Secret Agent Who Made the Pilgrimage to Mecca, Discovered the Kama Sutra, and Brought the Arabian Nights to the West* (New York: HarperPerennial, 1990), p. 1.

11. See Andrew Roberts, "The Imperial Mind," in Andrew Roberts, ed., *The Colonial Moment in Africa: Essays on the Movement of Minds and Materials, 1900–1940* (Cambridge: Cambridge University Press, 1990), pp. 24–76. See also Ronald Robinson and John Gallagher (with Alice Denny), *Africa and the Victorians: The Climax of Imperialism* (New York: St. Martin's, 1961).

12. See Thomas Packenham, *The Scramble for Africa: The White Man's Conquest of the Dark Continent from 1876 to 1912* (New York: Random House, 1991).

13. See J. K. Fynn, "Ghana-Asante (Ashanti)," in Michael Crowder, ed., *West African Resistance: The Military Response to Colonial Occupation* (New York: Africana, 1971), pp. 19–52. See also Robert B. Edgerton, *The Fall of the Asante Empire: The Hundred-Year War for Africa's Gold Coast* (New York: The Free Press, 1995).

14. *Ibid.*, p. 27.

15. *Ibid.*

16. See Michael Crowder, ed., *West African Resistance: The Military Response to Colonial Occupation* (New York: Africana, 1971), pp. 1–18.

17. See Prosser Gifford and Wm. Roger Louis, eds., *Britain and Germany in Africa* (New Haven: Yale University Press, 1967). See also Woodruff D. Smith, *The German Colonial Empire* (Chapel Hill: University of North Carolina Press, 1979).

18. The mandates were as follows: Togoland (France); Kamerun (France and Britain); Tanganyika (Britain); South-West Africa (South Africa).

19. For an overview, see Robert L. Hess, *Italian Colonialism in Somalia* (Chicago: University of Chicago, 1966).

20. For example, see Ibrahim Sundiata, *Equatorial Guinea* (Boulder: Westview, 1989).

21. See Sir F. D. Lugard, *The Dual Mandate in British Tropical Africa* (Edinburgh: Blackwood, 1922).

22. See Prosser Gifford and Wm. Roger Louis, eds., *France and Britain in Africa: Imperial Rivalry and Colonial Rule* (New Haven: Yale University Press, 1971).

23. For an overview, see Jean Suret-Canale, *Afrique noire: L'Ère Coloniale, 1900–1945* (Paris: Editions Sociales, 1964).

24. For an overview, see Crawford Young, *Politics in the Congo: Decolonization and Independence* (Princeton: Princeton University Press, 1965).

25. For an overview of Portuguese colonial policies, see Norrie MacQueen, *The Decolonization of Portuguese Africa: Metropolitan Revolution and the Dissolution of Empire* (London: Longman, 1997). See also Gerald J. Bendor, *Angola under the Portuguese: The Myth and the Reality* (London: Heinemann, 1978).

26. See "The Sources of the Status Quo and Irredentist Policies," in Carl G. Widstrand, ed., *African Boundary Problems* (Uppsala: Scandinavian Institute of African Studies, 1969), pp. 101–18. See also Naomi Chazan, ed., *Irredentism and International Politics* (Boulder: Lynne Rienner, 1991).

27. For a discussion of this theme, see Saadia Touval, *Somali Nationalism: International Politics and the Drive for Unity in the Horn* (Cambridge: Harvard University Press, 1963), pp. 49–50. See also David D. Laitin and Said S. Samatar, *Somalia: Nation in Search of a State* (Boulder: Westview, 1987).

28. See I. William Zartman, *Ripe for Resolution: Conflict and Intervention in Africa* (New York: Oxford University Press, 1985).

29. The breakdown by population is estimated as follows: Hausa-Fulani (29 percent); Yoruba (20 percent); and Igbo (17 percent). See Chris Cook and David Killingray, *African Political Facts since 1945,* 2nd ed. (New York: Facts on File, 1991), p. 235.

30. See Conrad Max Benedict Brann, "Democratisation of Language Use in Public Domains in Nigeria," *The Journal of Modern African Studies* 31, no. 4 (1993):644–45.

31. See Crawford Young, *The African Colonial State in Comparative Perspective* (New Haven: Yale University Press, 1994), p. 1.

32. See Myron Echenberg, *Colonial Conscripts: The Tirailleurs Sénégalais in French West Africa, 1857–1960* (Portsmouth: Heinemann, 1991).

33. Smith, *The German Colonial Empire,* pp. 97–99.

34. For an interesting discussion of this metaphor, see I. William Zartman, "The Sahara — Bridge or Barrier," *International Conciliation* 541 (1963):1–62.

35. See Sheldon Gellar, *Senegal: An African Nation between Islam and the West,* 2nd ed. (Boulder: Westview, 1995), pp. 12–13.

36. *Ibid.,* pp. 13, 60.

37. *Ibid.,* p. 12.

38. *Ibid.*, p. 13.

39. See Sembène Ousmane, *God's Bits of Wood* (Harare: Zimbabwe Publishing House, 1984).

40. Gellar, *Senegal: An African Nation between Islam and the West*, p. 12.

41. See Claude Ake, *A Political Economy of Africa* (New York: Longman, 1981), p. 68.

42. *Ibid.*

43. *Ibid.*, p. 64.

44. *Ibid.*, p. 64.

45. See, for example, the seminal work of Crawford Young, *The African Colonial State in Comparative Perspective* (New Haven: Yale University Press, 1994).

6

Nationalism and the Emergence of the Contemporary Independence Era (1951–Present)

Nigerians rally in support of their country's transition to democratic rule in 1999.

THE INDEPENDENCE OF LIBYA in 1951 marked the beginning of the end of European colonialism in Africa. Less than sixty-six years after European diplomats had sealed the fate of the precolonial independence era at the Conference of Berlin (1884–85), a new generation of African political leaders and popular movements witnessed the first fruits of a **decolonization process** that gradually encompassed the entire African continent and ushered in the contemporary independence era. Decolonization was for the most part peacefully accepted by European leaders, who ultimately recognized the impossibility of maintaining permanent control. Intransigence on the part of Portugal and the minority white-ruled regimes in Southern Africa nonetheless prompted the rise of revolutionary movements intent upon achieving independence by military force. Regardless of whether achieved peacefully or by force, decolonization resulted from the emergence of African nationalist movements that demanded independence and equality for their respective peoples. This process was largely completed in 1994, when democratic elections in South Africa ushered in a multiparty and multiracial government under the leadership of President Nelson Mandela. The remainder of this chapter is devoted to exploring the factors behind the rise of nationalism and the emergence of the contemporary independence era.

Trends in African Nationalism

The concept of **nationalism** is defined as a sense of collective identity in which a people perceives itself as different than (and often superior to) other peoples.[1] Nationalism also implies the existence of a variety of shared characteristics, most notably a common language and culture, but also race and religion, as shown by the rise of Islamic revivalist movements in North Africa and other regions of the world with sizable Muslim populations. In the case of the United States, for example, scholars traditionally described American society as a "melting pot," in which the varied languages and cultures of immigrants were gradually replaced by a common American language and American culture. Even more recent multicultural conceptions that portray American society as a "mixed salad," in which each individual group maintains its uniqueness, nonetheless recognize an overarching "American" culture and language.

The emergence of African nationalism and African demands for **national self-determination** (independence) of individual colonies followed a different pattern than its classic European counterparts of earlier centuries.[2] The emergence of European "nations" (i.e., cohesive group identities) generally preceded and contributed to the creation of European "states" (the structures of governance). The net result was the creation of viable nation-states that enjoyed the legitimacy of their peoples. This process was reversed in Africa. In most cases, the colonial state was created prior to the existence of any sense of nation. As a result, the creation and strengthening of a nationalist attachment to what in essence constituted artificially created African states became one of the supreme challenges of colonial administrators and the African leaders who replaced them during the contemporary independence era.

A second unique aspect of African nationalism was its inherently anticolonial character. African nationalist movements were sharply divided on political agendas, ideological orientation, and economic programs. Regardless of their differences, however, the leaders of these movements did agree on one point: the necessity and desirability of independence from foreign control. Anticolonial sentiment served as the rallying point of African nationalist movements to such a degree that African nationalism was equivalent to African anticolonialism.

The process of decolonization unfolded gradually in a series of waves, beginning in the 1950s with groups of countries becoming independent during specific historical periods (see Map 6.1).[3] Three countries, however, differed in this regard. Ethiopia was never colonized despite being occupied by fascist Italy from 1936 to 1941 during World War II. Liberia constituted at best a "quasi-American colony," which never fell under the direct authority of the U.S. government (see Box 5.2 in Chapter 5). Instead the country, principally founded in 1822 by freed American slaves, declared independence in 1847, and successfully avoided European colonization. Egypt too held a unique position in African history. Despite being subjected to British colonial rule, Egypt achieved its independence in 1922.

The **first wave of independence** took place during the 1950s, and was led by the heavily Arab-influenced North African countries of Libya (1951), Morocco (1956), Tunisia (1956), and the Sudan (1956).[4] Two countries outside of North Africa also obtained independence during this period: the former British colony of the Gold Coast (Ghana) in 1957, followed by the former French colony of Guinea in 1958. This latter case was especially noteworthy in that Guinea was the only French colony to cast a negative vote against a 1958 referendum concerning the creation of a revised "French community of states." A "yes" vote would have confirmed continued French sovereignty while at the same time granting some degree of political autonomy to Guinea and the other French colonies. The response of the French government was to order the immediate withdrawal of all French aid and advisors from Guinea. One infamous anecdote of the period suggested that departing French colonial administrators even went so far as to remove light bulbs from their sockets. Despite the acrimony involved in this latter case, the first wave of independence was marked by a relatively peaceful transfer of power to African authorities.

The **second** (and largest) **wave of independence** took place during the 1960s, when more than thirty African countries achieved independence.[5] The majority of these countries were former British and French colonies in East, Central, and West Africa. All three Belgian colonies (Burundi, Rwanda, and the Democratic Republic of the Congo [Congo-Kinshasa]) also acquired independence during this period, and were joined by the Republic of Somalia, which represented a federation of the former British and Italian Somaliland

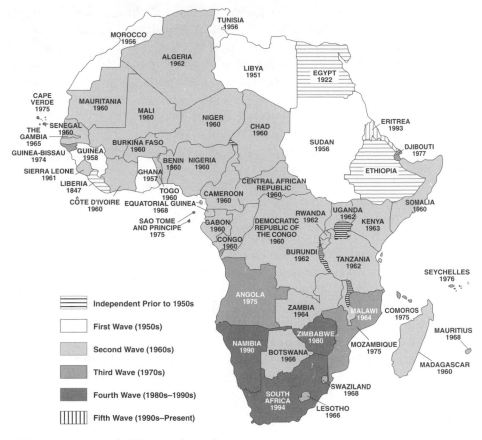

MAP 6.1   Waves of African Independence

territories. Aside from some noteworthy exceptions, most notably France's unsuccessful attempt to defeat a pro-independence guerrilla insurgency in Algeria and the emergence of the so-called Mau Mau guerrilla insurgency in Kenya, the decolonization process of the 1960s was also largely peaceful. The departing colonial powers had already accepted the inevitability of decolonization. Questions simply remained as to when and under what conditions.

The **third wave of independence** began in 1974. A military coup d'état in Portugal, led by junior military officers, resulted in a declaration that the Portuguese government intended to grant immediate independence to the colonies in Africa.[6] Coup plotters sought to end what they perceived as a series of African military quagmires that pitted poorly trained and unmotivated Portuguese military forces against highly motivated and increasingly adept African guerrilla insurgencies: the *Frente de Libertação de Moçambique* (FRELIMO, Front for the Liberation of Mozambique) in Mozambique; the *Partido Africano da Independência da Guiné e Cabo Verde* (PAIGC, Independence African Party of Guinea and Cape Verde) in Guinea Bissau and Cape Verde; and three guerrilla groups in Angola — the *Frente Nacional de Libertação de Angola* (FNLA, National Front for the Liberation of Angola); the *União Nacional para a Independência Total de Angola* (UNITA, National Union for the Total Independence of Angola); and the *Movimento Popular de Libertação de Angola* (MPLA, Popular Movement for the Liberation of Angola). The violent path to independence in the former Portuguese colonies was further complicated in 1975, when Angolan guerrilla groups began an extended civil war over who would lead an independent Angola. The former French colonies of Comoros (1975), Seychelles (1976), and Djibouti (1977), however, achieved independence under largely peaceful terms.

The **fourth wave of independence** emerged during the 1980s and was directed against the minority white-ruled regimes in Southern Africa.[7] Since 1948, South Africa was controlled by the descendants of white settlers known as Afrikaners. This minority elite established a highly racist system known as *apartheid* (apartness) in which blacks and other minorities (roughly 85 percent of the population) were denied political rights. The apartheid system was eventually exported to the former German colony of Namibia after it became a South African mandate territory in the aftermath of World War I. Similarly, white settlers in Southern Rhodesia (Zimbabwe) led by Ian Smith in 1965 instituted a regional variation of apartheid after they announced their Unilateral Declaration of Independence (UDI) from British colonial rule.

The minority white-ruled regimes of Southern Africa were confronted by guerrilla organizations that enjoyed regional and international support: the African National Congress (ANC) and the Pan-African Congress (PAC) in South Africa; the South-West Africa People's Organization (SWAPO) in Namibia; and the Zimbabwe African Nationalist Union (ZANU) and the Zimbabwe African People's Union (ZAPU) in Zimbabwe.[8] In all three cases, the military struggles were suspended after the white minority regimes agreed to negotiate transitions to black majority rule. Zimbabwe's transition in 1980 was followed by the creation of multiparty and multiracial democracies in Namibia in 1990 and South Africa in 1994. Except for the minor coastal enclaves of Ceuta and Melilla in present-day Morocco which remain under Spanish sovereignty, Nelson Mandela's emergence in 1994 as the first democratically elected leader of South Africa signaled the end of the decolonization process and the complete transition to the contemporary independence era (see Box 6.1).

Domestic Influences on the Rise of Nationalism

The socioeconomic and political systems of the precolonial independence era underwent immense social change due to the imposition of colonial rule. Although the principal duty of colonial administrators was to ensure European domination in the colonies, social changes unleashed by colonial rule unwittingly sowed the seeds for colonial demise. Three patterns of social change in particular contributed to the rise of African nationalism and African demands for decolonization.

Creation of Administrative Centers and the Rise of Urbanization

The creation of the colony itself, most notably the designation of regional administrative centers and a capital city, played an important initial role in providing the basis for the emergence of nationalism.[9] The urban areas served as "magnets" for Africans seeking employment and education, contributing to a process of urbanization in which Africans moved in increasing numbers from the countryside to the capital cities and towns. The "lure of the town," notes Kenneth Little, was due to the role of the urban areas as centers of politics, economics, and education.[10] In short, those who desired political and economic success within the colonial states were invariably drawn to emerging administrative centers.

Newly created towns dramatically expanded in terms of population. Abidjan, the former capital of Côte d'Ivoire, initially was a fishing village inhabited by approximately 700 people at the beginning of the twentieth century. The growing need for French colonial administrators in Abidjan fueled population growth, which exceeded 10,000 people by 1931. The 1951 completion of a canal linking Abidjan's lagoon with the Atlantic ocean further hastened urbanization. On the eve of independence in 1961, Abidjan's population exceeded 180,000 people; the figure exceeds 2.5 million at the end of the 1990s.[11]

The new towns served as the focal points of emerging national identities. In contrast to the relatively homogeneous nature of life in the villages, the colonial towns served as meeting grounds for the numerous ethnic groups that inhabited individual colonies. The towns served as "melting pots," in the sense that diverse ethnic cultures were gradually overshadowed by a sense of belonging to a larger political unit. It is important to note, however, that the promotion of nationalist sentiment did not necessarily mean a weakening of ethnic identity, nor the breaking of socioeconomic and political ties between the urbanized migrants and their villages of birth. It is precisely for this reason that the multicultural metaphor of a "mixed salad" is as relevant for most of Africa as it is for the United States at the beginning of the twenty-first century. Simply put, the colonial towns fostered the emergence of an overarching national culture and language while at the same time individuals maintained their specific cultural attachments — just as the separate ingredients of a mixed salad maintain their distinct flavors.

Educational Training and Development

The promotion of educational training for select groups of Africans served as a second pattern of social change that contributed to the rise of nationalism. The practical problem confronted by colonial administrators was that the small number of Europeans posted in each colony were incapable of managing all aspects of the colonial economic and political systems. In order to ensure

BOX 6.1

NELSON MANDELA'S "LONG WALK TO FREEDOM"

On May 10, 1994, Nelson Mandela was inaugurated as South Africa's first democratically elected leader. His inauguration in many respects represented the culmination of his "long walk to freedom" — to quote the title of his internationally acclaimed autobiography. Mandela spent nearly three decades (1962–91) as a political prisoner due to his firm conviction that all means, including guerrilla struggle, were to be employed to destroy the racist system of apartheid that existed in South Africa from 1948 to 1994. "I cannot pinpoint a moment when I became politicized, when I knew that I would spend my life in the liberation struggle," explains Mandela in his autobiography. "To be an African in South Africa means that one is politicized from the moment of one's birth, whether one acknowledges it or not."

A turning point in Mandela's political life occurred at the age of thirty-six when he became a formal member of the African National Congress (ANC), the oldest South African political party (established in 1912) and principal opponent of white minority rule. In its early years, the ANC was committed to the nonviolent transformation of South Africa's political system. However, the nonviolent approach of the ANC changed in the aftermath of the **Sharpeville massacre** of March 21, 1960. Without provocation, the South African police opened fire on marchers demonstrating against the "pass laws," legislation that controlled the movement of Africans throughout the country. Sixty-nine were killed and hundreds more were wounded. As demonstrations began to break out in other parts of the country, the South African government declared a state of emergency and outlawed all political organizations. The ANC was ultimately forced into exile.

Under the leadership of Mandela, the ANC moved away from its nonviolent approach and in 1961 formed a military wing, *Umkhonto we Sizwe* (Spear of the Nation), capable of carrying out acts of sabotage against the South African government. "This was a fateful step," explains Mandela. "We were embarking on a new and more dangerous path, a path of organized violence, the results of which we did not and could not know." From an organizational standpoint, this event marked the transformation of the ANC into a military organization capable of carrying out a sustained guerrilla struggle against the apartheid system. Concerning Mandela's personal life, however, this decision eventually earned him a life sentence in prison after he was captured by the South African police in 1962.

A significant portion of Mandela's sentence (nearly two decades) was spent at an isolated prison on Robben Island. Off the coast of Capetown, this small island is described by Mandela as the "harshest, most iron-fisted outpost in the South African penal system." At the beginning of his sentence, for example, Mandela was classified as a "Group D" prisoner: a political prisoner who threatened the national security. This classification allowed Mandela to receive only one visitor and to write and receive only one letter every six months. "I found this to be one of the most inhumane restrictions of the prison system," explains Mandela. "Communication with one's family is a human right; it should not be restricted by the artificial gradations of a prison system. But it was one of the facts of prison life."

Mandela's incarceration ended on February 11, 1991, in full view of the international media. At the age of seventy-three, his unrelenting opposition to the apartheid system, which had cost him nearly three decades of freedom, had transformed him into one of the most celebrated and admired political figures in the world. He became the symbol of a domestic and international anti-apartheid movement that culminated in South Africa's first multiracial, multi-party democratic elections in 1994. Rather than seeking to punish his former jailers once he and the ANC emerged victorious in those elections, Mandela magnanimously extended the olive branch of cooperation to all ethnic and racial factions in South Africa. It is this determination — to extend the hands of cooperation to all those interested in creating a South Africa devoid of racial and ethnic injustice — that has ensured Mandela's place as one of the greatest leaders of the twentieth century.

Quotations drawn from Nelson Mandela, *Long Walk to Freedom: The Autobiography of Nelson Mandela* (Boston: Little, Brown, 1994).

---

effective rule, colonial administrators oversaw a series of educational programs specifically designed to train the local peoples in the language and philosophy of the colonial power; create an auxiliary technical staff capable of performing a variety of technical tasks, such as accounting, plumbing, and electrical work; and train a select elite to collaborate with the colonial powers.[12] Each colony therefore went beyond the traditional literacy programs of missionaries by creating grade schools, high schools, and technical training institutes.

Rather than creating a subservient population and a collaborationist elite, colonial education served as one of the seeds of nationalism that contributed to colonialism's ultimate demise. Small numbers of secondary schools for the most part located in the capital city meant that students selected by colonial administrators would arrive from all regions of the colony. As a result, students who had most likely never traveled outside of their villages and who had rarely if ever met students their own ages from other ethnic groups suddenly found themselves in new surroundings with students from all over the colony. As time went by, friendships were created that transcended ethnic lines.

Students began seeing themselves as part of a larger entity (the colony) that was multiethnic in nature. In the British colony of Nigeria, for example, the vast majority of colonial civil servants were trained in the capital city at King's College, the standard name for such institutions throughout the British colonies. The formative years spent at this institution prompted students from various ethnic backgrounds, such as Yoruba, Igbo, and Hausa-Fulani, to think of themselves as belonging to a greater Nigerian nation that, in turn, formed part of the greater British Empire.

The sense of belonging to something larger than a particular ethnic group developed further when students were sent to study at regional colonial schools. Prior to the beginning of World War II, the only postsecondary school throughout *Afrique Occidentale Française* (AOF — French West Africa) was the *École Normale William Ponty* in Dakar, Senegal. The school was renowned as the "most important center" for elite training in francophone West Africa.[13] For the first time in their lives, students were able to interact with their counterparts from other colonies, realizing that they often shared much more in common with each other as colonized peoples than they did with their colonial educators, who in any case rarely accepted them as either political or intellectual equals. Furthermore, these institutions served as the training centers for individuals who often emerged as the Founding Fathers of the newly independent African countries. One of the most influential leaders to graduate from the *École Normale William Ponty* was Félix Houphouët-Boigny, one of the Founding Fathers of Côte d'Ivoire, who served as president from 1960 to 1993.

African students sent to Paris, London, and the capitals of other colonizing powers to pursue advanced education and training perhaps had the greatest impact on nationalist demands for independence. The sharing of ideas and the nurturing of lifelong friendships became possible, not only with students from colonies in other regions of the world, but with citizens from the host country itself. The extremely close personal relationship between Léopold Sédar Senghor, the first president of Senegal (1960–81), and Georges Pompidou, president of France from 1969 to 1974, was made possible by the fact that they were classmates during the same era at *Lycée Louis-le-Grand,* a prestigious secondary school in Paris.[14]

An equally important impact of studying abroad was direct exposure to the inherent contradictions between the colonizer's democratic heritage and traditions and the reality of authoritarian colonial rule at home. As any student who has studied in Paris can attest, the French curriculum has always underscored the importance of French democracy, with special emphasis being placed on the universal democratic ideals of the French revolution: *"Liberté, Égalité, Fraternité"* ("Liberty, Equality, Fraternity"). However, even the most enamored African student of French civilization and French culture was hard pressed to rationalize the realities of undemocratic rule throughout the French colonies. Indeed, regardless of whether they studied in Paris, Brussels, London, Lisbon, Madrid, or Rome, African students were inevitably confronted by the chasm that existed between the practice of democracy in Europe and the undemocratic realities of day-to-day life in the colonies. African students, once trained to serve as the colonial administrators of their respective colonies, more often than not returned home intent on doing everything in their power to achieve independence for their peoples.

Formation and Spread of Voluntary Associations

The emergence of **voluntary associations** also contributed to the rise of nationalist demands for independence. The initial rise of voluntary associations was based on the willingness of individuals to join groups and cooperate to achieve a certain goal. The proliferation of such groups was especially tied to the urbanization process. Individuals uprooted from the familiar setting of the village or simply interested in meeting people with shared interests joined a wide variety of organizations in rapidly expanding urban areas.

The vast numbers of voluntary associations could be divided into two major types, the first of which was based on ethnicity.[15] A common example of an **ethnic voluntary association** that remains influential today is a **mutual aid society.** A mutual aid society essentially served as a social welcome wagon and social welfare system for individuals who arrived in town from the village. Newcomers could count on the mutual aid society to provide essential information, such as where to go to acquire housing and meals with members of the same ethnic group. The mutual aid society also served as a social network in the sense that it sponsored dances and dinners. The accruement of monthly contributions of members allowed the mutual aid society to provide periodic financial assistance, including loans to start a business.

Membership in the second type of voluntary association was based on an individual's specific functional interest. The **functional voluntary association** transcended ethnic divisions by bringing together individuals who shared a common profession, such as nurses, or a specific social interest, such as playing soccer.[16] Some of these societies were even based on an individual's perceived social standing within the colony. In the Belgian Congo, for example, the *Association des Évolués du Stanleyville* (Association of Évolués of Stanleyville) served as an exclusive club for Congolese who had "evolved" into "civilized" members of the Belgian colony by embracing Belgian culture.[17]

The spread of voluntary associations during the colonial era played three prominent roles in the rise of nationalist sentiment and African demands for decolonization. First, the voluntary associations served as important meeting grounds where issues related to colonialism and independence could be discussed. Created in London in the 1920s, the West African Students' Union for at least two decades served as "the main political and social meeting place" of Nigerian students studying in England.[18] Voluntary associations also provided the organizational and leadership training for those individuals who led their countries to independence.[19] "Most of the early nationalist leaders were people who had benefited from the educational programs of the urban associations," explains Claude Ake, a Nigerian social scientist. "Many of them had their first experience of politics and organization through their involvement in these secondary organizations."[20] Nnamdi Azikiwe, who served as president of Nigeria from 1963 to 1966, was one of the principal founders in 1923 of the Young Man's Literary Association, which in 1940 joined with ten similar organizations to create the Federation of Nigerian Literary Societies and increasingly became involved in political issues.[21]

Most important, voluntary associations served as ready-made organizational structures for nationalist movements.[22] A group of associations, each created for very different reasons, often became the organizational nucleus of a political movement seeking independence. One of the Nigerian colony's first truly nationalist political organizations, the National Council of Nigeria and the Cameroons (NCNC), constituted a federation of numerous voluntary associations, including local Nigerian chapters of the West African Student Union and the Nigerian Union of Students.[23]

International Influences on the Rise of Nationalism

The process of social change taking place in each of the colonies was also influenced in varying degrees by the international environment. Four sets of international influences in particular contributed to the rise of African nationalism and African demands for decolonization.

Spread of Pan-Africanism

The first trend revolved around the emergence of pan-African linkages and organizations.[24] Inspired by the anticolonial and antiracist activities of peoples of African descent living in North America, the West Indies, and Europe during the nineteenth and twentieth centuries, African leaders sought to promote a unified African front against colonial rule.

Fascist Italy's 1935 invasion of Ethiopia (also known as Abyssinia) and defeat of Emperor Haile Selassie's 250,000-strong Ethiopian army marked a turning point in the emergence of pan-African sentiment. Ali A. Mazrui, the Kenyan historian, notes that foreign occupation of a country that served as a "proud symbol of African independence and black achievement" had a "resounding impact" on Africans and members of the African diaspora.[25] A noted example is found in the autobiography of Kwame Nkrumah, the first president of Ghana. At the time of Ethiopia's invasion, Nkrumah had just arrived in London to pursue his university studies. Nkrumah relates the moral outrage he felt when he first learned of the invasion while walking down a London street:

> At that moment it was if the whole of London had declared war on me personally. For the next few minutes I could do nothing but glare at each impassive face wondering if those people could possibly realize the wickedness of colonialism, and praying that the day might come when I could play my part in bringing about the downfall of such a system. My nationalism surged to the fore; I was ready and willing to go through hell itself, if need be, in order to achieve my object.[26]

What subsequently became known as the "pan-African ideal" was force-fully enunciated for the first time at the 1945 meeting of the Pan-African Congress held in Manchester, England. Participants adopted a resolution, "Declaration to the Colonial Peoples," that affirmed the "rights" of all colonized peoples to be "free from foreign imperialist control" and "to elect their own governments, without restrictions from foreign powers."[27] In a separate resolution, "Declaration to the Colonial Powers," participants further underscored that if the colonial powers were "still determined to rule mankind by force, then Africans, as a last resort, may have to appeal to force in the effort to achieve freedom."[28]

Involvement of African Soldiers in World War I and World War II

The outbreak of two world wars in Europe served as a second international influence that significantly affected the rise of African demands for decolonization. Each of the colonial powers maintained standing armies comprised primarily of African recruits, several of which clashed during skirmishes on the African continent during World War I.[29] During World War II, African conscripts played an increasingly important combat role in the European theater, especially in the case of France. By the beginning of 1939, seven African divisions of the *Tirailleurs Sénégalais,* a fighting force comprised of African recruits from francophone West Africa, constituted 7 percent of all French military forces stationed in Europe, with 20,000–25,000 soldiers dying during the course of World War II.[30]

The most decisive impact of African soldiers fighting in Europe was the shattering of colonially inspired images of whites as invincible and all powerful. The rank-and-file of the *Tirailleurs Sénégalais* were direct participants in numerous battles in which French military forces were overrun by other "white" (Nazi Germany) and "nonwhite" (Imperial Japan) military forces. The pace of Japanese victories was especially significant because Africans saw that European militaries could in fact be defeated by non-European armies. Indeed, many African soldiers concluded that Africans were militarily superior to Europeans in terms of both courage and valor. Laqui Condé, a *Tirailleur Sénégalais* recruited from Côte d'Ivoire, summarized a common belief among African soldiers:

> We were stronger than the whites. That bullet that hit my tooth would have killed a white. When the shooting came, the whites ran. They knew the area and we did not, so we stayed. Our officers? They were behind us.[31]

For many soldiers, a turning point in the development of nationalist sentiment occurred upon demobilization. Unlike their white French counterparts who were usually quickly demobilized, given "tumultuous welcomes," and provided with back pay and demobilization premiums, the African soldiers, many of whom spent several years in prisoner-of-war (POW) camps, "languished" in demobilization centers in southern France and West Africa.[32] African soldiers became especially disenchanted when French authorities sought to deny them the same financial benefits accorded white soldiers, resulting in a series of protests and uprisings, the most notable of which occurred at a military camp in Thiaroye, Senegal. A heavy-handed French military response resulted in at least thirty-five deaths and hundreds of casualties among the *Tirailleurs Sénégalais,* and further inflamed the sense of betrayal felt by soldiers who perceived themselves as having made sacrifices for France.[33]

Soldiers responded to the events of Thiaroye and other shortcomings of demobilization, such as the lack of jobs, by forming and joining a host of veterans associations. Collectively, veterans asserted that equal sacrifices required equal benefits.[34] The veterans associations not only fought for equal treatment for African veterans, they also played an integral role in the nationalist movements seeking independence.

BOX 6.2

AFRICA'S FIFTY-FOURTH COUNTRY?
SECESSION OF THE SOMALILAND REPUBLIC

Five days after achieving independence from colonial rule in 1960, the former British protectorate of northern Somalia voluntarily federated with the former Italian colony of southern Somalia to create the Republic of Somalia. In the eyes of northern leaders, however, this democratic compact was violated beginning in 1969 when a southerner, Mohammed Siad Barre, seized power in a military coup d'état and created a southern-dominated military dictatorship. Barre scrapped the constitution and destroyed the fragile political basis which had tenuously kept the democratic union together, most notably by carrying out a policy of genocide against the north during the 1980s, as part of a widening civil war. Even after Barre was overthrown in 1991 by a coalition of guerrilla armies, northern expectations of a government of national unity were dashed when southern guerrilla movements reneged on an earlier agreement and unilaterally named a southerner president. On May 17, 1991, northern leaders responded to over twenty years of perceived victimization by declaring the Somali union null and void, and reasserting their country's sovereign independence as the Somaliland Republic.

Despite enjoying de facto control over its domestic and international affairs, the Somaliland Republic has yet to be recognized by any other country or international body within the international system. Those in favor of the Somaliland Republic's recognition as the fifty-fourth independent African country criticize international inaction, especially in light of the strides that northern Somali leaders have made in fostering stability and democracy.

The cornerstone of northern efforts to secede is reliance on the Somali *shir*, a traditional conference dating back to the precolonial independence era, in which a broad cross section of northern Somali elders, religious leaders *(sheikhs)*, and clan leaders periodically engage in full and free debate on every issue affecting national peace and security. At one such *shir* held in the town of Boroma from December 1992 to April 1993, participants outlined the creation of a popularly elected eighty-two-member National Assembly, an eighty-two-member Senate (the *Gurti*) comprised of senior elders, an executive branch headed by an elected president, and an independent judiciary. A critical aspect of this democratization process was the marginalization of militia leaders (a problem still plaguing southern Somalia) in favor of a civilian transition government headed by President Mohamed Ibrahim Egal, one of the Somaliland Republic's most distinguished elder statesmen. Egal's stewardship of the transition process was renewed in 1997 for an additional four years, by an overwhelming 71 percent (223 out of 315) of those taking part in a special meeting held in the town of Hargeisa.

"The Somaliland Republic has earned the right to have its wishes taken seriously by the international community," explains Ahmed Jirreh, a northern Somali living in the United States, who favors independence for his land of birth. "At the very least, the international community should oversee some sort of referendum designed to poll the wishes of those living in the Somaliland Republic." One of the potential electoral models, often cited by proponents of independence, is that which led to Eritrea's independence from Ethiopian sovereignty in 1993: a two-year "cooling-off period" could be followed by a UN-sponsored referendum monitored by international observers. "We northern Somalis are not asking for international charity, nor are we asking foreigners to assume responsibility for what we ourselves are capable of accomplishing," explains Jirreh. "We simply seek international recognition of our sovereign right to withdraw from a union we once voluntarily joined."

Quotations are from a personal interview with Ahmed Jirreh in Chicago, Illinois. See also Hussein M. Adam, "Formation and Recognition of New States: Somaliland in Contrast to Eritrea," *Review of African Political Economy*, no. 59 (1994):21–38; and Gérard Prunier, "Somaliland Goes It Alone," *Current History* 97, no. 619 (1998):225–28.

Demonstration Effect of Decolonization in Asia

The decolonization of Asia constituted a third international trend with implications for the rise of African nationalism.[35] Numerous Asian countries became independent during the 1940s, providing an important "demonstration effect" for African nationalist movements. For those seeking independence by peaceful means, the experience of India under the leadership of Mohandas K. Gandhi (1869–1948) served as a tremendous inspiration. Gandhi had lived in

British-ruled South Africa from 1893 to 1915, where he led a series of protests denouncing discrimination against Indian immigrants. It was during this period that Gandhi developed and tested his nonviolent approach to challenging unjust colonial rules and regulations. The cornerstone of his approach was a campaign of civil disobedience known as *satyagraha* (holding to the truth). After returning to India in 1915, Gandhi's vision of nonviolent civil disobedience became the hallmark of a nationalist movement that forced Great Britain to cede independence to India in 1947.

African nationalist leaders drew inspiration from Gandhi's experiences for several reasons.[36] First, he had achieved a special level of legitimacy due to his personal involvement in the struggle for human dignity on the African continent. Second, the Christian faith shared by many African nationalist leaders, primarily in Sub-Saharan Africa, made them particularly receptive to nonviolent approaches, as one of the hallmarks of Christianity is the denunciation of war and conflict. Most important, civil disobedience had achieved a stunning success in India, leading to independence largely devoid of bloodshed and violence. If it could succeed in what at the time was considered to be the cornerstone of the British Empire, some African nationalists thought, then it surely could succeed in Africa.

The ultimate success of the nonviolent approach depended on the willingness of the colonial power to peacefully accede to nationalist demands for independence. For those nationalist leaders who believed that armed struggle was the only recourse to the military campaigns of the colonial powers, inspiration was drawn from the success of Asian liberation movements. African nationalist movements were tremendously affected by the dramatic 1954 defeat of French military forces at Dien Bien Phu: a geographical name that became synonymous with the beginning of French withdrawal from Indochina and eventual independence for the former French colonies of Vietnam, Cambodia, and Laos. Indeed, Ben Bella, a leader of the guerrilla insurgency that ultimately forced France to grant independence to Algeria in 1962, witnessed firsthand the promise of guerrilla insurgency while serving as a sergeant in the French army stationed in Indochina.[37]

The Asian nations furthermore provided concrete support to African nationalist organizations for achieving independence by creating a series of mechanisms designed to enhance African-Asian solidarity. The 1955 Bandung Conference held in Bandung, Indonesia, was one of the earliest manifestations of Asian support. Five Asian countries — Burma, Ceylon, India, Indonesia, and Pakistan — hosted representatives from twenty-four other countries, including the independent African countries of Egypt, Ethiopia, and Liberia, and representatives from the not-yet-independent states of Ghana and Sudan. The common denominator of all present was a principled opposition to colonial rule, and the conference resulted in a final communiqué underscoring the obligation of member states to promote the independence of those countries still suffering under colonial rule.

Shifting Structure of the International System

A final international trend with important implications for the emergence of African demands for independence was the shift in the structure of the international system. The end of World War II left European colonial powers economically, politically, and militarily devastated. Their power had been eclipsed by the rise of the United States and the former Soviet Union as the unparalleled superpowers of the post–World War II era. As a result, the center of gravity for African nationalists intent upon seeking independence for their respective colonies gradually shifted toward Moscow and Washington.[38]

The Soviet Union in many respects enjoyed several ideological advantages over the United States and the European colonial powers during the initial stages of the Cold War.[39] First, neither the former Soviet Union nor its communist allies had ever been colonial powers in Africa. Second, the history of the Soviet Union, at least from the vantage point of the 1940s and the 1950s, suggested that following the Soviet economic model could lead to rapid industrialization and socioeconomic development. Most important, the Soviet Union actively provided economic and military aid to liberation movements, most notably those opposed to white minority rule in Southern Africa. This latter activity in particular earned high marks among African leaders who, regardless of ideology, shared the common goal of eradicating all remaining forms of colonialism and apartheid on the African continent.

The United States similarly appealed to African nationalists due to the often vocal anticolonial rhetoric of American policymakers. The United States especially captured the imagination of African nationalists in 1941, when President Franklin D. Roosevelt enunciated the principles associated with the **Atlantic Charter**, the most important of which underscored strong U.S. support for the self-determination of African peoples from colonial rule. With the intensification of the Cold War, however, the United States was increasingly perceived by African nationalists as too closely tied to the interests of the colonial powers. Indeed, when African demands for decolonization clashed with policies considered crucial to U.S. security interests in Europe, U.S. policymakers often sided with Europe at the expense of Africa.[40]

A commitment to the principles of **nonalignment** often served as one of the rallying points of African nationalists. According to this view, African and other developing countries should seek a third path of development, independent of the liberal form of capitalism promoted by the United States and other Western powers, but also independent of the more critical form of Marxism promoted by the former Soviet Union and its communist bloc allies. In practice, however, African nationalists often aligned themselves with one of the two major ideological blocs, and sometimes even prompted virtual bidding wars between the United States and the former Soviet Union as each superpower sought to curry favor with particular nationalist movements. As succinctly noted in 1957 by Senator (and future president) John F. Kennedy, the perceived stakes of the Cold War contest were tied to whether the emerging leaders of Africa would "look West or East — to Moscow or to Washington — for sympathy, help, and guidance in their effort to recapitulate, in a few decades, the entire history of modern Europe and America."[41]

Self-Determination and the Rise of Secessionist Movements

The four waves of African independence that culminated in South Africa's transition to democracy in 1994 depended on the self-determination of individual colonial states. In the aftermath of the end of the Cold War and the largely successful transition to the contemporary independence era, a series of nationalist movements has emerged that seeks the **self-determination of peoples** within individual nation-states.[42] The leaders of what potentially constitutes a **fifth wave of independence** often underscore the historic mistreatment of their peoples as part of their pursuit of two overriding objectives: the secession of their territories from existing African nation-states; and international recognition of their territories as independent nation-states within the international system.

The emergence of secessionist movements is neither unique to Africa nor simply a product of the post–Cold War era. The end of the Cold War has indeed fostered the reemergence of ethnically based nationalism on a global scale. The most notable outcome of this trend was the fragmentation of the former Soviet Union into numerous independent republics. As demonstrated by the efforts of Nigeria's Igbo people to create an independent Republic of Biafra at the end of the 1960s, however, secessionist movements have existed in Africa since the beginning of the decolonization process (see Chapter 7).[43] The post–Cold War era is nonetheless unique in that the demands for the self-determination of individual peoples appear to have risen in both scope and intensity, and the African and international communities appear increasingly willing to entertain secessionist demands.

Eritrea serves as the only successful case of secession and independence during the fifth wave of African independence (see Box 6.2).[44] On May 24, 1993, an internationally monitored popular referendum resulted in a vote overwhelmingly in favor of independence. Out of a total of 1,100,260 eligible voters, 99.8 percent voted in favor of independence.[45] The referendum officially marked the end of a thirty-year guerrilla struggle against Ethiopian sovereignty, which began in 1961 against the United States–supported regime of Emperor Haile Selassie and ended in 1991 with the downfall of the Soviet-supported Marxist regime of Mengistu Haile Mariam. The guerrilla insurgency was initially led by the Eritrean Liberation Front (ELF), which was ultimately succeeded by the more powerful Eritrean People's Liberation Front (EPLF). It is estimated that nearly 65,000 guerrilla fighters and tens of thousands of civilians lost their lives during Eritrea's struggle for independence.

The strength and long-term viability of the fifth wave of independence depends on a variety of factors, most notably the responses of the Organization of African Unity (OAU) and the international community. As discussed in Chapter 13, the OAU opposes any attempts at secession, because one of the hallmarks of the OAU Charter is the inviolability of frontiers inherited from the colonial era. Due to the multiethnic nature of most African nation-states, African leaders remain fearful that changing even one boundary will open a Pandora's box of ethnically based secessionist movements and lead to the further **Balkanization** of the African continent into smaller and economically inviable political units.

Key Terms

decolonization process
nationalism
national self-determination
first wave of independence
second wave of independence
third wave of independence
fourth wave of independence
Sharpeville massacre
voluntary associations

ethnic voluntary associations
mutual aid society
functional voluntary associations
Atlantic Charter
nonalignment
self-determination of peoples
fifth wave of independence
Balkanization

For Further Reading

Afigbo, A. E., et al. *The Making of Modern Africa* (vol. 2): *The Twentieth Century*. London: Longman, 1986.

Carter, Gwendolen M., and Patrick O'Meara, eds. *African Independence: The First Twenty-Five Years*. Bloomington: Indiana University Press, 1985.

Davidson, Basil. *The Black Man's Burden: Africa and the Curse of the Nation-State*. New York: Times Books, 1992.

Freund, Bill. *The Making of Contemporary Africa: The Development of African Society since 1800* (2nd ed.). Boulder: Lynne Rienner, 1998.

Gifford, Prosser, and Wm. Roger Louis, eds. *The Transfer of Power in Africa: Decolonization, 1940–1960*. New Haven: Yale University Press, 1982.

Grimal, Henri (translated by Stephen DeVos). *Decolonization: The British, French, Dutch and Belgian Empires, 1919–1963*. Boulder: Westview, 1978.

Hargreaves, John D. *Decolonization in Africa* (2nd ed.). London: Longman, 1996.

Hodgkin, Thomas. *Nationalism in Colonial Africa*. New York: New York University Press, 1957.

Little, Kenneth. *West African Urbanization: A Study of Voluntary Associations in Social Change*. Cambridge: Cambridge University Press, 1970.

MacQueen, Norrie. *The Decolonization of Portuguese Africa: Metropolitan Revolution and the Dissolution of Empire*. London: Longman, 1997.

Mazrui, Ali A., and Michael Tidy. *Nationalism and New States in Africa from About 1935 to the Present*. London: Heinemann, 1984.

Neuberger, Benyamin. *National Self-Determination in Post-Colonial Africa*. Boulder: Lynne Rienner, 1986.

Rimmer, Douglas, et al. *Africa Thirty Years On: The Record and the Outlook after Thirty Years of Independence Examined for the Royal African Society*. London: James Currey, 1991.

Wilson, Henry S. *African Decolonization*. London: Edward Arnold, 1994.

Young, Crawford. *Politics in the Congo: Decolonization and Independence*. Princeton: Princeton University Press, 1965.

Notes

1. For an overview, see Hans Kohn, *The Idea of Nationalism* (New York: Macmillan, 1943); Ernest Gellner, *Nations and Nationalism* (Ithaca: Cornell University Press, 1983); and Eric Hobsbawm, *Nations and Nationalism since 1780: Programme, Myth, Reality* (Cambridge: Cambridge University Press, 1990).

2. For an overview of the various meanings of this term, see Benyamin Neuberger, *National Self-Determination in Post-Colonial Africa* (Boulder: Lynne Rienner, 1986).

3. For an overview, see Basil Davidson, *Modern Africa: A Social and Political History*, 3rd ed. (London: Longman, 1994).

4. See Henry S. Wilson, *African Decolonization* (London: Edward Arnold, 1994), pp. 112–33.

5. See John D. Hargreaves, *Decolonization in Africa*, 2nd ed. (London: Longman, 1996).

6. For an overview, see Norrie MacQueen, *The Decolonization of Portuguese Africa: Metropolitan Revolution and the Dissolution of Empire* (London: Longman, 1997).

7. For an overview, see William Minter, *King Solomon's Mines Revisited: Western Interests and the Burdened History of Southern Africa* (New York: Basic, 1986).

8. For an early overview, see Richard Gibson, *African Liberation Movements: Contemporary Struggles against White Minority Rule* (London: Oxford University Press, 1972). See also Sheridan Johns and R. Hunt Davis, Jr., eds., *Mandela, Tambo, and the African National Congress: The Struggle against Apartheid, 1948–1990: A Documentary Survey* (New York: Oxford University Press, 1991).

9. See Thomas Hodgkin, *Nationalism in Colonial Africa* (New York: New York University Press, 1957), pp. 63–83.

10. Kenneth Little, *West African Urbanization: A Study of Voluntary Associations in Social Change* (Cambridge: Cambridge University Press, 1970), pp. 7–23.

11. See Peter C. Lloyd, *Africa in Social Change: Changing Traditional Societies in the Modern World* (Middlesex: Penguin, 1971), pp. 109–24.

12. See Claude Ake, *A Political Economy of Africa* (London: Longman, 1981), pp. 72–73.

13. J. F. Ade Ajayi, Lameck K. H. Goma, and G. Ampah Johnson, *The African Experience with Higher Education* (Accra: Association of African Universities, 1996), p. 39.

14. See Janet G. Vaillant, *Black, French, and African: A Life of Léopold Sédar Senghor* (Cambridge: Harvard University Press, 1990), pp. 64–86.

15. See Little, *West African Urbanization*, 1970, pp. 24–65.

16. *Ibid.*, pp. 66–84.

17. *Ibid.*, pp. 74–75.

18. *Ibid.*, p. 77.

19. Ake, *A Political Economy of Africa*, 1981, p. 79.

20. *Ibid.*, p. 79.

21. Little, *West African Urbanization*, 1970, pp. 107–8.

22. Ake, *A Political Economy of Africa*, 1981, p. 79.

23. Little, *West African Urbanization*, 1970, p. 147.

24. See P. Olisanwuche Esedebe, *Pan-Africanism: The Idea and the Movement 1776–1963* (Washington: Howard University Press, 1982).

25. Ali A. Mazrui and Michael Tidy, *Nationalism and New States in Africa from About 1935 to the Present* (London: Heinemann, 1984), p. 7. For the reaction of African-Americans, see William R. Scott, *The Sons of Sheba's Race: African-Americans and the Italo-Ethiopian War, 1935–1941* (Bloomington: Indiana University Press, 1993).

26. Kwame Nkrumah, *Ghana: The Autobiography of Kwame Nkrumah* (London: Thomas Nelson and Sons, 1957), p. 27.

27. Adekunle Ajala, "Background to the Establishment, Nature and Structure of the Organization of African Unity," *Nigerian Journal of International Affairs* 14, no. 1 (1988):36.

28. *Ibid.*, p. 39.

29. See Byron Farwell, *The Great War in Africa (1914–1918)* (New York: W. W. Norton, 1986).

30. For an overview, see Myron Echenberg, *Colonial Conscripts: The Tirailleurs Sénégalais in French West Africa, 1857–1960* (Portsmouth: Heinemann, 1991).

31. Quoted in *ibid.*, p. 92.

32. *Ibid.*, p. 98.

33. *Ibid.*, pp. 96–104. The events of Thiaroye were depicted in a 1988 film, *Le Camp de Thiaroye* (The Thiaroye Military Camp), by the celebrated Senegalese novelist and filmmaker, Sembène Ousmane.

34. *Ibid.*, p. 104.

35. For a comparison, see Elie Kedourie, ed., *Nationalism in Asia and Africa* (New York: World, 1970). See also D. A. Low, "The Asian Mirror to Tropical Africa's Independence," in Prosser Gifford and Wm. Roger Louis, eds., *The*

Transfer of Power in Africa: Decolonization, 1940–1960 (New Haven: Yale University Press, 1982).

36. Mazrui and Tidy, *Nationalism and New States in Africa,* 1984, pp. 17–18.

37. Ibid, 1984, p. 16.

38. For an overview, see Zaki Laïdi, *The Superpowers and Africa: The Constraints of a Rivalry 1960–1990* (Chicago: The University of Chicago Press, 1990).

39. See Colin Legum, "African Outlooks toward the USSR," in David E. Albright, ed., *Africa and International Communism* (Bloomington: Indiana University Press, 1980), pp. 7–34. See also Jeffrey A. Lefebvre, "Moscow's Cold War and Post–Cold War Policies in Africa," in Edmond J. Keller and Donald Rothchild, eds., *Africa in the New International Order: Rethinking State Sovereignty and Regional Security* (Boulder: Lynne Rienner, 1996), pp. 206–26.

40. See Steven Metz, "American Attitudes toward Decolonization in Africa," *Political Science Quarterly* 99, 3 (1984):515–33. See also Peter J. Schraeder, *United States Foreign Policy toward Africa: Incrementalism, Crisis and Change* (London: Cambridge University Press, 1994).

41. John F. Kennedy, "The New Nations of Africa," in Theodore C. Sorenson, ed., *"Let the Word Go Forth": The Speeches, Statements, and Writings of John F. Kennedy* (New York: Delacorte, 1988), pp. 365, 368.

42. For an early analysis, see Benyamin Neuberger, *National Self-Determination in Postcolonial Africa* (Boulder: Lynne Rienner, 1986).

43. For a discussion of this and other cases, see Crawford Young, "Comparative Claims to Political Sovereignty: Biafra, Katanga, and Eritrea," in Donald Rothchild and Victor Olorunsola, eds., *State versus Ethnic Claims: African Policy Dilemmas* (Boulder: Westview, 1983), pp. 199–232.

44. See Ruth Iyob, *The Eritrean Struggle for Independence: Domination, Resistance, Nationalism 1941–1993* (Cambridge: Cambridge University Press, 1995).

45. *Ibid.,* fn. 27, p. 178.

7

Ethnicity and Class

An all-night celebration of the Tijaniyya Islamic brotherhood in Tivaouane, Senegal, attended by the brotherhood's revered leader Abdoul Aziz Sy "Dabakh" (left), his nephew Mansour Sy (who inherited the leadership role after Dabakh's death in 1997), and thousands of taalibe *(disciples).*

THE CONCEPTS OF ETHNICITY and class are analytical tools that identify the roles and interests that influence the choices of groups and individuals. Each concept has served as the basis of often competing interpretations of African politics and society. Scholars typically emphasize the importance of either one or the other, despite a recognition that both have influenced the socio-economic and political-military evolution of the African continent during the contemporary independence era. Ironically, Western scholars enamored with the unifying force of African nationalism during the 1950s initially overlooked the importance of ethnic or class differences. However, events of later decades, most notably the outbreak of ethnic tensions and the emergence of authoritarian ruling classes, clearly demonstrated the usefulness of ethnicity and class-based scholarship. Whereas interpretations based on ethnicity became especially prominent during the 1960s, class analysis emerged as a rich field of inquiry beginning in the 1970s. The intensification of ethnic competition and conflict that accompanied the end of the Cold War prompted a renewal of interest among scholars in understanding the ethnic dimensions of African politics and society. Other events associated with the Cold War's end — particularly the emergence of new classes at the head of pro-democracy movements — also fostered a reevaluation of class-based analyses. This chapter examines the evolving and often competing roles of ethnicity and class in African politics and society during the contemporary independence era.

Ethnic Dimension of African Politics and Society

Ethnicity defines a sense of collective identity in which a people (the ethnic group) perceives itself as sharing a common historical past and a variety of social norms and customs, including the roles of elders and other age groups within society, relationships between males and females, rites and practices of marriage and divorce, legitimate forms of governance, and the proper means of resolving conflict. The African continent is comprised of thousands of ethnic groups. One authoritative source, the *Encyclopedia of Africa South of the Sahara,* provides separate entries for nearly two hundred of the largest and most influential African ethnic groups, with an appendix offering short descriptions for more than one thousand others.[1] Although the total number of African ethnic groups differs depending on the source consulted and the system of classification used, all studies recognize that the ethnic and cultural diversity on the African continent is extremely rich.

Many ethnic groups are divided into subgroup identities and loyalties. Individual subgroups based on kinship, often referred to as **clans,** can usually trace their common lineage back hundreds, if not thousands, of years to a specific founding member or ruling family dynasty. For example, the Somali ethnic group of the Horn of Africa is divided among ten major clans, each of which has a genealogy of clan leaders that can be traced to the mythical founding member. Other ethnic groups are divided according to **age-sets,** a division based on the year or period in which one was born, that determines when an individual assumes various responsibilities within the ethnic group, such as entering the ranks of senior political leader or senior elder. Among the Maasai ethnic group of Kenya, for example, a series of age-sets determines when young boys enter the ranks of the *moran* (warrior recruits).

The Tswana ethnic group, which includes one million members comprising more than two-thirds of the total population of Botswana, illustrates the political ramifications of complexity within an ethnic group. Though the Tswana speak the same language (Setswana), share a common historical past, and share social norms and customs, including participation in public *kgotla* meetings in which community issues are freely debated, the Tswana are divided among eight major clan groups: Bamangwato, Bakwena, Bangwaketse, Bakgatla, Barolong, Batlokwa, Bamalete, and Batawana. Each of these clans inhabits a specific geographical region of Botswana and is headed by a traditional king who represents his people in the House of Chiefs, an advisory legislative chamber that functions alongside the popularly elected National Assembly. The political impact of clan differences among the Tswana is evident in the national election results from 1969 to 1994.[2] During this period, the ruling Botswana Democratic Front (BDF) averaged sixty-eight percent of the popular vote — for the leaders of the BDF are members of the Bamangwato clan family, the largest of the Tswana clan families, that constitutes more than 35 percent of Botswana's total population.[3]

The concept of ethnicity was largely ignored by foreign observers during the first decade of the contemporary independence period. One reason for this neglect was the strong belief, especially among American researchers and policymakers, that ethnic divisions would fade away as modernizing African societies set aside ethnic identities in favor of Western industrial and cultural practices. Modernization theory, the intellectual blueprint of development that was extremely popular among American scholars and policymakers in the 1950s and 1960s, proposed that the march of modern industrial and economic progress would eclipse the importance of "primitive" ethnic loyalties (see Chapter 2).

The concept of ethnicity was also ignored due to the shared belief of African leaders and Western observers that the future success of newly independent African countries depended on their ability to promote a unifying nationalism that transcended ethnic differences. Those who suggested that ethnic differences would endure and were a subject worthy of research ran the risk of being denounced by African leaders and Western observers alike as subverting the African continent's struggle for independence and dignity. "If nationalism was a progressive and worthy topic, ethnicity was a retrogressive and shameful one," explains Crawford Young, a leading scholar on ethnicity. "To dwell unduly upon it [ethnicity] was to summon forth from the societal depths demons who might subvert nationalism at its hour of triumph."[4]

Several political developments nonetheless ensured that the study of ethnicity would emerge in the 1960s as one of the most important fields of inquiry in

African studies.[5] The creation of single-party regimes and the outbreak of military coups d'état were associated with the emergence of authoritarian political systems often dominated by one ethnic group (see Chapters 11 and 12). More often than not, ethnic majorities made their power felt at the ballot box and then resisted relinquishing their power and privileges. Of even greater importance was the outbreak of ethnically inspired violence that threatened to unravel the gains of independence and lead to the breakup of multiethnic nation-states. "Only when it became apparent that, bidden or not, the demons of disunity were at hand," concludes Young in a retrospective essay on his experiences during the 1960s, "did ethnicity begin to receive systematic examination."[6] The resurgence of ethnically based African conflicts in the aftermath of the Cold War has once again prompted scholars to focus their attention on the importance of ethnicity in understanding African politics and society.

Ethnic Intermediaries and the Creation of Ethnic Compacts

A philosophical underpinning of Africa's multiethnic nation-states is that an **ethnic compact** can be achieved between the central government and ethnic leaders, that is minimally acceptable to all ethnic groups within society. This compact is based on the assumption that ethnic groups can compete peacefully within the established political framework for their rightful share of national resources, such as federal budget allocations for local education, health care, and infrastructural development; salaried positions in the various bureaucracies of the executive branch; and, perhaps most important, representation within the political system itself, including political appointments, party representation, and election to local and national offices. The ethnic compact also assumes that African governments can treat these ethnic groups equitably regardless of whether they represent the largest or the smallest portion of the overall population. In other words, the government is seen as capable of resolving conflicts between majorities and minorities, and of protecting individual rights.

An important participant who contributes to the success or failure of the ethnic compact is the **ethnic intermediary**: an ethnic leader or "go-between" who represents and channels the demands of his/her ethnic group to the national political leadership, and who also transmits the demands and expectations of that leadership to his/her ethnic constituents.[7] Ethnic intermediaries employ a variety of tactics to promote the interests of their respective ethnic groups in the national political arena. They may issue private appeals to politicians, public statements of support for sympathetic politicians, or public threats of noncompliance and noncooperation to those initially unwilling to listen.[8] The level of success is strongly influenced by the ethnic intermediary's diplomatic and political skills; ethnic intermediaries not only must seek agreement among potentially competing factions within their own ethnic group, but must also be capable of negotiating and seeking agreement with counterparts from other ethnic groups and regions when pressing their groups' demands in the national political arena.

The ethnic intermediary operates in all types of political systems — democratic or authoritarian, capitalist or socialist, civilian or military, secular or religious.[9] In the case of Ghana, for example, ethnic intermediaries have continuously engaged in promoting their ethnic groups' interests, despite numerous shifts in government since independence in 1957. During four periods (1957–60, 1969–72, 1979–81, and 1992–present) in which multiparty politics have dominated the Ghanaian political system, ethnic intermediaries have made "extensive use" of forums within the national legislature to focus the attention of national leaders on the need for regional development.[10] With the rise of the single-party state from 1960 to 1966, as well as the emergence of a succession of military regimes during 1966–69, 1972–79, and 1981–92, ethnic intermediaries needed to shift tactics in favor of quieter, more concealed approaches, such as "face-to face contacts" with individual leaders.[11] "What proved constant through all of these switches was the critical roles played by the ethnic intermediary," explains one collaborative analysis of African politics and society, "even if the means used to advance the interests of rural constituents at the political center changed noticeably with each shift in authority system."[12]

African leaders committed to pursuing an ethnic compact often seek to promote an **ethnic balance** in governance through the **proportionality principle**: the provision of state resources, such as government jobs, federal budget allocations, and even political representation, according to an ethnic group's percentage of the total population.[13] As shown by Donald Rothchild, a specialist of conflict resolution in Africa, African leaders committed to maintaining some level of ethnic balance can employ a variety of policies, several of which have appeared with some regularity during the contemporary independence era:

- the inclusion of major ethnoregional strongmen in the cabinet and/or party national executive committee;
- the decision not to drop a minister who has been reelected to parliament;
- the maintenance of an ethnic balance by replacing retiring ministers and high party officials with others from the same subregion;
- the preservation, when succession occurs, of a geographical balance in appointments to the president and prime minister as well as within the cabinet and party;
- special measures to include minority ethnic interests in the decision-making process;
- an understanding not to discuss highly emotional, ethnicity-related issues outside the political coalition.[14]

The concept of proportionality is in some ways similar to a patronage-style democracy, in which diverse groups are kept happy with the provision of their expected portion of economic resources and power. However, even the most authoritarian of African leaders, who fashioned political systems largely dominated by their own ethnic groups, nonetheless realized the importance of maintaining at least some semblance of ethnic balance in government. Indeed, the proportionality principle, like the efforts of the ethnic intermediary, can successfully operate regardless of whether the country is led by a democratically elected president, an authoritarian military dictator, a hereditary monarch, a revolutionary Marxist, or an Islamic revivalist. The cornerstone of the proportionality principle is the assumption that inclusiveness of diverse ethnic interests will provide for greater regime stability. "The benefits accruing from this exchange may well go to some groups disproportionately," explains Rothchild, "but if all partners gain some share, they may come to view continued participation in the process as serving their interests."[15]

The evolution of ethnic politics in Djibouti, a ministate in the Horn of Africa with a population of less than 500,000, shows how ethnic balancing has played a role in an authoritarian, single-party system.[16] Two ethnic groups, the Issa and the Afar, have increasingly competed for political power in Djibouti. The Issa, a clan of the Somali people, is Djibouti's largest ethnic group (33 percent of the population) and inhabits the southern one-third of the country. The Afar is the second largest ethnic group (20 percent) and inhabits the northern two-thirds of the country. The remainder of the population is divided among five major immigrant groups largely living in the capital, Djibouti City: Gadaboursi (15 percent) and Isaak (13 percent), also clans of the Somali people that migrated from northern Somalia during the twentieth century; Arabs, particularly Yemenis (6 percent), who work primarily in the commercial sector; French nationals and other Europeans (4 percent) working at all levels of the Djiboutian government, including 3,500 troops of the French Foreign Legion; and illegal economic migrants and refugees from neighboring countries, who together constitute 10 to 15 percent of the country's population.

Hassan Gouled Aptidon, an Issa politician and leader of a nationalist movement, the *Ligue Populaire Africaine pour l'Indépendance* (LPAI, African Popular League for Independence), emerged as Djibouti's first president in 1977, and Ahmed Dini, an Afar and secretary-general of the LPAI, became prime minister. Similar to other African leaders during the initial decades of the contemporary independence era, Gouled strengthened the single-party system by bringing the party and the government increasingly under his personal control and restricting popular debate. According to the National Mobilization Law passed by the National Assembly in October 1981, for example, Djibouti was transformed into a single-party political system, in which the only legal party prior to 1992 was the state-endorsed *Rassemblement Populaire pour le Progrès* (RPP, Popular Assembly for Progress), the party that succeeded the LPAI. Only those politicians approved by Gouled and the RPP were allowed to run on a single-party slate during election periods.

Despite his far-reaching powers, Gouled initially crafted a ruling coalition, inclusive of all ethnic groups, but which nonetheless ensured control by his Issa ethnic group. An unwritten power-sharing agreement made prior to independence ensured that the office of the president would be occupied by an Issa and the office of the prime minister would be occupied by an Afar. Another unwritten agreement provided for the apportionment of the sixty-five-seat National Assembly along ethnic lines. Whereas Issas and others of Somali origin, such as the Gadaboursis and Isaaks, were guaranteed a total of thirty-three seats, Afars were apportioned the slightly smaller number of thirty seats, and Arabs were guaranteed two seats. Gouled also put together an initial cabinet of advisors that included seven Afars and six Issas, as well as one representative each from the Isaak, Gadaboursi, and Arab groups. Gouled's successful ethnic balancing earned Djibouti the label "eye of the hurricane," for its ethnic stability in the troubled region of the Horn of Africa.[17]

Ethnic Violence and the Breakdown of Ethnic Compacts

African leaders and ethnic intermediaries who have been unsuccessful in creating or maintaining ethnic compacts have invariably found their regimes confronted by ethnically inspired opposition movements and guerrilla insurgencies.[18] In the case of Djibouti, Afar leaders increasingly became disenchanted with their second-class role in a political system essentially dominated by the Issa ethnic group, ultimately fueling Afar support for a variety of dissident movements.[19] In 1979, the Afar leaders of two Ethiopian-supported guerrilla movements, the *Mouvement Populaire de Libération* (MPL, Popular Movement of Liberation) and the *Union Nationale de l'Indépendance* (UNI, National Union for Independence), created a joint military organization, the *Front Démocratique pour la Libération de Djibouti* (FDLD, Democratic Front for the Liberation of Djibouti), and planned to overthrow the Gouled regime by force. In the political realm, former Prime Minister Ahmed Dini attempted to break the monopoly of the ruling RPP in 1981, by forming the *Parti Populaire Djiboutien* (PPD, Djiboutian Popular Party), an opposition political party that was quickly outlawed by the Gouled regime. Afar opposition to Gouled created an escalating cycle of violence as the government repressed Afar guerrilla attacks, particularly within the northern Afar-inhabited territories.

Rising frustrations within the Afar community reached a critical point in November 1991. At that time, the *Front pour la Restauration de la Démocratie* (FRUD, Front for the Restoration of Democracy), a military force of approximately three thousand guerrilla fighters primarily from the Afar ethnic group, launched a sustained military offensive that eventually captured all

BOX 7.1

TRANSCENDING ETHNICITY AND CLASS?
MARABOUTS AS RELIGIOUS INTERMEDIARIES

Religion plays an important role in African politics and society, most notably due to the ability of Christian, Muslim, and animist leaders to tap into religious beliefs that transcend ethnicity and class differences. In the case of Senegal, elected politicians historically have contended with the often competing interests of **marabouts**, the leaders of religious organizations known as Islamic brotherhoods, who represent the religious values of the country's heavily Muslim (94 percent) population.

Three Islamic brotherhoods, the Qadiriyya, the Tijaniyya, and the Mouridiyya, claim the allegiance of more than two-thirds of Senegalese Muslims, thereby making their marabouts particularly powerful within Senegalese politics and society. A marabout is capable of mobilizing the Muslim faithful through an intricate network of patron-client ties, in which thousands of lesser marabouts declare their allegiance to more senior leaders. The Mouridiyya, whose spiritual center is the holy city of Touba, are the most influential of the Senegalese marabouts. Their founder, Khalif General Amadou Bamba, is revered within Senegalese history as a charismatic leader who fought against French colonialism.

The power of Senegalese marabouts derives from the population's belief in the spiritual and often magical powers of their personal religious guides. The most revered, senior marabouts serve as spiritual leaders for the brotherhood as a whole and enjoy the largest degree of political power and prestige. During the 1960s, the term "marabout-cadillac" was coined to indicate the prestigious societal rank and financial success of these senior marabouts. Another type of marabout, the "marabout-teacher," is responsible for the religious instruction of his *taalibe* (disciples) in a variety of settings, most notably the koranic (Islamic) schools for young children. Finally, the "marabout-magician" is revered for his magical powers, such as an ability to predict and even alter the future. The "gris-gris" or talisman worn by most Senegalese for protection against evil is a visible manifestation of the disciples' faith in the magical powers of their respective marabout. All three types of marabouts enjoy financial independence thanks to a complex system of alms collection by their disciples who, depending on the charisma and power of the particular marabout in question, are capable of channeling enormous amounts of money into a designated cause.

Popular support has fostered the marabout's rise as an increasingly influential **religious intermediary** between the Senegalese government and the general population. Politicians actively court marabout support because of the religious leaders' ability to both facilitate and stymie government policies. During the colonial era, for example, the French government's decision to allow Khalif

General Bamba to return home from exile in 1902 marked the beginning of marabout financial participation in political campaigns. In 1914, the Mouridiyya brotherhood, grateful for the return of their leader, offered political and financial support to Blaise Diagne, helping him to become the first African deputy in the French Assembly. The Mouridiyya marabouts in return received important material advantages, most notably the deeds to large tracts of land for farming purposes.

A dramatic contemporary example of the political influence wielded by marabouts occurred in 1994, when Senegalese President Abdou Diouf was "rebuffed" by the religious leaders of the Mouridiyya and the Tijaniyya brotherhoods. Prior to this date, Diouf and his predecessor, Léopold Sédar Senghor, felt politically compelled to make internal "state visits" to the holy cities of these two brotherhoods, at least once every two months to personally consult with senior marabouts. In what amounted to a major political scandal, the marabouts unilaterally announced that such visits were no longer practical nor desirable. Simply put, senior marabouts had taken the extraordinary step of distancing themselves from the Diouf administration, due to growing concerns over President Diouf's ability to govern effectively.

For further reading, see Leonardo A. Villalón, *Islamic Society and State Power in Senegal: Disciples and Citizens in Fatick* (Cambridge: Cambridge University Press, 1995).

---

major areas in the north except for the towns of Tadjoura and Obock. The military operation amounted to a "reform" insurgency as the leaders intended to maintain Djibouti's territorial integrity while also reordering the existing ethnic compact in favor of greater political power for the Afar ethnic group (see Chapter 13). The Gouled regime sought to defuse this Afar-based military offensive, in part by holding multiparty legislative and presidential elections in December 1992 and May 1993. These elections were significantly marred, however, by massive electoral fraud by supporters of the Gouled regime and a FRUD-inspired boycott heeded by approximately 50 percent of the voting age population (primarily within the Afar ethnic group). As expected by most foreign observers, Gouled and the ruling RPP declared victory in these elections and subsequently launched a military offensive in July 1993 that defeated the FRUD guerrilla insurgency.

Despite ongoing pressures for democratization, principally from the Afar ethnic group, all organs of government remain firmly under the control of the Issa-dominated government. Gouled's age (he is an octogenarian) nonetheless has reduced his involvement in the regime to that of a figurehead. In 1999, Ismael Omar Guelleh, another Issa politician with extremely close ties to Gouled, succeeded Gouled as president, ensuring continued Issa domination of the country. Although the Issa regime's manipulation of multiparty elections appears to have ensured political stability in the short term, it has done little to resolve the long-term grievances of the political opposition. Indeed, events of the 1990s have prompted foreign observers to use a new metaphor; they now refer to Djibouti as the "boiling cauldron" for its potential for ethnic violence.[20]

The launching of separatist movements by aggrieved ethnic groups is a second, more drastic response to the failure of ethnic compacts during the contemporary independence era (see Chapter 13). In these cases, aggrieved ethnic leaders and their constituents believe that an ethnic compact is no longer viable, either under existing circumstances or in the future. Instead they believe that the only remaining option for their ethnic group is to secede and to seek recognition of their territory as an independent nation-state within the international system. All secessionist attempts in Africa have resulted in a military response from the centralized government; therefore leaders of the secessionist movement prepare for and expect to be engaged in a protracted civil war.[21]

The declaration of independence by the Somaliland Republic on May 17, 1991, offers an interesting case, due to its origins in a reformist guerrilla insurgency that was transformed into a separatist movement (see Box 6.2). The cornerstone of this conflict is the division of the Somali ethnic group into ten major clan families, the relations of which historically have alternated between peaceful competition and military conflict.[22] The Isaak clan represents approximately 70 percent of Somaliland's population, and the remainder is largely divided among four other clan groups: the Issa, Gadaboursi, Dulbahante, and Warsangeli.

The Isaak clan entered into an ethnic compact with the other Somali clans when they agreed in 1960 to voluntarily federate their territory (a former British colony) with the Italian colony of southern Somalia to create the Republic of Somalia.[23] The beginning of the end of this compact began in 1969, however, when Major-General Mohammed Siad Barre seized power in a military coup d'état and created a military dictatorship that revolved around the clans of his father (Marehan), mother (Ogadeni), and wife (Dulbahante), the so-called MOD alliance. In 1981, political opposition was transformed into military opposition with the creation of an Isaak guerrilla insurgency known as the Somali National Movement (SNM), which ultimately contributed to Barre's overthrow in 1991.

The Isaak-inhabited areas of the north paid a tremendous price for the SNM's guerrilla victory; Barre's forces engaged in a "systematic pattern" of attacks against unarmed Isaak villages throughout the 1980s that, in the eyes of Isaak clan leaders, bordered on genocide. The two major northern cities of Berbera and Hargeisa were virtually destroyed.[24] To make matters worse, a southern-based guerrilla army of the Hawiye clan, the United Somali Congress (USC), reneged on an earlier agreement to create a military government of national unity and took advantage of its control of the former capital of Mogadishu to name a Hawiye clan member president. This proved the final straw for Isaak leaders weary of twenty-two years of civil war and dictatorship. In 1991, Isaak clan leaders officially declared the ethnic compact of 1969 to be null and void. From this point forward, Somaliland would "go it alone."[25]

The fact that the Somaliland Republic remains unrecognized by any other country underscores some of the obstacles associated with the pursuit of ethnically based secession in Africa.[26] First and foremost, regional and international norms are stacked against the legitimacy of ethnically based secession and strongly favor existing nation-states. One of the cardinal principles of the Organization of African Unity (OAU) is the inviolability of inherited frontiers from the colonial era. Only Eritrea successfully seceded during the contemporary independence era.

Second, the African territories seeking to secede, including the Somaliland Republic, are never ethnically homogeneous, prompting critics to question whether secession is fair to potentially unwilling minorities in the proposed new state. Even if one could measure public opinion accurately, at what point does secession become both acceptable and desirable: a simple majority (51 percent), a clear majority (67 percent), or overwhelming support (90 percent or above)? In the case of Somaliland, for example, some Isaak clan members have called for a national referendum monitored by the United Nations. If the non-Isaak minorities decide to remain federated, as many as 30 percent could vote against secession. In short, the lack of clear-cut precedents and prevailing regional and international norms make it highly unlikely that any of Africa's separatist insurgencies will result in international recognition.

The most extreme outcome associated with the failure of ethnic compacts is the outbreak of **genocide**: the systematic killing or extermination of an entire ethnic group. Most often associated with the Nazi regime's execution of millions of Jews throughout Europe during World War II, the label of genocide in the African context has become synonymous with the killings that took place in Rwanda in 1994.[27] In the aftermath of Rwandan President Juvenal Habyarimana's death in a mysterious plane crash on April 6, 1994, extremists among the majority Hutu ethnic group unleashed a reign of terror against the Tutsi minority as well as against Hutu deemed sympathetic to the plight of the Tutsi. At least half a million unarmed civilians were executed. The carnage was only stopped when a Tutsi guerrilla force, the *Front Patriotique Rwandais* (FPR, Rwandan Patriotic Front), invaded from Uganda and captured the capital of Kigali, subsequently establishing a Tutsi-dominated regime. As is the case with all regions of the world, genocide has rarely occurred in the African context.

Class Dimension of African Politics and Society

The concept of **class** defines a group of individuals who share a common status in society based on cultural, political, or economic distinctions. For example, culturally based class distinctions served as the cornerstone of French colonial policies that distinguished between *évolués* ("evolved" or "civilized" Africans) and their "nonevolved" and "uncivilized" counterparts. French administrators granted *évolué* status to those Africans who had completely embraced French culture, including achieving fluency in the French language, converting to Christianity, obtaining at least a high school education, and becoming a property owner. The attainment of this status ensured access to a wide variety of privileges, such as protection under the French legal system and the right to pursue French citizenship, unavailable to most Africans within the colonies.

Some African societies, such as the African monarchies of both the precolonial and contemporary independence eras, are also stratified according to politically inspired class distinctions. In the case of the Oyo empire, which reached its zenith during the eighteenth century, only a member of the royal family could become the nation's supreme ruler, the Alafin, as well as the numerous *obas* (kings) who comprised the royal lineage (see Chapter 4). The Alafin's formal powers included the appointment of provincial governors and the ability to declare war. His informal powers, most notably the art of public persuasion, grew out of the sacred nature of his office. The Alafin represented the pinnacle of a ruling political class in which power was hereditary.

The classic understanding of class draws on the works of Karl Marx and focuses on an individual's economic position in the productive processes of a particular society (see Chapter 3). According to Marxian thought, all capitalist societies at the very least can be divided into a property-owning class that dominates society, and an exploited, propertyless working class that is forced to accept poor jobs and unsafe working conditions or starve. Numerous classes exist between these two extremes. The working class is trapped in a system in which its labor provides the only means for its own survival while serving to create more wealth for the property-owning class. According to Marx, the exploitative nature of capitalist society can only be changed through class revolution.

Sembène Ousmane, a renowned Senegalese novelist and filmmaker, captures the economic dimension of class distinctions in his novel, *Les Bouts de Bois de Dieu* (published in English as *God's Bits of Wood*).[28] The novel documents the historic six-month strike during 1947–48 on the railroad line that currently links Dakar, Senegal, with Bamako, Mali. The strike pitted African workers from Senegal and Mali against the French owners of the colonial railroad. The primary demand of the African workers was higher wages and benefits commensurate with those provided to the smaller group of European workers on the railroad. The strike constituted a classic encounter between the French owners who controlled the means of production (the railroad line) and an exploited, propertyless working class unrewarded for the efforts of their labor. "We are being robbed," explains Mamadou Keita, an elder in the novel who claims to have witnessed the epidemics, the famines, and the seizure of African lands associated with the railroad's advance. "Our wages are so low that there is no longer any difference between ourselves and animals."[29]

The scholarly community largely ignored the importance of class during the first two decades of the contemporary independence era.[30] African leaders and Western observers optimistically believed that the unifying forces of nationalism and modernization would erase any class differences that might exist, just as they predicted with regard to ethnicity. The Cold War competition between the United States and the former Soviet Union reinforced this neglect. Western, particularly American, policymakers denigrated class analysis as an intellectual propaganda tool of the communist bloc, with little if any relevance to the African continent.[31] African leaders and scholars trained within the Western, liberal tradition largely shared these beliefs despite a well-established Marxist tradition in Western Europe, particularly in France.[32] Even Soviet-inspired Marxism, itself "tainted and twisted" by Stalinist orthodoxy, "had little impact" on interpretations of African politics and society during the 1950s and the early 1960s.[33]

Several political developments brought about prolific class-based scholarship from the late 1960s to the present.[34] Critics who sought explanations for the widespread emergence of Western-supported authoritarian regimes were naturally drawn to critical perspectives, such as Marxian-inspired class analysis, that underscored the extent to which self-interested ruling classes can impede development. Rising domestic protests against America's involvement in the Vietnam War fostered disillusionment with the liberal model of development, prompting African scholars and policymakers to seek alternative models of development. African leaders increasingly adopted variants of socialism and Marxism as official models of development, subsequently seeking close ties with the Soviet Union, the People's Republic of China, and other members of the socialist bloc (see Chapter 8). This trend reached its height in 1975, when Portugal's withdrawal from its colonies in Africa led to the establishment of self-proclaimed Marxist regimes in Angola, Cape Verde, Guinea-Bissau, Mozambique, and Sao Tome and Principe. Although the decline of communism in the former Soviet Union and Eastern Europe reinforced the rejection of Marxist and socialist models of development by the beginning of the 1990s, class analysis remains a vital and important tool for understanding African politics and society.

Class Divisions within African Society

Debates over the origins and development of African classes have spawned a rich diversity of terms and categorizations for individual classes and **class factions** (divisions within classes).[35] Although scholars may disagree over specific titles, they agree on four general class categories.

The first class, the **foreign bourgeoisie**, originated in the Great Power rivalry in Africa, and is usually divided into two class factions. The most important class faction, the **metropolitan bourgeoisie**, includes the political and business leaders of the Great Powers, most notably the former colonial powers, which have cultivated economic ties with individual African countries. The metropolitan bourgeoisie is especially discussed in writings about the relationship between

France and its former colonies.[36] For example, Jacques Foccart, the architect of French foreign policy toward Africa under the administrations of Charles de Gaulle and Georges Pompidou, is recognized by both admirers and critics alike as having created an intricate web of ties that still closely links France to its francophone colonies.[37] Foccart and other members of the metropolitan bourgeoisie ensured that the end of direct colonial rule (1884–1951) was replaced by a series of neocolonial economic ties that permitted continued external domination.

A second faction of the foreign bourgeoisie, the **local expatriate class**, lives and works in individual African countries. The expatriate class ranges in number from less than a hundred to several thousand and plays the vital role of serving as a daily reminder of the metropolitan power's economic reach and influence. At the end of the 1990s, approximately fifteen thousand French nationals were living in Senegal, which received its independence in 1960. These French citizens work at all levels of the Senegalese government and economy as special advisors to Senegalese President Abdou Diouf, administrators of the French Cultural Center and other local offices of the French government, military advisors and troops stationed in the country as part of a bilateral French-Senegalese military agreement, and as directors and personnel of French companies, most notably those in the lucrative petroleum, telecommunications, and automobile industries.[38]

A second major class group, the **African bourgeoisie**, constitutes the dominant class in most African countries, and is often subdivided into four class factions.[39] The **political bourgeoisie**, which encompasses the political elite, including the head-of-state and his senior advisors, holds the reins of political power in all African countries. The political bourgeoisie includes both civilian and military leaders, and spans the ideological spectrum from proponents of capitalism to self-proclaimed socialists and Marxists. The political bourgeoisie plays a critical role in the appointment of the **bureaucratic bourgeoisie**, the upper division of the civil service and other senior employees who staff government bureaucracies. A nongovernmental faction, the **commercial bourgeoisie**, includes private businesspersons, most notably the senior executives of major local businesses. Finally, a **petty bourgeoisie**, often referred to as the lower middle class, includes small traders and shopkeepers, artisans, teachers, soldiers, and the lower ranks of government bureaucracies. The small size of the private sector has made the political and bureaucratic factions of the African bourgeoisie particularly important.

Kenya is often cited as one of the best examples of a well-developed and well-entrenched African bourgeoisie.[40] The country's founding father, President Jomo Kenyatta, served as the symbolic head of a political bourgeoisie that sought to maintain close ties with the major northern capitalist powers, most notably Great Britain, the former colonial power. As was the case in most African countries at the beginning of the contemporary independence era, Kenyatta's administration oversaw massive increases in public sector jobs, which established a very extensive bureaucratic bourgeoisie. Kenyatta also fervently supported national legislation, such as the Trade Licensing Act of 1967, that reserved significant portions of the Kenyan economy for Kenyan businesspersons and therefore fostered the rise of a commercial bourgeoisie. That this commercial bourgeoisie ultimately engaged in highly corrupt practices to ensure its economic monopoly was of little concern to the Kenyatta regime, as long as kickbacks and other forms of financial support were funneled to the political bourgeoisie. Even the Kenyan petty bourgeoisie was able to flourish, particularly in terms of trade, construction, and road transport, despite its general inability to achieve the scale of riches enjoyed by the other factions of the Kenyan bourgeoisie.

The **African proletariat** is a third major class category of African workers.[41] The proletariat is generally found in urban settings and earns a set wage that may range from an hourly to a monthly basis. The case of Zambia is particularly illuminating. Although the proletariat on average constitutes less than 20 percent of the wage-earning population in most African countries, their numbers exceed more than 50 percent of wage earners in Zambia. These large numbers are due to the substantial industrial demands surrounding the sale of copper, Zambia's largest export. Thousands of workers were needed to create and maintain a massive mining industry and a railroad line to transport the copper to ports for export. Often referred to as the "copperbelt," the broad territory following the railroad line from the copper fields to points of export is heavily urbanized. The urbanization of Zambian society and the development of a substantial proletariat has contributed to very powerful labor unions and movements.

An unemployed or underemployed urban working class, known as the **lumpenproletariat**, is an important class faction of the proletariat. In Senegal, for example, high unemployment rates among a growing urban population sometimes drive violent confrontations between government forces and heavily politicized student groups and workers unions.[42] As depicted in the film, *La Génération Sacrifiée?* (The Sacrificed Generation?), coproduced in 1995 by a Senegalese and an American filmmaker, rising numbers of increasingly educated, yet discouraged, Senegalese youth are entering a job market that, in their eyes, offers them nothing but positions as street vendors, maids, and cooks. The concept of a "sacrificed generation" has become especially poignant in the aftermath of France's 1994 decision to unilaterally impose a 50 percent devaluation on the common currency (CFA franc) shared by Senegal and thirteen other francophone members of the CFA Franc Zone. As a result, the francophone countries experienced a 50 percent decline in the purchasing power of an already economically marginalized population.

Finally, the **African peasantry** is usually the largest class category in most African countries.[43] The peasant is a rural dweller who grows food and raises livestock, either for personal consumption or for export to the urban areas and the wider international market. The most prosperous peasants, often referred to as **kulaks,** hire other peasants to work larger land holdings and often partic-ipate in regional trade. The peasantry historically has been the most exploited class of African societies.[44] During the initial decades of the contemporary independence era, for example, state-controlled marketing boards often fixed the price of agricultural goods well below market value to ensure the availabil-ity of cheap foodstuffs for the urban areas. The peasantry's response to these price controls — most notably selling crops illegally in the informal economy or simply deciding to only grow crops for personal consumption — demon-strated the "uncaptured" nature of the peasant class.[45] Members could opt out of the formal market economy and concentrate on their local interests and needs, or what has been referred to as the **economy of affection.**[46] It is pre-cisely this dynamic that was responsible for the decline of food production throughout Africa from the 1950s to the 1980s.

Tanzania offers one of the most widely examined cases of the role of the African peasantry.[47] Approximately 77 percent of the population lives in the rural areas and is involved in agricultural production.[48] Under the leadership of Julius Nyerere, Tanzania's first president, the government launched a social-ist development strategy known as *ujamaa* (the Kiswahili word for brother-hood), which sought to regroup the peasant population in new communal villages. One of the goals of *ujamaa* was to create new educational, health care, and agricultural extension services in the modern centralized villages, in order to better serve the peasant class.[49] However, the gradual withdrawal of the peasantry from the formal economy and the tremendous decline in national food production ultimately ensured the failure of the economic dimension of the *ujamaa* strategy. Although this strategy was ultimately dis-carded by Nyerere's successor, President Ali Hassan Mwinyi, in the late 1980s, it nonetheless recognized the centrality of the African peasant in the pursuit of development (see Chapter 8).

Class Cooperation and Conflict

According to Marxist theorists, the "relations of production" that determine who owns and controls the means of economic production, such as property, factories, and investment capital, are crucial to understanding the evolving nature of class relationships within capitalist societies. They further argue that the exploitative nature of the relations of production within capitalist societies leads to class conflict and ultimately revolution (see Chapter 3). Marxist theo-rists who apply this model to Africa generally conclude that only class-based, national liberation struggles will be capable of promoting true change throughout the African continent.[50]

In a pathbreaking article that significantly altered thinking within African-ist intellectual circles, Richard L. Sklar argues for the need to "liberate" class analysis from the economic preconceptions of Marxism and to focus instead on the *political* basis of class relations.[51] Sklar notes that the Marxist belief in the inevitable class conflict and revolution must be tempered in favor of a more nuanced understanding, which recognizes the possibility of class cooperation in the pursuit of national development. "Class relations, at bottom," explains Sklar, "are determined by relations of power, not production."[52] In short, politics, not economics, are the defining aspect of class relations throughout Africa.

Four possible combinations of class cooperation and conflict deserve special mention. First, it is important to underscore the possibility of **interclass cooperation** in the peaceful pursuit of national development. In the case of Ghana, for example, an interclass alliance between the political bourgeoisie and the peasantry turned Ghana into one of the most widely touted development success stories of the 1980s.[53] Under the leadership of Flt. Lt. Jerry Rawlings, a strong-willed — and at times, iron-fisted — charismatic leader with his "hand on the popular pulse," the political bourgeoisie implemented a series of structural adjustment economic reforms largely designed by the International Monetary Fund (IMF) and the World Bank.[54] Ghana succeeded where many other African countries had failed. This is in part because the political bourgeoisie overcame the protests of two urban-based classes that would be negatively affected by the economic reforms: the commercial bourgeoisie and the proletariat. The successful strategy was based on Rawlings' cultivation of an interclass alliance with the rural peasantry, which in 1985 constituted approximately 78 percent of the general population.[55] Indeed, voting in the 1988–89 district assembly elections clearly demonstrated strong peasant support for the Rawlings regime in all regions except that of "Greater Accra," the primary urban area inhabited by the commercial bourgeoisie and the proletariat which suffered under reform policies.[56]

A second, more common class dynamic during the contemporary independence era is **transnational class cooperation** between the political bourgeoisie and the international bourgeoisie. In many cases, a threatened political bourgeoisie turns to its class allies within the international system in order to maintain its own power. French intervention in the Democratic Republic of the Congo (Congo-Kinshasa) in 1977 is a striking example of transnational class cooperation.[57] On March 8, 1977, 2,500 guerrillas associated with the Front for the National Liberation of the Congo (FLNC) invaded Congo-Kinshasa from Angola with the intent of capturing Shaba province, the source of nearly 75 percent of Congo-Kinshasa's export earnings. The combined appeals of President Mobutu Sese Seko, the head of the Congolese political bourgeoisie, and the local European expatriate class, most notably French and Belgian nationals working in Shaba's mining industry, prompted French President Giscard d'Estaing to authorize French military intervention in conjunction with Morocco. This and later French interventions would maintain Mobutu in power until 1997, despite the emergence of overwhelming rural and urban

BOX 7.2

TRANSCENDING ETHNICITY AND CLASS?
GENDER AND THE DEBATE OVER FEMALE CIRCUMCISION

In May 1996, Fauziya Kasinga, a nineteen-year-old African woman from the country of Togo, was involved in a precedent-setting case for the U.S. Immigration and Naturalization Service. Kasinga argued that her family would force her to undergo **female circumcision** if she were deported. She fled Togo at the age of fifteen to avoid being circumcised as part of a marriage that had been arranged for her after the death of her father. The U.S. Justice Department's Board of Immigration Appeals ruled favorably on Kasinga's case, thereby adding female circumcision to the list of factors that constituted a "well-founded fear of persecution," the legal basis for seeking political asylum in the United States. Previously, political asylum was only granted to individuals who demonstrated a well-founded fear of persecution due to their race, religion, nationality, political opinions, or membership in a social group.

Female circumcision, also referred to as **female genital mutilation**, is practiced throughout Africa, Asia, and the Middle East. The mildest form, **clitoridectomy**, involves the partial or total removal of the clitoris. A more severe type, referred to as **excision**, involves the removal of the clitoris and some or all of the labia minora (inner lips) and the labia majora (outer lips). The most severe form, **infibulation**, concludes the process of excision with the suturing of the raw tissue such that a scar tissue forms across the vaginal opening. A small opening is left to allow for urination and menstruation.

Female circumcision is not limited to a particular religious, ethnic, or class group on the African continent. It is common throughout West, North, and East Africa, with its most severe forms being practiced in the countries of Djibouti, Eritrea, Mali, Somalia, and the Sudan. The practice is often associated with a rite of passage. "In some areas, such as for the Gikuyu and Maasai [ethnic groups] of Kenya, excision is performed to mark a girl's transition to womanhood: by the Maasai just weeks prior to marriage and by the Gikuyu prior to the first menstruation," explains Ellen Gruenbaum, a specialist of circumcision and infibulation. "In many societies, however, the age at which the circumcisions are performed is so young [sometimes as early as the age of three] that it is clearly not intended to mark the onset of womanhood," Gruenbaum continues. "The reasons for this in some cultures are explicitly related to the goal of attenuating sexual desire in preadolescent girls and women, and, in the case of infibulation, preventing illicit intercourse by constructing a barrier of scar tissue."

The publicity surrounding Kasinga's asylum case was indicative of growing international condemnation of female circumcision. African feminists, such as Raqiya Haji Dualeh Abdalla, a Somali woman who wrote *Sisters in Affliction: Circumcision and Infibulation of Women in Africa* (1982), have joined with a variety of international organizations, such as the New York–based Research, Action, and Information Network for Bodily Integrity of Women (RAIN-BOW), in their quest to outlaw female circumcision throughout Africa and other regions of the world. Health concerns are usually at the forefront of anticircumcision efforts. Circumcised women are often afflicted with chronic urinary tract infections, menstrual problems, and difficult childbirth, not to mention the deaths that occur due to shock and hemorrhaging during the circumcision process itself. Other concerns involve the circumcised woman's ability to experience sexual pleasure and the psychological scarring that accompanies the circumcision. Although activist measures, such as educational drives and the promotion of national legislation, have led to the steady decline of female circumcision, it continues to be annually performed on approximately two million African girls, primarily between the ages of four and twelve.

Quotations are from Ellen Gruenbaum, "Clitoridectomy and Infibulation," in John Middleton, ed., *Encyclopedia of Africa South of the Sahara*, vol. 2 (New York: Charles Scribner's Sons, 1997), pp. 382–83. See also Nahid Toubia, *Female Genital Mutilation: A Call for Global Action* (New York: Research, Action, and Information Network for Bodily Integrity of Women, 1993).

support for his removal from power. In short, the FLNC insurgency, which voiced growing popular discontent with the failed policies of the increasingly corrupt Mobutu regime, was defeated primarily due to the interclass alliance between the Congolese political bourgeoisie, the local European expatriate class, and the French metropolitan bourgeoisie.

A third class dynamic explains how **intraclass conflict** within the African bourgeoisie can undermine democratic transitions by preserving politics as usual. Critics of the democratization process that swept the African continent during the first half of the 1990s are particularly wary of the false appearance of change associated with the holding of multiparty elections. According to Claude Ake, what one is witnessing in even the most widely heralded success stories of democratic elections can be characterized as the "democratization of disempowerment": a process whereby newly established multiparty political systems merely allow rotating and competing class factions of the African bourgeoisie to exploit the proletariat and the peasantry who remain disempowered from the political process (see Chapter 3).[58] In the case of Zambia, the initial optimism associated with President Frederick Chiluba's victory in that country's first multiparty elections in 1991 has been sobered by growing concerns with the new administration's drift toward authoritarianism. Despite the fact that he was a distinguished union activist whose father was a mine-worker, Chiluba has increasingly been denounced as more interested in protecting his newfound status as a member of the ruling political bourgeoisie than in promoting the needs and interests of those who voted him into office — the peasantry and the proletariat. Indeed, he engineered several highly questionable political tactics to ensure victory in the 1996 presidential elections (see Chapter 12).

A final class dynamic is revolutionary **interclass conflict** and the reordering of class relations. Under such a scenario, rising popular dissatisfaction within the proletariat and the bourgeoisie prompts disenfranchised classes to seek to overthrow a weakened political bourgeoisie. The downfall of the Ethiopian regime of Emperor Haile Selassie offers one of the most-documented cases of revolution within an African context. As explained by Edmond J. Keller, a noted observer of the Ethiopian revolution, widespread drought and famine at the beginning of the 1970s ensured the "relentless worsening" of the peasant condition and the rising militancy of a small, urbanized proletariat.[59] Although the combined dissatisfaction of the peasantry and the proletariat was insufficient to ensure a revolutionary outcome, by 1974 the Selassie regime found itself abandoned by significant factions of the bourgeoisie, most notably the petty bourgeoisie.[60] Even U.S. policymakers, the most important faction of the international bourgeoisie that maintained close ties with Ethiopia, at best ignored the unfolding of the revolutionary situation and in any case were unwilling to provide the support necessary to maintain Emperor Selassie in power.[61]

The intensification of a revolutionary situation prompted a military coup d'état and the replacement of the Selassie regime with a Provisional Military Administrative Council (PMAC), a group of approximately 120 junior grade and noncommissioned officers of the Ethiopian military who became known as the Dergue. As is the case in the aftermath of most revolutions, bloody infighting led to the emergence of a group of self-proclaimed Marxists under the leadership of Colonel Mengistu Haile Mariam, which assumed control over the political reins of government. Rather than overseeing the transformation of the relations of production in favor of proletarian and peasant interests, however, Mengistu and the other members of his junta unleashed a reign of terror against their former class allies, as well as against the remnants of the former ruling bourgeoisie. Mengistu's class faction ultimately transformed itself into a political bourgeoisie intent on maintaining power at all costs, only to be overthrown in 1991 by the combined forces of several guerrilla armies. Revolutions are extremely rare in Africa, and successful revolutions that reflect the interests of the peasant and proletariat classes are even rarer still.[62]

Competing Explanations of the Nigerian Civil War (1967–70)

As artfully described by Richard L. Sklar and C. S. Whitaker, Nigeria was the "brightest star in the galaxy of new African states" when it achieved independence in 1960.[63] A democratically elected government took power in Africa's most populous and richly endowed country. Nigerians and outside observers alike thought that Nigeria was destined to play a leadership role on the African continent.

A brutal three-year civil war (1967–70) tainted Nigeria's image as a potential role model for the continent. The civil war began with the May 1967 decision of Nigeria's Eastern Province to secede from the Nigerian federation and declare itself the independent Republic of Biafra, an act that had been preceded by two military coups d'état in January and July of 1966. Although the secessionist province was militarily defeated in January 1970, the civil war and associated coups served as harbingers of more than three decades of military rule and authoritarianism.[64]

The Nigerian civil war is therefore an important turning point in both Nigerian and African history. As such, it offers a unique opportunity to understand how the concepts of ethnicity and class have contributed to significantly different interpretations of African politics and society. Although most analyses of the Nigerian civil war include references to both ethnicity and class, they often emphasize the importance of one approach at the expense of another.[65] The following two brief narratives of the Nigerian civil war — one from the perspective of ethnicity and the other from the perspective of class — demonstrate the implications of ethnicity- and class-based interpretations of African politics and society. Each narrative portrays three crucial elements of the Nigerian civil war: historical origins prior to Nigeria's independence in 1960, mounting social tensions during Nigeria's First Republic (1960–66), and the unfolding of events specifically associated with the military coups that preceded the actual outbreak of military hostilities in 1967.

Perceiving Events through an Ethnic Lens

One way to understand the historical origins of the Nigerian civil war is to begin with the multiethnic country created by Great Britain during the colonial era.[66] The colony was comprised of over 250 ethnic groups, three of which constituted 66 percent of the total population and primarily resided in three geographical areas: the Igbo in the southeast; the Yoruba in the southwest, and the Hausa/Fulani in the north (refer back to Map 5.3 in Chapter 5). Upon independence in 1960, Nigerian leaders faced the challenge of creating an ethnic compact that balanced the interests, needs, and often highly diverse political cultures of this ethnic mosaic inherited from the colonial era. For example, the Hausa/Fulani practiced a highly centralized political culture that demanded the complete deference of its subjects to the proclamations of traditional kings known as *emirs*. By contrast, in the egalitarian political culture of the Igbo it is considered the citizen's duty to publicly challenge and criticize the errors of political leaders. When multiplied by 250 ethnic groups, the differences in Hausa/Fulani and Igbo political cultures suggested that the possibility for ethnic competition and conflict was significant, even under the best of circumstances.

The Nigerian ethnic compact eroded and social tensions mounted in the six years (1960–66) preceding the outbreak of civil war. This was due to rising perceptions among ethnic intermediaries and their constituents that some ethnic groups were gaining more than their rightful share of national resources. The southern ethnic groups, most notably the Igbo, embraced British religious practices and colonial educational opportunities, prompting their preferential placement at all levels of colonial administration significantly beyond their respective share of the Nigerian population. This practice carried over into the contemporary independence era, as the more Westernized Igbo and other southern ethnic groups were well positioned to take advantage of expanding government positions and economic opportunities in the private sector. The more numerous Hausa/Fulani, who had resisted Westernization more than the southerners, increasingly feared that the Igbo and other southern ethnic groups would turn their educational advantages into long-term control of the civil service and the political system.[67]

Disputes over the 1962 national census, the first of its kind during the contemporary independence era, aptly demonstrated the political impact of Hausa/Fulani fears. Fully aware that the census would serve as the primary vehicle for determining each ethnic group's future share of national resources, ethnic intermediaries fraudulently inflated the numbers of their respective ethnic groups. "Controversy flared when the initial results revealed much larger population increases in the South — sufficient to end the North's population majority — and demographic tests showed some of the Eastern Region's figures to have been 'grossly inflated'," explains Larry Diamond, a specialist of Nigerian politics and society. "When the North then claimed to have discovered eight million more people in a 'verification check' (thus preserving its population majority), the ensuing crisis forced Prime Minister Tafawa Balewa to cancel the census and order a new one for 1963."[68] The entire process had become tainted. "The result was a still greater fiasco," explains Diamond, "an 'altogether incredible' national increase of 83 percent in ten years and a continued Northern population majority."[69]

Rising ethnic tensions, particularly among Nigeria's three major ethnic groups, culminated in the military coups of January and June 1966, which in turn triggered the Nigerian civil war. In the case of the January coup, for example, there was an "undeniable ethnic selectivity" in terms of both leaders and victims: "Six of the seven majors involved were Igbo; of the seven senior officers killed who outranked the majors, only one was Igbo," explains Young. "The two regional governors who were murdered were not Igbo; the two who survived were."[70] What was increasingly perceived among the general population as a power grab on the part of the Igbo ethnic group was followed by a series of anti-Igbo riots that culminated in a countercoup led by Hausa-Fulani military officers. "This time," explains Young, "twenty-seven of the thirty-nine officers (including General Ironsi), and most of the 191 of other ranks who were murdered, were Igbo."[71] Confronted with spiraling ethnic violence and a northern-based military government unwilling to compromise, Colonel Chukwuemeka Ojukwu, the Igbo governor and military commander of the

Eastern Region, announced his region's decision to secede and to establish the independent Republic of Biafra.

Perceiving Events through a Class Lens

A second way to understand the historical origins of the Nigerian civil war begins with the crucial role played by the British metropolitan bourgeoisie during the colonial era.[72] At the end of the colonial era, the British encouraged the development of a Nigerian bourgeoisie that would accept a peaceful transfer of power and protect British financial interests after independence. The strategy worked, in that the anti-British rhetoric of Nigerian nationalist movements essentially masked the emergence of a political bourgeoisie that shared Britain's belief in the strength of liberal capitalism. The Nigerian bourgeoisie was far from unified, however, with individual factions competing for power within the newly independent country. Different factions were part of the Nigerian bourgeoisie for different reasons: the northern *emirs* played a part, due to their role in traditional society during the precolonial and colonial eras; other factions, such as a rising economic bourgeoisie in southeastern Nigeria, owed their status to the regional structures created during the colonial era and maintained during the early independence years. Political and economic bourgeoisies emerged in each of Nigeria's three major regions, setting the stage for intraclass conflict within the Nigerian bourgeoisie as a whole.[73]

Intraclass competition, within the Nigerian bourgeoisie, over control of the means of production caused mounting tensions during the six years (1960–66) preceding the civil war. In the case of Eastern Nigeria, for example, an emerging regional economic bourgeoisie was in competition with other factions of the national bourgeoisie over control of a booming industrial zone that included at least twenty-four major industries.[74] The most lucrative industry exploited the region's massive oil reserves. A quadrupling of oil prices, engineered by the Organization of Petroleum Exporting Countries (OPEC) in 1973–74, ensured that oil rights would be severely contested. Even as early as 1966, the economic and political bourgeoisies of the Eastern Region were locked in a struggle with other regional bourgeoisies over the exploitation of the region's oil resources. "Some of the members of the bourgeoisie [of the Eastern Region] began to dream dreams," explains Ikenna Nzimiro, a participant in the Nigerian civil war and an avid proponent of the class approach of understanding Nigerian politics and society.[75] Foremost in their minds was that control over the economic resource of oil would allow them to emerge as the dominant class within the economic and the political bourgeoisie.[76]

The workers' strike of June 1964 crippled the national economy for thirteen days and was a crucial turning point in mounting social tensions during the First Republic.[77] The strike pitted the urban proletariat against the political bourgeoisie. Although it originated in workers' demands for higher pay and greater benefits, it captured popular "disgust" with the corrupt and extravagant lifestyles of the Nigerian political bourgeoisie.[78] The net effect of the strike, which received widespread public support especially within the urban areas, was to "further weaken" the already threatened legitimacy of the Nigerian political bourgeoisie "and to expose the weakness of its authority."[79]

Rising intraclass conflict within the Nigerian bourgeoisie, particularly between the petty bourgeoisie and the political bourgeoisie, culminated in the military coups of January and June 1966. The progressive faction of the petty bourgeoisie was made up of the young army majors and captains who led the January coup in order to end the corrupt practices of the dominant political bourgeoisie. Despite the fact that they were primarily Igbo, these officers were motivated by a higher commitment to create a more progressive Nigerian regime that served all ethnic groups. However, the progressive coup plotters ultimately failed to achieve all of their military objectives, most notably the execution of J. T. U. Aguiyi Ironsi, an Igbo general who rallied federal troops in the defense of a unified Nigeria, and who ultimately emerged as Nigeria's military leader in the aftermath of the failed coup.

General Ironsi's assumption of power, and subsequent execution in the countercoup of July 1966, signaled the intensification of intraclass struggle within the political bourgeoisie over control of national economic resources. Although successful in bringing down Nigeria's First Republic and destroying its ethnic base, the January coup nonetheless failed to win power for the progressive military officers.[80] "The top echelon of the officer corps, many of whom already identified, in terms of class interests, with the ousted politicians, grabbed power," explains Nzimiro.[81] In this regard, the decision of Colonel Ojukwu to declare Biafra's independence and to lead a protracted military campaign against the Nigerian central government was motivated less by his allegiance to the Igbo nation than by his desire to protect the class interests of an emerging regional political bourgeoisie, of which he was a member.[82]

The two preceding analyses of the Nigerian civil war demonstrate important differences between ethnicity and class analysis. Despite general agreement over most of the facts associated with the Nigerian civil war, specific interpretations of those facts have widely varied, depending on whether one focuses primarily on the role of class or ethnicity as the defining characteristic of African politics and society. The interpretations vary by picking out different significant events and assigning different intentions and identities to the principal actors.

Uncertain Debate

The concepts of ethnicity and class have contributed to the development of extremely rich and provocative analyses of African politics and society. However, comprehensive understanding of the relationship between these two concepts has been hindered by their division into two separate and highly divided fields of analysis. "An invisible wall has separated ethnicity and class analysis, which has only infrequently been scaled," explains Young. "On both sides of the wall, analysts tend to concede that the other exists, then proceed to ignore or trivialize it."[83]

The ideological Cold War between the Western and Eastern blocs played an especially prominent role in strengthening this invisible wall. Western, and particularly American, scholars implicitly held the belief that class was a tainted concept of Soviet-led Marxism, with little if any relevance to African politics and society. Although scholars optimistically believed in the declining importance of ethnic attachments as part of the modernization process, ethnicity was an important concept of the Western intellectual tradition and therefore remained an acceptable topic of research. Most important, the Cold War reinforced the ideological divide separating ethnicity and class analyses; the concept of ethnicity was associated with an acceptable, mainstream liberal tradition, whereas the concept of class was associated with a critical tradition of scholarship considered on the fringe of intellectual debates (see Chapters 2 and 3).

The Cold War's end removed the ideological foundations of the invisible wall, and thereby set the stage for reinterpretations of African politics and society that allowed for a creative reevaluation of the concepts of class and ethnicity. At a minimum, such a synthesis would recognize the important interplay between ethnicity and class, underscoring the importance of both concepts. "Although a creative synthesis of the concepts of class and ethnicity that is capable of explaining social stratification and politics in African states and societies has yet to appear," explains Patrick Boyle, "both concepts are in danger of becoming increasingly irrelevant in the absence of a post–Cold War reinterpretation of their place in contemporary Africa."[84] Although each concept is capable of explaining one piece of the African puzzle, neither is capable of explaining the puzzle as a whole. Future generations of ethnicity scholars will need to explain how systematic domination by particular ethnic groups differentiates them from a ruling class, while those scholars who emphasize class analysis will have to explain the persistence of ethnic divisions in societies seemingly divided into conflicting classes. Both concepts are necessary and relevant to a contemporary understanding of African politics and society.

Key Terms

ethnicity	genocide
clans	class
age-sets	class factions
ethnic compact	foreign bourgeoisie
ethnic intermediary	metropolitan bourgeoisie
ethnic balance	local expatriate class
proportionality principle	African bourgeoisie
marabouts	political bourgeoisie
religious intermediary	bureaucratic bourgeoisie

commercial bourgeoisie

petty bourgeoisie

African proletariat

lumpenproletariat

African peasantry

kulaks

economy of affection

interclass cooperation

transnational class cooperation

female circumcision

female genital mutilation

clitoridectomy

excision

infibulation

intraclass confict

interclass conflict

For Further Reading

Freund, Bill. *The African Worker*. Cambridge: Cambridge University Press, 1988.

Horowitz, Donald. *Ethnic Groups in Conflict*. Berkeley: University of California Press, 1985.

Huntington, Samuel P. *The Clash of Civilizations and the Remaking of World Order*. New York: Simon & Schuster, 1996.

Kasfir, Nelson, ed. *State and Class in Africa*. London: Frank Cass, 1984.

Laitin, David D. *Hegemony and Culture: Politics and Religious Change among the Yoruba*. Chicago: University of Chicago Press, 1986.

Lloyd, Peter C. *The New Elites of Tropical Africa*. London: Oxford University Press for International African Institute, 1966.

Lubeck, Paul M., ed. *The African Bourgeoisie: Capitalist Development in Nigeria, Kenya, and the Ivory Coast*. Boulder: Lynne Rienner, 1987.

Markovitz, Irving Leonard. *Power and Class in Africa*. Englewood Cliffs: Prentice-Hall, 1977.

Markovitz, Irving Leonard, ed. *Studies in Power and Class in Africa*. New York: Oxford University Press, 1987.

Robertson, Claire, and Iris Berger, eds. *Women and Class in Africa*. New York: Africana, 1986.

Rothchild, Donald. *Managing Ethnic Conflict in Africa: Pressures and Incentives for Cooperation*. Washington: Brookings Institution, 1997.

Rothchild, Donald, and Victor Olorunsola, eds. *State versus Ethnic Claims: African Policy Dilemmas*. Boulder: Westview, 1983.

Sklar, Richard. "The Nature of Class Domination in Africa." *The Journal of Modern African Studies* 17, no. 4 (1979):531–52.

Young, Crawford. *The Politics of Cultural Pluralism*. Madison: University of Wisconsin Press, 1977.

Young, Crawford. *The Rising Tide of Cultural Pluralism: The Nation-State at Bay?* Madison: University of Wisconsin Press, 1993.

Notes

1. John Middleton, ed., *Encyclopedia of Africa South of the Sahara* (4 vols.), (New York: Charles Scribner's Sons, 1997).
2. See Andreas Danevad, "Responsiveness in Botswana Politics: Do Elections Matter?" *The Journal of Modern African Studies* 33, no. 3 (1995):381–402.
3. The leading opposition party, the Botswana National Front (BNF), increasingly has made inroads in national politics (winning 37 percent of the popular vote in 1994), at least partially due to the fact that its leaders are from the Bangwaketse clan family, the second largest of the Tswana clan groupings.
4. Crawford Young, "Nationalism, Ethnicity, and Class in Africa: A Retrospective," *Cahiers d'Etudes Africaines* 26, no. 6 (1986):443.
5. For an introduction to this vast literature, see Crawford Young, *The Politics of Cultural Pluralism* (Madison: University of Wisconsin Press, 1975). See also Crawford Young, "Evolving Modes of Consciousness and Ideology: Nationalism and Ethnicity," in David E. Apter and Carl G. Rosberg, eds., *Political Development and the New Realism in Sub-Saharan Africa* (Charlottesville: University Press of Virginia, 1994), pp. 61–86.
6. Young, "Nationalism, Ethnicity, and Class in Africa," p. 443.
7. See Naomi Chazan, Robert Mortimer, John Ravenhill, and Donald Rothchild, *Politics and Society in Contemporary Africa* (Boulder: Lynne Rienner, 1992), pp. 110–16.
8. *Ibid.*, p. 114.
9. *Ibid.*, p. 112.
10. *Ibid.*, pp. 114–15.
11. *Ibid.*
12. *Ibid.*, p. 115.
13. See Donald Rothchild, "State-Ethnic Relations in Middle Africa," in Gwendolen M. Carter and Patrick O'Meara, eds., *African Independence: The First Twenty-Five Years* (Bloomington: Indiana University Press, 1985), p. 83. See also Donald Rothchild, *Managing Ethnic Conflict in Africa: Pressures and Incentives for Cooperation* (Washington: Brookings Institution, 1997).
14. Rothchild, "State-Ethnic Relations," p. 82.
15. *Ibid.*, p. 82.
16. For an overview, see Peter J. Schraeder, "Ethnic Politics in Djibouti: From 'Eye of the Hurricane' to 'Boiling Cauldron'," *African Affairs* 92, no. 367 (1993):203–23. See also Absieh Omar Warsame and Maurice Botbol, *Djibouti: Les institutions politiques et militaires* (Paris: Banque d'Information et de Documentation de l'Océan Indien, 1986).
17. See Schraeder, "Ethnic Politics in Djibouti."
18. For an excellent overview, see Donald Rothchild and Victor A. Olorunsola, eds., *State versus Ethnic Claims: African Policy Dilemmas* (Boulder: Westview, 1983).

19. For an overview, see Kassim Shehim and James Searing, "Djibouti and the Question of Afar Nationalism," *African Affairs* 19, no. 315 (1980):209–26.

20. See the English-language translation of an article written by Catherine Simon for *Le Monde:* "Influx of Refugees Heightens Vulnerability," FBIS, *Daily Report Sub-Saharan Africa* (July 28, 1991):6.

21. For discussion of the major attempts at secession during the contemporary independence era, see Rothchild and Olorunsola, *State versus Ethnic Claims.*

22. The classic statement on the Somali clan system is I. M. Lewis, *Somalia: A Pastoral Democracy* (London: Oxford University Press, 1960).

23. For an overview of this history, see David Laitin and Said Samatar, *Somalia: Nation in Search of a State* (Boulder: Westview, 1987).

24. See Robert Gersony, *Why Somalis Flee: Synthesis of Accounts of Conflict Experience in Northern Somalia by Somali Refugees, Displaced Persons and Others* (Washington: Bureau for Refugee Programs, Department of State, August 1989); and Africa Watch, *Somalia: A Government at War with Its Own People; Testimonies about the Killings and the Conflict in the North* (London: Africa Watch, 1990).

25. See Gérard Prunier, "Somaliland Goes It Alone," *Current History* 97, no. 619 (1998):225–28.

26. For a more extended analysis, see Crawford Young, "Comparative Claims to Political Sovereignty: Biafra, Katanga, Eritrea," in Rothchild and Olorunsola, *State versus Ethnic Claims,* pp. 199–232.

27. For example, see Alain Destexhe (translated from the French by Alison Marschner), *Rwanda and Genocide in the Twentieth Century* (New York: New York University Press, 1995).

28. Sembène Ousmane, *God's Bits of Wood* (London: Heinemann, 1970).

29. Quoted in *ibid.,* p. 8.

30. See Young, "Nationalism, Ethnicity, and Class in Africa," p. 423.

31. See Martin Staniland, *American Intellectuals and African Nationalists, 1955–1970* (New Haven: Yale University Press, 1991).

32. The recognized leading light in the French tradition is J. Suret-Canale, *Afrique Noire, Occidentale et Centrale* (vol. 2): *L'Ère Coloniale 1900–1945* (Paris: Editions Sociales, 1964). Cited in Young, "Nationalism, Ethnicity, and Class," p. 422.

33. Young, "Nationalism, Ethnicity, and Class," p. 422.

34. *Ibid.,* p. 423.

35. For an introduction to this literature, see Irving Leonard Markovitz, ed., *Studies in Power and Class in Africa* (New York: Oxford University Press, 1987).

36. See Stephen Smith and Antoine Glaser, *Ces Messieurs Afrique: Le Paris-Village du Continent Noir* (Paris: Calmann-Lévy, 1992). See also Guy Martin, "Francophone Africa in the Context of Franco-African Relations," in John W. Harbeson and Donald Rothchild, eds., *Africa in World Politics: Post-Cold War Challenges* (Boulder: Westview, 1995), pp. 163–88.

37. For example, see Pierre Péan, *L'Homme de l'Ombre: Eléments d'Enquête Autour de Jacques Foccart, l'Homme le Plus Mystérieux et le Plus Puissant de la Ve République* (Paris: Fayard, 1990).

38. For an early analysis of the evolving French presence in Senegal, see Rita Cruise O'Brien, *White Society in Black Africa: The French of Africa* (London: Faber & Faber, 1972).

39. For a general discussion of the African bourgeoisie, see Paul M. Lubeck, ed., *The African Bourgeoisie: Capitalist Development in Nigeria, Kenya, and the Ivory Coast* (Boulder: Lynne Rienner, 1987). See also Richard L. Sklar, "Social Class and Political Action in Africa: The Bourgeoisie and the Proletariat," in David E. Apter and Carl G. Rosberg, eds., *Political Development and the New Realism in Sub-Saharan Africa* (Charlottesville: University Press of Virginia, 1994), esp. pp. 121–27.

40. For example, see Colin Leys, *Underdevelopment in Kenya: The Political Economy of Neo-Colonialism 1964–1971* (Berkeley: University of California Press, 1975). See also Gavin Kitching, *Class and Economic Change in Kenya: The Making of an African Petite Bourgeoisie, 1905–1970* (New Haven: Yale University Press, 1980); and Leys, "Learning from the Kenya Debate," in Apter and Rosberg, eds., *Political Development*, pp. 220–46.

41. For a general overview, see Bill Freund, *The African Worker* (Cambridge: Cambridge University Press, 1988). See also Sklar, "Social Class and Political Action in Africa," esp. pp. 127–34.

42. See Momar Coumba Diop and Mamadou Diouf, *Le Sénégal sous Abdou Diouf: Etat et Société* (Paris: Editions Karthala, 1990), especially chs. 5, 9, and 12.

43. For an introduction, see John S. Saul and Roger Woods, "African Peasantries," in Teodor Shanin, ed., *Peasants and Peasant Societies* (Harmondsworth: Penguin, 1971), pp. 80–88.

44. See Jonathan Barker, *Rural Communities Under Stress: Peasant Farmers and the State in Africa* (Cambridge: Cambridge University Press, 1989).

45. See Goran Hyden, *Beyond Ujamaa in Tanzania: Underdevelopment and an Uncaptured Peasantry* (Berkeley: University of California Press, 1980).

46. See James C. Scott, *The Moral Economy of the Peasant: Rebellion and Subsistence in Southeast Asia* (New Haven: Yale University Press, 1976).

47. For example, see Hyden, *Beyond Ujamaa in Tanzania*.

48. United Nations Development Program (UNDP) and the World Bank, *African Development Indicators* (Washington: UNDP and the World Bank, 1992), p. 317.

49. For a sympathetic overview, see Issa G. Shivji, *Class Struggles in Tanzania* (London: Heinemann, 1976).

50. For example, see Georges Nzongola-Ntalaja, *Class Struggles and National Liberation in Africa* (Roxbury: Omenana, 1982).

51. Richard L. Sklar, "The Nature of Class Domination in Africa," *The Journal of Modern African Studies* 17, no. 4 (1979):531–52. For an update and application

of Sklar's view, see Larry Diamond, "Class Formation in the Swollen African State," *Journal of Modern African Studies* 25, no. 4 (1989):567–96.

52. *Ibid.*, p. 537.

53. For an overview, see Jeffrey Herbst, *The Politics of Reform in Ghana, 1982–1991* (Berkeley: University of California Press, 1993).

54. *Ibid.*, p. 33.

55. UNDP and World Bank, *African Development Indicators,* p. 317.

56. See *ibid.* for election results.

57. See Alain Rouvez (with the assistance of Michael Coco and Jean-Paul Paddack), *Disconsolate Empires: French, British and Belgian Military Involvement in Post-Colonial Sub-Saharan Africa* (Lanham: University Press of America, 1994), pp. 169–71.

58. Claude Ake, *Democracy and Development in Africa* (Washington: Brookings Institution, 1996).

59. See Edmond J. Keller, *Revolutionary Ethiopia: From Empire to People's Republic* (Bloomington: Indiana University Press, 1988), pp. 142, 149.

60. See Robert D. Grey, "The Petite Bourgeoisie in the Ethiopian Revolution," in Markovitz, *Studies in Power and Class in Africa,* pp. 118–30. See also John Markakis and Nega Ayele, *Class and Revolution in Ethiopia* (Lawrenceville: Red Sea, 1986).

61. For a historical overview, see Jeffrey A. Lefebvre, *Arms for the Horn: U.S. Security Policy in Ethiopia and Somalia 1953–1991* (Pittsburgh: University of Pittsburgh Press, 1991).

62. For discussion, see Nzongola-Ntalaja, *Revolution and Counter-Revolution in Africa: Essays in Contemporary Politics* (London: Zed, 1987).

63. Richard L. Sklar and C. S. Whitaker, "Nigeria: Rivers of Oil, Trails of Blood, Prospects for Unity and Democracy," *CSIS Africa Notes* no. 179 (December 1995):1.

64. For a good overview, see Paul A. Beckett and Crawford Young, eds., *Dilemmas of Democracy in Nigeria* (Rochester: University of Rochester Press, 1997).

65. One of the most noteworthy attempts at achieving a balance between ethnicity and class-based analyses is Richard A. Joseph, *Democracy and Prebendal Politics in Nigeria: The Rise and Fall of the Second Republic* (Cambridge: Cambridge University Press, 1987).

66. The ethnic interpretation primarily draws on Crawford Young, "Comparative Claims to Political Sovereignty: Biafra, Katanga, Eritrea," in Donald Rothchild and Victor A. Olorunsola, eds., *State versus Ethnic Claims: African Policy Dilemmas* (Boulder: Westview, 1983), pp. 199–232. See also Robert Melson and Howard Wolpe, eds., *Nigeria: Modernization and the Politics of Communalism* (East Lansing: University of Michigan Press, 1971).

67. See David Abernethy, *The Political Dilemma of Popular Education: An African Case* (Stanford: University of California Press, 1969).

68. Larry Diamond, "Nigeria: The Uncivic Society and the Descent into Praetorianism," in Larry Diamond et al., eds., *Politics in Developing Countries: Com-*

paring Experiences with Democracy, 2nd ed. (Boulder: Lynne Rienner, 1995), p. 425.

69. *Ibid.,* pp. 425–26.
70. Young, "Comparative Claims to Political Sovereignty," pp. 206-7.
71. *Ibid.,* p. 207.
72. The class interpretation primarily draws on Ikenna Nzimiro, *The Nigerian Civil War: A Study in Class Conflict* (Lagos: Frontline, 1982). See also Sakah Saidu Mahmud, *State, Class and Underdevelopment in Nigeria and Early Meiji Japan* (New York: St. Martin's, 1996).
73. Larry Diamond, *Class, Ethnicity and Democracy in Nigeria: The Failure of the First Republic* (Syracuse: Syracuse University Press, 1988), pp. 31–32.
74. Nzimiro, *The Nigerian Civil War,* pp. 109–12.
75. *Ibid.,* p. 112.
76. *Ibid.*
77. Diamond, "Nigeria: The Uncivic Society," p. 426.
78. *Ibid.,* p. 426.
79. *Ibid.,* p. 426.
80. Nzimiro, *The Nigerian Civil War,* p. 88.
81. *Ibid.,* p. 88.
82. See Nzimiro, *The Nigerian Civil War,* esp. pp. 109–27.
83. Young, "Nationalism, Ethnicity, and Class in Africa," p. 471.
84. Personal correspondence. For an overview of such attempts, see Young, "Nationalism, Ethnicity, and Class," pp. 470–74. For a specific formulation applied to the case of Nigeria, see Joseph, *Democracy and Prebendal Politics in Nigeria.*

8

Ideology and the Politics of Development

Mother and son withdrawing money from a cash machine in Harare, Zimbabwe.

DURING THE 1960S, the leaders of Kenya and Tanzania engaged in an acrimonious ideological debate over the proper path to development. Tanzanian President Julius Nyerere sharply criticized Kenyan capitalism as an inherently flawed "man-eat-man" system, in which only a few would prosper at the expense of society as a whole. Kenyan President Jomo Kenyatta responded by denouncing Tanzanian socialism as a "man-eat-nothing" system, in which the lack of production incentives would stall the economy and impoverish everyone. This ideological debate widened in East Africa after the Ethiopian revolution of 1974 and the emergence of a Marxist regime under the leadership of Mengistu Haile Mariam. Together these regimes exemplified the three major ideologies — capitalism, socialism, and Marxism — that have competed for influence in the development strategies of African leaders during the contemporary independence era.[1] Though capitalism was the legacy of the departing colonial powers, socialist and Marxist alternatives began appearing in the 1950s and the 1960s, and together represented nearly 30 percent of all African regimes during the 1970s. By the mid-1990s, both socialism and Marxism had fallen into disrepute and most African leaders adopted a capitalist path to development. This chapter examines the evolution and impact of ideology on the development of the African continent.

Evolution of African Ideologies of Development

Ideology refers to the principles that guide a country's political and economic policies. In Africa, ideology has particularly guided national development strategies. It can also serve as the basis for cooperation among like-minded elites, or as an important source of competition and conflict. Especially during the Cold War, ideology tended to intensify existing regional rivalries, such as that between Kenya and Tanzania, sometimes transforming them into ideological flashpoints between the United States and the former Soviet Union.

African leaders who took power at the beginning of the 1950s inherited economic systems largely based on capitalist principles of development, the most important of which is a belief in the benefits of a free-market economy (see Map 8.1).[2] In the aftermath of World War II, the European colonial powers shared a belief in the universality of a **capitalist model of development** and had implanted its basic elements in their African colonies. The willingness of the vast majority of Africa's new leaders to embrace capitalist economic policies suggested that this model would dominate African development thinking throughout the remainder of the twentieth century. After independence, former colonies approached capitalist development strategies differently. Some countries, such as Côte d'Ivoire under the leadership of Félix Houphouët-Boigny, pursued a brand of capitalism that relied heavily on close links with the former colonial power (in this case, France). Others, such as Nigeria, pursued a more nationalist brand of capitalism that sought to reduce the influence of the other major capitalist powers, most notably the United States and Great Britain.

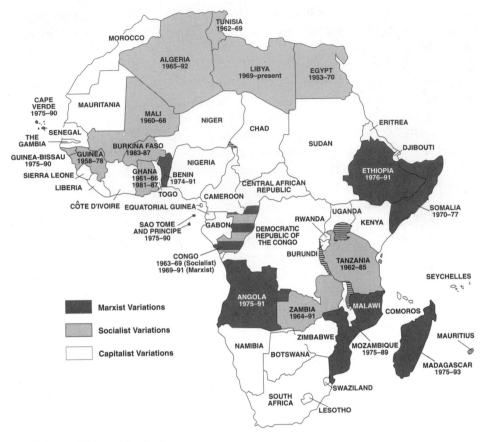

MAP 8.1   African Ideologies

A **socialist model of development** emerged in the early 1950s as the first ideological challenge to the capitalist orthodoxy of African development thinking.[3] This socialist alternative, often called **populist socialism**, is philosophically grounded in African populism and advocates state control over the national economy. Its initial adherents, Gamal Abdel Nasser of Egypt and Ahmed Sékou Touré of Guinea, displayed a strident anti-West populism that, in the case of Egypt, also included a pan-Arabist populism. In other cases, such as Algeria and Guinea-Bissau, popular support for socialist alternatives stemmed directly from extended guerrilla insurgencies against the former colonial powers. It is important to note, however, that anti-West populism is not a necessary ingredient of socialism. In Zambia, for example, President Kenneth Kaunda promoted a unique brand of "humanist" socialism, while maintaining close ties with a variety of Western powers. Indeed, some of Africa's most eloquent proponents of socialism, such as Léopold Sédar Senghor, the first president of Senegal, not only maintained extremely close ties with the West, but oversaw a national development strategy that largely drew from capitalist principles.

A second challenge to capitalist development orthodoxy, the **Marxist model of development**, emerged in the late 1960s, and was inspired by the works of Karl Marx and the communist regimes of the Soviet Union and Eastern Europe.[4] The Marxist alternative, also called **scientific socialism**, is based on the belief that revolutionary struggle will eventually lead to the development of communism throughout the world. The first African-Marxist regime emerged in Congo-Brazzaville in 1969, as a result of a military coup led by a self-proclaimed Marxist leader, Marien Ngouabi. His assumption of power, which overthrew a populist-socialist regime, underscored the Marxist disdain for capitalist and populist-socialist regimes alike and marked the beginning of a trend in which military rulers in Somalia (1970), Benin (1974), Madagascar (1975), and Ethiopia (1976) also announced the creation of Marxist regimes. A second wave of Marxist regimes emerged in Angola, Cape Verde, Sao Tome and Principe, and Mozambique in the latter half of the 1970s, after extended guerrilla insurgencies and a military coup d'état in Lisbon prompted Portuguese authorities to grant independence to their colonies in Africa. To the great concern of Western, particularly American, policymakers, Marxism was becoming increasingly popular among African leaders.[5]

A series of political and economic developments in the 1980s gradually spurred the ideological transformation of socialist and Marxist regimes. Economic decline and the emergence of pro-democracy movements throughout the African continent forced African leaders of all ideological persuasions to reassess the economic and political dimensions of their national development strategies (see Chapter 12). These reassessments were strongly influenced by the end of the Cold War and the decline of communism in the former Soviet Union and Eastern Europe. "If communism could not succeed in its birthplace," explained Bathie Mbodj, a Senegalese student, "why should we continue to debate its relevance to the African experience?"[6] More important, the International Monetary Fund (IMF) and the World Bank became increasingly influential in the restructuring of African development strategies and economies. In order to obtain access to desperately needed international financial capital, socialist and Marxist regimes were forced to implement structural adjustment programs designed to restructure African economies and political systems according to free-market principles (see Chapter 14).

The 1990s witnessed the resurgence of capitalist ideology in African development thinking. All of Africa's Marxist regimes renounced their Marxist ideologies, and Libya (under the leadership of Muammar Qaddafi) remained the only African country officially committed to a version of populist socialism, albeit one largely informed by pan-Arabism.[7] The case of South Africa is particularly illuminating. During the guerrilla struggle against the former apartheid regime, the leaders of the African National Congress (ANC) underscored the usefulness of populist-socialist, and especially Marxist, ideological models of development in the future transformation of South Africa into a nonracist society. "Marxism's call to revolutionary action was music to the ears of a freedom fighter," explains Nelson Mandela in his autobiography. "In my reading of Marxist works, I found a great deal of information that bore on the type of problems that face a practical politician."[8] Upon entering office in 1994, however, Nelson Mandela and the ruling ANC embarked on a development program strongly influenced by capitalist ideology. We will return to this point in the concluding section.

Ideology and Development Choice

Except for Crawford Young's thought-provoking book, *Ideology and Development in Africa,* published in 1982, the field of African studies lacks comprehensive, comparative analyses of the degree to which different ideologies influence the development choices of individual African regimes.[9] A careful reading of Young's book suggests that the potentially different policy implications of Africa's three major ideologies — capitalism, socialism, and Marxism — are aptly demonstrated by how their African proponents respond to five questions:

- What is the primary purpose of development?
- What is the primary engine of development?
- What is the role of agriculture in development?
- What is the role of the peasantry in development?
- What is the role of foreign powers and investment in development?

The answers to each of these questions are drawn from in-depth analyses of one representative case for each of our three broad ideological categories. The ideological choices associated with African capitalism are represented by the Kenyan regime of President Jomo Kenyatta (1963–78).[10] Kenyatta led his country to independence in 1963 and was an ardent defender of capitalist values. He was also an extremely popular leader who was respectfully referred to by Kenyans as the *mzee* (the wise old man). After his death in 1978, Kenyatta was succeeded by his vice president, Daniel arap Moi, who has maintained Kenya's adherence to the capitalist model of development.

African socialism is represented by the Tanzanian regime of President Julius Nyerere (1962–85).[11] Nyerere led his country to independence in 1962, and subsequently emerged as Africa's most ardent proponent of socialism. Affectionately referred to by Tanzanians as the *mwalimu* (teacher), Nyerere is best known for his launching of Tanzania's socialist experiment in development known as *ujamaa* (brotherhood). Nyerere voluntarily stepped down from power in 1985, and his successors have gradually dismantled the major components of Tanzania's experiment in socialism.

Finally, African Marxism is represented by the Ethiopian regime of Mengistu Haile Mariam (1976–91).[12] Mengistu initiated a Marxist "revolution from above" two years after he and several other members of the Ethiopian military took power in a military coup d'état in 1974. Mengistu never achieved a wide degree of popular support beyond his core Amhara ethnic group. As a result, his regime was plagued by popular unrest that ultimately developed into a series of regime-threatening guerrilla insurgencies. Ethiopia's experiment in Marxism ended in 1991, when the Tigrean People's Liberation Front (TPLF), one of several guerrilla armies opposed to Mengistu's rule, captured the capital city of Addis Ababa. Mengistu lives in exile in Harare, Zimbabwe. Together these three cases — Kenyan capitalism, Tanzanian socialism, and Ethiopian Marxism — offer important insights as to how ideological beliefs affect development choices.

Primary Purpose of Development

Different ideologies manifest different purposes of development. African capitalists seek evolutionary change within the confines of their existing socioeconomic systems. They share an overriding concern with ensuring the industrialization of their societies, particularly as measured by the growth rate of the gross national product (GNP). As a result, African capitalists are wary of state-promoted measures designed to ensure economic equality at the expense of economic growth. For advocates of capitalist economic strategies, the socioeconomic benefits of a rising GNP will eventually "trickle down" to all levels of society. The growth-oriented nature of African capitalists is clearly captured in the Kenyan government's blueprint for economic development, *African Socialism and Its Application to Kenya,* which, despite its misleading title, firmly placed Kenya within the capitalist sphere of development.[13] "The most important [policy] is to provide a firm basis for rapid economic growth," explains the report. "Other immediate problems such as Africanization of the economy, education, unemployment and welfare services and provincial policies must be handled in ways that do not jeopardize growth. . . . Growth then is the first concern of planning in Kenya."[14]

African socialists perceive the primary purpose of development as an attempt to gradually return to a socialist past — the indigenous communal economies that existed prior to the colonial era. They argue that African development historically was based on a "communitarian ethos" in which successes and failures were shared by the community as a whole.[15] Both then and now, development was and remains correctly targeted toward satisfying the basic human needs of every member of the overall community. It is precisely for this reason that Nyerere chose *ujamaa* — the Kiswahili term for brotherhood — as the symbolic title of Tanzania's experiment in socialism. "Both the 'rich' and the 'poor' were completely secure in [precolonial] African society," explains Nyerere in his treatise on Tanzanian socialism, *Ujamaa: Essays on Socialism,* which was originally published in 1962. "Nobody starved, either of food or of human dignity, because he lacked personal wealth; he could depend on the wealth possessed by the community of which he was a member. That was socialism. That is socialism."[16]

African Marxists seek a revolutionary break with both present and past forms of African development. They argue that the primary goal of development is the revolutionary transformation of class relationships to create a classless society. African Marxists often cite the Ethiopian revolution (1974–77) that brought the Mengistu regime into power as a unique example of revolutionary transformation of an African society. During that four-year period, an aging and unresponsive monarchy under the leadership of Emperor Haile Selassie was overthrown and replaced by the Provisional Military Administrative Council (PMAC), a group of approximately 120 progressive officers of the Ethiopian military who became known as the Dergue. Despite initial policy pronouncements that emphasized the importance of *hebrettesebawinet* (Ethiopian socialism) and *Ethiopia Tikdem* (Ethiopian unity), the Dergue in 1977 announced its firm ideological commitment to the transformation of Ethiopian society according to the Marxist principles of scientific socialism.[17] The Marxist faction under Mengistu's leadership assured its ascendancy by unleashing a wave of "revolutionary red terror" that resulted in the execution of ten thousand members of the civilian opposition in 1977 alone. To deter future anti-Marxist opposition, the regime terrorized citizens by "leaving [the] bodies of their assassinated victims in the streets with signs marking them as 'counterrevolutionaries' attached to their clothes."[18]

Primary Engine of Development

Different ideologies also lead to different policy choices as to what should constitute the primary engine of development. African capitalists share an unabiding faith in the free-market economy as the most important engine of development. An emphasis is placed on the private ownership of capital and the entrepreneurship of private businesspersons. As a result, the role of the African state theoretically should be limited to that of regulating an essentially free-market economy. Kenyan capitalism nonetheless demonstrates the highly interventionist role of the state even in African capitalist systems. Often referred to as **nurture capitalism**, this particular brand of African capitalism assumes that the state must actively promote the emergence and protection of private businesses that can successfully compete with foreign enterprises.[19] It is precisely for this reason that the Kenyan state actively promoted a rich body of national legislation, such as the Trade Licensing Act of 1967, designed to reserve significant portions of the Kenyan economy for Kenyan businesspersons. The Kenyan state also authorized the transfer of ownership of 1.5 million acres of land from white settler families (approximately 21 percent of their total holdings) to nearly 500,000 Kenyan farmers and their families.[20] The authorized transfer of land served as a powerful symbol of the role of the state under nurture capitalism. "Africans had cracked the hitherto impenetrable sanctuary of the white highlands," explains Young, "while domestic and external private sector interests were reassured by the market-centered principles that had guided the operation."[21]

African socialists are suspicious of private ownership because of its proclivity toward an unequal distribution of wealth. For socialists, the public sector is the primary engine of development. At the local level, African socialists usu-ally favor the creation of communally owned lands and enterprises under the guidance of local leaders. A cornerstone of Tanzania's *ujamaa* strategy, for example, was the resettlement of all Tanzanian peasants to new communally owned villages known as *ujamaa vijijini* (Kiswahili for "village socialism" or "rural socialism"). At the national level, African socialists favor state control over the **commanding heights of the economy**, including all major financial and commercial enterprises. In Tanzania, banking was the first industry to be nationalized under an aggressive nationalization campaign, which by the mid-1970s had assumed control over 80 percent of all large-scale economic activ-ity.[22] Tanzania's two-tiered approach to public sector involvement in the economy demonstrates that the socialist state usually serves as the coordinator of national development, setting forth the major principles of national social-ism while allowing communally owned villages a great deal of latitude in local economic affairs.

African Marxists are strongly opposed to private sector involvement in the economy. African Marxists agree with their socialist counterparts that the public sector should serve as the primary engine of development. However, African Marxists advocate highly centralized economies in which the state achieves total control over the process of development. Immediately after the Ethiopian revolution, the Marxist regime brought all aspects of the economy under state rule. In early 1975, the Derg nationalized the financial and bank-ing industries and completely abolished private ownership over land.[23] In order to enforce these efforts in the countryside, the Mengistu regime dis-patched over fifty thousand students who were to educate and guide the rural peasantry. During that same year, all urban land and housing was placed under the control of radical urban associations known as *kebeles*. These associations served as the primary tools — and battlegrounds — of the red terror of 1977–78 that ensured Mengistu's rise as the unparalleled leader of Ethiopia.

Role of Agriculture in National Development

The policy implications of different ideologies are particularly relevant to the role of agriculture in national development.[24] African capitalists traditionally have formulated national development strategies that favor urban-based industrialization at the expense of rural-based agriculture. However, they encourage private ownership of agricultural production and limited state involvement, typically in the form of agricultural extension services that dis-seminate agricultural innovations, such as new fertilizers and high-yield seeds. Kenya was exemplary among the African capitalist countries due to the Ke-nyatta regime's strong support of agricultural development. Kenyatta whole-heartedly embraced a colonial development strategy, *A Plan to Intensify the Development of African Agriculture in Kenya*, that proposed the registration and provision of private land titles.[25] The privatization of Kenyan lands was designed to strengthen agricultural production by making individual owners

BOX 8.1

IVORY TRADE AND THE POLITICS OF CONSERVATION

African policymakers, regardless of ideology, not surprisingly have looked upon their countries' natural resources, whether oil, gold, or ivory, as important tools in the quest for national development. Interestingly, whereas few would question the sale of oil or gold in the pursuit of this goal, the sale of ivory has contributed to one of the most vociferous debates in the field of African development.

The legal and illegal trade of African ivory is a time-honored tradition dating back hundreds of years. "The earliest records of ivory trade in Africa date to the Sixth Dynasty of ancient Egypt (2420–2258 B.C.E.) and later records, including royal burials, make it clear that ivory was among the most prized possessions of its rulers," explains Edward A. Alpers. "Following the collapse of the Roman Empire, India and China emerged as the main markets for ivory from northeastern and eastern Africa by the tenth century." By the end of the twentieth century, Japan had earned the distinction of being the world's most insatiable market for ivory, typically using the material to manufacture chopsticks, signature seals for letters and documents, and ornamental decorations.

On June 19, 1997, the Convention on International Trade in Endangered Species (CITES) ratified an exception to the international ban on trading ivory that had been put in place in 1989. According to the exception, Botswana, Namibia, and Zimbabwe were permitted during April 1999 to make a one-time sale to Japan of nearly sixty tons of stockpiled ivory that had been culled from overpopulated elephant herds. This decision unleashed a firestorm of international debate that pitted international conservation groups against African conservation groups, and African governments against each other, in the process illuminating the **politics of conservation** on the African continent.

Opponents of the exception argue that even the smallest opening in the worldwide ban will encourage the resurgence of illegal poaching that previously led to an alarming decline in Africa's elephant population from approximately 1.3 million in 1979 to 500,000 in 1989. They also question the ability and, in some cases, the resolve of international monitors to ensure that illegal ivory will not be mixed with legal ivory stocks, and that the emergence of parallel illegal markets will be aggressively contained. African opponents to any easing of the ban note that their conservation services will be hard-pressed to effectively stem the expected rise in illegal poaching. In the case of Kenya, for example, which depends on tourism for nearly 40 percent of its foreign exchange earnings, the Kenya Wildlife Services managed to stem the rising tide of poachers in the country's national parks only beginning in the mid-1990s. Kenyan leaders are opposed to any renewal of the ivory trade that will potentially embolden Kenyan poachers.

Proponents of lifting the ban, most notably policymakers in Botswana, Namibia, and Zimbabwe, argue that their countries should not be penalized for successfully protecting their elephant herds. Indeed, the wildlife services in each of these countries are forced to cull an annual percentage of their elephant herds in order to prevent the overpopulation of national wildlife parks. In their eyes, why should they not be allowed to reap the profits of culled ivory, especially when it is primarily destined to further enhance national wildlife programs? If the one-time exception is successfully monitored, these countries are sure to seek further exceptions to sell nearly one hundred tons of additional existing ivory stocks, as well as that to be gleaned from the further culling of national elephant stocks.

Quotations are from Edward A. Alpers, "Ivory Trade," in John Middleton, ed., *Encyclopedia of Africa South of the Sahara*, vol. 2 (New York: Charles Scribner's Sons, 1997), pp. 403-4. See also Doran Ross, ed., *Elephant: The Animal and Its Ivory in African Culture* (Los Angeles: University of California Press, 1992).

responsible for their own profits. The program was in progress in all provinces in 1965, and accounted for more than 15 percent of government expenditures on agricultural development during the first half of the 1970s.[26]

African socialists typically focus more attention on agricultural development than either their capitalist or Marxist counterparts. In Tanzania during the experiment with *ujamaa* socialism, the leadership treated the communal ownership of land as the cornerstone of agricultural development. Indeed, *ujamaa* was the most far-reaching attempt at promoting agrarian socialism on the African continent. From 1967 to 1976, more than ninety percent of Tanzania's rural population was resettled into communal villages.[27] These villages were responsible for coordinating agricultural development, in addition to providing health care and education. Although land was communally owned, farmers were provided with individual plots of land that could be passed on from generation to generation. Farmers were allowed to keep the profits generated by their cultivation of agricultural products, but were not allowed access to lands beyond that which they could till by themselves. Limiting access to land precluded farmers from hiring other peasants, which, socialists argued, provides the basis for exploitation and runs counter to the egalitarian goal of African socialism. Although initially voluntary, the villagization program ultimately became coercive, especially from 1974 to 1976, when an "astonishing" 70 percent of peasants were coerced into taking part.[28]

African Marxists agree with African socialists that the private ownership of agricultural lands and production contradicts socialist and Marxist ideals. They nonetheless espouse a more centralized approach to agriculture that goes beyond socialist communalism. Inspired by the collective farms of the Soviet Union and the peasant communes of the People's Republic of China (PRC),

African Marxists claim all agricultural lands for the state and set production standards for individual collectives.[29] Ethiopia is recognized as the African Marxist country which most closely mirrored the Soviet Union's approach to collectivization.[30] Less than one year after taking power, the Derg in 1975 issued decrees that nationalized all land and called for the creation of voluntary peasant associations. Four years later, the Derg issued another decree calling for the voluntary creation of peasant collectives and began investing heavily in the creation of large-scale, mechanized collectives patterned after the Soviet model. Unhappy with the rate of collectivization — only 7 percent of all peasants had joined peasant collectives or the larger state-controlled collectives — the Derg in 1985 issued yet another decree that essentially sought the forced collectivization of all peasants.[31]

Perception of the Rural Peasantry

Though most African regimes share an urban bias and perceive the rural peasantry as both backward and resistant to change, there are important distinctions between the three ideologies' treatment of the peasantry.[32] African capitalists are the most likely of the three ideological groups to ignore the importance of the peasant in national development. The urban, industrially biased capitalist development programs place the peasantry near the bottom of national development concerns. Even the Kenyatta regime of Kenya, known for its support of rural agriculture, focused its agricultural policies on the **progressive farmer**, not the peasantry in general. The progressive farmer typically is a wealthy, land-owning individual who hires other peasants to work the land and who is perceived by the government as more open to innovative ideas and therefore more capable of expanding national agricultural production. It is precisely due to the progressive farmers' perceived openness to innovation that they are primarily targeted for help with extensive agricultural extension services.

African socialists are the most likely of the three ideological groups to focus on the role of the peasantry in development and to even "exalt" that group as "the carrier of the moral values of society."[33] Nyerere's speeches and writings glorify the peasant as the cornerstone of *ujamaa* socialism. However, the rhetorical glorification of the peasantry did not deter senior Tanzanian policymakers from implementing the forced villagization of unwilling Tanzanian peasants. Even as representatives of socialist values, the peasants were manipulated by the architects of socialist policy. Whereas the progressive farmer was exalted under African capitalist systems, he was derisively referred to as a *kulak* by Tanzania and its socialist counterparts throughout Africa. A Russian term popular during the Soviet era, kulak refers to peasants who opposed collectivization in the Soviet Union. As was the case in the Soviet Union, the Tanzanian kulak represented the portion of the peasantry that needed to be crushed in order to advance the egalitarian goals of Tanzanian socialism.

African Marxists perceive the entire peasantry, but particularly the kulak, as an inherently conservative portion of society, likely to oppose the radical changes associated with the movement toward scientific socialism. As a result, the African Marxists at best view the peasantry with suspicion, and at worst perceive them as a potential threat to the consolidation of communist rule. In Ethiopia, the vast majority of the peasantry, particularly in southern Ethiopia, strongly welcomed the Derg's nationalization decree of 1975. This support was not primarily due to the peasantry's support for Marxism-Leninism, but to the fact that the decree essentially removed hated rural landlords who had systematically exploited the rural population for centuries.[34] However, when the Derg issued decrees in 1979 and 1985 that sought the collectivization of the new peasant holdings, the peasantry fought back to maintain their new-found independence.

Role of Foreign Powers and Investment

A final point of comparison is the impact of ideology on African foreign relations, especially concerning a regime's openness to foreign investment.[35] African capitalists traditionally have maintained their closest relations with the world's major capitalist countries. Whereas African capitalists heavily courted the former colonial powers, particularly France, and the United States during the Cold War, Japan and Germany have become increasingly prominent in African capitalist foreign relations since the end of the Cold War (see Chapter 14). In the case of Kenya, for example, the Kenyatta regime maintained close financial ties with Great Britain (the former colonial power), while successfully diversifying its economic links with other major capitalist powers, most notably the United States. The inherently open nature of capitalist free-market economies ensures that African capitalists are also the least likely of the three ideological types to impose significant restrictions on foreign investment. However, when national leaders do implement investment restrictions, they do so in order to protect or ensure the entry of national capitalists into a specific industry or area of economic competition. In the case of Kenya, for example, national investment policies ensured the entry of Kenyan businessmen, particularly those closely allied with the Kenyatta regime, into the tea and coffee plantation industries. During the colonial era, these highly lucrative industries were exclusively reserved for white plantation owners.

African socialists publicly profess their aversion to free-market enterprise and therefore highly regulate or prohibit multinational corporations (MNCs). As a result, African socialist countries provide a relatively inhospitable economic environment to foreign investment. Tanzania under Nyerere was particularly restrictive of foreign investment in order to boost "self-reliance," one of the guiding principles of *ujamaa* socialism. Nyerere argued that "true" development, free from external domination and exploitation, could only be achieved if Tanzanians relied upon their own labor and national resources. Interestingly enough, Nyerere's aversion to foreign investment did not preclude the acceptance of foreign aid, especially when it was provided in the form of grants. In 1977, an astonishing 59 percent of Tanzania's development budget was underwritten by foreign assistance, making that country the largest African foreign aid recipient on a per capita basis.[36] A significant portion of these funds was provided by countries that shared Nyerere's socialist ideals, such as Sweden and other Scandinavian countries, as well as the People's Republic of China (PRC), which provided one of the models for Tanzania's agrarian socialism. Tanzania also received lucrative foreign aid packages from the United States and Japan, effectively demonstrating that adherence to socialism did not preclude fruitful economic relationships with the international proponents of other ideologies.

African Marxists have often sought close ties with the former Soviet Union and other members of the Eastern Bloc.[37] However, some Marxist countries established important relationships with noncommunist states. Especially in the case of francophone West Africa, self-proclaimed African Marxists usually maintained their privileged economic, political, and even military relationships with France. Despite a shared aversion to capitalism, African Marxists are more open to foreign investment than their socialist counterparts. However, the Marxist policy to seize the commanding heights of the economy, which invariably involves the nationalization of foreign-owned industries, creates an environment of distrust that makes meaningful levels of foreign investment highly unlikely. In the aftermath of the Ethiopian revolution, for example, the Derg nationalized twenty U.S.–owned industries, the largest of which was the Ethiopian subsidiary of the Michigan-based Kalamazoo Spice Extraction Company (valued at roughly $11 million). This action not only made U.S. investors wary of future investments, but triggered congressionally mandated financial sanctions that prohibited any further U.S. foreign aid (except for disaster relief) to the Mengistu regime.

The preceding discussion of Kenyan capitalism, Tanzanian socialism, and Ethiopian Marxism illustrates how an African regime's commitment to a specific ideology significantly influences development choices (see Table 8.1 for a summary overview). African leaders can choose from a wide array of policy alternatives, but historically choices concerning development are largely determined by regime ideology. In short, different ideologies lead to different development choices.

Ideology and Development Performance

Ideology's impact on development choice raises the much-debated issue of ideology's impact on **development performance**. Does the selection of different ideological pathways lead to varied development performance, or have all African ideologies performed equally well during the contemporary independence era? This question has led to much debate largely because development is defined differently by different people. Whereas an economist might focus on the economic dimensions of development and a political scientist might focus on its political dimensions, a sociologist might reject both views and

TABLE 8.1

Policy Implications of African Ideologies

	African Capitalists	African Socialists	African Marxists
Primary Purpose of Development	promote economic growth; evolutionary change	promote basic human needs; return to African past	promote classless society; revolutionary change
Primary Engine of Development	individual entrepreneurs in free-market economy; state as regulator	public sector, especially communal villages; state as coordinator	state in highly centralized economy; state has total control
Role of Agriculture	private ownership of land; state-provided extension services	communal ownership of land; communal villages manage agricultural production	state ownership of land; ideally creation of large-scale, state-managed mechanized collectives
Perception of Rural Peasantry	ignored in favor of urban, industrial bias; preference for "progressive farmers"	exalted as carrier of moral values; cornerstone of development efforts; opposition to *kulaks*	suspiciously viewed as inherently conservative and opposed to change; opposition to *kulaks*
Role of Foreign Powers and Investment	close ties with the major capitalist powers, especially the United States; very favorable toward MNCs and foreign investment	close ties with the Nordic countries and the PRC; adverse to MNCs and foreign investment; strategy of self-reliance	close ties with the major communist countries, especially the former Soviet Union; open to MNCs and foreign investment

instead focus on the social aspects of development. Any realistic assessment of ideology's impact on development performance ultimately depends on how one actually *defines* the concept of development.

Young argues in *Ideology and Development in Africa* that one can evaluate Africa's experience with capitalism, socialism, and Marxism according to five different dimensions of development performance: economic growth; socioeconomic equality; autonomy from foreign control; human dignity; and political participation.[38] It is important to note that a wide variety of statistics could be employed to characterize each dimension of development performance. The following analysis focuses on the one or two most widely used or representative indicators for each performance dimension. In so doing, the analysis seeks to highlight general trends. Each ideological pathway is once again represented by the three model cases: Kenyan capitalism under the Kenyatta regime (1963–78); Tanzanian socialism under the Nyerere regime (1962–85); and Ethiopian Marxism under the Mengistu regime (1976–91).

Economic Growth

Economic growth, typically measured in terms of the per capita growth rate in a country's GNP, serves as an important starting point for understanding the varied development histories of the African continent's three ideological pathways.[39] This statistic offers a crude, yet widely recognized, indicator of the overall health of an African country's economy. "Certainly no African leader would dismiss it," explains Young. "Indeed, without growth none of the other goals [of development] can be achieved."[40] Statistics compiled by the World Bank suggest that the African capitalist countries have usually outperformed their socialist and Marxist counterparts in terms of GNP per capita.[41] The Kenyatta regime oversaw a capitalist economy that witnessed a 3.4 percent annual increase in GNP per capita from 1963 to 1978. In contrast, socialist Tanzania averaged a negative growth rate of 5.5 percent during the Nyerere administration, and Marxist Ethiopia averaged a negative growth rate of 2.75 percent during the Mengistu administration. If each of these countries truly represents the model of their respective ideologies, African capitalism clearly emerges as the most capable of promoting economic growth.

Socioeconomic Equality

The promotion of socioeconomic equality, most notably meeting the **basic human needs** (BHN) of a given population, is a second dimension of development performance.[42] BHN encompasses a wide variety of specific socioeconomic indicators of development, such as life expectancy, access to health care, and literacy rates. The African socialist countries have typically outperformed their capitalist and Marxist counterparts in this dimension of development performance due to a strong commitment to social equality. The socialist *ujamaa* policies of the Nyerere regime ensured that 53 percent of Tanzania's population, including 46 percent in the rural areas, were guaranteed access to safe water by the mid-1980s.[43] Tanzania achieved its goal, whereas only 28 percent (21 percent in the rural areas) had access to clean water in capitalist Kenya and a meager 18 percent (11 percent in the rural areas) in Marxist Ethiopia during the same period.[44] Tanzania's *ujamaa* policies were equally effective in the realm of health care, with nearly 85 percent of children under one year of age being immunized against tuberculosis, diphtheria, polio, and measles by the beginning of the 1980s.[45] Kenya approached this total with a 72 percent average, followed distantly by Ethiopia with only 14 percent.[46] In short, Tanzania managed to fulfill the socialist commitment to providing for basic human needs.

Autonomy from Foreign Control

A third measure of development performance, autonomy from foreign control, is the African leadership's ability to pursue a path of development that is not heavily dependent on external involvement and resources, most notably foreign aid.[47] This dimension of development performance is based on the assumption that countries heavily dependent on external sources of financing are more likely to pursue development programs that serve foreign interests, as opposed to the true development needs of their own peoples. For example, Nyerere's brand of *ujamaa* socialism was heavily dependent on foreign aid despite the call for self-reliance. During the second half of the 1970s, foreign aid accounted for 10.5 percent of Tanzania's Gross Domestic Product (GDP), compared with only 4.5 percent for both capitalist Kenya and Marxist Ethiopia.[48] The legacy of socialist Tanzania's dependence on foreign economic resources is particularly striking when examined in terms of its debt-GDP ratio (the country's foreign indebtedness as a percentage of GDP). By the end of the

---

BOX 8.2

POLITICAL RISK AND INVESTMENT

The rising importance of trade and investment in international relations has prompted the emergence of a wide variety of consulting firms that specialize in providing **risk assessments** for companies doing business in all regions of the world. Entrepreneurs interested in expanding their companies, or simply starting new ones in the various emerging markets of the twenty-first century, need guidance in terms of the economic and political risks that they will face, and are willing to pay handsomely for such information. As a result, private companies providing economic and political risk data have become somewhat of a growth industry in the northern industrialized democracies.

Credit Risk International, a London-based firm, is unique among these firms in that it offers comprehensive risk analyses for every country on the

African continent (see Map 8.2). Information provided by Credit Risk allows the potential investor to assess countries according to four general levels of investment risk: (1) low risk: high degree of political stability, very favorable to foreign investors; (2) weak risk: solid political and economic institutions, occasional political or economic instability; (3) medium risk: weak political and economic institutions, political and economic stability in the short term, latent threat of military intervention or other illegal actions by the government in power; (4) high risk: very vulnerable economic and political institutions, strong possibility of a military coup d'état or intervention by an international peace-keeping force; in the extreme, government is hardly functioning and the economy is in ruin.

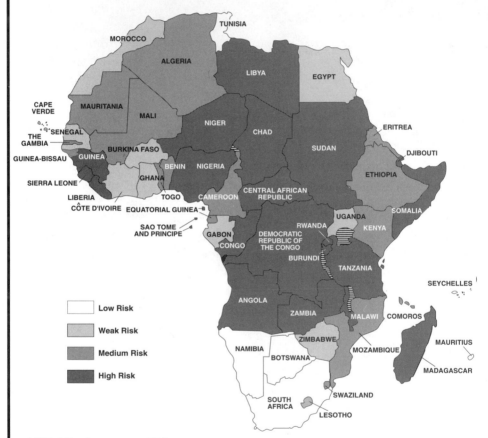

MAP 8.2   Investment Risk

Discussion drawn from Credit Risk International (London), and Jocelyne Muhutu, "Évaluer le risque politique," *L'Autre Afrique*, no. 10 (July 23–29, 1997):16–17. For a summary of the methods used by eleven leading commercial suppliers of political risk analyses, see William D. Coplin and Michael K. O'Leary, eds., *Political Risk Services: The Handbook of Country and Political Risk Analysis* (East Syracuse: Political Risk Analysis, 1994).

1980s, Tanzania's average debt-GDP ratio was a staggering 85 percent, followed by 34 percent for capitalist Kenya and 25 percent for Marxist Ethiopia.[49] If we assume that foreign aid and indebtedness are valid indicators of dependency, African socialism clearly emerges as the least capable of promoting autonomy from foreign control, with Kenyan capitalism and Ethiopian Marxism faring about the same.

A focus on the military dimension of the dependency equation suggests that Kenyan capitalism is more autonomous than Ethiopian Marxism. Similar to the experience of other Marxist countries in Africa, the Mengistu regime was heavily dependent on communist-bloc military aid to stem domestic dissent and the spread of regime-threatening guerrilla insurgencies. From 1977 to its demise in 1991, the Mengistu regime reportedly received more than $5 billion in communist-bloc military aid.[50] Indeed, Soviet and Cuban military aid was decisive in preventing the fragmentation of Ethiopia during the 1977–78 Ogaden war between Ethiopia and Somalia. With northern secessionists on the verge of military victory and Somali military forces in control of the eastern provinces, the Soviet Union began a massive airlift of fifteen thousand Cuban troops from bases in Cuba, Angola, and Congo-Brazzaville. Accompanied by Soviet tactical commanders and nearly $2 billion in Soviet military weaponry, the Cuban troops spearheaded a series of Ethiopian counteroffensives in spring 1978 that forced Somali troops to flee across the border and ensured a military stalemate in the north. Marxist Ethiopia was so dependent on communist-bloc military aid that the Mengistu regime was overthrown not long after the end of the Cold War and the Soviet Union's disengagement from the Horn of Africa.[51]

Human Dignity

The promotion of human dignity, often conceived in terms of the protection of civil liberties and human rights, is the fourth dimension of development performance.[52] In 1972, Freedom House, a conservative think tank located in Washington, D.C., began annually rating the protection of civil liberties in individual countries. The checklist of questions, which subsequently forms the basis of the civil liberties assessment, includes the following:

- Are there free and independent media, literature, and other cultural expressions?
- Is there open public discussion and free private discussion?
- Is there freedom of assembly and demonstration?
- Is there freedom of political or quasi-political organization?
- Are citizens equal under the law, with access to an independent, nondiscriminatory judiciary, and are they respected by the security forces?
- Is there protection from political terror, and from unjustified imprisonment, exile or torture, whether by groups that support or oppose the system, and freedom from war or insurgency situations?

- Are there free trade unions and peasant organizations or equivalents, and is there effective collective bargaining?
- Are there free professional and other private organizations?
- Are there free businesses or cooperatives?
- Are there personal social freedoms, which include such aspects as gender equality, property rights, freedom of movement, choice of residence, and choice of marriage and size of family?
- Is there equality of opportunity, which includes freedom from exploitation by or dependency on landlords, employers, union leaders, bureaucrats, or any other type of denigrating obstacle to a share of legitimate economic gains?
- Is there freedom from extreme government indifference and corruption?[53]

The Freedom House ratings suggest that African countries across the ideological spectrum fared poorly in the protection of civil liberties during the initial decades of the contemporary independence era. In many African countries, ruling regimes put constraints on the freedom of speech of individuals, organizations, and the independent media. Capitalist countries nonetheless fared better on average than their socialist or communist counterparts. On a scale of 1 to 7 ("1" being the best score and "7" being the worst), the Kenyatta regime consistently received a score of "5," whereas Marxist Ethiopia under the Mengistu regime consistently received the worst possible score of "7." Socialist Tanzania under Nyerere found itself consistently between these two extremes with an average score of "6."[54] Whereas Ethiopia's poor score was primarily due to state-sponsored political terror against its own population, Tanzania's low score was primarily due to the lack of freedom of organization for independent trade unions, peasant organizations, and private businesses.

Political Participation

The quality of political participation is the final measure of development performance.[55] Freedom House also annually rates the protection of political rights in individual countries. The checklist of questions, which subsequently forms the basis of the political rights assessment, includes the following:

- Is the head of state and/or head of government or other chief authority elected through free and fair elections?
- Are the legislative representatives elected through free and fair elections?
- Are there fair electoral laws, equal campaigning activities, fair polling, and honest tabulation of ballots?
- Are the voters able to endow their freely elected representatives with real power?
- Do the people have the right to organize in different political parties or other competitive political groupings of their choice, and is the system open to the rise and fall of these competing parties and groupings?

- Is there a significant opposition vote, de facto opposition power, and a realistic possibility for the opposition to increase its support or gain power through elections?
- Are the people free from domination from the military, foreign powers, totalitarian parties, religious hierarchies, economic oligarchies, or any other powerful group?
- Do cultural, ethnic, religious, and other minority groups have reasonable self-determination, self-government, autonomy, or participation through informal consensus in the decision-making process?[56]

The Freedom House survey shows that African countries across the ideological spectrum fared poorly in the promotion of political participation during the initial decades of the contemporary independence era. During this time, many African leaders established single-party regimes that prohibited true political competition (see Chapter 12). In each of our three model cases of African ideology, for example, opposition parties were intimidated or completely banned, in favor of a single state-sponsored party: Kenya African National Union (KANU) in Kenya; Chama Cha Mapinduzi (CCM) in Tanzania; and the Workers Party of Ethiopia (WPE). Capitalist countries nonetheless fared better on average than their socialist or communist counterparts. On a scale of 1 to 7, the Kenyatta regime consistently received a score of "4" or "5," whereas Marxist Ethiopia under the Mengistu regime consistently received a "7." Socialist Tanzania under Nyerere once again found itself consistently between these two extremes with an average score of "6."[57] Whereas Kenya scored the best, due to the Kenyatta regime's willingness to permit a limited degree of opposition party activity, Tanzania's single-party system was recognized for its ability to allow for genuine electoral competition within the party ranks. Ethiopia's highly centralized single-party system scored the worst, due to its unwillingness to allow for any internal political dissent.

The preceding discussion of Kenyan capitalism, Tanzanian socialism, and Ethiopian Marxism clearly suggests that an African regime's commitment to a specific ideological pathway leads to varied development performance (see Table 8.2 for a summary overview). African capitalism outperformed its socialist and Marxist counterparts in four out of five categories, with socialism performing best in one and Marxism performing best in none. Perhaps for this reason neither socialist nor Marxist regimes, except for the unique case of Libya, exist at the beginning of the twenty-first century.

These results are nonetheless tentative and must be treated with a great deal of caution. The results could change with the selection of different statistical indicators, the inclusion of new dimensions of development performance, or an examination of different model case studies of capitalism, socialism, and Marxism. Indeed, the field of African studies is still awaiting a comprehensive statistical comparison of the development performance of competing ideologies during the contemporary independence era.

TABLE 8.2

Comparative Development Performance
of African Ideologies (× = best performer)

	African Capitalists	African Socialists	African Marxists
Economic Growth	×		
Socioeconomic Equality		×	
Autonomy from Foreign Control	×		
Human Dignity (human rights)	×		
Political Participation	×		

Toward a Capitalist Hybrid?

The one undeniable result of ideological competition between capitalism, socialism, and Marxism during the contemporary independence era is that capitalism emerged in the 1990s as the ideology of African development. African leaders and foreign observers alike agree that some form of private enterprise is the key to the future development success of the African continent.[58] Richard Sklar, a noted observer of African ideology, refers to this phenomenon as a **capitalist movement**, the turning point of which was marked by the attendance of African ministers and civil servants at the Conference on the Enabling Environment for Private Sector Contributions to Development, held in Nairobi, Kenya, in October 1986.[59] According to Sklar, this conference signaled the "confluence of various currents of African capitalist thought," setting the stage for its widespread resurgence in the post–Cold War era.[60]

The emergence of capitalism as the predominant African ideology is partially due to the widespread perception among African policymakers and foreign observers that socialism and Marxism lack convincing incentives for individual producers to expand production.[61] In both Nyerere's Tanzania and Mengistu's Ethiopia, for example, coercion was ultimately used to force recalcitrant peasants to take part in villagization or collectivization programs. "In this century," concludes Sklar, "revolutionary socialists from [Leon] Trotsky and [Josef] Stalin to Mao Zedong, [Fidel] Castro, and Sékou Touré have tried to compensate for the weakness of socialist incentives for both workers and managers by resorting to combinations of moral suasion and coercion — poor substitutes for personal motivation."[62]

It is important to note that Africa's growing embrace of capitalist ideology does not mean that African policymakers are blind to its negative outcomes nor necessarily willing to forsake all elements of African socialism or Marxism.[63] African policymakers recognize that African capitalism has failed to deliver in the one area that African socialism has registered at least some short-term success: the promotion of social equality and justice. The dilemma, of course, is how best to balance the perceived trade-offs between growth and equality. Whereas the capitalist regimes typically have fostered economic growth at the expense of equality, their socialist counterparts have pursued equality at the expense of economic growth. A focus on one at the expense of another is a recipe for disaster. In Tanzania, for example, the lack of economic growth ultimately wiped out any short-term gains of *ujamaa* socialism in the realm of equality. In Kenya, unbalanced support of economic growth strengthened socioeconomic inequalities that have contributed to growing societal strains in contemporary Kenya.[64]

South Africa's experiment in development, since the election of President Nelson Mandela in 1994, is indicative of a new hybrid form of African capitalism that may prove capable of simultaneously promoting both growth and equality. "Any South African leader is bound to be preoccupied with the economy, which must generate enough employment to ease chronic black impoverishment," explains Michael Bratton, a specialist of democratic transition. "As the government's own targets reflect, economic growth must reach 6 percent per year to keep up with population growth and at the same time lift the poor."[65] However, the ANC gained power under the leadership of President Mandela with the mandate of aggressively redistributing the wealth of the South African economy, in order to make up for the injustices of the apartheid era. Indeed, the administration's two major sources of support beyond the ANC — the Confederation of South African Trade Unions (COSATU) and the South African Communist Party (SACP) — were particularly vocal in terms of the need for quick redistributional justice.

The hybrid solution of the Mandela administration was the formulation of a development strategy known as Growth, Employment, and Redistribution (GEAR), that simultaneously pursues the economic objectives of promoting economic growth, reducing unemployment, and ensuring the redistribution of national resources. Economic growth is the most important development objective, without which the other two objectives would be impossible. GEAR is nonetheless unique in that its third objective — the socialist-inspired goal of redistribution — is expected to be aggressively pursued by Mandela's successor, Thabo Mbeki, who was elected president in 1999. If successful, South Africa's hybrid form of capitalism could serve as a model of development for the rest of the African continent.[66]

Key Terms

ideology

capitalist model of development

socialist model of development

populist socialism

Marxist model of development

scientific socialism

nurture capitalism

commanding heights of the economy

politics of conservation

progressive farmer

development performance

basic human needs

risk assessments

capitalist movement

For Further Reading

Babu, Abdul Rahman Mohamed. *African Socialism or Socialist Africa?* Harare: Zimbabwe Publishing House, 1981.

Berman, Bruce J., and Colin T. Leys, eds. *African Capitalists in African Development*. Boulder: Lynne Rienner, 1993.

Cohen, Robin, and Harry Goulbourne, eds. *Democracy and Socialism in Africa*. Boulder: Westview, 1991.

Coplin, William D., and Michael K. O'Leary, eds. *Political Risk Services: The Handbook of Country and Political Risk Analysis*. East Syracuse: Political Risk Analysis, 1994.

Friedland, William H., and Carl G. Rosberg, eds. *African Socialism*. Stanford: Stanford University Press, 1964.

Gordon, April A. *Transforming Capitalism and Patriarchy: Gender and Development in Africa*. Boulder: Lynne Rienner, 1996.

Hughes, Arnold, ed. *Marxism's Retreat from Africa*. London: Cass, 1992.

Keller, Edmond J., and Donald Rothchild, eds. *Afromarxist Regimes: Ideology and Public Policy*. Boulder: Lynne Rienner, 1987.

Kennedy, Paul. *African Capitalism: The Struggle for Ascendancy*. Cambridge: Cambridge University Press, 1988.

Lubeck, Paul M., ed. *The African Bourgeoisie: Capitalist Development in Nigeria, Kenya, and the Ivory Coast*. Boulder: Lynne Rienner, 1987.

Ottaway, Marina, and David Ottaway. *Afrocommunism* (2nd ed.). New York: Africana, 1986.

Rosberg, Carl G., and Thomas M. Callaghy, eds. *Socialism in Sub-Saharan Africa: A New Assessment*. Berkeley: University of California Institute of International Studies, 1979.

Sender, John, and Sheila Smith. *The Development of Capitalism in Africa*. London: Methuen, 1986.

Young, Crawford. *Ideology and Development in Africa*. New Haven: Yale University Press, 1982.

World Bank, *African Development Indicators*. Washington: World Bank, published annually.

Notes

1. Michael Chege, "Swapping Development Strategies: Kenya and Tanzania after Their Founding Presidents," in David E. Apter and Carl G. Rosberg, eds., *Political Development and the New Realism in Sub-Saharan Africa* (Charlottesville: University Press of Virginia, 1994), p.248.
2. For an introduction, see John Sender and Sheila Smith, *The Development of Capitalism in Africa* (Methuen: London, 1986). See also Paul Kennedy, *African Capitalism: The Struggle for Ascendancy* (Cambridge: Cambridge University Press, 1988).

3. For an introduction, see William H. Friedland and Carl G. Rosberg, eds., *African Socialism* (Stanford: Stanford University Press, 1964). See also Abdul Rahman Mohamed Babu, *African Socialism or Socialist Africa?* (Harare: Zimbabwe Publishing House, 1981).

4. For an introduction, see Marina Ottaway and David Ottaway, eds., *Afrocommunism*, 2nd ed. (New York: Africana, 1986).

5. For an overview, see Peter J. Schraeder, *United States Foreign Policy toward Africa: Incrementalism, Crisis and Change* (Cambridge: Cambridge University Press, 1994).

6. Personal correspondence, Dakar, Senegal, May 1996.

7. For an overview, see Edmond J. Keller, "Whither Afromarxist Regimes? A Comparative Preliminary Analysis," *Journal of Third World Studies* 9, no. 2 (1992):285–312. See also Arnold Hughes, ed., *Marxism's Retreat from Africa* (London: Frank Cass, 1992).

8. Nelson Mandela, *Long Walk to Freedom: The Autobiography of Nelson Mandela* (Boston: Little, Brown, 1994), pp. 120–21.

9. Crawford Young, *Ideology and Development in Africa* (New Haven: Yale University Press, 1982). Other studies typically have focused on one ideology. For example, see Edmond J. Keller and Donald Rothchild, eds., *Afro-Marxist Regimes: Ideology and Public Policy* (Boulder: Lynne Rienner, 1987); Carl G. Rosberg and Thomas M. Callaghy, eds., *Socialism in Sub-Saharan Africa: A New Assessment* (Berkeley: Institute of International Studies, 1979); and Bruce J. Berman and Colin T. Leys, eds., *African Capitalists in African Development* (Boulder: Lynne Rienner, 1993).

10. For a general introduction, see Norman N. Miller, *Kenya: The Quest for Prosperity* (Boulder: Westview, 1993).

11. For a general introduction, see Rodger Yeager, *Tanzania: An African Experiment* (Boulder: Westview, 1991).

12. For a general introduction, see Mulatu Wubneh, *Ethiopia: Transition and Development in the Horn of Africa* (Boulder: Westview, 1987).

13. Republic of Kenya, *African Socialism and Its Application to Planning in Kenya* (Nairobi: Government Printer, 1965), as cited in Chege, "Swapping Development Strategies," p. 248.

14. *Ibid.*

15. Young, *Ideology and Development*, p. 98.

16. Julius Nyerere, *Ujamaa: Essays in Socialism* (London: Oxford University Press, 1966), pp. 3–4, as quoted in Young, *Ideology and Development*, p. 98.

17. Ottaway, *Afrocommunism*, p. 130.

18. *Ibid.*, pp. 152–54.

19. For an overview, see John Iliffe, *The Emergence of African Capitalism* (London: Macmillan, 1983). See also Young, *Ideology and Development*, p. 189.

20. Young, *Ideology and Development*, p. 209.

21. *Ibid.*, p. 210.

22. *Ibid.*, p. 106.
23. *Ibid.*, pp. 74–75.
24. For a general introduction, see Robert H. Bates, *Markets and States in Tropical Africa: The Political Basis of Agricultural Policies* (Berkeley: University of California Press, 1981).
25. R. J. M. Swynnerton, *A Plan to Intensify the Development of African Agriculture in Kenya* (Nairobi: Government Printer, 1955), as discussed in Colin Leys, *Underdevelopment in Kenya: The Political Economy of Neo-Colonialism 1964–1971* (Berkeley: University of California Press, 1975), pp. 52–53, 69.
26. Leys, *Underdevelopment in Kenya*, p. 69.
27. Young, *Ideology and Development*, p. 114.
28. Jackson and Rosberg, *Personal Rule in Black Africa*, p. 225.
29. Marina and David Ottaway, *Afrocommunism*, pp. 138–46.
30. *Ibid.*
31. See Marina Ottaway, *Africa's New Leaders: Democracy or State Consolidation?* (Washington: Carnegie Endowment for International Peace, 1999), p. 53.
32. See Peter J. Schraeder, "Involuntary Migration in Somalia: The Politics of Resettlement," *The Journal of Modern African Studies* 24, no. 4 (1986):641–62.
33. Young, *Ideology and Development*, pp. 102–3.
34. Ottaway, *Afrocommunism*, p. 139.
35. For an overview, see Young, *Ideology and Development*, pp. 253–97.
36. Jackson and Rosberg, *Personal Rule*, p. 229.
37. For an early analysis, see David E. Albright, ed., *Africa and International Communism* (Bloomington: Indiana University Press, 1980).
38. Young, *Ideology and Development*, ch. 6. Young also adopts a sixth measure, "expansion of societal capacity," which essentially refers to the "ability of the state to respond to new challenges and demands and to adapt to changing needs" (p. 19). I discuss the role of the state in Chapter 10.
39. Young, *Ideology and Development*, pp. 15–16, 298–301.
40. *Ibid.*, p. 298.
41. Data are from *World*Data 1995: World Bank Indicators on CD-ROM.*
42. Young, *Ideology and Development*, pp. 16, 302–308.
43. World Bank, *African Development Indicators 1996* (Washington: World Bank, 1996), p. 339.
44. *Ibid.*
45. *Ibid.*, p. 336.
46. *Ibid.*, p. 336.
47. Young, *Ideology and Development*, pp. 16–17, 308–313.
48. United Nations Development Program and World Bank, *African Development Indicators* (Washington: World Bank, 1992), p. 298.
49. *Ibid.*, p. 163.
50. See Robert G. Patman, *The Soviet Union in the Horn of Africa: The Diplomacy of Intervention and Disengagement* (Cambridge: Cambridge University Press, 1990).

51. *Ibid.*
52. Young, *Ideology and Development,* pp. 17–18, 313–19.
53. Freedom House, *Freedom in the World: The Annual Survey of Political Rights and Civil Liberties, 1996–1997* (New Brunswick: Transaction, 1997), pp. 573–74.
54. *Ibid.,* various years.
55. Young, *Ideology and Development,* pp. 18–19, 319–20.
56. Freedom House, *Freedom in the World, 1996–1997,* p. 573.
57. *Ibid.,* various years.
58. For an early view, see Bruce R. Bartlett, "Capitalism in Africa: A Survey," *The Journal of Developing Areas* 24 (1990):327–50. See also the review essay of E. Wayne Nafziger, "African Capitalism, State Power, and Economic Development," *The Journal of Modern African Studies* 28, no. 1 (1990):141–50.
59. Richard L. Sklar, "Beyond Capitalism and Socialism in Africa," *The Journal of Modern African Studies,* 26, no. 1 (1988):12.
60. *Ibid.*
61. See Richard L. Sklar, "The Future of Socialism in Africa: The Failure of Economic Statism," *Dissent* (1992):399–407.
62. *Ibid.,* p. 15.
63. See Robin Cohen and Harry Goulbourne, eds., *Democracy and Socialism in Africa* (Boulder: Westview, 1991).
64. For a comparison of Kenyan and Tanzanian development efforts in the post-Kenyatta and post-Nyerere era, see Chege, "Swapping Development Strategies."
65. Michael Bratton, "After Mandela's Miracle in South Africa," *Current History* 97, no. 619 (May 1998):215.
66. Indeed, as aptly noted by Sklar, the "baton of leadership" concerning alternative development strategies has passed from Tanzania to South Africa. See Sklar, "The Future of Socialism in Africa," p. 401.

9

Politics of the African Novel

Wole Soyinka — Nigerian novelist, Nobel laureate in literature, and outspoken opponent of military rule in Nigeria — walking with Professors Cornell West (center) and Henry Louis Gates, Jr. (right) at Harvard University prior to giving a lecture in 1997.

SOCIAL SCIENTISTS HAVE typically sought to understand African politics and society by focusing on the structure and development of African political institutions, such as national legislatures and political parties, or the historical evolution of political events on the African continent, such as the dramatic rise in military coups d'état during the 1960s. These classic building blocks of knowledge can be enriched by an examination of the political and historical content of African arts and literature, including filmmaking, oral and written poetry, novels and short stories, and theater.[1] One form of African literature — the African novel — is increasingly recognized by social scientists as a unique means of gaining insight into the evolution of African politics and society.[2] In essence constituting a Western form of literature that African writers gradually adopted during the colonial era, the African novel has flourished throughout the contemporary independence era. The African novel is particularly suited to the teaching goals of social scientists interested in African politics, due to the highly politicized nature of this genre of African writing. In addition to raising a variety of politically inspired themes, ranging from critiques of colonialism to the trials and tribulations of the contemporary independence era, African writers in the extreme have used their novels as platforms to call for the overthrow of authoritarian regimes in their respective countries. The primary purpose of this chapter is to provide an introduction to these politically inspired novelists, most notably in terms of the evolving political content of their novels.[3]

Political Dilemmas Faced by the African Novelist

A much-debated dilemma facing African novelists is the **politics of language choice**. Should they write in the indigenous languages of the African continent, such as Kiswahili in Eastern and Central Africa, Hausa in northern Nigeria, and the Arabic dialects found primarily in North Africa, or should they employ the imported languages of the colonial era, most notably French, English, and Portuguese? One of the most famous African proponents of writing in indigenous languages is the Kenyan writer, Ngugi wa Thiong'o, whose widely acclaimed book, *Decolonising the Mind: The Politics of Language in African Literature,* has fostered a lively debate in African academic circles.[4]

Ngugi's basic argument is that, since the majority of the populations in most African countries do not speak the inherited European languages, the African novelist adopting this medium speaks only to a very small national elite and foreign audiences, which in turn reinforces an intellectual dependency on the former colonial powers. According to Ngugi, true independence means writing in African languages. As underscored by the image contained in the title of another of his works, *Barrel of a Pen: Resistance to Repression in Neo-Colonial Kenya,*[5] African writers must be political activists, meaning that their words must be employed to transform African politics and society in accordance with socialist principles. In order to match words with deeds, Ngugi made a conscious decision in 1977 to stop writing novels in English in favor of the indigenous languages of Kenya, resulting in the publication in 1980 of his first novel in the Kikuyu language, *Caitaani Mutharaba-ini,* which subsequently was translated into English for publication in 1980 as *Devil on the Cross.*

The proponents of writing in the inherited colonial languages advance equally compelling arguments. As explained by the famed Nigerian novelist, Chinua Achebe, if the goal of the writer is to reach the widest audience possible, writing in an ethnic language accessible to only a small group simply will not do.[6] Even in countries with a national indigenous language (such as Kiswahili in Kenya), illiteracy, especially in the countryside, prevents active readership by a significant portion of the population. The most important argument for writing in the European languages, however, is the potential for linguistically unifying numerous ethnic groups, leading to the national integration of the country.[7] In short, a literature in a national language, even if it did not originate on the African continent, provides a basis for creating a national identity in countries such as Nigeria, where three major ethnic groups (Igbo, Yoruba, and Hausa/Fulani) and over 250 minor ethnic groups speak dozens of languages (see Chapter 7).

A second dilemma facing the African writer is **official censorship** by African governments that often denounce their critics within the literary world as instigators of "antigovernment propaganda."[8] Topics often considered taboo within government circles include the ethnic makeup of the ruling regime, the moral character of the president, the nature of political rule (especially "attacks" on military regimes and civilian-based single-party systems), or the ideology and foreign relations of the country. Although official censorship is on the decline in countries making a transition to more democratic forms of governance (see Chapter 12), in more cases than not, African writers still do not share the same liberty of expression enjoyed by their Western counterparts. Under these constraints, African writers are forced to make a conscious decision as to whether to make politics an issue of their novels. This choice can result not only in the banning of a book, but the jailing of the author. As a result, dozens of African authors have been forced to flee their countries, as they continue to write from exile.[9]

Books by the noted Cameroonian novelist, Alexandre Biyidi, who has written under the pseudonyms of Eza Boto and Mongo Beti, have been banned for political reasons.[10] Born in Cameroon and educated in France, Biyidi wrote four novels severely criticizing French colonial rule that were banned in Cameroon prior to independence in 1960.[11] A Marxist, Biyidi also found himself at odds with the French colonial authorities due to his support for the *Union des Populations du Cameroun* (UPC, Union of the Populations of Cameroon), a political-turned-military nationalist organization that was banned by the French. Rather than being embraced by the Cameroonian leadership that assumed power in the aftermath of French colonial rule, Biyidi's novels were instead banned as the works of a radical who threatened stability.

In his novels, Biyidi had criticized Cameroon's first independence regime, led by President Ahmadou Ahidjo, as a "neocolonial" puppet of the French government. He also supported the UPC, which was seeking to gain power by promoting guerrilla warfare in the countryside.[12]

Finally, African writers must choose which **publishing outlet** to use for their works, a choice that affects both content and style.[13] Since most African publishing companies are owned by governments historically unfavorable to political critiques, a decision to publish in the writer's home country usually means that works must be apolitical in nature, or, if political, must reflect the political orientation of the current regime. It is precisely for this reason that numerous African authors have sought foreign publication of their works, most notably with the London-based African Writers Series of Heinemann Press.

It is important to recognize, however, that publication by foreign publishing houses is not cost-free in terms of intellectual freedom of expression. Such a decision not only virtually guarantees that the work must be written in the language of the foreign press, it also favors a publishing process often more sensitive to foreign, as opposed to African, editorial concerns. For example, Western presses during the Cold War era often refused to consider "radical" works, leading several African writers within the critical tradition to pursue publication of their novels with Eastern bloc publishing houses, such as Seven Seas Press in the former Eastern Germany.

Even when a foreign press decides to publish a book, political concerns may still intrude upon the process. The French government was successful in banning the sale upon publication of one of Biyidi's books, *Main Basse sur le Cameroun: Autopsie d'une Décolonisation* (1972; *Heavy Hand on Cameroon: Autopsy of Decolonization*), despite the fact that he maintained a French passport and the book was published by a French publishing house. The primary reason for the ban, which lasted five years, was a desire on the part of the French government to stifle a stinging critique of political repression under President Ahidjo and Cameroon's "neocolonial" relationship with France.

Political Themes of the African Novel

The African novel has undergone several thematic revolutions during the contemporary independence era. Though these thematic changes are presented in chronological fashion, it is important to remember that all themes are employed by contemporary African novelists.

Re-creation of Africa's Past

The earliest African novelists sought to re-create Africa's political heritage of the precolonial independence era, to emphasize that Africa had a noble past prior to the arrival of the colonial powers. Writing in the Sesotho language in 1908, Thomas Mofolo's *Chaka* provided a historical romance set against the rule of the renowned Zulu leader, Shaka. Although publication was initially delayed by Mofolo's missionary patrons, due to what they perceived as anti-Christian, "pagan" elements within the text, the novel was eventually published in 1925.[14]

Colonial Intrusion

During the 1950s, African novelists continued to glorify the African past and added a new twist: the intrusion of colonial cultures on traditional African cultures. The classic work of this type is Chinua Achebe, *Things Fall Apart* (1958), which seeks to re-create the dignity and integrity of Igbo culture in what constitutes present-day Nigeria.[15] The protagonist is Okonkwo, a great wrestler of the village of Umuofia, who achieves a level of success unparalleled by his contemporaries, but who falls from grace and is exiled from the village due to acts of sacrilege committed against his "chi" (personal god) and the "earth goddess" of the land. When Okonkwo seeks to follow traditional customs and return to the village in a triumphant manner, he is virtually ignored by a culture that is in the process of "falling apart," and he ultimately commits suicide. British colonialism during the nineteenth century had an extremely negative impact on Igbo culture, causing turmoil in the village and fragmentation of Igbo culture. According to Achebe, the combination of British administration, trading practices, and, most important, missionary influence severely undermined traditional Igbo values to such a degree that the harmony of the past was lost forever.

BOX 9.1

POLITICS OF AFRICAN CINEMA

Unlike their counterparts in other regions of the world, African filmmakers are perceived by foreign film critics as especially "militant" in terms of the films they produce. One reason for this reputation is the very powerful political messages that African filmmakers transmit to audiences, such as the destructive impact of colonialism on African political systems, the emergence of corrupt "neocolonial" elites more interested in acquiring wealth than promoting broadly shared development, the horrors of racially based authoritarian rule under the apartheid regime of South Africa, and the destruction of traditional values and ways of living due to urbanization, modernization, and the importation of Western values. In this regard, many African filmmakers firmly believe that their art should serve a political function, in the sense of promoting the "African struggle" for dignity and equality within the international system. As precisely noted by Gaston Kaboré, a Burkinabé filmmaker and former secretary general of the Fédération Panafricaine des Cinéastes (FEPACI, Pan-African Film-Makers Federation), the primary goal of African films is to "develop African cinema as an art, industry, and mass media that can aid the African people in their full social, cultural, and political liberation."

It would be wrong to assume, however, that all African filmmakers are interested in solely politically based films. As evident at the 1999 Festival Panafricain du Cinéma de Ouagadougou (FESPACO, Pan-African Film Festival of Ouagadougou), held every two years in the capital of Burkina Faso, the African filmmaking industry is rapidly growing and diversifying, in terms of both numbers of films produced and themes portrayed. Whereas the first FESPACO held in 1969 offered a small selection of films from five African countries, the 1999 event enjoyed an extremely vigorous competition among over two hundred films from sixty countries worldwide.

Despite the emergence of an extremely vibrant African cinema, critics cite two major problems within the industry. First, cash-starved African filmmakers often find themselves heavily dependent on financing from their own governments, private interests in the former colonial powers, and international development agencies. The different priorities of such sources can often lead to constraints placed on the political themes of a particular film. Second, African filmmakers find it difficult to reach African audiences because the majority of Africans live in rural areas where few movie theaters exist, and urban theater chains are dominated by U.S. and Indian films that specialize in what Patrick Ilboudo, another Burkinabé film critic, has labeled "cultural toxic waste" — karate flicks, grade-C Hollywood war pictures, and cop stories.

Quotations are from Marco Werman, "African Cinema: A Market in the U.S.?", *Africa Report* 34, no. 3 (1989):69; and David Turcamo, "Culture: A Celebration of Cinema," *Africa Report* 38, no. 3 (1993):69. See also Manthia Diawara, *African Cinema* (Bloomington: Indiana University Press, 1992); F. Pfaff, *Twenty-Five African Filmmakers* (Westport: Greenwood, 1988); and N. F. Ukadike, *Black African Cinema* (Berkeley: University of California Press, 1993).

Colonial Injustice

A third genre of the African novel that also emerged in the 1950s focused on the cruelty and injustice of colonial rule, especially the inherent contradiction between European rhetorical promotion of democracy in Africa and the authoritarian reality of colonial regimes. One of the most noted writers in this genre is the Cameroonian author, Ferdinand Oyono, whose French-language works have been translated into English. In one of his most well-known books, *Une Vie de Boy* (appearing in English in 1956 as *Boy!*), Oyono severely criticizes the French policy of assimilation, by which Africans could theoretically achieve total acceptance as French citizens. The main character of the book is Toundi, a Cameroonian boy who runs away from home to work as a houseboy, first for a local French missionary, and then later for the local French commandant. A variety of actions taken by local French administrators, such as the savage beating, whipping, and chaining of two Africans simply because they are accused of stealing (a charge never proven and, indeed, false), slowly make Toundi question and ultimately flee the inhumanity of the culture he previously sought to emulate.

Nationalism and Independence

The 1950s also witnessed the emergence of novels that portrayed African nationalist leaders as saviors fighting to bring an end to colonial rule and leading their nations to independence. One of the most celebrated writers of this theme is Peter Abrahams, a South African writer who lived in London just prior to the initial wave of African independence, and had the opportunity to interact with several future African leaders, including Kwame Nkrumah of Ghana. In *A Wreath for Udomo* (1956), for example, Abrahams describes the life of a fervent nationalist (Udomo) who returns home from London to lead a fictitious African country (Panafrica) to independence. Abrahams paints an idyllic view of the commitment and integrity of the African nationalist leaders of the 1950s and the 1960s; his story is based on the independence experience of Ghana and the nationalist fervor of its first leader, Kwame Nkrumah.

Disenchantment with Elites

After the initial honeymoon period enjoyed by African leaders in the first decades of independence, a variety of negative trends — socioeconomic decline, the rise of single-party rule, the increase in military rule, and the general authoritarianism inherent in numerous African states — led African novelists of the 1960s to begin articulating themes of disenchantment with national elites and disillusionment with previously held ideas of progress.[16] The Malawian writer, David Rubadiri, in his novel, *No Bride Price* (1967), portrays African elites as unscrupulous, immoral, and corrupt individuals whose primary concern is maintaining themselves in power at any cost. The despicable nature of African elites is underscored by Rubadiri's portrayal of government ministers who force lower-grade civil servants to set them up with Indian and European prostitutes, and who fire those workers who refuse or fail to deliver. Ironically, Rubadiri implies that only the military is capable of restoring order and ending corruption. In the novel, the people rejoice when the military overthrows the inept government that has wielded power since independence. This image of the military changed as it soon became clear that military coups d'état often led to new forms of military-led authoritarianism as bad as, if not worse than, its civilian counterparts.

Freedom as Despair

Disillusionment with African leaders became so prevalent during the 1960s that several novelists, such as the Ghanaian author, Ayi Kwei Armah, in *The Beautyful Ones Are Not Yet Born* (1962), emphasized a theme of despair in which the amelioration of dismal living conditions in Africa was portrayed as a near impossibility. "So wicked, so dirty and so corrupt is humanity that there is no point in the individual's trying to change it," as one reviewer explains Armah's main theme. "The individual has got to learn to live in the midst of the filth and must try to secure his own private salvation."[17] Indeed, the "senses of the reader are assaulted to the point of being numbed" by such images as a child's nose overflowing with mucus while a mother sucks it, women disfigured by creases of prematurely dried skin, littered streets overflowing with trash, and lavatory walls streaked with excrement. The title confirms that "the beautyful ones are not yet born," and those that are living are "corrupt, greedy, selfish, and dishonest."[18]

Politically Committed African Novelists

The 1970s and the 1980s witnessed the coalescence of a group of **politically committed novelists** who, perceiving highly unjust forms of governance in their respective countries, called for the overthrow of those governments. Unlike the previous period of despair, these authors believe in the ability of people to change their history and unite in a struggle toward a particular social ideal. Many, if not all, of these authors have written novels that have been banned in their country of birth, and have been jailed and/or forced to write from exile. Whereas African governments have attempted to explain away such acts of official censorship by claiming that novelists have wrongfully and maliciously misrepresented the intentions and contributions of their regimes, their opponents, most notably the novelists themselves, claim more effectively that such novels have been banned because they represent the authoritarian and degenerative nature of domestic politics all too well. In addition to incorporating several of the themes already noted, the politically committed African novelist often focuses on at least one of three topics often neglected by other writers.

Neglected Popular Elements of Society

Many committed novelists exalt the values and ideals of neglected popular elements of society — the rural peasantry, urban workers, and popular guerrilla movements — all of which are perceived as being oppressed by authoritarian elites more interested in acquiring personal power and wealth rather than promoting the well-being of the majority of the population. One of the most notable writers in this regard is Ngugi wa Thiong'o, who, in addition to publishing several novels, created a rural-based theater company that sought to actively involve the Kenyan peasantry in theater productions focusing on sensitive social and political topics. In 1977, the publication of *Petals of Blood*, a novel highly critical of the Kenyan ruling elite, as well as the production in Kikuyu of an equally critical play, *Ngaahika Ndeenda* ("I Will Marry When I Want"), led to his imprisonment for nearly one year, after which he left the country and continued to write from exile.[19]

Destructive Nature of Societal Divisions

A second topic explored by committed African novelists is the destructive nature of racial, ethnic, and class divisions within African societies, and how these are manipulated by the "divide-and-rule" policies of authoritarian African regimes. One of the most celebrated writers on this theme is Alex La Guma, a South African novelist who portrayed the racist apartheid system of South Africa as one that promoted frustration, aggression, and violence. As demonstrated in one of his most noted novels, *In the Fog of the Season's End* (1972), La Guma celebrated the activities of organizations such as the African National Congress (ANC), which prior to 1992 sought to overthrow the apartheid system by force of arms. The novel also denounces the police-state mentality that led to the imprisonment, torture, and, finally, death of numerous antiapartheid activists, including Steven Biko, the founder and leader of the Black Consciousness Movement. Arrested and imprisoned at various times in his life, most notably as a defendant in the famous Treason Trial of 1956, La Guma left South Africa in 1966 and continued to write his novels — all of which were banned by the South African regime — in exile in Britain and Cuba until his death in 1985.

Status of Women in African Society

A final important theme of many committed African novelists is the status of women in African societies. These authors argue that African women are underprivileged and unequal members of African societies, who need to be more fully included within their respective political systems. One of the most famous African proponents of greater equality for African women is Sembène Ousmane, the famous Senegalese novelist and filmmaker who died in 1998. In one of his most acclaimed novels, *Xala* (1973), which he turned into a film (1974) by the same name, Ousmane severely criticizes the custom of polygamy by weaving a tale of a rich African businessman who is struck by *xala* (the Wolof term for sexual impotence) upon the taking of a third wife. His most famous novel, however, *Les Bouts de Bois de Dieu* (1960; appearing in English as *God's Bits of Wood*), describes the events surrounding the historic 1947–48 workers' strike against the colonial railroad system that currently links Dakar, Senegal, and Bamako, Mali. Describing this book as Ousmane's "novelistic masterpiece," one reviewer perceptively notes that it is "an eloquent account of the strength, courage and foresight of women — not educated or aristocratic, but ordinary, illiterate womenfolk of modest origin and rank in society, including a prostitute and a common blind woman beggar" who became involved in the railroad strike.[20]

The importance of gender among politically committed novelists is reflective of the growing voice of female African novelists during the contemporary independence era. Flora Nwapa, a Nigerian novelist, served as a pathbreaker in this regard. The publication of her first novel, *Efuru* (1966), signaled the formal emergence and critical acceptance of an entire generation of world-renowned female African novelists, including Buchi Emecheta of Nigeria, Ama Ata Aidoo of Ghana, Aminta Sow Fall of Senegal, and Bessie Head of South Africa.[21]

Although their writings reflect many of the same socioeconomic and political themes raised by their male African counterparts, female African novelists are particularly vocal about the simple reality that male-dominated (and authoritarian) African regimes have paid insufficient attention to a variety of gender-related challenges of the contemporary independence era. Female African novelists raise many issues, including the much lower literacy rates and higher mortality rates for African women compared to African men; the rise of prostitution and rape as African societies become increasingly urbanized; the significant underrepresentation of African women in wage labor; the injustices involved in polygamous marriages; and culturally inspired constraints, which range from the veiling of women in Muslim societies to the physical mutilation of women associated with the practices of circumcision and infibulation (see Box 7.2 in Chapter 7).

One of the most celebrated female African novelists is Mariama Bâ, a Senegalese author who wrote *Une si Longue Lettre* (1979; published in English in 1981 as *So Long a Letter*). This novel is written in the form of a letter from Ramatoulaye, a widowed Senegalese woman living in Dakar, to her childhood friend, Aîssatou, who has emigrated to the United States. Ramatoulaye's letter represents an exercise in self-awareness as she explains her feelings of sorrow and betrayal over her late husband's decision to take a second wife after nearly twenty years of marriage, as permitted by Islamic law. Unlike her friend, Aîssatou, who divorced her husband when he did the same thing, Ramatoulaye remained with her husband, only to be left neglected, penniless, and responsible for the care of twelve children after his death. This tragic and moving tale became a best-seller in Senegal, due to its insightful exploration of the nature and impacts of polygamy. "Ramatoulaye's life story resonated with many women, which explains the novel's extraordinary reception in Senegal and the fact that it is now a classic of African letters," explains one reviewer of the novel. "But the great appeal of the text resides not in its reflection of the life drama lived by so many but in the vitality of Ramatoulaye, a woman among many who became a heroine and a role model in spite of herself."[22]

Nuruddin Farah and the Politics of Commitment in Somalia

An in-depth analysis of the evolving political themes of Somali novelist Nuruddin Farah — one of the most provocative writers within the tradition of the politically committed African novelist — offers important insights into the invaluable role of African novels in any understanding of African politics and society. Somali politics, particularly the dictatorial practices of the Siad Barre regime, which seized power in a military coup d'état in 1969 and ruled until its overthrow in 1991, are at the center of a series of novels that Farah has written since the late 1960s.[23] Fluent in several languages, Farah decided to write his novels in English rather than in his native language of Somali. Although a desire to reach the broadest international audience contributed to this decision, the Siad regime left him with little choice when it banned the publication and distribution of any of his works, thereby denying him access to the most significant potential market of literature written in Somali.[24] Most important, Farah's firm commitment to writing about social and political injustice in Somalia, coupled with government threats that his writings were subversive and could lead to imprisonment, led him to begin writing from voluntary exile beginning in 1974.[25] The political content of Farah's novels can be analyzed according to four phases, in which an early commitment to exploring social issues is gradually replaced by acute political engagement with perceived injustice in Somalia.[26]

Early Years as Critic of Social Injustice

Farah's first novel, *From a Crooked Rib* (1970), focuses on the unequal status of women in Somali society,[27] and was written in 1968 while he was a student of literature and philosophy at the Punjab University of Chandigarh, India. During this period, Somalia enjoyed a functioning multiparty political system, in which national elections in 1967 led to a peaceful change in government, from the administration of President Aden Abdulla Osman (who served since independence in 1960) to that of President Abdirashid Ali Shermarke. Both regimes were generally pro-Western in orientation, and sought to maintain strong links with Britain and Italy (the former colonial powers), as well as with the United States.[28]

The main character of the novel is Ebla, a rural woman from the Somali-inhabited Ogaden region of Ethiopia, who desires emancipation from her subservient status in Somali society. Ebla first runs away from her family to the city of Belet Wene because she refuses to accept her arranged marriage with Giumaleh, "an old man of forty-eight fit to be her father." Once established at the house of her cousin Gheddi, however, Ebla learns that, to pay off some debts, he had secretly offered her hand in marriage to a "broker" friend. Ebla thus flees a second time by eloping to Mogadishu, the capital of Somalia, with a civil servant named Awill, only to become infuriated when she learns that he is cheating on her. Ebla gains revenge by secretly marrying Tiffo, a wealthy man of the city with whom she trades sexual favors for money. Ebla has learned to manipulate men through a brand of prostitution in which she realizes that her body is "my treasure, my only treasure, my bank, my money, my existence." Eventually Ebla discards Tiffo and confronts Awill upon his return. Rather than bringing each other's infidelity into the open, however, the pair leave resolution of this issue for "tomorrow."

Farah continually emphasizes the unequal status of women in Somali society: "From experience [Ebla] knew that girls were materials, just like objects, of items on the shelf of a shop. They were sold and bought as shepherds sold their goats at market-places, or shopowners sold their goods to customers. To a shop-keeper what was the difference between a girl and his goods? Nothing, absolutely nothing." Farah is particularly opposed to the circumcision and infibulation of young Somali girls, a traditional ritual that he describes as "barbaric"[29] and that often leads to severe health problems ranging from urinary tract diseases to complications during childbirth (see Box 7.2 in Chapter 7).

Qualified Optimism after the 1969 Military Coup d'Etat

Farah's second novel, *A Naked Needle* (1976), was written in Mogadishu in 1972, three years into the preliminary successes, failures, and effects of the 1969 military coup d'état that ushered in Siad's dictatorship.[30] Announcing the creation of a "revolutionary," single-party socialist state under the stewardship of the Somali Revolutionary Council, Siad rationalized his seizure of power as necessary to overcome the corrupt excesses of the civilian era — a perception generally shared by the Somali people who initially rallied around the military government. Siad was especially vocal about the necessity of creating a national political identity capable of transcending clan divisions within Somali society, and initially expected the educated class of Somalia to aid him in this quest.[31] Although Farah was initially sympathetic to the general goals of the revolution, his decision to criticize political corruption and clan-based patronage practices at the highest levels of government placed him in conflict with the Siad regime.

The main character of the novel is Koschin, a university professor and fervent revolutionary committed to the advancement of socialism and the welfare of the masses. Espousing an idealist faith in the goals and aims of the 1969 Somali revolution, Koschin is appalled by the "tribalist" and immoral tendencies of his immediate superior at the university, ultimately choosing to resign from his position rather than compromise his revolutionary ideals. In addition, Koschin is nervously awaiting the arrival of Nancy, a woman he had met in London and had agreed to marry if within two years neither had found someone else. Koschin wonders how Nancy, a white non-Muslim who has never been to his country, will fit into Somali society. The rekindling of their relationship is set against those of Koschin's Somali friends and acquaintances who have married foreign white women.

The marital relationships of Somali men with foreign women symbolize Somalia's international relationships with foreign powers.[32] Mirroring the regime's increasingly strained relationship with the United States, due to Siad's socialist rhetoric and growing ties with the former Soviet Union, Barre's relationship with his American wife is fraught with problems and viewed with disdain by Koschin. Warsan's Soviet wife irritates Koschin with her overbearing manner, indicative of Somali perceptions of Soviet racism and paternalism toward African countries, even those of a socialist orientation. Representing Somalia's love-hate relationship with the former colonial powers, the relatively successful relationship of Mohamed and his British wife nonetheless disgusts Koschin due to their reactionary statements concerning the revolution. Koschin thinks only British-born Barbara, perhaps of the lower class and of socialist sympathies (her former fiancé and her father were both revolutionaries), understands the true principles of the Somali revolution.

Several other aspects of the initial years of the Siad regime are probed in Farah's second novel, through the character of Koschin. For example, Koschin is disturbed by the "tribalistic" practices of his superior and the revelation that the top echelons of the government, despite socialist rhetoric to the contrary, are hesitant "to take any steps to bring this ill-practice and what it entails to an end." "I do not owe any loyalty to any tribe," emphatically proclaims Koschin, "I owe loyalty to the nation, the government in power." In fact, a dialogue between Koschin and his friend Mohamed is perhaps indicative of Farah's attempt to understand the necessity of the 1969 military coup d'état. Koschin states that "Somalia very badly needed a revolution," and Mohamed replies: "Was Somalia in need of terror and horror from dawn to dusk?" Koschin responds by noting that revolution "is a pill that tastes bitter, the benefits of which are felt only when one has gone through the preliminary pain and pestilence." The reader has the impression that although there are questionable aspects of the revolution, a "wait-and-see" attitude was appropriate in order to judge whether it would remain true to its goals. Indeed, Farah shows initial approval as Koschin proclaims, "Why Somali is a written language! Bless the Revolution!" indicating that Siad's successful introduction in 1972 of a written script for the Somali language was an important and constructive outcome of the 1969 revolution (see Box 9.2).

Opposition to the Dictatorship of Siad Barre

The qualified optimism of the second novel is firmly rejected in a subsequent trilogy of works that Farah entitled "Variations on the Theme of an African Dictatorship."[33] This trilogy represents the most politically committed phase of Farah's literary career, as he comes out adamantly opposed to the Siad regime (referred to as the "General") and begins writing his novels from exile in England and Italy. The growing authoritarianism of the Siad regime, as well as its gradual movement away from the socialist ideals of the early years of the revolution, served as the pivotal factors in this stage of Farah's writing.[34] During the mid to late 1970s, for example, a variety of state-sponsored instruments of repression, such as the National Security Service, the National Security Court, the Somali Revolutionary Council, and the *Gulwadhayal* (Victory Pioneers), were increasingly being utilized to silence anyone deemed "antisocialist," "antirevolutionary," or "anti-Siad" by the military regime.[35]

This authoritarian trend intensified in the aftermath of Somalia's defeat in the 1977–78 Ogaden War with Ethiopia, an event which led to the influx of thousands of refugees, the devastation of the economy, and a rupturing of ties with the former Soviet Union (which supported Ethiopia) in favor of the renewal of ties with the United States.[36]

The first part of the trilogy, *Sweet and Sour Milk* (1979), virulently attacks the authoritarian practices of the Siad regime, its links with the former Soviet Union, and self-serving Somali elites who compromised their principles to acquire positions with the government. The novel begins with the mysterious death of Soyaan, an economic adviser answerable only to the General, and a leading member of a clandestine opposition movement composed of Somali intellectuals and professionals. Soyaan's twin brother, Loyaan, is gradually drawn into a personal investigation of the mysterious circumstances surrounding his brother's death, eventually learning his brother was "silenced" by the regime because he secretly wrote and distributed antigovernment pamphlets. In order to discredit the movement and keep Soyaan's true actions from reaching the general populace, the government proclaims him a "hero of the revolution" whose last words were, "Labour is honour and there is no General but our General." Loyaan's efforts to keep the government from making a mockery of his deceased brother's true political beliefs eventually bring him into direct opposition with the regime. The novel ends with Loyaan facing either exile overseas or imprisonment if he refuses to leave.

The novel further portrays how a burgeoning opposition within the educated upper classes of Somalia leads to the preparation and distribution of clandestine material that violates national security statutes imposed by the ruling elite. Farah's opinion of the ruling elite is summarized in a secret memo penned by Soyaan: "Clowns. Cowards. And (tribal) upstarts: these are who I work with. The top civil service in this country is composed of them. Men and women whose pride has been broken by the General's security; men and women who have succumbed and accepted to be humiliated." Special ridicule is directed toward Siad. In Soyaan's words: "Listen to these ludicrous eulogies of the General. The father of the nation. The carrier of wisdom. The provider of comforts. A demi-god. I see him as a Grand Warden of a Gulag." Even more disturbing to Farah is the degree of control and influence that the Soviets maintained with the Siad regime. This is portrayed in the novel by Loyaan's anger when told that an accomplice of Soyaan was arrested for anti-Soviet activities. Loyaan proclaims: "But we are not in the Soviet Union. We are in the Somali Democratic Republic, a sovereign African state. Not in the Soviet Union. We are *not*."

Sardines (1981), the second part of Farah's antigovernment trilogy and fourth novel, breaks new ground by exploring the role of women in opposing the Siad regime. The story revolves around Medina, an avowed feminist and sole female member of the antigovernment clandestine movement composed of members of Somalia's educated upper class. Medina has been banned from

BOX 9.2
ALPHABET POLITICS

On October 21, 1972, the military dictatorship of Siad Barre ushered in a linguistic milestone in Somali history by announcing that it had chosen a slightly modified version of the Latin script as the official alphabet for the Somali language. Prior to this date, the lack of an official script contributed to a less than ideal linguistic mosaic in which the Somali language — spoken by the vast majority of Somalia's population — served as the primary means for oral communication, but all written forms of communication, such as newspapers, government documents, and literature, depended on the uneven usage of three nonindigenous languages: English, Italian, and to a lesser degree, Arabic. The most curious aspect of this event was not that it took place, but that its arrival took as long as it did in a society that has a deep respect and love for its language and bestows great honors on those who can skillfully use its rich poetic heritage in oral discourse.

Political infighting among powerful adherents to three different types of proposed scripts served as the primary stumbling block to the creation and dissemination of a nationally accepted form of written Somali. Powerful *wadaads* (men of religion) forcefully argued for the adoption of the Arabic script for the Somali language, due to Somalia's status as an Islamic country (over 99 percent of the population is Muslim) situated at the crossroads of the Middle East, as well as the fact that almost all Somali children learn the Arabic script in order to study the *Qur'an* (the Muslim holy book). These arguments were countered by Somali nationalists who sought to establish their uniqueness as a people free from any external control, including the Arabs, whom Somalis have traditionally mistrusted. According to this group, adoption of the Arabic script would weaken the Somali identity and make it more susceptible to Arab influence.

The Latin script constituted the second alternative for a written Somali language, and proponents included the former colonial powers and Somali administrators trained in either English or Italian. These groups argued that adoption of the Latin script not only would place Somalia securely within the camp of the "modern" world, but would facilitate the utilization of existing technologies (such as typewriters and printing presses) in the dissemination of written materials. Such arguments were dismissed by Somali nationalists who associated the Latin script with Somalia's subjugation by the former colonial powers. As explained by one Somali intellectual, Ibraahiim Xaashi, "Somalia came in contact with the Latin script as a result of colonialism. We were compelled to learn it. Now that we are free, we must get rid of all colonial roots — and Latin would just remind us of the dark deeds of the colonialists." The *wadaads* reinforced these arguments by portraying the Latin script as a tool of foreign "infidels" (nonbelievers) seeking to replace Islam with Christianity, and developed a religious slogan that become commonplace during the debates: *Laatiin waa Laa Diin* ("Latin is without God").

A third and final major competitor within Somali alphabet politics — the Cismaaniya script — was invented by a Somali scholar, Cismaan Yuusuf Keenadiid. From a nationalist point of view, the script was attractive in that it did not rely upon the "foreign" scripts of either Arabic or Latin, and represented a Somali creation underscoring the uniqueness of the Somali people and language. However, in addition to being opposed by the *wadaads* and Somali administrators, Cismaaniya was criticized as an attempt by its creator's clan grouping (the Majertein) to achieve an unwarranted level of political influence within an independent Somalia. Critics also noted that adoption of Cismaaniya would impose undesired educational costs by requiring Somalis to learn at least three separate scripts: Cismaaniya (for Somali); Arabic (for religious training); and Latin (for contact with the Western world). In short, competing political interests — each of which was strong enough to block the adoption of another script but not strong enough to impose its will — postponed the adoption of written language in Somalia until the seizure of power by the Siad regime.

Quotations are from David D. Laitin, *Politics, Language, and Thought: The Somali Experience* (Chicago: University of Chicago Press, 1977). See also B. W. Andrzejewski, "Language Reform in Somalia and the Modernization of the Somali Vocabulary," *Northeast African Studies* 1, no. 3 (1979–80):59–71.

publishing and fears that Ubax, her daughter, will be forced to undergo the traditional circumcision and infibulation performed on the vast majority of young women in Somalia. Medina also guides the intellectual development of her friend's daughter, Sagal, a nationally recognized swimming star who potentially will be taking part in a sporting event sponsored by the communist bloc in Budapest, Hungary. Furthermore, Medina's husband, Samatar, has been blackmailed by the regime into accepting a cabinet position — from which he ultimately resigns — and is eventually jailed.

This fourth novel is unique in that the opposition is comprised of women and female students, representative of Farah's concern for Somali women. Medina, for example, typifies the educated, cosmopolitan woman who seeks a better life for her daughter. Medina is extremely concerned about the intellectual freedom of Ubax and is disgusted with the traditional customs that harm women. Farah seems to speak through his protagonist when, in an impassioned speech, Medina asserts: "I want to spare my daughter these and many other pains. She will not be circumcised. Over my dead body."

Individuals comprising a second group of opposition within the novel are female students, indicative of Farah's impression of growing student unrest in Somalia. Sagal, who has always dreamed of "painting the dawn" with antigovernment slogans, is extremely jealous when her two closest competitors are arrested for committing this act. The girls had painted the slogan: "Down with the one-man, one-tribe dictatorship! Down with the General's regime." However, despite the rise of opposition groups within Somali society, Farah warns through Samatar that most of the educated class is corrupt and self-serving: "We the intellectuals are the betrayers; we the so-called intellectuals are the entrance the foreign powers use so as to dominate, designate, name and label; we the intellectuals are the ones who tell our people lies."

Close Sesame (1984) is the final and most politically engaged novel of Farah's antigovernment trilogy, in which he seemingly calls for Siad's assassination and seeks to rationalize such a call. The plot of the novel revolves around Deeriye, a principled Somali nationalist and pan-Africanist who had been a Sayyidist all his life — a reference to Sayyid Mohamed Abdulle Hassan, the most revered nationalist in Somali history who fought against British colonialism.[37] Unfortunately, Deeriye had paid for his beliefs by spending eight years in colonial prisons and four in postindependence jails. A respected man within Somali society in the 1980s, Deeriye is confronted with a personal dilemma when he learns that his son Mursal, with three other accomplices, is plotting the General's assassination. Originally stating that he would never make use "of violent means to overthrow a tyrannical regime," Derriye changes political opinions when the General seeks to isolate him from his clan and discredit his public image. Upon learning that his son presumably has been killed by the regime, Deeriye is finally driven to attempt to assassinate the General, "not to avenge his son but to vindicate justice." Deeriye dies in his unsuccessful attempt.

This novel is especially powerful because the call for the overthrow of the Siad regime comes not only from the upper-class intellectuals but also from Deeriye, an extremely nationalist Somali and former hero of the revolution who is revered by his peers. Drawing parallels with the colonial past, the plot suggests that the Siad regime's attempt to isolate and intimidate Deeriye replicates the Italian colonialists' imprisonment of Deeriye in 1934. Just as the Italian authorities had wanted Deeriye to hand over a suspected assassin and disassociate himself from the individual's actions, so Siad is portrayed as attempting the same thing. "The only difference, *if there is a difference*," explains Farah, "is that in 1934 the enemy and the famine-creating power was colonial and foreign; and now it is neo-colonial and local."

Evolving African Identity

The completion of Farah's trilogy of novels on the authoritarian abuses of the Siad regime marked a turning point in his career as a politically committed novelist. Although still set in Somalia, Farah's subsequent novels represent an effort to move beyond the specific abuses of the Siad regime and to return to the dilemmas confronted by all African countries, most notably the **evolving**

African identity. Farah wrote the most provocative example of this new trend, *Maps* (1986), while living in Lagos, Nigeria.

Maps takes place within the historical context of the 1977–78 Ogaden War between Ethiopia and Somalia. The primary character of the story is Askar, an orphaned Somali boy who was born in the Ogaden region of Ethiopia and is adopted by Misra, an Amharic-speaking Oromo woman from the highlands of Ethiopia. Askar and Misra are separated when the young boy is sent to Mogadishu to live with his Uncle Hilaal and Aunt Salaado, and are only reunited after Misra arrives as a refugee from the fighting in the Ogaden. The relationship between Askar and Misra at first is extremely strained, due to accusations that Misra — a non-Somali — had betrayed the positions of the Western Somali Liberation Front (WSLF), an act which in turn contributed to the massacre of over six hundred Somali fighters at the hands of Ethiopian forces. The story ends with Askar being interrogated concerning his involvement in the death of Misra, who apparently was brutally murdered by the WSLF despite her vehement disavowal of any complicity in the massacre which took place.

The cornerstone of the novel is the shifting "maps" of Africa, both geographical nation-states and individual emotional attachment to ethnic and national identity. In a geographical sense, one of the primary origins of the Ogaden War dates back to the colonial era, when the Somali-inhabited territories of the Horn of Africa were arbitrarily divided among four European and African powers into five separate territories: the British Somaliland Protectorate and Italian Somaliland (both of which joined together upon independence in 1960 to create the Republic of Somalia), the French Territory of the Afars and the Issas (as of 1977, the Republic of Djibouti), the Northern Frontier District (the Northern Province of Britain's former colony of Kenya), and the Ogaden region controlled by Ethiopia (see Chapter 5). As symbolized by the five-pointed star emblazoned on the Somali flag — one point for each of the five "lost" portions of the Somali nation — Somali nationalists from the 1950s through the 1970s pursued an "irredentist" policy seeking to unite all the Somali peoples in the Horn of Africa under one state.[38] This policy reached its height in 1977, when Somalia militarily invaded and managed to capture the majority of the Ogaden. However, a Soviet-managed airlift to Ethiopia of nearly $2 billion in military weaponry and fifteen thousand Cuban troops began a military counteroffensive that quickly overwhelmed the outnumbered and internationally isolated Somali troops within a matter of weeks, ultimately destroying the short-lived Somali dream of a "Greater Somalia."[39] As concluded by Askar's Uncle Hilaal: "There is truth in maps. The Ogaden, as Somali, is truth. To the Ethiopian map-maker, the Ogaden as Somali, is untruth."

The most devastating map of this novel, however, is the ethnic one that inhabitants of the Horn of Africa carry within their psyches. Despite the fact that Misra raised and loved an orphaned Somali boy, learned the Somali language, and adopted a local Somali village in the Ogaden as her own, she inevitably finds herself scapegoated and ultimately killed by ethnic Somalis consumed by their hate for Ethiopians who, for their part, have also committed acts of hatred during war. Indeed, socially reinforced ethnic divisions, which historically have been intensified by colonialism and self-interested African elites, lie at the center of this tragic tale in which a young boy is forced to choose between his love for his adopted mother and his love for a reunited Somali nation.

Politics of the African Novel in Perspective

The novels of Nuruddin Farah, like those of other African writers who have made a conscious decision to integrate political ideals into their writings, offer unique insights into the evolution of African politics and society. Espousing his perception of the role of literature within the political realm, Farah once characterized African novelists (and undoubtedly himself) as managing to "touch the raw nerve of the reader." Alluding to what drives his critical novels, Farah stated: "There is something virgin about writing in Africa. There are certain aspects of this writing which are like social documentation, writing about things which have never before been written about."[40]

It is important to remember, however, that African novelists do not deliver mere **documentary realism** (i.e., exact portayals) of political events within their respective countries. They instead capture the concept and the image of a particular political situation or historical period, which is then presented in story form to the public, who may judge it upon its own merits. African novelists therefore should not be regarded as simple recorders of events, but rather as interpreters acting upon their perceptions of specific events. In the end, it is up to the reader to determine how well the African novelist captures the socioeconomic and political-military realities of the country and period in question.

Key Terms

politics of language choice
official censorship
publishing outlet

politically committed novelists
evolving African identity
documentary realism

For Further Reading

Awoonor, Kofi. *The Breast of the Earth: A Survey of the History, Culture and Literature of Africa South of the Sahara.* New York: Nok Publishers International, 1975.

Bruner, Charlotte, ed. *The Heinemann Book of African Women's Writing.* Portsmouth: Heinemann, 1993.

Egejuru, Phanuel A. *Toward African Literary Independence: A Dialogue with Contemporary African Writers.* Westview: Greenwood, 1980.

Gakwandi, Shatto Arthur. *The Novel and Contemporary Experience in Africa.* London: Heinemann, 1977.

Harrow, Kenneth W., ed. *Faces of Islam in African Literature.* Portsmouth: Heinemann, 1991.

Harrow, Kenneth W. *Thresholds of Change in African Literature: The Emergence of a Tradition.* Portsmouth: Heinemann, 1997.

Hay, Jean, ed. *African Novels in the Classroom.* Boulder: Lynne Rienner, 1999.

Irele, Abiola. *The African Experience in Literature and Ideology.* Bloomington: Indiana University Press, 1990.

Lindfors, Bernth. *Long Drums and Canons: Teaching and Researching African Literatures.* Trenton: Africa World, 1995.

Maja-Pearce, Adewale. *Who's Afraid of Wole Soyinka? Essays on Censorship.* Portsmouth: Heinemann, 1991.

Mortimer, Mildred, ed. *Journeys through the French African Novel.* Portsmouth: Heinemann, 1990.

Ngara, Emmanuel. *Art and Ideology in the African Novel: A Study of the Influence of Marxism on African Writing.* London: Heinemann, 1985.

Ngugi wa Thiong'o. *Barrel of a Pen: Resistance to Repression in Neo-Colonial Kenya.* Trenton: Africa World, 1982.

Ngugi wa Thiong'o. *Decolonising the Mind: The Politics of Language in African Literature.* London: James Currey, 1981.

Wilkinson, Jane, ed. *Talking with African Writers: Interviews with African Poets, Playwrights and Novelists.* Portsmouth: Heinemann, 1992.

Notes

1. For a general overview, see Kofi Awoonor, *The Breast of the Earth: A Survey of the History, Culture and Literature of Africa South of the Sahara* (New York: Nok Publishers International, 1975). See also Jane Wilkinson, ed., *Talking with African Writers: Interviews with African Poets, Playwrights and Novelists* (Portsmouth: Heinemann, 1992).

2. For a brief discussion of this trend, see Mark W. DeLancey, December Green, and Kenneth Menkhaus, "African Politics at American Colleges and Universities: Topics, Approaches and Readings," *The Political Science Teacher* 2, no. 2 (1989):3.

3. For some general overviews of the African novel, see Simon Gikandi, *Reading the African Novel* (London: James Currey, 1987); Emmanuel Ngara, *Art and Ideology in the African Novel: A Study of the Influence of Marxism on African Writing* (London: Heinemann, 1985); and Shatto Arthur Gakwandi, *The Novel and Contemporary Experience in Africa* (London: Heineman, 1977).

4. Ngugi wa Thiong'o, *Decolonising the Mind: The Politics of Language in African Literature* (London: James Currey, 1986). See also Feroza Jussawalla, "The Language of Struggle: Ngugi wa Thiong'o on the Prisonhouse of Language," *Transition* 54 (1991):142–54.

5. Ngugi wa Thiong'o, *Barrel of a Pen: Resistance to Repression in Neo-Colonial Kenya* (Trenton: Africa World, 1982). See also Ngugi's *Moving the Centre: The Struggle for Cultural Freedom* (Portsmouth: Heinemann, 1993).

6. See, for example, Chinua Achebe, *Hopes and Impediments: Selected Essays 1965–1987* (Oxford: Heinemann, 1988).

7. For a discussion of this theme, see David D. Laitin, "Can Language Be Planned?" *Transition* 54 (1991):130–41.

8. For a general overview, see Adewale Maja-Pearce, *Who's Afraid of Wole Soyinka? Essays on Censorship* (Portsmouth: Heinemann, 1991).

9. For a general overview, see Roger G. Thomas, "Exile, Dictatorship and the Creative Writer in Africa: A Select Annotated Bibliography," *Third World Quarterly* 9, no. 1 (1987):271–96.

10. This summary is drawn from *ibid.*, pp. 276–77.

11. Under the pseudonym Eza Boto, see *Ville Cruelle* (1954). Under the pseudonym Mongo Beti, see *Le Pauvre Christ de Bomba* (1956; published in English in 1971 as *The Poor Christ of Bomba*); *Mission Terminée* (1957; published in English in 1958 as *Mission Accomplished*); and *Le Roi Miraculé: Chronique des Essazam* (1958; published in English in 1960 as *King Lazarus*).

12. See, for example, *Remember Ruben* (1974; published in English in 1980 under the same title); and *Perpétue et l'Habitude du Malheur* (1974; appeared in English in 1974 as *Perpetua and the Habit of Unhappiness*).

13. See, for example, Philip G. Altbach, Amadio A. Arboleda, and S. Gopinathan, eds., *Publishing in the Third World: Knowledge and Development* (Portsmouth: Heinemann, 1985).

14. See Gakwandi, *The Novel and Contemporary Experience in Africa*, p. 3.

15. For an overview of Achebe's works, see Simon Gikandi, *Reading Chinua Achebe: Language of Ideology in Fiction* (London: James Currey, 1991). For an analysis of the scholarship that Achebe's works have inspired, see Anna Rutherford and Kirsten Holst Petersen, eds., *Chinua Achebe: A Celebration* (Portsmouth: Heinemann, 1991).

16. See, for example, Bernth Lindfors, "The African Politician's Changing Image in African Literature in English, *The Journal of Developing Areas* 4 (1969):13–28.

17. Gakwandi, *The Novel and Contemporary Experience in Africa*, p. 97.

18. *Ibid.*, p. 98.

19. For a more extensive analysis of the evolution of Ngugi's career, see G. D. Killam, *An Introduction to the Writings of Ngugi* (London: Heinemann, 1980), esp. pp. 1–19.

20. See Edris Makward, "Women, Tradition, and Religion in Sembène Ousmane's Work," in Kenneth W. Harrow, ed., *Faces of Islam in African Literature* (Portsmouth: Heinemann, 1991), p. 195.

21. See Sonia Lee, "Women Writers," in John Middleton, ed., *Encyclopedia of Africa South of the Sahara*, vol. 3 (New York: Charles Scribner's Sons, 1997), p. 42. For a discussion of these and other female African novelists, see Adeoloa James, ed., *In Their Own Voices: African Women Writers Talk* (London: James Currey, 1990). For a selection of novels and short stories written by African women, see two volumes edited by Charlotte Bruner: *Unwinding Threads* (Portsmouth: Heinemann, 1983); and *The Heinemann Book of African Women's Writing* (Portsmouth: Heinemann, 1993).

22. Lee, "Women Writers," p. 47.

23. Farah also has written several short stories and plays, including *Why Dead So Soon?* (1966); *A Dagger in Vacuum* (1969); *The Offering* (1976); and *Yussuf and His Brothers* (1982). For an overview of his works, Derek Wright, *The Novels of Nuruddin Farah* (Bayreuth, Germany: Eckhard Breitinger, 1994).

24. See Nuruddin Farah, "A Combining of Gifts: An Interview," *Third World Quarterly* 11, no. 3 (1989):173–74.

25. See Nuruddin Farah, "Why I Write," *Third World Quarterly* 10, no. 4 (1988): 1591–99.

26. Parts of this portion of the chapter were drawn from Peter J. Schraeder, "The Novels of Nuruddin Farah: The Socio-Political Evolution of a Somali Writer," *Northeast African Studies* 10, no. 2–3 (1988):15–26.

27. For a discussion of this theme in this and other of Farah's novels, see Juliet I. Okonkwo, "Nuruddin Farah and the Changing Roles of Women," *World Literature Today* 58, no. 2 (1984):215–21.

28. For a discussion of this era, see David D. Laitin and Said S. Samatar, *Somalia: Nation in Search of a State* (Boulder: Westview, 1985).

29. Farah, "A Combining of Gifts," p. 179.

30. For discussion, see I. M. Lewis, "The Politics of the 1969 Coup," *The Journal of Modern African Studies* 10, no. 3 (1972):383–408.

31. For examples of his speeches, see Somali Ministry of Information and National Guidance, *My People and My Country: Selected Speeches of Jaalle Major General Mohammad Siad Barre* (Mogadishu: State Printing Agency, 1979).

32. For an overview of these relationships, see Jeffrey A. Lefebvre, *Arms for the Horn: U.S. Security Policy in Ethiopia and Somalia, 1953–1991* (Pittsburgh: University of Pittsburgh Press, 1991); Robert G. Patman, *The Soviet Union and the Horn of Africa: The Diplomacy of Intervention and Disengagement* (Cambridge: Cambridge University Press, 1990); and Harold G. Marcus, *Ethiopia, Great Britain, and the United States, 1941–1974: The Politics of Empire* (Berkeley: University of California Press, 1983).

33. For a discussion of this theme, see Barbara Turfan, "Opposing Dictatorship: A Comment on Nuruddin Farah's 'Variations on the Theme of an African Dictatorship'," *Journal of Commonwealth Literature* 24, no. 1 (1989): 193–206. See also Jacqueline Bardolph, "L'Evolution de l'Écriture dans la Trilogie de Nourredine Farah: Variations sur le thème d'une Dictature Africaine," *Nouvelles du Sud* 6 (1986–87):79–92.

34. For discussion, see David D. Laitin, "The Political Economy of Military Rule in Somalia," *The Journal of Modern African Studies* 14, no. 3 (1976):449–68.

35. Mohamed Hassan, "Status of Human Rights in Somalia," *Horn of Africa* 3, no. 2 (1980):4.

36. For discussion, see Harry Ododa, "Somalia's Domestic Politics and Foreign Relations since the Ogaden War of 1977–78," *Middle Eastern Studies* 21, no. 3 (1985):285–97.

37. See Said S. Samatar, *Oral Poetry and Somali Nationalism: The Case of Sayyid Mahammad Abdille Hasan* (Cambridge: Cambridge University Press, 1982).

38. For a discussion of this theme, see Saadia Touval, *Somali Nationalism: International Politics and the Drive for Unity in the Horn* (Cambridge: Harvard University Press, 1963); and I. M. Lewis, *A Modern History of Somalia: Nation and State in the Horn of Africa* (Boulder: Westview, 1988).

39. For discussion, see Tom J. Farer, *War Clouds on the Horn of Africa: The Widening Storm* (New York: Carnegie Endowment for International Peace, 1979).

40. Quoted in "Close Sesame: The End of a Trilogy," *Africa Now* 32 (1983):82.

10

State and Civil Society

Honor guard standing in front of the gates of the presidential mansion in Dakar, Senegal.

THE RELATIONSHIP BETWEEN the state and civil society is an important foundation of African politics and society. Whereas the **African state** encompasses the formal institutions of power within African political systems, including but not limited to the presidency, judiciary, government bureaucracies, national legislature, and military forces, **African civil society** incorporates the vast array of voluntary associations throughout society, such as political parties, labor unions, student organizations, and religious groups that seek access to that power. From the 1950s to the 1970s, the **state-society relationship** was marked by the creation of highly authoritarian and centralized states seeking to co-opt or silence those very elements of civil society that had contributed to the independence struggles. However, the expansion of state power was significantly challenged during the 1970s and the 1980s by the reemergence of civil societies intent on seeking greater political and economic rights. Hobbled by decades of corruption and economic mismanagement, authoritarian states were increasingly incapable of maintaining control over their respective territories. The net result of what became known as the **crisis of the African state** was the emergence, during the 1990s, of efforts to restructure state-society relations in light of the legitimate interests and needs of both states and civil societies. The primary purpose of this chapter is to assess three broad trends in the evolution of state-society relations in Africa: the concentration of state power at the expense of civil society from the 1950s to the 1970s; the crisis of the state and the resurgence of civil society during the 1970s and the 1980s; and the emergence of new efforts to restructure state-society relationships during the 1990s and the beginning of the twenty-first century.

Concentration of State Power at the Expense of Civil Society

The first generation of African leaders, who took office at the beginning of the 1950s, was immediately challenged by what can be termed the **great expectations–minimal capabilities paradox**. First and foremost, the newly elected leaders had to contend with popular expectations that the fruits of independence, most notably higher wages and better living conditions, would be quickly and widely shared after the departure of the former colonial powers. In almost every case, however, the former colonial state simply did not have the capabilities to satisfy public demands. In addition to being heavily dependent on the former colonial power for trade, investment, and even personnel to staff key governmental ministries, the newly independent African states were often constrained by export-oriented mono-crop and mono-mineral economies, low levels of education among the general population, and perverse infrastructural development favoring the maintenance of external links at the expense of national development and regional cooperation (see Chapter 5).

The vast majority of African leaders resolved this paradox of independence by promoting the concentration of state power at the expense of civil society.

Even the most democratic of African leaders agreed that the numerous challenges of the contemporary independence era, such as the rapid achievement of socioeconomic development, the creation of a sense of "nation" among numerous ethnic groups, and the maintenance of political-military order, required the creation of powerful, centralized states. This process continued the authoritarian colonial model of state-society relations known as "Bula Matari" ("he who breaks all rocks," see Chapter 5). In the context of state-society relations, Bula Matari embodied the vision of a state that "crushes all resistance."[1]

Six distinct patterns illustrate the ways in which the concentration of state power generally unfolded throughout the African continent from the 1950s to the mid-1970s. Each of these patterns is highlighted by the details and events surrounding the evolution of state-society relations in the Democratic Republic of the Congo (Congo-Kinshasa), from independence in 1960 to 1974.[2] Congo-Kinshasa serves as an excellent case study because Congolese citizens and foreign observers alike shared high expectations that the country would emerge as one of the leaders of the African continent. Moreover, Congo-Kinshasa has often been cited as a "model" for all that could potentially succeed or fail throughout the African continent. Indeed, the concentration of state power that unfolded in Congo-Kinshasa was representative of similar processes throughout Africa.

Africanization of the State

The first and most immediately visible form of state concentration of power revolved around the **Africanization of state institutions**: the replacement of departing colonial administrators with African politicians and civil servants. In the case of Congo-Kinshasa, the process of almost "instantaneous"[3] Africanization of the civil service, which accompanied independence in 1960, took on several interesting dimensions after Joseph Désiré Mobutu assumed power in a military coup d'état in 1965. In 1971, Mobutu announced a broad policy of "authenticity" that sought to replace the remaining cultural vestiges of Belgian colonialism with more "authentic" forms of African consciousness. Similar to an earlier edict that renamed the country "Zaire" (a designation that ended after the fall of the Second Republic in 1997), all citizens were to drop their Christian forenames in favor of African names. In order to set the example for the rest of the nation, Mobutu renounced his Christian forenames of Joseph Désiré and assumed the new name of Mobutu Sese Seko. The policy of authenticity also changed the ways in which Congolese spoke and dressed. The formal French titles of *Monsieur* and *Madame* were replaced by *Citoyen* for men and *Citoyenne* for women, terms derivative of the French Revolution that literally mean "Citizen." European suits were replaced by the *abacost,* a collarless suit worn without either a shirt or a tie.[4] (The term *abacost* is actually shorthand for the chant, "A bas le Costume" ["Down with Suits"], associated with the anti-West policy of authenticity.)

A second dimension of Africanization, the "Zairianization campaign" of 1973, was targeted toward immigrants of Asian or Mediterranean origins.[5] As was the case in many African countries at the beginning of the contemporary independence era, Congo-Kinshasa's commercial sector was dominated by immigrant groups, most notably Greeks, Jews, Italians, and Portuguese, who had migrated to the territory and who had been given preferential treatment during the colonial era. These immigrant groups, especially the owners of local shops that sold traditional food staples, were often viewed with derision by the local population as "foreigners" who charged unfair prices and monopolized the market. These outsiders were tempting targets for newly formed governments seeking to curry the favor of public opinion. On November 30, 1973, Mobutu announced that all small and medium foreign-owned commercial businesses were to be handed over to the state authorities for redistribution to Congolese nationals. Within less than three months, the vast majority of such businesses had been turned over to Congolese, who became known as *acquéreurs* (acquirers), with little if any compensation to their original owners, many of whom ultimately fled the country in either fear or disgust.

Bureaucratic Expansion and the Growth of Parastatals

African leaders also sought to strengthen state power by expanding the number of civil servants working in the various bureaucracies of the executive branch. According to one study, African civil services grew at such a rapid rate during the 1960s — an annual average of 6 percent — that by 1970 approximately 60 percent of all African wage earners were employed by their respective governments.[6] In the case of Congo-Kinshasa, the number of civil servants had grown to approximately 400,000 by 1973, more than double the number employed at the time of independence. These positions were divided into a three-fold hierarchy: the top-level *fonctionnaires de commandement* (command civil servants, 2 percent); the mid-level *agents de collaboration* (collaboration officers, 7 percent); and the lower-level *agents d'exécution* (executing officers, 91 percent). Such positions were highly coveted due to the popular perception of the state as the most lucrative source of wage employment and privileges, including government-provided cars, chauffeurs, and housing. From the state's perspective, the doling out of ever-increasing numbers of jobs was an important form of political patronage intended to win public approval.

The creation and expansion of state-owned or state-controlled corporations known as **parastatals** illustrates the process of bureaucratic expansion. In some cases, the parastatals existed during the colonial era and were responsible for providing a public service, such as electricity. In Congo-Kinshasa, the state-owned electric utility company, *Société Nationale de l'Electricité* (National Electric Company), not only expanded in size and civil servant slots, but strongly supported several massive public works projects designed to enhance the country's energy infrastructure. One of the most ambitious undertakings in this regard was the Inga-Shaba project: a 1,800 kilometer power transmission line between the massive hydroelectric dam at Inga, which cost $140 million to construct, and an electricity grid centered in Kolwezi, the capital of the Shaba Province, to supply energy for Congo-Kinshasa's sizable mining industry. Almost all African states continued this "public" direction of services and industry, and neither encouraged nor facilitated the expansion of the private sector.

The process of bureaucratic expansion was further fueled by the **nationalization** of foreign corporations, a process whereby the state names its own agents to the boards of directors of companies formerly owned and governed privately. The state, when in this mode, attempts to bring under its control all economic activity, especially economic decision making. The purpose, generally speaking, is obtaining power. But equally important is the economic power that derives from the *revenues* of all these activities. In 1966, for example, the Mobutu regime nationalized the Belgian mining conglomerate, *Union Minière*, which generated more than 50 percent of government revenues during the colonial era. The new Congolese conglomerate, *Générale Congolaise des Minérais* (GECOMIN, Congolese General of Minerals), was renamed *Générale des Carrières et des Mines* (GECAMINES, General of Quarries and Mines) during the Zairianization campaign of 1971, and served as the precursor of a later, more widespread nationalization campaign. On December 30, 1974, after spending a month with Mao Zedong in the People's Republic of China (PRC), Mobutu announced the beginning of a ten-point "radicalization campaign" that included the nationalization of large-scale industries in a variety of sectors, including construction, manufacturing, publishing, food processing, and transportation.[7]

One of the most common forms of parastatals was the **marketing board**: a state agency that set the prices and maintained monopolistic control over the buying and selling of primary products. Originally derivative of the colonial era, this particular form of parastatal dramatically expanded in both size and scope to include almost all forms of primary products, including both natural resources (such as mineral wealth) and agricultural products (such as cotton). In Congo-Kinshasa, for example, nearly all mineral production, including copper, cobalt, and diamonds, was marketed by the *Société Zairoise pour la Commercialisation des Minérais* (SOZACOM, Zairian Company for the Commercialization of Minerals). Similarly, fourteen agricultural enterprises personally acquired by the Mobutu family were grouped together under the conglomerate, *Cultures et Elevages du Zaire* (CELZA, Farms and Ranches of Zaire). In each case, the process of nationalization and/or the creation of parastatals served the dual function of creating state-oriented revenue streams and adding to the growing number of state-provided jobs for the local population.

Dismantling of Institutional Checks-and-Balances

Many African leaders also concentrated state power by undertaking presidential actions designed to limit, and in some cases completely destroy, the ability of other state actors to challenge the decision-making supremacy of the presidential mansion. Presidential actions essentially dismantled the ill-conceived systems of checks-and-balances that were hastily constructed by the departing colonial powers. In short, African leaders sought to create highly centralized states in which the executive mansion reigned supreme.

The case of Congo-Kinshasa demonstrates that the dismantling of institutional checks-and-balances usually followed three patterns. First and foremost, leaders sought to underscore the unitary nature of the state by dismissing any federalist arrangements that allowed for the political autonomy of groups or regions based on ethnic, linguistic, or religious claims. After assuming power in 1965, Mobutu effectively ended the unitary-federalist debate that dominated the politics of the First Republic (1960–65) in favor of a highly unitary state.[8] For example, the number of administrative regions, which in the past had increased to take into account regional and especially ethnic differences, was reduced from twenty-one to nine.[9] The Founding Constitution of 1960 was replaced by a new constitution that gave the office of the president sweeping powers. This new constitutional framework, supported by "spectacular margins of approval" in a national referendum held in 1967, underscored the belief of both the Congolese population and the Mobutu regime that federalist arrangements were at least partially responsible for the ethnic and regional political instability of the First Republic.[10]

The dismantling of institutional checks-and-balances also included the marginalization, and sometimes even the disbanding, of independent parliaments and judiciaries. On November 30, 1965, less than one week after assuming power, Mobutu announced that all of the constitutionally mandated powers attributed to the national legislature, such as the authority to pass legislation, henceforth were vested in the head-of-state. Although the legislature continued to meet and hold debates, generating nearly 1,400 pages of proceedings during 1966 alone, Mobutu's edict had "rendered it powerless."[11] The charade of powerless legislators publicly debating national priorities was ended on March 23, 1967, when Mobutu announced the formal dissolution of the national legislature. Although a new legislative body was created in 1970, it constituted at best a "rubber stamp" institution that merely endorsed Mobutu's legislative initiatives.

The dismantling of institutional checks-and-balances usually culminated in the outlawing of all opposition political parties and the creation of a single-party system subservient to the presidential mansion (see Chapter 12). Mobutu had suspended all activities by political parties on November 24, 1965. He subsequently established his own political party, the *Mouvement Populaire de la Révolution* (MPR, Popular Movement of the Revolution). Although the constitution of 1967 provided for a two-party system, the MPR was the only political party officially allowed to exist by the Mobutu regime. The MPR's single-party status was formalized in 1970 by a constitutional amendment that recognized the party as the "supreme institution" of the land.[12]

Co-optation and Silencing of Civil Society

The desire of African leaders to ensure the concentration of state power around the presidential mansion invariably conflicted with the increasingly vocal demands of **civil society**: the vast array of voluntary associations throughout African societies that seeks access to state power.[13] Numerous components of African civil society, including but not limited to political parties, labor unions, student organizations, and religious groups, had played important roles in the ultimate downfall of colonialism and the transition to independence during the 1950s. After independence these groups expected to wield equal or greater levels of influence in their newly independent countries (see Chapter 6). These expectations proved ill-founded, however, as African leaders consistently employed two sets of policies — co-optation and repression — to effectively silence the dissident demands of civil society, in their pursuit of the concentration of state power.

Mobutu's handling of opposition political figures from Congo-Kinshasa's First Republic clearly demonstrated tactics used to co-opt and silence civil society. Potential opponents were wooed with the offer of important and lucrative positions in the Second Republic. For example, Kamanda wa Kamanda, one of the "most articulate" leaders of an influential student umbrella group, the *Union Générale des Etudiants Congolais* (UGEC, General Union of Congolese Students), was given the powerful post of general secretary to the presidency.[14] As demonstrated by Mobutu's response to the so-called Pentecost Plot of 1966, however, political opponents who became either a real or perceived threat to the regime were dealt with harshly. On May 30, 1966, Mobutu ordered the arrest of four First Republic politicians — Prime Minister–designate Evariste Kimba, Defense Minister Jérôme Anany, Finance Minister Emmanuel Banda, and Minister of Mines and Energy Alexander Mahamba — on the charge of plotting a military coup against the government. Three days later they were publicly executed before a crowd of fifty thousand spectators. This swift, public act had a "tremendous psychological effect" on politicians and civil society in general: "opposition, it was now clear, carried mortal perils."[15]

Co-optation and repression were also employed with initial success against other elements of Congolese civil society. In June 1967, all existing labor unions were forced to join one government-approved umbrella union, the *Union Nationale des Travailleurs Congolais* (UNTC, National Union of Congolese Workers). In June 1969, all student organizations were banned in favor of the *Jeunesse du Mouvement Populaire de la Révolution* (JMPR, Youth of the Popular Movement of the Revolution), the youth wing of the sole ruling party. As part of this process, all institutions of higher learning were nationalized by the government and placed under the authority of the *Université Nationale du Zaire* (UNAZA, National University of Zaire). Even the Catholic Church, which represented 40 percent of the Congolese population,

BOX 10.1

THE "EXIT OPTION":
AFRICAN EMIGRATION TO THE UNITED STATES

Emigration to other African countries and continents historically has served as an important **exit option** for Africans seeking to better their lives and those of their families. This took on new meaning in the 1970s as the emerging "crisis of the African state" contributed to rising levels of political persecution, civil conflict, and socioeconomic hardship throughout the African continent. For many Africans, emigration literally meant the difference between freedom and prison and even life and death.

The largest numbers of Africans historically have chosen Europe as their destination of choice due to the impact of European colonialism and the continuation of privileged ties during the contemporary independence era. Beginning in the 1970s, however, increasing numbers of Africans have sought to emigrate to the United States. According to an important study carried out by April A. Gordon, the number of visas that the U.S. Immigration and Naturalization Service annually grants to African citizens increased from less than 10,000 in 1975 to more than 40,000 in 1995. Statistics compiled by the U.S. Census Bureau confirm this upward trend. The 1990 census documents that 205,316 Africans born outside of the United States are currently either temporary or permanent residents or have become naturalized U.S. citizens, with 67 percent of that total (137,746 immigrants) having arrived since 1980.

Three types of African immigrants are favored by immigration legislation passed by the U.S. Congress in 1965 and 1990. First and foremost, preference is given to the immediate family members, most notably spouse and children, of a U.S. permanent resident or naturalized citizen. This **family reunification program** became increasingly important during the 1980s, as larger numbers of African immigrants decided to make the United States their permanent home. Preference is also given to African immigrants with special employment skills, favoring educated professionals. Forty-three percent of African immigrants who are fifteen years of age or older have at least some college education, with many holding advanced degrees. (The average for the U.S. population as a whole is only 20 percent.) The final and smallest category includes political refugees who demonstrate a "well-founded fear of persecution" based on ethnic background, political beliefs, or religious affiliation, should they be forced to return to their country of birth. A precedent-setting case in 1996 expanded this definition to include a woman's fear of being forced to submit to the still common practice of female genital mutilation known as circumcision (see Chapter 7).

The African continent nonetheless has constituted the smallest source of immigrants relative to all other regions of the world, accounting for less than 5 percent of the U.S. total throughout the 1990s. In response to growing criticism that this low number reflected a racial bias in U.S. immigration policy toward Africa and other regions of the developing south, the U.S. Immigration and Naturalization Service launched a **diversity immigration lottery** in 1995 that grants 55,000 additional visas through a random selection process. Out of this total, 20,623 slots (37 percent) were reserved for African immigrants in 1997. The lottery has not only increased the number of Africans entering the United States as legal immigrants, but has emerged as one of the most popular and reported U.S. programs throughout the African continent. For many African families, the "winning" of the visa lottery by one of their members ignites dreams of a better life in America, by establishing a foothold that they hope will become the basis for other family members to follow.

Statistics are drawn from April Gordon, "The New Diaspora: African Immigration to the United States," *Journal of Third World Studies* 15, no. 1 (1998):79–103. See also Joel Millman, *The Other Americans: How Immigrants Renew Our Country, Our Economy, and Our Values* (New York: Viking, 1997).

was forced to succumb to the centralizing tendencies of the state, especially after an August 1969 conference of Congolese bishops noted the "dictatorial tendencies" of the Mobutu regime.[16] Beginning in 1972, the Mobutu regime banned all religious broadcasts and dissolved church-sponsored youth networks, subsequently nationalizing religious school networks.[17] All Protestant denominations were similarly reorganized under one state-imposed umbrella group, *Les Eglises du Christ au Zaire* (Churches of Christ in Zaire).

Expansion of the Coercive Apparatus

Leaders intent on dismantling institutional checks-and-balances and silencing outspoken elements of civil society depended on loyal military troops and police forces that were both willing and able to enforce presidential directives. As a result, the creation and rapid expansion of a **coercive apparatus**, comprising a wide variety of security forces, served as a critical component of the concentration of state power. According to one study, military spending as a percentage of gross national product (GNP) nearly doubled throughout the African continent, from 1.8 percent in 1963 to 3.4 percent in 1971.[18]

Mobutu oversaw a vast coercive apparatus that operated at three major levels in Congo-Kinshasa. As a former Lieutenant-General and the leader of the 1965 military coup that brought his regime into power, Mobutu first and foremost relied upon the *Armée Nationale Congolaise* (ANC, Congolese National Army), which was subsequently renamed the *Forces Armées Zairoises* (FAZ, Zairian Armed Forces). The number of troops was increased from 23,100 in 1960 to 63,200 in 1970, and included the creation of elite paracommando battalions, such as the *Division Spéciale Présidentielle* (DSP, Special Presidential Division), staffed with soldiers from Mobutu's Equateur province.[19] A national police force known as the *Guarde Civile* (Civil Guard) served as the second general level of the coercive apparatus. A presidential decree authorized the expansion of the police force from 9,000 in 1960 to 25,000 in 1966.[20] By 1974, this force was buttressed by approximately 29,000 local police. The secret police were the third and most feared level of Mobutu's coercive apparatus. Originally known as the *Sûreté de l'Etat* (State Security) and subsequently renamed the *Centre National de Documentation* (CND, National Documentation Center), this highly secretive organization was responsible for the arrest, interrogation, and torture of anyone considered to be a threat to the Mobutu regime.

Mobutu's coercive apparatus was further enhanced by extensive reliance on foreign security advisors and military forces, especially those from Belgium, France, and the United States. During the fall of 1963, for example, the U.S. Central Intelligence Agency (CIA) contracted with Cuban exiles (who had taken part in the Bay of Pigs invasion of Cuba in 1961) to pilot T-6 planes against a guerrilla insurgency in Congo-Kinshasa's Kwilu province. In the spring of 1964, when the insurgency had spread to other eastern provinces, the CIA hired additional Cuban paramilitary fighters to pilot six T-28 fighters recently delivered by the U.S. Department of Defense. Maintenance for the fighters was carried out by European mechanics associated with the Western International Ground Maintenance Organization (WIGMO), a CIA front organization based in Liechtenstein. CIA efforts were buttressed by the Pentagon's establishment of a U.S. military mission in Congo-Kinshasa in the fall of 1963, as well as the arrival, in the spring of 1964, of three mobile training teams (MTTs) and approximately seventy technicians to offer guidance in counterinsurgency tactics against the guerrillas. This case indicated the beginning of a pattern in which the United States and the other northern industrialized democracies, most notably Belgium and France, periodically came to Mobutu's aid to thwart a series of regime-threatening guerrilla insurgencies and external invasions.[21]

Creation of Personal Rule Networks

A final trend associated with the concentration of state power was the creation of **personal rule networks**: a system of governance in which power is ultimately vested in an individual leader, as opposed to legally based institutions.[22] The system is based on a series of concentric circles of **patron-client relationships,** in which the leader at the center of the system personally selects senior government appointees, who in turn select their appointees, and so on. The leader is exalted in this system and seeks to instill loyalty through a delicate combination of charisma and the provision of economic and political patronage. In extreme cases, the inherently personal nature of patron-client systems ensures that they often do not survive the death of the leader. However, as long as the leader is capable of maintaining and increasing the level of political and economic resources provided through the patronage network, he can at least ensure his continued domination of the political system.

Mobutu distinguished himself as a master tactician of personal rule.[23] He fostered a virtual "cult of the personality" in which he was popularly referred to as Congo-Kinshasa's Founding President, Father of the Nation, Guide of the Revolution, and Helmsman of the Nation. He even went so far as to declare "Mobutuism" the official ideology of the state. As exemplified in a public declaration by Interior Minister Baanga Engulu, Mobutu was even successful in making his rule synonymous with a virtual "third coming of Christ":

> In our religion, we have our own theologians. In all religions, and at all times, there are prophets. Why not today? God has sent us a great prophet, our prestigious Guide Mobutu — this prophet is our liberator, our Messiah. Our church is the MPR. Its chief is Mobutu, we respect him like one respects a Pope. Our gospel is Mobutuism. This is why the crucifixes must be replaced by the image of our Messiah.[24]

The cornerstone of Mobutu's personal rule network was the judicious use of political-economic rewards and sanctions. Supporters were rewarded with high-paying government positions and easily doubled their salaries through state-approved corruption and/or state-obtained private businesses.[25] Mobutu also kept administrators and cabinet members on the move from post to post so that none of them could establish a firm power base. Mobutu's response to the Pentecost Plot, however, demonstrates that potential claimants to the presidency and opponents in general were dealt with harshly. This combination of reward and punishment ensured that by 1974, the year marking the height of Mobutu's political and financial success, "there was literally no one in the state domain who held a position other than through presidential grace."[26]

Crisis of the State and the Resurgence of Civil Society

The rise of centralized, authoritarian African states at the expense of civil society was significantly challenged during the 1970s and the 1980s by a series of economic, political, and military developments often referred to as the crisis of the African state.[27] African leaders found their hold on power simultaneously threatened by the economic demands of faltering national economies, the resurgence of civil society, and in some cases the emergence of civil unrest and conflict. Hobbled by decades of corruption and economic mismanagement, the **predatory states**[28] of the earlier independence era increasingly proved incapable of maintaining control over their respective territories, and became known as **lame Leviathans**[29] and **shadow states**.[30]

Four patterns in particular exemplify the process of state decline that generally occurred throughout the African continent from the mid-1970s to the beginning of the 1990s. Each of these patterns is once again illustrated by the evolution of state-society relations in Congo-Kinshasa.

Deepening Economic Crisis

A continent-wide economic crisis during the 1980s severely threatened the economic foundations of the African state. The first symptom of this crisis which appeared during the second half of the 1970s as extremely weak economic growth, was followed by sharp economic decline during the 1980s. A simple yet telling indicator — per capita income — captured the economic dilemma confronted by African policymakers. From 1975 to 1979, per capita income for the African continent registered less than 1 percent annual growth rate. During the decade of the 1980s, this meager growth rate turned into a 2.2 percent annual *decline* in per capita income.[31] African leaders had expanded the scope of state power without also increasing the state's capacity to use that power to create wealth. As a result, African leaders were increasingly incapable of mustering the resources to maintain the African state's unparalleled control of the economic and political systems. The growing indebtedness of the African continent further compounded the problem. From 1980 to 1989, Africa's debt burden nearly tripled in size, from $55 billion to $160 billion.[32] Indeed, nearly every economic indicator compiled by the World Bank and the International Monetary Fund suggested an emerging economic crisis of epic proportions.

The economic turning point in Congo-Kinshasa occurred when the international price of copper declined 62 percent, from an all-time high of $1.40 a pound in 1974 to $.53 a pound one year later.[33] Since copper was the mainstay of the economy, the dramatic price decline ensured the 1975 loss of nearly $600 million in purchasing power for the state, causing a short-term financial crisis of confidence in the Mobutu regime.[34] This short-term crisis coincided with the dramatic oil price increases adopted by the Organization of Petroleum Exporting Countries (OPEC), significantly diminishing the ability of developing countries like Congo-Kinshasa to maintain their balances of payments. From this point forward, Congo-Kinshasa was confronted with hyperinflation that averaged 60 to 80 percent annually throughout the 1980s.[35]

The most important outcome of the copper and oil "shocks" of 1974–75 was that they revealed the Mobutu regime's ill-fated policies of economic development and the sheer economic mismanagement associated with the drive to concentrate power around the presidential mansion. The Zairianization and radicalization campaigns of 1973 and 1974 proved utter failures, with most of the *acquéreurs* either stripping the stores of stocks for short-term gain or financially mismanaging their businesses into bankruptcy. As was the case throughout Africa, the rapidly expanding parastatal sector did equally poorly, leading to massive financial losses. The marketing boards in particular hampered the Congolese agricultural economy for the simple reason that rural farmers were paid below-market prices to ensure a steady flow of cash into the state's coffers. For example, the government-index price paid for manioc, a food staple for rural dwellers, actually decreased by more than 70 percent from 1960 to 1974.[36] The net result of such pricing policies was a dramatic decline in food production and thus the growing inability of Congo-Kinshasa to feed itself.

Pervasive and widespread corruption at all levels of government, often referred to as *"le mal Zairois"* (the Zairian sickness), served as both the cement that held together Mobutu's personal rule network and the primary impediment to economic growth and development. Although **petty corruption**, such as police officers seeking bribes from defenseless motorists, has always existed in Africa and other regions of the world, the Mobutu regime fostered extreme corruption best described as a **kleptocracy**: a political system in which the state's wealth is systematically plundered by the ruling elite. The politically and economically ambitious looked upon all forms of state employment, including that with the civil service, parastatals, marketing boards, or the ruling party, as the principal path to getting rich. For example, as the manager of a marketing board, one drew a regular salary, skimmed a portion of the profits from the products regulated by that board, and pocketed bribes from buyers and sellers seeking "special" consideration. "A regional economic affairs inspector confided [in me] that his superiors had showed him the way to making $2,000 monthly in illegal bribes (although his official salary was $120), on condition, however, that he offer substantial kickbacks to them," explains David J. Gould, a specialist of corruption in Africa. "At a higher level, a regional commissioner in 1974–75 had so misused the 'Zairianized' property entrusted to him by the state, that he let the former owners manage it in return for a $100,000 kickback (fifty times his salary)."[37] Mobutu himself not surprisingly set the standard for this system by amassing a personal fortune that reportedly exceeded $5 billion and included luxurious châteaux in Belgium, France, Italy, and Switzerland. His only "warning" to state employees was made in a oft-cited public speech on May 20, 1976: *"Yibana mayele"* (steal cleverly) so as to avoid inflaming public opinion.[38]

Growing Inability to Provide Social Goods

The crisis of the African state was also demonstrated by the growing inability of the state to provide a wide variety of **social goods**, expected by civil society and normally taken for granted in the northern industrialized democracies, including effective transportation and telecommunications networks, access to electricity and clean water, and educational training in a public school system. Decline in public services was often due to cuts in government social spending devoted to these sectors, in favor of increases in government military spending for the police and other portions of the coercive apparatus.

The combination of corruption and economic mismanagement in Congo-Kinshasa fostered a severe decline in social services by the beginning of the 1990s. As explained by John Clark, a scholar who carried out field research in

Congo-Kinshasa during 1994, an expansive and effective road network that had crisscrossed the country in the early 1960s had deteriorated to such a degree as to become virtually nonexistent.[39] Something seemingly as simple as traveling sixty miles by car between the capital of Kinshasa and a neighboring town had become a "grueling, four-hour journey" due to the extremely poor condition of the road system.[40] The telephone system had also deteriorated to the point that the only effective means of telephone communication was through a variety of cell-phone systems offered by private companies. To make matters worse, power and water service outages became so frequent as to constitute the norm, and most public hospitals had declined to the point that local residents found "little use in going to them."[41]

An analysis of Congo-Kinshasa's federal budget clearly demonstrates the conscious trade-off that was taking place between the rising security focus of the presidential mansion and the social demands of civil society. The portion of the federal budget devoted to the presidency and national defense rose from 23 percent in 1982 to 58 percent in 1988.[42] According to one figure, the presidency alone was consuming an incredible 95 percent of all government expenditures as of 1992.[43] By contrast, federal expenditures for education had sharply declined from 23 percent in 1982 to 10 percent in 1988.[44] By the beginning of the 1990s, federal support for education had all but vanished, with the public education system in a state of near total collapse. Those with the financial means placed their children in foreign schools or in one of the hundreds of private schools that emerged in Congo-Kinshasa at the beginning of the 1990s.[45] Unfortunately, the vast majority of the nation's school children, especially those at the primary school level, would receive no education. These children, like others throughout Africa, have literally become a **génération sacrifiée** (sacrificed generation), often discouraged by the fact that a poor job market offers them nothing but positions as street vendors, maids, and cooks.

The state's inability to provide social goods was compounded by its declining control over the country except for a few urban areas, control that was at best sporadic and incomplete, even at the height of state power during the early independence era.[46] Despite devoting ever-increasing amounts of the federal budget to the security apparatus, Congo-Kinshasa had become a shadow state in which large areas of the national territory were no longer effectively governed by the central authorities.[47] Several regions, such as the southeastern Shaba province, achieved a large degree of autonomy, with local leaders controlling the local economy and pursuing foreign relations independent of — and sometimes contrary to — the wishes of the enfeebled central government in Kinshasa.[48]

The intrusiveness of state-sponsored corruption further impairs the effectiveness of state control, while strengthening the spread of **informal economies**: webs of economic activities that are "unmeasured, unrecorded and, in varying degrees, illegal."[49] Vast amounts of previously unrecorded smuggling along Congo-Kinshasa's southern, northeastern, and western borders linked those regions more closely with neighboring countries than with their own capital of Kinshasa or other national provinces during the 1980s.[50] The illegal trade in coffee, an important primary product, offers an important insight. From 1975 to 1979, 30 to 60 percent of the national coffee crop was illegally smuggled out of the country, costing the Congolese state nearly $350 million in lost revenues.[51] During the 1985–86 planting season, the Lubero coffee zone of northeastern Congo-Kinshasa "officially" exported 32 percent (41,117,000 kilograms) of a total estimated harvest of 129,000,000 kilograms; hence nearly 68 percent of that harvest was illegally smuggled through the informal market.[52] When this one harvest is multiplied by dozens of regions and dozens of other primary products, the potential negative impact on the national economy is staggering.

A final trend that accompanied the declining socioeconomic reach of the African state was the rising influence of international financial institutions, such as the International Monetary Fund (IMF) and the World Bank, in the restructuring of African economies and political systems in the image of the northern industrialized democracies (see Chapter 14). During the 1980s, African leaders were increasingly forced to accept externally imposed reform measures, referred to as "structural adjustment programs" (SAPs), in order to obtain IMF and World Bank loans. However, in Congo-Kinshasa and other African countries, the maneuvering between African leaders and the international financial institutions often turned into what Thomas Callaghy aptly called the "ritual dance of the debt game." No sooner had loans been granted did the Mobutu regime renege on its promised reform package, subsequently promising one year later to abide by a new set of reforms, only to be followed once again by a rejection of those reforms after funds had been disbursed, and, one year later, an entirely new set of promised reforms.[53]

Resurgence of Civil Society

The crisis of the African state was paralleled by the resurgence of increasingly vocal civil societies intent on opening up the political space within their respective countries.[54] Student organizations and trade unions that played a role in the independence struggle reemerged as vocal opponents of existing regimes, in response to the often severe deterioration of national educational systems, the lack of professional jobs for university graduates, and insufficient and often declining wages for workers in general. Student organizations became particularly politicized in Congo-Kinshasa, leading to violent clashes with security forces. On May 11, 1990, at least twelve (though some estimates go as high as 150) students at Lubumbashi University were killed when members of Mobutu's Special Presidential Division attacked the dormitories of students who had led a series of antigovernment protests. In response to this and other acts of government repression, students formed an umbrella organization, the *Union Progressiste des Etudiants Zairois* (UPEZA, Progressive Union of Zairian Students), that together with a variety of independent union groups regularly launched public demonstrations and one-day strikes known as *villes mortes* (dead cities).

Religious groups and organizations also emerged as vocal elements of civil society.[55] In the case of Congo-Kinshasa, the Catholic Church and particularly local Catholic bishops took the lead in advocating for the transformation of the Congolese state.[56] In April 1990, a letter addressed to Mobutu and signed by twelve Congolese Catholic bishops was made public. In this letter the bishops denounced the Mobutu regime as the "principal cause" of paralysis in governance and the intensifying crisis of the Congolese state. The letter marked a shift in the Catholic church's historic position of remaining removed from politics to one in which church leaders spoke out against injustices within the political system.[57] Indeed, several Congolese religious figures, most notably Archbishop Monsengwo Pasyina, sought to position themselves as "honest-brokers" in negotiations between the Mobutu regime and other portions of civil society seeking to transform the Congolese state.[58]

An important component of the resurgence of civil society was the formation and expansion of opposition political parties, particularly after single-party regimes had become thoroughly discredited by their decline in Eastern Europe and the former Soviet Union at the end of the 1980s (see Chapter 12). In the case of Congo-Kinshasa, the leading opposition party, the *Union pour la Démocratie et le Progrès Social* (UDPS, Union for Democracy and Social Progress), was formed in 1981 by thirteen members of the National Assembly and headed by Etienne Tshisekedi. Although the party was banned and its members ultimately jailed or co-opted into the ruling MPR, it reemerged in 1990 under the leadership of Tshisekedi after Mobutu bowed to political pressure and allowed for the creation of opposition political parties. Dozens of new parties appeared literally overnight. One year later, Tshisekedi oversaw the creation of an opposition coalition, the *Union Sacrée de l'Opposition Radicale* (USOR, Sacred Union of Radical Opposition), comprised of the UDPS and the vast majority of new political parties opposed to the Mobutu regime.

Opposition politicians sought to force the Mobutu regime into taking part in a "national conference": an extended national gathering of leaders from the state and civil society that debates the outlines of a new democratic order (see Chapter 12). Although such a conference was sporadically convened between August 1991 and December 1992, it largely failed in its overall objective, due primarily to Mobutu's continued co-optation of significant portions of its membership. The national conference nonetheless succeeded in further expanding Congo-Kinshasa's political space, and cemented Tshisekedi's role as the leader of that portion of the political opposition seeking peaceful change in Congo-Kinshasa.

Intensification of Domestic Violence and Conflict

A final dimension of the crisis of the African state was the state's inability to contain the intensification of domestic violence and conflict. In the case of

Congo-Kinshasa, the almost routine manner in which the military and other portions of the coercive apparatus preyed on civil society had created an atmosphere of fear and distrust, even among foreign diplomats who are normally exempt from these types of practices. As explained by Helen Winternitz, who visited Congo-Kinshasa during the 1980s, a common form of harassment involved the creation of roadblocks to extort money from motorists, under the pretense of checking the validity of driver's licenses and vehicle paperwork:

> Better not to be grabbed at all, which is the strategy the American Embassy recommends to its staff. It issues a manual to arriving Americans that tells them never to roll down the windows of their cars when they are stopped by police officials and never to hand over their driver's licenses or travel documents. They are to show their papers through a rolled up window and from behind a locked door. The gendarmes are known for robbing with impunity not only on the city streets but also at fraudulent roadblocks, where passage is granted for money or an impromptu gift, like a pack of cigarettes or a wristwatch.[59]

Despite Mobutu's periodic promises to rein in corruption and to punish those who went beyond the realm of acceptability, by the beginning of the 1990s his regime was increasingly incapable of asserting its authority in this realm, particularly because it could not adequately train, feed, or control its own military.

A second dimension of domestic violence and conflict included the periodic outbreak of spontaneous protests, riots, and uprisings. In September 1991, for example, nearly three thousand mutinous troops protesting the lack of pay touched off several days of violent riots and looting in Congo-Kinshasa's capital which quickly spread to regional capitals and cities, most notably in Shaba province, leaving thirty dead and more than 1,250 injured. The mutinous soldiers are said to have "systematically plundered" the most affluent areas of town.[60] "Expatriate observers described scenes of drunken soldiers driving around in cars stolen from dealerships, firing their weapons into the air indiscriminately," explains Winsome Leslie, a specialist of Congo-Kinshasa. "Ordinary citizens suffering economic hardship soon followed the soldiers, taking whatever they had left behind."[61] Fearful that the mobs were going to turn on Western nationals living within the country, approximately 1,750 French and Belgian troops intervened on September 24 (with the blessing of Mobutu) to ensure the evacuation of nearly eight thousand foreigners, including over seven hundred U.S. citizens. Another sign of the domestic conflict in Congo-Kinshasa was the inability of the Mobutu regime to successfully handle and contain the influx of Rwandan refugees beginning in 1994. The eastern provinces, especially Kivu, were overrun by Rwandans, especially Hutus, fleeing westward.

Similar to the sporadic outbursts of civil unrest and conflict that have occurred throughout Africa during the independence era, the 1991 riots in

BOX 10.2

REBUILDING TRUST: SOUTH AFRICA'S
TRUTH AND RECONCILIATION COMMISSION

Numerous countries have grappled with the dilemma of how best to heal the psychological, emotional, and political wounds left behind by state-sponsored atrocities against their own peoples, and in the process rebuild trust between the state and civil society. In the aftermath of World War II, the victorious Allies held the Nuremberg trials to prosecute Nazi war criminals who had committed crimes against humanity. Other forms of reckoning with the past have included the purging of discredited elites, the granting of blanket amnesties, offering compensation to victims and their families, and the construction of national monuments.

In the case of South Africa, a political consensus supported the creation of a **Truth and Reconciliation Commission** as the best vehicle for overcoming forty-six years of violence between the apartheid state of South Africa (1948–94) and a variety of liberation movements led by the African National Congress (ANC). Headed by Archbishop Desmond Tutu, a Nobel Peace Prize laureate, the commission was given a triple mandate: (1) uncover the truth concerning human rights abuses committed between March 1, 1960, and the inauguration of Nelson Mandela as president of South Africa on May 10, 1994; (2) bestow amnesty upon those owning up to and asking forgiveness for their politically motivated crimes; and (3) assess and provide reparations to the victims of those human rights abuses. The actual process was relatively simple and straightforward. Those requesting amnesty provided sworn testimony in a public hearing, including responses to questions by members of the commission and victims and their families. The commission subsequently used the power of subpoena to pursue additional corroborating evidence.

The testimony of victims and perpetrators alike produced tearful, shocking, and gruesome revelations. Extensive documentation has now become public as to how state security officers routinely extracted confessions through a variety of grisly techniques, such as the attachment of electrodes to a prisoner's genitals or the administering of the "black bag," the use of a tightly wrapped cloth to repeatedly bring a prisoner to the brink of asphyxiation. Former opponents of the apartheid state have similarly confessed to their involvement in the execution of informants, most notably by the use of "necklacing," in which a automobile tire doused in gasoline is wedged around the informant's body and set on fire.

The commission was not without controversy. The family of Steve Biko, a famous antiapartheid activist who founded the Black Consciousness Movement and whose life is documented in the celebrated movie, "Cry Freedom," successfully challenged the applications of five officers whose actions led to Biko's death while in police custody in 1977. The Biko family and others whose family members were murdered by agents of the apartheid state understandably desired those petitioning for an official pardon to be tried for murder and sentenced accordingly in a criminal court. In short, they do not recognize the right of the commission to pardon those responsible for murder.

Defenders of the commission's work countered that the issue of amnesty, however flawed, constituted a necessary political compromise that allowed for a peaceful transition to democracy in South Africa. "We could have chosen the revolution and overthrow route, but we chose the negotiations route," notes Dullah Omar, an ANC member of the South African parliament, "and that means having to live and work with and rebuild the country together with people who have treated us very badly in the past and against whom we have very strong feelings." Defenders also noted that the public chronicling of past abuses represented an important first step in healing a nation still seriously divided by racial and ethnic differences. "It is important that victims be allowed to tell their stories; survivors often feel misunderstood and ignored, their sacrifice unacknowledged, their pain unrecognized, and their identity destroyed," explains Lyn S. Graybill. "Reconciliation requires that there be some general agreement between both sides as to the wrongs committed."

Quotations are drawn from Lyn S. Graybill, "South Africa's Truth and Reconciliation Commission: Ethical and Theological Perspectives," *Ethics and International Affairs* 12 (1998):43–62. See also Truth and Reconciliation Commission, *Truth and Reconciliation Commission of South Africa Report* (5 vols.), (New York: Grove, 1999); and the Truth and Reconciliation Commission's homepage: <http://www.truth.org.za/back/bill.htm>.

Congo-Kinshasa were directed at neither explicit political goals nor the issue of regime change.[62] They were instead triggered by one disgruntled portion of the state — the Congolese military — over a specific economic concern: the lack of pay. These riots nonetheless represented a turning point in Congolese political history, in that they represented the beginning of a growing spiral of lawlessness and civil conflict. In 1993, for example, renewed rioting led to pitched battles in several cities between loyalist and dissident portions of the Congolese military. These battles resulted in the deaths of more than three hundred citizens, including the newly appointed French ambassador, who was killed by a stray bullet.

An especially threatening form of domestic conflict, from the perspective of the state, was the rise and spread of guerrilla insurgencies intent on reordering state-society relations by force. The contemporary independence era has witnessed four types of insurgencies.[63] First and foremost, **liberation insurgencies** were directed against colonial empires unwilling to cede power peacefully, as well as against white minority regimes in Southern Africa (see Chapter 6). Other guerrilla groups sought greater rights for specific regions of already independent nation-states. In the extreme, such **separatist insurgencies** sought the secession and ultimate recognition of their territories as independent nation-states within the international system. Although another group of **reform insurgencies** sought to maintain the territorial integrity of existing nation-states, their leaders were nonetheless committed to overthrowing existing regimes and reordering state-society relations. A fourth group, best referred to as **warlord insurgencies**, lacked a coherent vision of the future beyond the more immediate goal of overthrowing the regime in power. Such insurgencies were usually unable to reestablish centralized states after achieving victory, often leading to the continuation of conflict among competing warlords and their respective armies.

Beginning in 1996, a reform insurgency led by Laurent-Désiré Kabila, a guerrilla fighter who had taken part in a series of insurgencies during the 1960s, threatened the Mobutu regime. Kabila's guerrilla forces, the *Alliance des Forces Démocratiques pour la Libération* (AFDL, Alliance of Democratic Forces for Liberation), originated in eastern Congo-Kinshasa and received the strong backing of neighboring countries, including weapons from the Ugandan regime of Yoweri Museveni and troops from the Rwandan regime of Paul Kagame and the Angolan regime of José Eduardo dos Santos. The AFDL was able to capitalize on widespread public dissatisfaction with the Mobutu regime and the decay of the Congolese state, particularly the highly corrupt and incapable coercive apparatus. The Congolese Armed Forces had neither the financial resources nor the organizational capacity to mount a defense against either domestic or foreign foes. The AFDL therefore was able to advance westward across Congo-Kinshasa with almost lightning speed. Confronted with an impending guerrilla victory, Mobutu and his family fled to Côte d'Ivoire on May 15, 1997. Two days later, Kabila's forces entered Kinshasa and in so doing ended nearly twenty-seven years of dictatorship under the Mobutu regime.

Toward a State-Society Balance?

The most important outcome associated with the crisis of the African state was the emergence of efforts to restructure state-society relationships during the 1990s. The crisis of the African state had clearly demonstrated that highly authoritarian and centralized states were ineffective managers of Africa's economic, political, and social systems. It also highlighted the rising importance of African civil societies. As was the case just prior to their marginalization in the immediate postindependence era, African civil societies had played limited, but important, roles in the downfall of authoritarian African states during the 1990s, and expected to wield equal or greater levels of influence in their newly restructured societies. The international dimension had also changed with the Cold War's end. African leaders could no longer count on the diplomatic, financial, or even military support of foreign powers to compensate for the African state's increased inability to manage its economic, political, and military affairs.

Whether a new generation of African leadership will be successful in refashioning state-society relationships that will both foster and reinforce an economic and political renaissance on the African continent has emerged as a topic of considerable debate.[64] Skeptics note, for example, that Kabila's actions in the aftermath of overthrowing the Mobutu regime in 1997 do not bode well for the future of creating more equitable state-society relations.[65] Rather than establishing democratic practices and setting a timetable for national elections, Kabila's victory ushered in a new dictatorship that has failed to resolve the crisis of the Congolese state. In a series of moves that harkened back to the rise of authoritarianism under the Mobutu regime, the Kabila regime banned all opposition party activity, arrested several leading opposition political figures, including sending Tshisekedi into internal exile, banned leading human rights organizations, and arrested journalists who severely criticized the new regime.[66] Kabila's actions suggest a desire to re-create, rather than reformulate, the state-society relationships that existed under Mobutu. In an ironic but not surprising twist of fate, the Kabila regime as of 1999 has found itself confronted with a guerrilla insurgency in the eastern provinces that is funded by Kabila's former military benefactors of Uganda and Rwanda.

There are, however, other situations where new conceptualizations of state-society relations are making a difference. One form of restructuring has been implemented by a group of victorious guerrilla leaders, often referred to as the **new bloc of African leaders**, who have succeeded in overthrowing their discredited states through their leadership of strong, disciplined, and battle-tested guerrilla armies.[67] Among the leaders included in this group are Issaias Afwerki of Eritrea, Meles Zenawi of Ethiopia, Yoweri Museveni of Uganda, and Paul Kagame of Rwanda. Each of these leaders share a common belief in creating "responsible and accountable" state-society relationships that are, at least in principle, based on a commitment to the free-market economy, the reduction of corruption at all levels of governance, observance of the rule of law, and the creation of a disciplined security apparatus. However, this new bloc of leaders also tends to view the creation of multiparty democracy as a "luxury" that must take a back seat to the promotion of political-military stability and socioeconomic development. In the case of Uganda, for example, Museveni's regime has instituted a "no-party" system, which prohibits political candidates from campaigning under the banner of opposition parties (see Box 12.1, Chapter 12). As a result, this bloc of leaders increasingly finds itself criticized by dissident elements of civil society, as well as by sympathetic international observers who question the long-term wisdom of stifling political dissent.

A second form of state-society restructuring that has fostered a tremendous amount of debate revolves around Ethiopia's ethnically based federal system.[68] In 1991, after nearly thirty years of civil war, the Ethiopian People's Revolutionary Democratic Front (EPRDF) overthrew a highly authoritarian and centralized state that had been ruled by the U.S.-supported monarchy of Emperor

Haile Selassie (1930–74) and the Soviet-supported Marxist regime of Mengistu Haile Mariam (1974–91). The EPRDF leadership firmly believed that the highly centralized, authoritarian state of both the Selassie and Mengistu years was the principal contributor to the rise and intensification of ethnic hatreds and polarizing tendencies. A crucial outcome of this overthrow was the determination of Eritrean leaders to field a guerrilla army that not only contributed to the ultimate defeat of the Mengistu regime, but ensured the eventual independence of the Eritrean province. In a referendum in May 1993, 99.8 percent of all Eritreans voted in favor of independence (see Chapter 6). The EPRDF leadership believed that the only way to "save" the remaining portions of the multiethnic Ethiopian state was to create a federal system comprised of twelve ethnically based local states and two autonomous cities. Although critics have argued that such an arrangement will further polarize ethnic politics as ethnic leaders compete for federal resources, proponents have countered that further separatist tendencies have been quelled. This experiment in ethnically based federalism has been marred by the authoritarian practices of the Tigrean People's Liberation Front (TPLF), the political-military core of the EPRDF, which controls both the presidency and 88 percent of the seats in the Council of People's Representatives, the national legislature.

The most comprehensive example of state-society restructuring is the continued transformation of South Africa's former apartheid system into a multiracial and multiethnic democratic political system.[69] The historic turning point in this process was Nelson Mandela's victory in 1994 as the first president of South Africa elected by a majority vote. Prior to 1994, South Africa had been ruled by a white minority regime that instituted unequal racial, social, and political segregation. As part of the democratization process, South Africans were challenged to confront their collective past and to create a democratic culture of forgiveness through involvement in the public hearings of the Truth and Reconciliation Commission (see Box 10.2). Subsequent negotiations and debates among all the major political parties resulted in the adoption of a new constitutional framework in February 1997, which enshrined the separation of powers between the executive, legislative, and judicial branches of the federal government; the creation of a three-tiered structure of governance in which specific powers are outlined for local municipalities, nine provincial governments, and the federal government; and a bill of rights detailing an extensive array of political, economic, and social rights for the individual and civil society. Although the constitution recognizes the importance of protecting the "cultural" rights of individual racial and ethnic groups, the federal system is nonetheless "unitary" in that representation is not based on race or ethnicity.

South Africa's carefully crafted state-society balance is nonetheless threatened by dramatically rising crime levels and the continued poverty of a large portion of the nation's population. Constitutional guarantees of political freedoms may mean very little to working parents who cannot safely walk about their townships or earn enough money to move their families out of poverty. Indeed, the suggestion that the new constitution will eventually evolve into a living testament to the multiracial and multiethnic ideals of the African National Congress (ANC) misses the crucial point associated with political transition and the restructuring of state-society relations through constitutional means: the vast majority of South Africa's population *expects* and *demands* immediate rewards and benefits to make up for the past injustices of the apartheid system.[70] "However it evolves, it seems safe to conclude that the [South African] constitution nonetheless provides a solid basis for representative, transparent, and accountable governance, with meaningful protection and promotion of fundamental rights," explained a report of Carnegie Foundation's Commission on Preventing Deadly Conflict. "As such, it does hold promise as an inspiration for other countries in transition, particularly those that are attempting to build viable state-society coalitions under conditions of diverse cultures, deep economic disparities, and limited political authority and financial resources."[71]

Key Terms

African state
African civil society
state-society relationship
crisis of the African state
great expectations–minimal
    capabilities paradox
Africanization of state institutions
parastatals
nationalization
marketing board
civil society
exit option
family reunification program
diversity immigration lottery
coercive apparatus
personal rule networks

patron-client relationship
predatory state
lame Leviathan
shadow state
petty corruption
kleptocracy
social goods
génération sacrifiée (sacrificed
    generation)
informal economies
Truth and Reconciliation Commission
liberation insurgencies
separatist insurgencies
reform insurgencies
warlord insurgencies
new bloc of African leaders

For Further Reading

Bayart, Jean-François, Stephen Ellis, and Béatrice Hibou. *The Criminalization of the State in Africa*. Oxford: James Currey, 1999.

Bayart, Jean-François. *The State in Africa: The Politics of the Belly*. London: Longman, 1993.

Chabal, Patrick, and Jean-Pascol Daloz. *Africa Works: Disorder as Political Instrument*. London: James Currey, 1999.

Clapham, Christopher, ed. *African Guerrillas*. Oxford: James Currey, 1998.

Fatton, Robert. *Predatory Rule: State and Civil Society in Africa*. Boulder: Lynne Rienner, 1992.

Harbeson, John W., Donald Rothchild, and Naomi Chazan, eds. *Civil Society and the State in Africa*. Boulder: Lynne Rienner, 1994.

Jackson, Robert H., and Carl G. Rosberg. *Personal Rule in Black Africa: Prince, Autocrat, Prophet, Tyrant*. Berkeley: University of California Press, 1982.

Joseph, Richard, ed. *State, Conflict and Democracy in Africa*. Boulder: Lynne Rienner, 1998.

Olukoshi, Adebayo O., and Liisa Laakso, eds. *Challenges to the Nation-State in Africa*. Helsinki: Institute of Development Studies, 1996.

Osaghae, Eghosa, ed. *Between State and Civil Society in Africa: Perspectives on Development*. Dakar: CODESRIA, 1994.

Parpart, Jane L., and Kathleen A. Staudt, eds. *Women and the State in Africa*. Boulder: Lynne Rienner, 1990.

Reno, William. *Warlord Politics and African States*. Boulder: Lynne Rienner, 1998.

Rothchild, Donald, and Naomi Chazan, eds. *The Precarious Balance: State and Society in Africa*. Boulder: Westview, 1988.

Villalón, Leonardo, and Phillip Huxtable, eds. *The African State at a Critical Juncture: Between Disintegration and Reconfiguration*. Boulder: Lynne Rienner, 1998.

Young, Crawford. *The African Colonial State in Comparative Perspective*. New Haven: Yale University Press, 1994.

Notes

1. See Crawford Young, *The African Colonial State in Comparative Perspective* (New Haven: Yale University Press, 1994), p. 1.
2. The discussion of Congo-Kinshasa primarily draws on Crawford Young and Thomas Turner, *The Rise and Decline of the Zairian State* (Madison: University of Wisconsin Press, 1985). See also Winsome J. Leslie, *Zaire: Continuity and Political Change in an Oppressive State* (Boulder: Westview, 1993); Thomas M. Callaghy, *The State-Society Struggle: Zaire in Comparative Perspective* (New York: Columbia University Press, 1984); Michael G. Schatzberg, *The Dialectics of Oppression in Zaire* (Bloomington: Indiana University Press, 1988); and Nzongola-Ntalaja, ed., *The Crisis of Zaire: Myths and Realities* (Trenton: Africa World, 1986).
3. Patrick Boyle, "A View From Zaire," *World Politics*, 60, no. 2 (1988):270.
4. See Young and Turner, *Rise and Decline*, pp. 43, 65, 68, 117.
5. *Ibid.*, pp. 326–50.
6. See Irving Leonard Markovitz, "Bureaucratic Development and Economic Growth," *Journal of Modern African Studies*, 14, no. 2 (1970):183–200, as

cited in Naomi Chazan et al., *Politics and Society in Contemporary Africa* (Boulder: Lynne Rienner, 1992), p. 55.

7. Young and Turner, *Rise and Decline,* pp. 350–62.
8. *Ibid.,* pp. 40–42.
9. *Ibid.,* p. 55.
10. *Ibid.,* p. 59.
11. *Ibid.,* pp. 54–55.
12. *Ibid.,* p. 192.
13. See Donald Rothchild and Naomi Chazan, eds., *The Precarious Balance: State and Society in Africa* (Boulder: Westview, 1988).
14. Young and Turner, *Rise and Decline,* p. 56.
15. *Ibid.,* p. 57.
16. *Ibid.,* p. 67.
17. *Ibid.,* p. 68.
18. U.S. Arms Control and Disarmament Agency, *World Military Expenditures and Arms Trade 1963–1973* (Washington: U.S. Government Printing Office, 1975), p. 16, as quoted in Chazan et al., *Politics and Society,* p. 58.
19. Young and Turner, *Rise and Decline,* p. 267.
20. *Ibid.,* p. 273.
21. See Peter J. Schraeder, *United States Foreign Policy toward Africa: Incrementalism, Crisis and Change* (Cambridge: Cambridge University Press, 1994), ch. 3. See also Michael G. Schatzberg, *Mobutu or Chaos? The United States and Zaire, 1960–1990* (Lanham: University Press of America, 1991).
22. See Robert H. Jackson and Carl G. Rosberg, *Personal Rule in Black Africa: Prince, Autocrat, Prophet, Tyrant* (Berkeley: University of California Press, 1984).
23. See J. C. Williame, *Patrimonialism and Political Change in the Congo* (Stanford: Stanford University Press, 1972). See also Jackson and Rosberg, *Personal Rule in Black Africa,* pp. 167–81; and Young and Turner, *Rise and Decline,* ch. 6.
24. Quoted in Young and Turner, *Rise and Decline,* p. 169.
25. *Ibid.,* p. 166.
26. *Ibid.,* p. 165.
27. See Leonardo Villalón and Phillip Huxtable, eds., *The African State at a Critical Juncture* (Boulder: Lynne Rienner, 1998).
28. Robert Fatton, *Predatory Rule: State and Civil Society in Africa* (Boulder: Lynne Rienner, 1992).
29. Thomas Callaghy, "The State as Lame Leviathan: The Patrimonial Administrative State in Africa," in Zaki Ergas, ed., *The African State in Transition* (Basingstoke: Macmillan, 1987), pp. 87–116.
30. William Reno, *Corruption and State Politics in Sierra Leone* (Cambridge: Cambridge University Press, 1995).
31. John Ravenhill, "A Second Decade of Adjustment: Greater Complexity, Greater Uncertainty, " in Thomas M. Callaghy and John Ravenhill, eds., *Hemmed In:*

Responses to Africa's Economic Decline (New York: Columbia University Press, 1993), p. 18.

32. *Ibid.*

33. Young and Turner, *Rise and Decline,* p. 307.

34. *Ibid.,* p. 307.

35. *Ibid.,* p. 71.

36. *Ibid.,* p. 94.

37. David J. Gould, *Bureaucratic Corruption and Underdevelopment in the Third World: The Case of Zaire* (New York: Pergamon, 1980), p. xiv.

38. *Ibid.,* p. xiii.

39. John F. Clark, "Zaire: The Bankruptcy of the Extractive State," in Villalón and Huxtable, eds., *The African State at a Critical Juncture,* pp. 109–25.

40. *Ibid.,* p. 116.

41. *Ibid.*

42. Leslie, *Zaire,* p. 116.

43. William Reno, "Sovereignty and Personal Rule in Zaire," *African Studies Quarterly* 1, no. 3 (1997):5.

44. Leslie, *Zaire,* p. 116.

45. See Patrick M. Boyle, "Class Formation and Civil Society: The Politics of Education in Sub-Saharan Africa," forthcoming.

46. See Crawford Young, "Zaire: The Shattered Illusion of the Integral State," *The Journal of Modern African Studies* 32, no. 2 (1994):247–63.

47. See William Reno, *Warlord Politics and African States* (Boulder: Lynne Rienner, 1998).

48. See Christopher Clapham, *Africa and the International System: The Politics of State Survival* (Cambridge: Cambridge University Press, 1996).

49. Janet MacGaffey, *The Real Economy of Zaire: The Contribution of Smuggling and Other Unofficial Activities to National Wealth* (Philadelphia: University of Pennsylvania Press, 1991), p. 12.

50. *Ibid.,* p. 23.

51. *Ibid.,* p. 19.

52. *Ibid.,* pp. 49–50.

53. Thomas M. Callaghy, "The Ritual Dance of the Debt Game," *Africa Report* (September–October 1984):22–26.

54. See John W. Harbeson, Donald Rothchild, and Naomi Chazan, eds., *Civil Society and the State in Africa* (Boulder: Lynne Rienner, 1994).

55. For example, see Jeff Haynes, *Religion and Politics in Africa* (London: Zed, 1996).

56. Patrick M. Boyle, "Beyond Self-Protection to Prophecy: The Catholic Church and Political Change in Zaire," *Africa Today* (1992):49–66. See also Boyle, "School Wars: Church, State, and the Death of the Congo," *The Journal of Modern African Studies* 33, no. 3 (1995):451–68.

57. Patrick M. Boyle, "Bishops as Brokers: Ecclesiastics, Political Reform, and Regime Transitions in Sub-Saharan Africa," unpublished paper.

58. *Ibid.*

59. Helen Winternitz, *East along the Equator* (New York: Atlantic Monthly, 1987), p. 19, quoted in Leslie, *Zaire,* pp. 44–45.

60. *Ibid.*, p. 45.

61. *Ibid.*

62. For a discussion, see Michael Bratton and Nicolas van de Walle, *Democratic Experiments in Africa: Regime Transitions in Comparative Perspective* (Cambridge: Cambridge University Press, 1997), pp. 101–103.

63. See Clapham, *Africa and the International System,* pp. 208–44.

64. For example, see Jeffrey Herbst, "Responding to State Failure in Africa," *International Security* 21, no. 3 (Winter 1996–97):120–44; Richard Joseph and Jeffrey Herbst, "Correspondence: Responding to State Failure in Africa," *International Security* 22, no. 2 (Fall 1997):175–84.

65. For example, see Michael G. Schatzberg, "Beyond Mobutu: Kabila and the Congo," *Journal of Democracy* 8, no. 4 (1997):70–84.

66. See Peter Rosenblum, "Kabila's Congo," *Current History* 97, no. 619 (1998): 193–99.

67. See Don Connell and Frank Smyth, "Africa's New Bloc," *Foreign Affairs* 77, no. 2 (March–April 1998):80–94.

68. See Kidane Mengisteab, "New Approaches to State Building in Africa: The Case of Ethiopia's Ethnic-Based Federalism," *African Studies Review* 40, 3 (1997):111–32; John Young, "Ethnicity and Power in Ethiopia," *Review of African Political Economy* 70 (1996):531–42; and Walle Engedayehu, "Ethiopia: Democracy and the Politics of Ethnicity," *Africa Today* 40, no. 2 (1993):29–52.

69. John Stremlau (with the cooperation of Helen Zille), *A House No Longer Divided: Progress and Prospects for Democratic Peace in South Africa* (Washington: Carnegie Corporation of New York, 1997).

70. See Michael Bratton, "After Mandela's Miracle in South Africa," *Current History* 97, no. 619 (1998):214–19.

71. *Ibid.*, p. 17.

11

Military Coups d'Etat
and Military Governance

Senegalese military in the Casamance region of Senegal.

AFRICAN MILITARIES EMERGED from the shadows of obscurity during the 1950s to become one of the most important institutional actors in African politics and society. The primary means for African military personnel to achieve power and influence over their respective political systems was the **military coup d'état**: the sudden and illegal overthrow of an existing government by a portion of the state's armed forces. By the end of the 1960s, military leaders had launched over twenty-five successful coups, ushering in a period of militarization that soon left more than 50 percent of all African countries governed by military regimes. Even in cases where they led their troops back to the barracks after turning over power to elected civilian regimes, military leaders maintained — and often enhanced — their newfound levels of political influence. Once having enjoyed the fruits of power, military leaders, often referred to as the **men on horseback** or **leaders in khaki**, were prone to return to presidential mansions in later coups, leading foreign observers to characterize African militaries as the primary forces for change throughout the African continent. By the end of the 1980s, however, the emergence of pro-democracy movements and several successful transitions to democracy led to a rebirth of civilian regimes intent on permanently returning African militaries to their barracks. The primary purpose of this chapter is to examine the nature and evolution of military intervention in African politics and society.

Trends in Military Coups d'Etat

Scholars initially overlooked the role of the military in African politics and society during the initial decade of the contemporary independence era. At the time of independence, the militaries inherited by newly elected African leaders were usually very small and lacked sophisticated weapons, such as armored vehicles, combat aircraft, and guided missile systems.[1] African militaries were therefore more symbols of sovereignty and independence than independent actors capable of significantly influencing their respective political systems. Most African militaries played little if any role in the largely peaceful decolonization process during the initial independence decade of the 1950s. Even after a series of coups overthrew five civilian governments from 1958 to 1965, scholars perceived these events as mere aberrations from the expected consolidation of multiparty democracies.[2]

An early inkling that the so-called aberrations were becoming the norm of African politics occurred in 1966, when military coups overthrew eight civilian regimes, ranging from the monarchy of King Ntare V of Burundi to the multiparty democracy of Prime Minister Abubakar Tafawa Balewa of Nigeria. From this point forward, scholars and analysts took serious note of the explosion of military involvement. According to one authoritative study, the first thirty-five years (1951–85) of the contemporary independence era witnessed 131 attempted military coups, of which 60 (46 percent) were successful. If one also includes reported **military plots** in which coup leaders were arrested

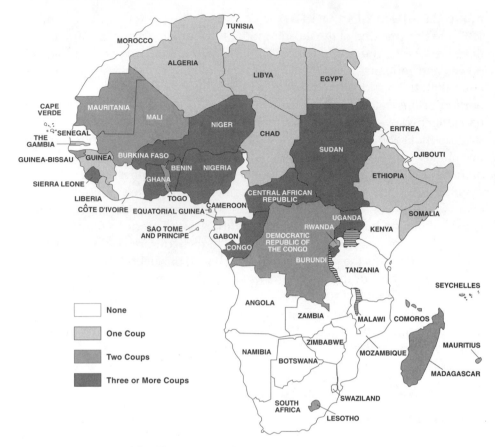

MAP 11.1   Successful Military Coups d'Etat

before they were able to launch any sort of military action, the total number of attempted coups during this same period rises to 257, and the success/failure ratio changes to 23 percent and 77 percent.[3]

The prevalence of military coups is graphically demonstrated in Map 11.1. Most African countries have experienced at least one successful military coup, and several have experienced two or more. The record for the greatest number of successful military coups (six) is jointly held by Benin, Burkina Faso, and Nigeria. The pervasiveness of military leaders as the principal agents of regime change is demonstrated by the unfolding of eighty-three successful military coups from 1951 to 1999. Only six African countries — Botswana, Djibouti, Cape Verde, Eritrea, Namibia, and South Africa — have never faced armed challenges (successful or unsuccessful) from their military, police, or other security personnel.

The majority of coups share several characteristics. First, military leaders have been able to intervene successfully within their respective political systems, due to the weak nature of the African state in the immediate postindependence era (see Chapter 10). Weak state power was often exacerbated by the rise to power of illegitimate leaders, whose corrupt and authoritarian practices led to widening gaps between the self-interested policies of incumbent regimes and the needs and demands of their respective populations. Indeed, regardless of regime type (e.g., monarchical, democratic, or authoritarian) or ideology (capitalist, socialist, or Marxist), African states increasingly incapable of responding to their citizens fell prey to military leaders professing a special capability to undertake political-military reforms and socioeconomic development.

African coups are also similar in the sense that they are usually carried out by members of African armies as opposed to other branches of the armed services, such as the air force or the navy. The primary reason for this similarity is that African navies and air forces are usually the smallest and most poorly equipped branches of African militaries, therefore lacking both the capability and the prestige to carry out a coup that can garner the support of officers within the army. The only exceptions to this general rule are the successful coups in Ghana in 1979 and 1981 that were led by Air Force Flight Lieutenant Jerry Rawlings, and the unsuccessful military bid for power in Kenya in 1982 that was led by the Air Force. No African country has ever experienced a coup led by naval personnel.

A third similarity involves what can be termed **coups of descending order**. The first coup that occurs within a country is usually led by the most senior members of the military establishment, most notably generals, who command the respect of lower-ranking military officers. Once they assume control of the political system, however, their refusal to relinquish the perks of their new-found political power often leads to grumbling within the lower ranks. The lower-ranking officers often regard their commanders as pursuing a lifestyle as bad as, if not worse than, their deposed civilian counterparts. The response is a **palace coup** in which the senior commanders are overthrown by junior officers who, after assuming power, can fall prey to yet another coup by even lower ranking officers. In the case of Burkina Faso, for example, President Maurice Yaméogo was overthrown in 1966 by Lieutenant Colonel Sangoulé Lamizana, who in turn was overthrown by Colonel Sayé Zerbo in 1980. Zerbo was overthrown by noncommissioned officers in 1982, followed by three further coups led by Major General Jean Baptiste Ouedraogo (1983), Captain Thomas Sankara (1983), and Captain Blaise Compaoré (1987). In each of these cases senior officers were overthrown by other officers of lower or equal rank.

The **contagion effect** constitutes a fourth common characteristic of military coups.[4] The underlying principle of this phenomenon is that once a coup occurs in one country, there exists a greater possibility of a coup taking place in a neighboring country. As in the case of a contagious illness, military leaders are affected by the activities of their neighbors, and perhaps become emboldened by the thought: "If *they* can do it, so can we!" This trend also holds true in terms of successive coups within a single country. Once the military intervenes against civilian leaders, military leaders become much more confident and willing to pursue similar actions in the future.

Role of the Military in Political Governance

The range of military involvement in African politics and society is best characterized as a **continuum of civil-military relations**, in which each successive model represents a greater degree of military influence over civilian politicians. Drawing on the work of J. Gus Liebenow, one can distinguish between five specific models of civil-military relations (see Figure 11.1).[5]

Civilian Supremacy Model

At one extreme is the **civilian supremacy model**, in which the military is firmly under the control of civilian politicians. "Essentially," explains Liebenow, "the civilian supremacy model requires that civilians, rather than the military, control decision making with respect to the issue of war and peace, the determination of the size and general shape of the military establishment, the basic methods of recruiting both officers and enlisted personnel, the allocation of major privileges and rewards within the service, and, most important, the allocation of government revenues for the funding of all military and paramilitary activities."[6] This is the model adhered to and promoted by the northern industrialized democracies.

Botswana offers the most clear-cut example of the civilian supremacy model.[7] Often referred to as Africa's "oldest democracy," Botswana did not create a national army until 1976, ten years after independence. The Botswana Defence Force (BDF) is headed by Lieutenant General Seretse Khama Ian Khama, the son of Botswana's first president, Sir Seretse Khama. Botswana's president is recognized by the constitution as commander in chief of the armed forces. He is responsible for appointing members to a civilian-dominated Defence Council, which also includes BDF Commander Khama as an *ex-officio* member. The Defence Council oversees all matters related to the military. The BDF constitutes a highly professional corps of officers and soldiers that has never militarily intervened in Botswana's domestic political system.

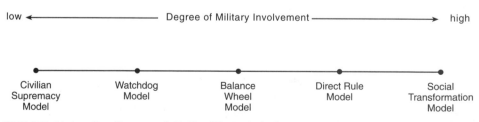

FIGURE 11.1 Continuum of Civil-Military Relations

Source: Derived from J. Gus Liebenow, *African Politics: Crises and Challenges* (Bloomington: Indiana University Press, 1986), pp. 250–54.

Watchdog Model

A second type of civil-military relations, known as the **watchdog model**, represents a greater degree of military intervention within the domestic political system.[8] Similar to the civilian supremacy model, the cornerstone of the watchdog model is the military's strong support for the supremacy of civilian rule. However, the officer corps perceives the military as the ultimate guarantor of democracy. As a result, military intervention in the domestic political arena, including the launching of a military coup, is considered acceptable if the country's democratic principles are threatened (e.g., a defeated incumbent refuses to step down after losing a democratically held election). The hallmark of this model is a short-term military intervention with a very specific objective in mind (e.g., ensuring that the victor in democratically held elections assumes office). According to this model, the restoration of democratic principles is followed by the military's swift return to the barracks.

A military coup in Mali in 1991 reflected the watchdog model.[9] A group of military officers headed by Lieutenant Colonel Amadou Toumani Touré (nicknamed "A.T.T.") took power after President Moussa Traoré's brutal suppression of a pro-democracy movement led to over one hundred deaths and seven hundred wounded. Touré's forces arrested President Traoré, formed a National Reconciliation Council, and pledged a return to democracy within one year. During the next twelve months, the military government convened a national conference that debated the outlines of a new democratic political system, conducted a national referendum on a new constitution, and oversaw the holding of legislative and presidential elections. After President Alpha Oumar Konaré assumed office on June 6, 1992, the Malian army returned to the barracks and Lieutenant Colonel Touré retired.

Balance Wheel Model

The military plays a stronger role in the **balance wheel model**, which constitutes a civil-military coalition.[10] Unlike the short-term and limited nature of military involvement under the watchdog model, military leaders under the balance wheel model proclaim that full decision-making authority is vested in the military. However, the military leaders have neither the interest nor the ability to staff individual ministries and government offices with military bureaucrats. As a result, the actual running of government ministries is left in the hands of civilian bureaucrats.

The military government of Liberia, led by Master Sergeant Samuel K. Doe from 1980 to 1986, is an example of the balance wheel model.[11] After seizing power through a military coup, Doe created a People's Redemption Council (PRC), which underscored the supreme authority of the new military government. As explained by Liebenow, who also is a specialist of Liberian politics, Doe's PRC had "no intentions of immediately returning to the barracks" in the aftermath of the 1980 coup.[12] "On the other hand, they recognized that they lacked the talents to perform the broad spectrum of duties which the Liberians had come to associate with the government," explains Liebenow. "This was signaled early by the co-optation of a number of prominent Liberian civilians to undertake many of the responsibilities with respect to economic development, foreign affairs, health delivery, and other governmental functions."[13]

Direct Rule Model

The military officers who adhere to the **direct rule model** of civil-military relations assume that the overthrown civilian leaders, including the heads of individual bureaucracies, are "creatures of their own pasts" and therefore incapable of providing adequate leadership for the country.[14] As a result, the new military leadership announces the establishment of direct rule, in which military officers assume responsibility for the day-to-day functioning of the central government, including individual bureaucracies and government agencies.

BOX 11.1

HIDDEN KILLERS:
LANDMINES IN AFRICA

Sometimes referred to as the "hidden killer" or the "maiming machine," the landmine remains one of the greatest scourges of African wars and civil conflicts. The International Campaign to Ban Landmines, corecipient of the 1997 Nobel Peace Prize with its director, Jody Williams, estimates that eighteen African countries are afflicted by the presence of thirty million landmines. The devastating impact of these weapons has been most strongly felt in Angola, where one in every 470 people is an amputee. Angola has earned the sad distinction of being the "amputee capital of the world."

The use of landmines is extremely popular among guerrillas seeking to overthrow existing governments. In addition to being relatively inexpensive ($3–$7), the landmine is a potent weapon that greatly restricts the freedom of movement of government troops. The sowing of landmines around villages and within crop-growing regions also exerts a heavy toll on the national economy. Farmers scared to plant or harvest their crops become the unwilling allies of guerrilla warfare.

The greatest scourge of landmines is that they remain hidden and lethal long after the combatants have settled their differences. In Mozambique, a country roughly twice the size of California, the 1992 peace accord ending three decades of civil war left one to two million landmines. Each month these hidden weapons on average maim and kill fifty innocent civilians, one-third of whom are women and children.

The government of President Joaquim Alberto Chissano has collaborated with the international donor community and the Mozambique Association for the Handicapped to launch several "de-mining" programs, including the creation of a school to train local specialists in the systematic clearing of mine-fields. Despite the best of intentions, such efforts are hampered by extraordinary costs (it is estimated that each mine costs $1,000 to remove), donor fatigue in the post–Cold War era, and the limited capacities of Mozambique's impoverished national economy. "The magnitude of the problem is staggering, and provides just one illustration why a return to normalcy in a landmined territory takes years if not decades," explains Isebill V. Gruhn. "Meanwhile, vehicles drive over unsafe tracks and people walk along mined pathways and fields, compounding the death toll and loss of limbs, and making villagers fearful of returning to their homes and farms."

Growing international pressures to eliminate the landmine threat prompted the ratification of an international treaty on landmines in December 1997. Signed by 125 countries, the treaty calls for a complete ban on the manufacture and sale of landmines, as well as the destruction of existing stockpiles. The treaty's effectiveness is hampered by the lack of support among important regional and global powers, such as China, India, Iran, and the United States, several of which are also major arms exporters. Approximately 68 percent (thirty-six) of all African countries have signed the treaty.

Discussion draws on Andrew Meldrum, "The Maiming Machines," *Africa Report* 40, no. 3 (May-June 1995):18–21; and Isebill V. Gruhn, "Land Mines: An African Tragedy," *The Journal of Modern African Studies* 34, no. 4 (1996):687–99.

The military government established in Nigeria in July 1966 by Lieutenant Colonel Yakabu Gowon offers an interesting example of this model.[15] Gowon favored portrayals of himself as the Abraham Lincoln of Nigeria, due to his successful management of the 1967–70 Nigerian civil war that preserved the federal union. At the end of the war, however, the vast majority of important administrative posts remained headed by military officers. The dramatic rise in state-controlled corruption, which resulted from the highly lucrative oil boom at the beginning of the 1970s, reinforced the desires of military officers to maintain control over the reins of power. Despite early assurances to swiftly return Nigeria to democratic rule, the transition process was continually delayed and finally indefinitely postponed in a major address to the nation on October 1, 1974. Gowon's military regime remained in power for a total of nine years, only to be overthrown by yet another military coup, led by Brigadier General Murtala Mohammed on July 29, 1975.

Social Transformation Model

A final form of civil-military relations, known as the **social transformation model**, is similar to that of direct rule in that military officers take charge of individual bureaucracies and government agencies.[16] However, this model represents an even greater level of military involvement, due to the explicit intentions of the new military leaders to seek the complete transformation of their country's socioeconomic and political systems. The military leaders who adopt this model are often driven by an ideology that differs from that of the displaced civilian elite. As a result, the military coup becomes the vehicle for the radical transformation of society, according to the military's understanding of the new ideology.

The emergence of a Marxist-inspired military regime in Ethiopia from 1974 to 1977 constitutes a clear-cut example of the social transformation model.[17] A series of mutinies within the Ethiopian Armed Forces over demands for higher pay and better living conditions led to the overthrow of Emperor Haile Selassie and his replacement by the Provisional Military Administrative Council (PMAC), a group of approximately 120 junior-grade and noncommissioned officers of the Ethiopian military who became known as the Derg. Factional infighting favored the emergence of Colonel Mengistu Haile Mariam, a self-proclaimed Marxist officer, as the unparalleled leader of Ethiopia. Among the radical steps undertaken by the Mengistu-led Derg in the months that followed were the execution of fifty-seven officials of the deposed monarchy, the creation of a single-party communist state, the nationalization of all financial institutions and major companies, and the initiation of a full-scale military offensive to end a guerrilla insurgency in the northern province of Eritrea. The military coup of 1974 served as the basis for a full-scale **revolution from above**, in which ideologically driven military leaders sought the complete transformation of Ethiopian society.

Myths Concerning the Effectiveness of Military Governance

Not surprisingly, African military leaders seek to justify their seizure of power and the institution of military rule. Most often these rationales are at best a misinterpretation of political and social realities, and at worst a thinly disguised attempt at obtaining and maintaining control over the reins of power. Indeed, the common assumption of African military leaders — that they as opposed to their civilian counterparts have more effectively governed during the contemporary independence era — is based on a variety of myths that have been strongly challenged by four decades of military governance. Drawing once again on the work of Liebenow, one can distinguish five sets of myths.[18]

Military Enjoys Greater Legitimacy

The first myth of military governance is that military leaders enjoy greater levels of legitimacy than their civilian counterparts.[19] The primary reason for this claim is the outpouring of public support that usually follows the military's assumption of power. It is important to note, however, that public support is usually not due to public preferences for military rule, nor the perception of military leaders as more effective rulers. To the contrary, the public often greets military intervention as a blessing due to strong disenchantment with the perceived shortcomings of civilian leadership. As a result, the public is willing to grant military leaders a brief "honeymoon period" in which to correct any deficiencies within the socioeconomic and political systems. The longer the military remains in power, however, the greater the likelihood that the honeymoon period will dissipate amidst popular demands for a return to civilian government.

In Somalia, public opinion overwhelmingly favored Major General Mohammed Siad Barre's seizure of power through a military coup on October 21, 1969.[20] In the days that followed, Siad created a Supreme Revolutionary Council (SRC) comprised of twenty-four military officers, replaced civilian leaders at the regional and local levels with military governors and district commissioners, and named senior military personnel to head Somalia's diplomatic missions abroad. Overwhelming popular support for the essentially **bloodless coup** was fostered by widespread dissatisfaction with the extremely corrupt practices of the civilian governments of the 1960–69 era. The civilian politicians, especially legislators of the National Assembly, were widely perceived as primarily driven by the self-interest of financial gain, while the nation's business and the national economy stagnated. Popular support for the military coup quickly subsided, however, as it became increasingly clear that the Siad regime had no intention of ever ceding political power to a new generation of civilian politicians. Rising disenchantment throughout the mid-1970s ultimately coalesced in the form of a ten-year guerrilla insurgency that succeeded in overthrowing the Siad regime in 1991.

Military Rule Is More Efficient

A second myth often posited by military leaders is that the very nature of military organization makes military rule more efficient than that of its civilian counterparts.[21] The core of this argument is that military personnel are members of a hierarchical chain of command and trained in discipline. Lower-ranking military personnel are expected to follow orders without question. This hierarchical structure theoretically allows military leaders to avoid the "inefficient compromises" of civilian governance. Even if one accepts the basic premise of the argument that military rule is efficient rule, most African militaries are incapable of staffing all civilian positions with adequately trained personnel. As a result, civil-military coalitions become the norm, and the presumably "inefficient" civilian politicians remain at various levels of governance. Even the most extreme form of military involvement within the political system requires some level of civilian participation.

The most serious contradiction associated with the "efficiency" argument is that the military's direct entry into the political system via military coup invariably politicizes that organization and makes it subject to the same political demands and shortcomings confronted by civilian politicians. In the simplest sense, the newfound access to the privileges associated with leadership, such as luxury housing and access to state wealth, almost invariably "creates a gulf between senior and junior grade officers as well as between officers and the rank and file."[22] It is precisely for this reason that one often witnesses coups of descending order, as more junior members of the military chain of command seek access to the privileges enjoyed by their superiors.

The corruption associated with the long series of coups and military regimes in Nigeria is but one counterpoint to military claims of greater efficiency.[23] In the aftermath of Major General Ibrahim Babangida's seizure of power in August 1985, official promises of prosecuting the corrupt civilian officials of the Second Republic "quietly evaporated" as military-dominated patterns of corruption steadily emerged.[24] According to Larry Diamond, a noted specialist in Nigerian politics and society, Babangida acquired the status of the "most massively corrupt ruler" in Nigerian political history.[25] "Numerous recipients and one-time insiders confirmed the pattern of largesse, and one former top-ranking officer and longtime associate of Babangida's claimed he entered the presidency with a net worth in the tens of millions of dollars from previous corruption in weapons purchases and other transactions," explains Diamond. "As in the Second Republic, foreign business leaders privately estimated the personal wealth of top [military] officials in the hundreds of millions, and objective evidence pointed to annual leakages of revenue in the billions of dollars, approximating 10 percent of the country's total annual output of goods and services!"[26] As is the case in both civilian and military regimes alike, however, the extreme corruption of Babangida's regime was a double-edged sword. "It oiled the wheels of a constantly whirring political machine, buying support, compliance, and alliances within and outside the military," explains Diamond. "But it also greatly intensified public alienation and revulsion toward the regime, the sense of acute injustice, the readiness to protest, and the need for [government] repression to suppress that protest (as well as any concrete exposure of what was happening)."[27]

Military Is Best Able to Maintain Stability

A third myth associated with military regimes is that they are better able than their civilian counterparts to maintain stability.[28] Militaries control and are trained in the use of the instruments of violence within society and are theoretically capable of ensuring stability by force. Even if one assumes that militaries are well-positioned in the short-term to take power and provide some semblance of stability, over time the military increasingly finds itself discredited and prone to the same types of attacks experienced by its civilian predecessors. The inherent problem associated with military rule is that long-term stability is not based on the military officer's natural tendency to ensure compliance through the use of force, but on the civilian politician's ability to create political compacts through the use of political bargaining. Political understandings imposed and maintained by the barrel of the gun are ultimately destined to fail.

The Ethiopian military regime (1974–91) headed by the Marxist Mengistu offers important insights into the inability of military-based regimes to maintain stability over the long term.[29] The primary pillar of Mengistu's dictatorship was one of the African continent's largest and best-equipped standing armies. By the end of the 1980s, over 500,000 troops maintained an impressive and extremely lethal military arsenal that included sophisticated fighter aircraft and thousands of tanks and other armored personnel carriers. However, the regime's reliance on force to promote its narrow political vision ultimately ensured the emergence and growing strength of antigovernment guerrilla insurgencies. A northern secessionist insurgency was led by the Eritrean People's Liberation Front (EPLF). Other, more ethnically dominated guerrilla groups committed to maintaining the territorial integrity of the Ethiopian state included the Tigrean People's Liberation Front (TPLF) and the Oromo Liberation Front (OLF). Together, these and other guerrilla groups formed a loose coalition of opposition forces, the Ethiopian People's Revolutionary Democratic Front (EPRDF), that succeeded in overthrowing the Mengistu regime on May 25, 1991. Ultimately, the largest military organization on the African continent was incapable of maintaining stability over the long term.

Military Constitutes a Better Unifying Structure

A fourth myth promoted by military leaders is that the military is more capable than its civilian counterparts of forging a national identity.[30] This argument is based on the assumption that the military constitutes one of the few (if not the only) national organizations inherited from the colonial era that socializes new recruits into serving the state regardless of their race or ethnicity. A sense of national identity presumably is forged due to the camaraderie associated with a common training experience, as well as the unifying mission of protecting the integrity of the state rather than serving an individual administration. In practice, however, African militaries historically have reflected the ethnic and racial divisions and conflicts of their larger societies. This shortcoming is primarily due to the tendency of the first generation of African leaders to employ recruits and officers from their personal ethnic or racial groups. The consequence of biased recruitment patterns is that African militaries in actuality promote societal competition and conflict, in the extreme leading to the complete breakdown of central authority along ethnic or racial lines.

The military dictatorship established in Liberia in 1980 by Master Sergeant Doe is an example of how African militaries become the focal points of ethnic conflict and contribute to ethnic fragmentation. After successfully leading a military coup against the popularly hated government of President William Tolbert, Doe ordered the purging of "distrustful" ethnic groups and their replacement with officers and recruits from his own Krahn ethnic group.[31] The ethnic tensions that resulted from the Krahn's newfound political status were aggravated in 1985 by further purges. In response to an attempted military coup primarily associated with the Mano and Gio ethnic groups, the Krahn-dominated military expelled their remaining numbers from the military and

BOX 11.2
FEMALE GUERRILLAS AFTER THE WARS

African women have served in combat roles in several successful guerrilla insurgencies during the contemporary era. One of the earliest examples of this phenomenon was the active involvement of female guerrillas in Algeria's nationalist war for independence against France at the end of the 1950s. Several years later in 1967, the military leaders of the Front for the Liberation of Mozambique (FRELIMO) created a female combat unit that served as the precursor of widespread female involvement in the guerrilla struggle against Portuguese colonialism in Mozambique. In these and other cases, however, the expectations of female guerrillas — that the common male-female struggle for independence would translate into a common male-female struggle against gender inequality in their respective societies — were not borne out. "Time and time again, a pattern has emerged where women play a significant role during the armed struggle," explains noted anthropologist Henrietta L. Moore, "but once the revolutionary government is installed, women's needs and interests fade from political agendas, and the political rhetoric fails to give rise to active programs for women's emancipation."

The evolution and aftermath of Eritrea's successful guerrilla struggle for independence from Ethiopia (1961–93) highlights evolving gender relations. The insurgency was led by the Eritrean People's Liberation Front (EPLF), which fully embraced the integration of women at all levels of the guerrilla struggle. Approximately 35 percent of the EPLF's active guerrilla fighters were women at the time of military victory in 1991. When the victorious guerrilla units marched into the capital on May 24, the female soldiers were reported to have been "treated with awe." "Teenage girls began to imitate their distinctive style," explained one account, "growing their neat plaited corn-rows into a wilder Afro hairstyle, swapping traditional dresses for men's trousers and volunteering for military training."

The EPLF actively promoted gender equality during the civil war. The guerrilla organization sponsored the formation of the National Union of Eritrean Women (NUEW), a national organization designed to promote women's rights, and passed a series of gender-related laws. In all areas controlled by the TPLF, "bride prices" (dowries) were outlawed, the age of consent to marriage was raised to eighteen, and it became legal for women to own property. In 1977, the EPLF also began to permit marriages between guerrilla fighters in forward operational areas, leading to a dramatic increase in the number of "guerrilla marriages."

With the end of the guerrilla struggle, the government's decision to demobilize, especially the female guerrilla fighters, served as but one issue of a renewed national debate over the proper role of women in Eritrean society. Demobilized female guerrillas found themselves returning to a civilian world dominated by traditional images of women as inferior to men and primarily responsible for family and home. This clash of gender images resulted in a divorce rate of at least 50 percent for the guerrilla marriages that took place in the field. "Women fighters say many of their male colleagues have buckled under family pressure to divorce their soldier wives for younger — and preferably virgin — brides," explained one report. "The women face tremendous pressure to leave the army and stay at home with the children."

Amair Adhana, a former guerrilla fighter who joined the TPLF at the age of fourteen and became a journalist after demobilization, is critical of government policies. "In the field, the men respected us — our brains, our strength — but in this society of ours, they now respect make-up, nice hair, being a proper house-wife. . . . If we kneel down now to what they want, we'll end up back in the kitchen." It is precisely for this reason that several former female guerrillas founded the Eritrean Women War Veterans Association, which aids women in the process of achieving financial independence. "We need to change laws and ways of thinking," concludes Adhana. "This new fight is only beginning."

Quotations are from "Eritrea: Changing the Status of Women," *WIN News* 21, no. 2 (1995):52; and "The Kitchen Calls: Eritrea," *The Economist* 331, no. 7869 (June 25, 1994). See also Meredeth Turshen and Clotilde Twagiramariya, eds., *What Women Do in Wartime: Gender and Conflict in Africa* (New York: St. Martin's, 1998).

---

subsequently carried out "brutal assaults" against the Mano and Gio civilian populations.[32] The rising spiral of ethnic violence further intensified in 1990, when the Doe regime was overthrown by the National Patriotic Front of Liberia (NPFL), a guerrilla army primarily composed of fighters from the Gio and Mano ethnic groups and led by Charles Taylor. An Interim Government of National Unity (IGNU) ultimately broke down amidst rising conflict between Taylor's NPFL and other ethnically dominated guerrilla armies, most notably the United Liberation Movement of Liberia (ULIMO), which primarily drew its support from the Krahn and Mandingo ethnic groups. Seven years of civil war finally ended in July 1997, when the country's first democratic elections resulted in Charles Taylor and his New Patriotic Party (NPP) assuming the presidency.

Military Is Best Prepared to Promote Development

A final myth often promoted by military leaders is that the military is better qualified than its civilian leaders to promote economic development.[33] According to this argument, African militaries, unlike other national institutions such as political parties, are the best trained in using modern technology, and therefore are presumably the best prepared to harness this technology for the overall modernization of the national economy. The primary problem with this view is that an ability to use technology for destructive purposes does not automatically translate into an ability to use technology to promote economic development. Indeed, according to the logic promoted by military leaders, the reverse of their argument should also hold true: civilian managers significantly trained in advanced technology within the civilian economy should be well prepared to manage the use of such technology in combat situations. The obvious response of military leaders to such an argument, of course, is to note the "special" characteristics associated with being a military officer and leading troops into battle.

The debate over whether military or civilian governments have more successfully promoted development has been the subject of numerous statistical studies.[34] One conclusion of these studies is that military-dominated regimes tend to increase military budgets and the size and technological capabilities of their respective militaries. Second, the statistics demonstrate that military regimes at best fare no better, and usually slightly worse, than their civilian counterparts with respect to the promotion of expanding gross national products (GNPs), greater levels of domestic investment, and higher levels of exports. It is widely accepted that these two trends are not only related but mutually reinforcing: the military's tendency to divert scarce national resources to expanding military establishments constitutes at least one reason for the poor economic performance of military regimes. It is important to note, however, that forty years of comparative evidence does not conclusively suggest the greater effectiveness of civilian regimes. As suggested by Robin Luckham, a noted specialist of the role of the military in African politics and society, perhaps only one general pattern exists: "So far *neither* military nor civilian governments have been able to resolve the development crises facing African states."[35]

Demilitarization and Transitions to Civilian Rule

The common assumption of African public opinion is that civilian-dominated political systems constitute the proper norm of civil-military relations. Even military leaders intent on maintaining themselves in power are forced to offer, at minimum, rhetorical support for an eventual "return" to civilian rule, usually accompanied by some sort of specific timetable. The notion of **demilitarization**, sometimes referred to as promoting the **civilianization** of military regimes, became increasingly important in the post-1989 era as African policymakers and pro-democracy movements sought to consolidate transitions to democracy (see Chapter 12).[36]

South Africa offers a splendid case for understanding the process of demilitarization, despite the fact that it was technically ruled by a civilian regime during the apartheid era. From its creation in 1948 to its ultimate demise in 1994, the apartheid system, based on separation of the races and a white minority's political domination of a black majority, maintained itself in power through the widespread militarization of South African society.[37] The South African Defense Force (SADF) doubled in size to 85,000 soldiers from 1975 to

1989, and could count on nearly 400,000 reserve forces which had received military training. The SADF also oversaw the military training of white children in a cadet program that expanded from 56,000 members in 1975 to 250,000 in 1987. Even the South African Police, which exceeded over 100,000 officers in 1994, received extensive military training and maintained a large arsenal of military equipment, including tanks and armored personnel carriers. The primary purpose of this highly militarized security apparatus was to prevent the emergence of a black majority-ruled regime, led by the African National Congress (ANC) and its guerrilla allies.

The historic transition in 1994 to a multiracial democratic system headed by Nelson Mandela, the leader of the ANC who spent nearly three decades (1962–91) in apartheid prisons, represented the worst-case scenario for at least some of the senior white officers in the SADF and other security-related offices of the former apartheid state. As a result, numerous commentators publicly worried whether elements of the SADF and its allies would seek to derail the transition process by organizing a military coup against the last apartheid-era government of F. W. DeKlerk, who agreed to cede power after losing the elections of 1994. Although fears of a military coup proved unfounded, the Mandela administration was nonetheless confronted with the difficult task of assuming control over a highly racist security apparatus that once was entirely devoted to using all legal and illegal means to keep the ANC from assuming power. One of the Mandela administration's most delicate tasks has been to oversee a demilitarization process designed to restore civilian control over a security apparatus that had become too powerful in the formulation of South African domestic and foreign policies.[38]

The Mandela administration's initial success in demilitarizing highlights the prospects and dilemmas associated with similar programs throughout Africa, including in those countries undergoing a transformation from a military to a civilian-based regime. The first and most obvious conclusion revolves around the timing of negotiations.[39] Specifically, agreement over the military's future role in the domestic political system should be sought during the transition process. The logic behind this simple, yet often neglected, element of democratic transitions is that failure to reach agreement on a demilitarization process leaves in place "non-reformed and possibly disloyal" security forces that may seek to undermine the new political order.[40] It is imperative to seek agreement "when previous government officials who are committed to change have not been completely delegitimized and still have some influence and leverage over the state security apparatus."[41]

In South Africa, the military leaders of the apartheid regime and the ANC outlined the structure and missions of the new South African National Defence Force (SANDF) prior to the presidential elections of 1994.[42] A clandestine agreement was reached between the old SADF and *Umkhonto we Sizwe,* the military wing of the ANC, after negotiations at Simonstown, South Africa, in April 1993.[43] The negotiations and the agreement were critical to the success of the transition process, especially in terms of dispelling any doubts concerning the loyalty of the largely white SADF. "What is remarkable," explains William Gutteridge, a specialist of the South African military, "is that the military, in spite of their more direct antagonism [toward Mandela and the ANC government], had by the time the election took place in April 1994 gone further in preparing the future than any other department of state."[44]

A second conclusion drawn from the South African case is the importance of clearly outlining the exact nature of civil-military relations in a popularly accepted constitutional document.[45] Democratic mechanisms for ensuring civilian oversight of the military must be created, including a civilian-managed ministry of defense, civilian control of the military budget, and ultimate approval of senior promotions and professional training.[46] The South African constitution even stipulates that the South African security forces, including the South African Defense Force, "must teach and require their members to act in accordance with the Constitution and the law, including customary international law and international agreements binding on the [South African] Republic" (Art. 5, Para. 6). It is important to recognize, however, that constitutions merely establish the guidelines of civil-military relations. The true test of the demilitarization process is the actual application of constitutional principles.

A third conclusion that can be drawn from the South African case is that the military must reflect the ethnic and racial diversity of the country's population. This commonsense approach was the hallmark of a series of regional conferences on civil-military relations, held in Burundi (1993), Benin (1995), Mozambique (1996), and Sierra Leone (1997), that were jointly sponsored by the African-American Institute (AAI) and the U.S. Agency for International Development.[47] This lesson was particularly challenging in the South African context, due to the necessity of integrating previously opposed military forces into a unified SANDF, including 85,000 SADF soldiers, 30,000 guerrilla fighters from *Umkhonto we Sizwe,* 6,000 guerrilla fighters from the Azanian People's Liberation Army (the military wing of the Pan-African Congress, PAC), and 7,000 soldiers from four black "homelands" created by the apartheid state.[48] Despite ongoing tensions over salaries and ranks, particularly among the newly integrated *Umkhonto we Sizwe* forces, the new SANDF serves as a model for integrating previously opposed military forces.[49]

A fourth conclusion, centering on the desire to trim oversized defense budgets and standing armies, is particularly applicable to countries attempting to consolidate democracy in the aftermath of civil conflict.[50] Although logic demands demobilization of both guerrilla fighters and the national army, in order to focus scarce resources on promoting socioeconomic development, practical political concerns often call for the expansion of the national military. In the short term, it is more important to first establish a unified national army that is inclusive of former guerrillas and standing armies, than to disenfranchise any given group. In the transition to an inclusive democracy, one is better off maintaining once-opposed troops within a newly unified command.

In South Africa, the competing goals of long-term socioeconomic development and short-term political-military stability were resolved in favor of the latter. Joe Modise, a former guerrilla commander of *Umkhonto we Sizwe* and Minister of Defense under the Mandela administration, has underscored his intention to maintain an oversized SANDF of at least 70,000 soldiers. As succinctly noted by South African President Thabo Mbeki, "We could hardly take 30,000 combatants from the ANC and throw them on the streets."[51] Similar to their counterparts from other portions of the SANDF, these guerrilla fighters were "proud of their role" in the struggle to create a multiracial and democratic South Africa and understandably "wanted to keep their jobs in an economy where unemployment is high."[52]

The greatest threat of the demilitarization process, of course, is that previously powerful militaries return to their barracks, but remain poised for reintervention. The evolving threat of military coups to African politics and society is clearly illustrated in Figure 11.2. In contrast to the 1960s, when the number of military coups reached its peak, the second half of the 1980s and the 1990s have witnessed a sharp decline and a leveling off in military intervention. This trend may suggest the declining importance of military intervention due to the growing strength of democratic transitions in the post–Cold War era.

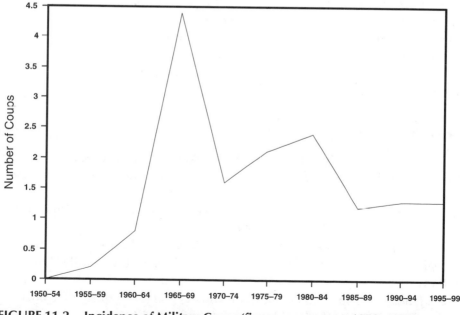

FIGURE 11.2   Incidence of Military Coups (five-year averages, 1950–1999)

Recall, however, that the transition to independent civilian governments during the 1950s ultimately stalled, only to be followed by an explosion of coups that made the 1960s the **decade of the military**. Contemporary African civilian leaders in particular are raising concerns over the potential reemergence of African militaries — the so-called **khaki contagion**[53] — as threats to the democratization process throughout Africa. On January 27, 1996, a military coup in Niger, led by Colonel Ibrahim Mainassara Baré, toppled the civilian regime headed by Alpha Oumar Konaré. This coup was important in that it marked the first such action against a democratically elected government in francophone Africa since the beginning of the democratization process in 1989. Even long-standing democracies are not immune to military influence. In July 1994, a successful military coup, led by Captain Yahya A. J. J. Jammeh, ended nearly thirty years of uninterrupted democratic rule in The Gambia since independence in 1965.[54] In this regard, the only permanent solution to the demilitarization dilemma will be the strengthening of democratic cultures where military elites are socialized into serving and protecting the supremacy of civilian democratic rule.

Key Terms

military coup d'état
men on horseback
leaders in khaki
military plots
coups of descending order
palace coup
contagion effect
continuum of civil-military relations
civilian supremacy model
watchdog model

balance wheel model
direct rule model
social transformation model
revolution from above
bloodless coup
demilitarization
civilianization
decade of the military
khaki contagion

For Further Reading

Bienen, Henry. *Armies and Parties in Africa*. New York: Africana, 1978.

Decalo, Samuel. *Coups and Army Rule in Africa: Motivations and Constraints* (2nd ed.). New Haven: Yale University Press, 1990.

Decalo, Samuel. *The Stable Minority: Civilian Rule in Africa, 1960–1990*. Gainesville: Florida Academic, 1998.

Foltz, William J., and Henry S. Bienen, eds. *Arms and the African: Military Influences on Africa's International Relations*. New Haven: Yale University Press, 1985.

Frazer, Jendayi. "Conceptualizing Civil-Military Relations during Democratic Transition." *Africa Today* 42, no. 1–2 (1995):39–48.

Harbeson, John B., ed. *The Military in African Politics*. New York: Praeger, 1987.

Khadiagala, Gilbert M. "The Military in Africa's Democratic Transitions: Regional Dimensions." *Africa Today* 42, no. 1–2 (1995):61–74.

Liebenow, J. Gus. "The Military Factor in African Politics: A Twenty-Five-Year Perspective." In Gwendolen M. Carter and Patrick O'Meara, eds. *African Independence: The First Twenty-Five Years*. Bloomington: Indiana University Press, 1985. pp. 126–59.

Luckham, Robin. "The Military, Militarization and Democratization in Africa: A Survey of Literature and Issues." *African Studies Review* 37 (1994): 13–76.

McGowan, Pat, and Thomas H. Johnson. "African Military Coups d'État and Underdevelopment: A Quantitative Historical Analysis." *The Journal of Modern African Studies* 22, no. 4 (1984):633–66.

McGowan, Pat, and Thomas H. Johnson. "Sixty Coups in Thirty Years: Further Evidence regarding African Military *Coups d'État*." *The Journal of Modern African Studies* 24, no. 3 (1986):539–46.

Nyang'oro, Julius E. "National Security and Defense Expenditure in Africa: A Political and Economic Analysis." *Africa Development* 17, no. 4 (1992): 5–28.

Odetola, Olatunde. *Military Regimes and Development: A Comparative Analysis of African Societies*. London: George Allen and Unwin, 1982.

Pateman, Roy. "Intelligence Agencies in Africa: A Preliminary Assessment." *The Journal of Modern African Studies* 30, no. 4 (1992):569–86.

Turshen, Meredeth, and Clotilde Twagiramariya, eds. *What Women Do in Wartime: Gender and Conflict in Africa*. New York: St. Martin's, 1998.

Notes

1. For a listing of personnel strengths and military equipment of African militaries during this period, see William G. Thom, "Sub-Saharan Africa's Changing Military Environment," *Armed Forces and Society* 11, no. 1 (1984):34–38.

2. The countries were Benin, Congo, Sudan, Togo, and Zaire. See J. Gus Liebenow, "The Military Factor in African Politics: A Twenty-Five-Year Perspective," in Gwendolen M. Carter and Patrick O'Meara, eds., *African Independence: The First Twenty-Five Years* (Bloomington: Indiana University Press, 1985), p. 127.

3. See Pat McGowan and Thomas H. Johnson, "African Military Coups d'État and Underdevelopment: A Quantitative Analysis," *The Journal of Modern African Studies* 22, no. 4 (1984):634–35; and Pat McGowan and Thomas H. Johnson. "Sixty Coups in Thirty Years: Further Evidence regarding African Military *Coups d'État*." *The Journal of Modern African Studies* 24, no. 3 (1986):539–46.

4. For example, see Richard P. Y. Li and William R. Thompson, "The 'Coup Contagion' Hypothesis," *Journal of Conflict Resolution* 19, no. 1 (1975): 63–88.
5. J. Gus Liebenow, *African Politics: Crises and Challenges* (Bloomington: Indiana University Press, 1986), pp. 237–66.
6. *Ibid.*, p. 251.
7. See James J. Zaffiro, "Foreign Policymaking in an African Democracy: Evolution of Structures and Processes," in Stephen John Stedman, ed., *Botswana: The Political Economy of Democratic Development* (Boulder: Lynne Rienner, 1993), pp. 154–55.
8. See Liebenow, *African Politics*, pp. 251–52.
9. See Michael Bratton and Nicolas van de Walle, *Democratic Experiments in Africa: Regime Transitions in Comparative Perspective* (Cambridge: Cambridge University Press, 1997), pp. 212–13.
10. See Liebenow, *African Politics*, p. 252.
11. See J. Gus Liebenow, *Liberia: The Quest for Democracy* (Bloomington: Indiana University Press, 1987), pp. 197–211.
12. *Ibid.*
13. *Ibid.*
14. Liebenow, *African Politics*, p. 252.
15. See Larry Diamond, "Nigeria: The Uncivic Society and the Descent into Praetorianism," in Larry Diamond, Juan J. Linz, and Seymour Martin Lipset, eds., *Politics in Developing Countries: Comparing Experiences with Democracy* (Boulder: Lynne Rienner, 1995), pp. 417–91.
16. Liebenow, *African Politics*, p. 252.
17. See Edmond J. Keller, *Revolutionary Ethiopia: From Empire to People's Republic* (Bloomington: Indiana University Press, 1988); and John W. Harbeson, *The Ethiopian Transformation: The Quest for the Post-Imperial State* (Boulder: Westview, 1988).
18. Liebenow, *African Politics*, pp. 255–64.
19. *Ibid.*, pp. 255–56.
20. See I. M. Lewis, "The Politics of the 1969 Coup," *The Journal of Modern African Studies* 10, no. 3 (1972):383–408.
21. Liebenow, *African Politics*, pp. 254–55.
22. *Ibid.*, p. 255.
23. Diamond, "Nigeria: The Uncivic Society," pp. 442–64.
24. *Ibid.*, p. 444.
25. *Ibid.*, p. 449.
26. *Ibid.*, pp. 449–50.
27. *Ibid.*, p. 450.
28. Liebenow, *African Politics*, p. 257.
29. Edmond Keller, "Remaking the Ethiopian State," in I. William Zartman, ed., *Collapsed States: The Disintegration and Restoration of Legitimate Authority* (Boulder: Lynne Rienner, 1995), pp. 125–39. See also Edmond Keller, *Revolu-*

tionary Ethiopia: From Empire to People's Republic (Bloomington: Indiana University Press, 1988).

30. Liebenow, *African Politics*, pp. 257–60.
31. See Martin Lowenkopf, "Liberia: Putting the State Back Together Again," in Zartman, *Collapsed States*, pp. 91–108.
32. *Ibid.*, p. 92.
33. Liebenow, *African Politics*, pp. 261–64.
34. For an introduction, see John Ravenhill, "Comparing Regime Performance in Africa: Limitations of Cross National Aggregate Analysis," *The Journal of Modern African Studies* 18, no. 1 (1980):99–126; K. Gyimah-Brempong, "Defense Spending and Economic Growth in Sub-Saharan Africa: An Econometric Investigation," *Journal of Peace Research* 26, no. 1 (1989):79–90.
35. Robin Luckham, "The Military, Militarization and Democratization in Africa: A Survey of Literature and Issues," *African Studies Review* 37, no. 2 (1994):52.
36. See William Gutteridge, "Undoing Military Coups in Africa," *Third World Quarterly* 7, no. 1 (1985):78–89. See also Michael Chege, "The Military in the Transition to Democracy in Africa: Some Preliminary Observations," *CODESRIA Bulletin* 3 (1995):13.
37. For an overview, see Neta C. Crawford, "South Africa's New Foreign and Military Policy: Opportunities and Constraints," *Africa Today* 42, no. 1–2 (1995):88–121. See also Jacklyn Cock and Laurie Nathan, eds., *Society at War: The Militarization of South Africa* (New York: St. Martin's, 1989).
38. See Nelson Mandela, "South Africa's Future Foreign Policy," *Foreign Affairs* 72, no. 5 (1993):86–97.
39. For discussion, see Jendayi Frazer, "Conceptualizing Civil-Military Relations during Democratic Transition," *Africa Today* 42, no. 1–2 (1995):42–44.
40. *Ibid.*, p. 43.
41. *Ibid.*
42. See Crawford, "South Africa's New Foreign and Military Policy," pp. 89, 101.
43. Norma Kriger and Patrick Bond, "Negotiations and the Military in South Africa," *Africa Today* 42, no. 1–2 (1995):125.
44. Quoted in Kriger and Bond, "Negotiations and the Military," p. 129.
45. See William J. Foltz, "Officer Politicians," *Africa Report* 38, no. 3 (May-June 1993):66.
46. See Bratton and van de Walle, *Democratic Experiments*, p. 245.
47. See in particular two early reports published by AAI: *The Bujumbura Conference. Democratization in Africa: The Role of the Military. Bujumbura, Burundi, February 1-4, 1993* (New York: AAI, 1993); and *Democratization in Africa: The Role of the Military. Report of the Second Regional Conference. The African-American Institute. Cotonou, Benin* (New York: AAI, 1995). Reports were not published for the latter two conferences.
48. Crawford, "South Africa's New Foreign and Military Policy," p. 90.
49. See Kriger and Bond, "Negotiations and the Military," pp. 128–32.

50. See Donald Rothchild, "On Implementing Africa's Peace Accords: From Defection to Cooperation," *Africa Today* 42, no. 1–2 (1995):8–38; and Kimberly Mahling Clark, "The Demobilization and Reintegration of Soldiers: Perspectives from USAID," *Africa Today* 42, no. 1–2 (1995):49–60.

51. Quoted in *ibid.*, p. 101.

52. *Ibid.*

53. See François Soudan, "La Contagion Kaki," *Jeune Afrique,* no. 1833 (February 21–27, 1996):19–20.

54. See John A. Wiseman, "Military Rule in The Gambia: An Interim Assessment," *Third World Quarterly* 17, no. 5 (1996):917–40.

12

Democratic Experiments
and Multiparty Politics

Olusegun Obasanjo — victor in Nigeria's 1999 presidential elections — addressing a crowd of political supporters from the Igbo ethnic group.

DOZENS OF COUNTRIES in Africa, Asia, Latin America, and Eastern and Southern Europe made transitions from authoritarian to democratic forms of governance during the last quarter of the twentieth century. This global trend has prompted proponents of democracy to speak of the **third wave of democratization** in world history (the first two waves began in the 1820s and the 1940s).[1] In the case of Africa, this third wave was sparked by the fall of the Berlin Wall in 1989. The collapse of single-party regimes throughout Eastern Europe and the former Soviet Union set powerful precedents for African pro-democracy activists who already had begun organizing against human rights abuses and political repression. Severe economic stagnation and decline in most African economies served as the internal spark for political discontent. The most notable outcome of this historic turning point, often referred to as **Africa's second independence** or **Africa's second liberation,** was the discrediting of more than thirty years of experimentation with single-party political systems in favor of more democratic forms of governance based on multiparty politics and the protection of human rights. This chapter is devoted to exploring the evolution of the extremely rich and varied forms of democratic experimentation that are presently unfolding throughout the African continent.[2]

Establishment of Single-Party Political Systems

The political frameworks bequeathed to the African continent at the beginning of the contemporary independence era embodied an **authoritarian-democratic paradox** in which African leaders, educated in authoritarianism during the colonial era, were expected to perform like seasoned experts in democracy. Despite their almost complete disregard for the promotion of democratic values during the colonial era, departing colonial administrators hastily constructed political arrangements that purported to embody Western democratic ideals, such as **systems of checks-and-balances**, in which offices of the president, legislatures, and judiciaries would balance each other's power and check the emergence of authoritarianism. The relatively decentralized **Westminster model** of parliamentary governance was grafted onto the authoritarian structures of colonial rule in the former British colonies, and the more centralized **Elysée model** was similarly introduced into France's former colonies.[3] For the most part, however, the so-called democracies left behind by the departing colonial powers represented largely untested and ill-suited political practices and procedures that in any case were not grounded in African traditions or political cultures.

Except in the unique case of Botswana, the first generation of African leadership resolved this paradox of independence by replacing the political systems left behind by the former colonial powers with more authoritarian forms of governance based on a centralization of power and personal rule.[4] Even the most principled of African leaders invariably turned to a variety of authoritarian measures to enhance their political power and ensure political survival at the expense of competing political interests. Among those actions taken were:

- the staffing of bureaucracies, militaries, and police forces with members of the leader's ethnic or clan groups, as well as with those of their principal ethnic or clan allies;
- the rejection of "federalist" arrangements, such as constitutional amendments, that allowed for the political autonomy of groups or regions based on ethnic, linguistic, or religious claims;
- the marginalization or even disbanding of independent parliaments and judiciaries that at best became "rubber stamp" organizations incapable of serving as a check on the powers of the executive;
- the imprisonment or exile of vocal critics from civil society, including labor unions, student organizations, and religious groups;
- the outlawing of rival political parties (see Chapter 10).

The creation of **single-party political systems** constituted the most significant political act undertaken by African leaders during the contemporary independence era.[5] These parties ranged from Chama Cha Mapinduzi (CCM), a mass-mobilizing party created by Julius Nyerere, the former socialist leader of Tanzania; to the Workers Party of Ethiopia (WPE), a vanguard party created by Mengistu Haile Mariam, the former Marxist leader of Ethiopia; and the Kenya African National Union (KANU), the sole ruling party of capitalist-oriented Kenya that was created by former President Jomo Kenyatta, and strengthened by his successor, Daniel arap Moi (see Chapter 8). In short, regardless of their political ideology, nearly all African leaders exhibited authoritarian tendencies that inevitably resulted in the creation of single-party political systems.[6]

African leaders offered numerous rationales to justify the establishment of political monopolies over their respective political systems.[7] The first justification was that single-party systems were reflective of traditional African political systems as they existed prior to the imposition of direct colonial rule.[8] According to this argument, the single-party system was not to be perceived as a "temporary aberration" from a universal norm of multiparty democracy, but rather as a "modern adaptation of traditional African political behavior."[9] Unlike the divisive nature of Western multiparty systems in which one party emerges dominant and the others are marginalized, the concept of single-party democracy was heralded as conducive to promoting the traditional African norm of **consensus building** in which every participant has the right to voice his/her opinion (although women were normally excluded from decision-making during the precolonial independence era) and decisions are made only when agreed upon by all present. It is precisely for this reason that Tanzanian President Nyerere chose *ujamaa* (the Kiswahili term for brotherhood) as the symbolic guiding principle of the CCM and his country's "return" to traditional African socialism.[10]

A second rationale for creating single-party systems was the imperative of responding to existing and potential crises. African leaders argued against "wasting" scarce resources on competitive politics when their countries were confronted with crises of development ("How can we quickly develop our society?"), crises of administration ("How do we quickly educate the required leaders?"), and, most important, crises of governance ("How do we quickly satisfy rising popular demands for the fruits of independence?").[11] Just as unity was crucial to the attainment of independence, argued those who led the nationalist struggles during the 1950s, so too was unity important once that independence had been achieved. Equally important, African leaders feared that multiparty systems would foster the fragmentation of ethnically diverse African societies, and therefore perceived the single-party system as one of the most important tools for transforming colonially inspired, artificial states into true nations.

A third rationale, offered especially by African leaders from the Marxist tradition, underscored the **vanguard role** that single parties were expected to play. Drawing upon the Leninist concept that the "masses" of individual African societies needed to be led by an "enlightened elite," the single party was envisioned as serving to protect and promote Marxist revolutions on the African continent.[12] The single party was particularly oriented toward the future evolution of African societies, especially in terms of ensuring industrial development and the promotion of basic human needs, such as guaranteed access to adequate food, shelter, and health care.

The nearly thirty-year experiment with single-party rule achieved few positive results.[13] Even in the most benevolent of examples, such as Nyerere's *ujamaa* experiment in Tanzania, the country made significant strides in promoting mass literacy and the provision of basic human needs only at the expense of a failed overall economy that witnessed an annual average decline of seven percent in agricultural output. One of the primary reasons for this failure was that the initially voluntary villagization program, the centerpiece of the *ujamaa* development strategy in which peasants were grouped together in new communal villages, ultimately became coercive in nature. Many peasants were forced to move from their traditional lands to village projects that were either poorly conceived or simply inappropriate for farming practices. If the state inevitably became coercive and therefore counterproductive to the goal of development in the most benevolent of single-party systems, one has only to imagine its impact on the development of the most authoritarian single-party systems, such as the Marxist-inspired tyranny created in Mengistu's Ethiopia.

The most notable problem associated with the single-party experiment of Tanzania and its contemporaries was that it led to a stagnation of ideas. For example, although Tanzanian legislative candidates were allowed to run against each other under the unified banner of the CCM, they were not permitted to question either the socialist domestic ideology or the foreign policy of the Nyerere regime. Candidates could debate the instrumental aspects of carrying out party-approved policies, but were unable to offer alternatives to misguided policies. In this and other cases, African leaders who felt they "knew best" restricted the range of political debate to such a degree that the single party ultimately became a means for maintaining control rather than a dynamic tool for promoting change and development.

The growing stagnation of single-party rule from the 1950s to the end of the 1980s was matched by the growing power and influence of African militaries and African military leaders (see Chapter 11). The sharp increase in military coups d'état led to the replacement of entrenched civilian leaders with their military counterparts, and became one of the most important forms of regime change in African politics during the initial decades of the contemporary independence era. Most important, the emergence of military leaders as power brokers within African presidential mansions and parliaments did not usher in a new period of democracy and prosperity, but instead led to new forms of military-led authoritarianism as bad as, if not worse than, their civilian counterparts.

Experimentation with Multiparty Politics

The downfall of single-party communist systems throughout Eastern Europe and the former Soviet Union sent shock waves throughout the African continent.[14] The rejection of single-party rule in its intellectual heartland ensured that African leaders could no longer justify the continuation of this model on the African continent. "If the owners of socialism have withdrawn from the one-party system," proclaimed Frederick Chiluba, the leader of the Zambian prodemocracy movement and future president of Zambia, "who are the Africans to continue with it?"[15] Equally important, authoritarian leaders could no longer use Cold War rhetoric as the means for ensuring superpower attention and therefore the financial and military support necessary to prevent opposition movements from taking power; the former Soviet Union had ceased to exist and a new Russian regime preoccupied with domestic economic restructuring had largely withdrawn from African politics, while the United States and its Western allies were increasingly prone to link African support for democratization and economic liberalization to future commitments of foreign assistance and preferential trade agreements (see Chapter 14).

The emergence of a Western consensus in favor of promoting democratic principles coincided with the rise of increasingly vocal and powerful African pro-democracy movements. Popular protests and demands for political reform often emerged as a response to the intensification of government-sponsored political repression and human rights abuses throughout the 1980s. This trend peaked in 1991, when a total of eighty-six popular protests were recorded in

BOX 12.1

NONPARTY SYSTEMS? UGANDA'S "MOVEMENT DEMOCRACY"

Uganda has successfully avoided the multiparty demands of the "third wave of democratization" in Africa by establishing and expanding a **nonparty system,** which is referred to by its supporters as **movement democracy.** This unique brand of political system was inspired by the political thought of Yoweri Kaguta Museveni, whose guerrilla movement, the National Resistance Army (NRA), assumed power in 1986.

The defining characteristic of movement democracy is the illegality of any political party involvement in local and national elections. The political system is instead based on **mass participatory democracy** in which all citizens are members of the national movement and therefore eligible to vote; all forms of "sectarianism," including ethnically, religiously, and regionally based differences are eliminated, and human rights are supported. Although originally inspired by Marxist economic strategies, Museveni has emerged as one of Africa's most fervent supporters of free-market capitalism.

The administrative structure of movement democracy is a series of councils known as Local Committees that, at the individual village level, are comprised of representatives directly elected by citizens of the village. Each successive, higher level of council, including the parish, the county, and finally the district, is comprised of representatives elected by the previous level of governance. The political system therefore embodies a pyramidal structure, the top of which is dominated by Museveni. This system of governance was widely legitimized in free and fair presidential elections in 1996, in which Museveni won 75 percent of the popular vote on the campaign slogan: "No Change!"

The simple and understandable reason for this dramatic victory, according to J. Oloka-Onyango, a Ugandan scholar, is that Museveni delivered on his pledge of building a "lasting sense" of peace and security out of political and economic chaos. From 1962 to 1986, hundreds of thousands of Ugandans died under the dictatorial abuses of Apollo Milton Obote and Major General Idi Amin, the latter who embodies the dubious distinction of having led one of Africa's most tyrannical regimes. By the beginning of the 1980s, Uganda had become economically chaotic — smuggling, *magendo* (black marketeering), and triple-digit inflation dominated a failing national economy. "In the event that some might have forgotten this, the NRM [National Resistance Movement] used the image of skulls . . . and the sound of gunshots in its electoral campaign advertising," explains Oloka-Onyango. "The message was simple: a vote against Museveni was a vote for a reversion to the chaos of the past."

Despite Museveni's resounding victory in the 1996 presidential elections, his concept of movement democracy is being challenged on several fronts. First, as the pre-1986 era becomes increasingly distant in the collective memory of the Ugandan people, the demands of opposition politicians for the restoration of multiparty politics is gaining in popularity. Similar to the concerns voiced by critics of the single-party systems that dominated the African landscape from the 1950s to the 1980s, opposition politicians claim that Museveni's movement democracy stifles debate and therefore runs the risk of ultimately becoming the means for maintaining control, rather than a dynamic tool for promoting change and development. Indeed, Museveni's political monopoly has proved incapable of resolving guerrilla insurgencies in northern Uganda, most notably the Holy Spirit Movement led by Alice Lakwena.

The most significant long-term challenge, however, is that the survival of movement democracy inherently depends on the continued vitality of Museveni himself. "The movement system has failed to institutionalize mechanisms of governance distinct from the personality of Museveni," explains Oloka-Onyango. "The success of the Ugandan experiment will be sealed only if it can extricate itself from reliance on a single individual." If history is any guide, personalized political systems such as Uganda's movement democracy rarely, if ever, survive the death of the political leader.

Quotations are from J. Oloka-Onyango, "Uganda's 'Benevolent' Dictatorship," *Current History* 96, no. 610 (1997):212–16. See also Nelson Kasfir, "'No-Party Democracy' in Uganda," *Journal of Democracy* 9, no. 2 (1998):49–63; and Yoweri Kaguta Museveni, *Sowing the Mustard Seed: The Struggle for Freedom and Democracy in Uganda* (London: Macmillan, 1997).

thirty African countries.[16] Protestors were emboldened by the adoption of continent-wide human rights norms, which was confirmed by the ratification of the African Charter of Human and Peoples' Rights by the majority of African countries at the beginning of the 1990s. Protesters were also driven by the severe deterioration of African economies that made it increasingly difficult for individual families — already perilously close to abject poverty — to acquire basic foodstuffs and other necessities of day-to-day living.[17]

The convergence of these domestic and international trends resulted in a period of democratic transition previously unknown in African history. Whereas many of these experiments resulted in the replacement of single-party systems with more inclusive forms of multiparty politics, several potential transitions to democracy have either stalled, are being co-opted, or have been completely derailed by authoritarian leaders intent upon maintaining power. Drawing on the work of Guy Martin, one can distinguish between six types of political change.[18]

Change via Multiparty Elections

The impact on Africa of the third wave of democratization is demonstrated by the dramatic expansion of **multiparty competition** within African political systems from 1990 to 1994.[19] During the preceding five-year period (1985–89), truly competitive elections were held in only five African countries: Botswana,

The Gambia, Mauritius, Senegal, and Zimbabwe. From 1990 to 1994, more than thirty-eight countries held competitive elections. Most important, twenty-nine of the multiparty contests of the 1990–94 era constituted **founding elections** in which "the office of the head of government is openly contested following a period during which multiparty political competition was denied."[20]

South Africa's founding election of April 26–29, 1994, serves as one of the most heralded examples of African democratic transition. For the first time, voters of all races cast ballots in free and fair elections that ushered in South Africa's first multiracial, multiethnic, and multiparty democracy. Nelson Mandela, who had spent nearly twenty-eight years in prison under the previous apartheid system, was elected president, and the party he represents, the African National Congress (ANC), won 63 percent of the popular vote, 252 of 400 seats in the National Assembly, and a majority share of seats in seven of the nine provincial legislatures. F. W. de Klerk, the last president of the apartheid era, and his Afrikaner-based National Party (NP) that dominated South African politics from 1948 to 1994, won only 21 percent of the popular vote (82 National Assembly seats), but majority control of the legislature in the Western Cape province, which is predominantly inhabited by Afrikaners. The third most influential presidential candidate was Chief Mangosuthu Buthelezi, a prominent Zulu leader. His predominantly Zulu-based political party, the Inkatha Freedom Party (IFP), won 10 percent of the popular vote, ensuring forty seats in the National Assembly as well as a majority victory in the KwaZulu-Natal province, which is largely inhabited by the Zulu ethnic group. The fact that both the NP and the IFP won at least 10 percent each of the popular vote ensured their inclusion in a constitutionally mandated government of national unity. "From the moment the results were in and it was apparent that the ANC was to form the government, I saw my mission as one of preaching reconciliation, of binding the wounds of the country, of engendering trust and confidence," explains Nelson Mandela in his autobiography. "At every opportunity, I said all South Africans must now unite and join hands and say we are one country, one nation, one people, marching together into the future."[21]

Change via the National Conference

A second important vehicle of the transition process, which became particularly influential in francophone Africa, is the **national conference**.[22] In this scenario, a broad coalition of leaders from all sectors of society, including elders and the heads of women's organizations, ethnic and religious leaders, labor and student activists, and ruling and opposition political leaders, holds an extended national gathering that serves as the basis for debating the outlines of a new democratic political order. In its ideal form, such a conference builds upon the traditional African concept of consensus building, in which every participant has the right to voice his/her opinion, and decisions are made only when agreed upon by all members present (unlike the more widespread Western concept of majority rule).

The democratization process under the guidance of the national conference generally follows five major steps.[23] First, a broad coalition of leaders responds to a growing crisis of governance in the country by convening a national conference in the capital city. The guiding principle of this body is its self-appointed "sovereignty" (i.e., independence) from either the existing constitutional framework or any interference on the part of the ruling regime. Second, the national conference appoints a transitional government that initially seeks a dialogue with the ruling regime. Over time, however, a weakened president is either gradually robbed of his executive powers or is simply declared an illegitimate authority who no longer has the authority to lead. In either case, the president is usually reduced to a figurehead. Fourth, the national conference transforms itself into a transitional legislative body (often referred to as the High Council) that, in turn, formally elects a prime minister who manages the transition process. Finally, the transitional government adopts a new constitution and holds legislative and presidential elections, subsequently dissolving itself upon the inauguration of the newly elected democratic regime.

The strong appeal of the national conference model was primarily due to the dramatic success achieved in Benin.[24] More than eighteen years of authoritarian rule under the Marxist dictatorship of Mathieu Kérékou were peacefully overcome by a 488-member national conference that lasted ten days. During February 19–28, 1990, the national conference declared its sovereignty, provided Kérékou with political amnesty while at the same time stripping him of his official powers, and drafted a timetable that ultimately led to the successful holding of multiparty elections in 1991. The critical element that contributed to the success of this democratization process was Kérékou's peaceful acceptance of the national conference's self-declared right to take control of the political process. As observed by Jacques Mariel Nzouankeu, director of the Center for Study and Research on Plural Democracy in the Third World (CERDET), Kérékou still enjoyed the loyalty of the Beninois Armed Forces, and presumably could have crushed the opposition with military force.[25] Moreover, the military elite itself constituted a potential threat to the national conference in that the transition to a civilian regime inevitably ensured a reduction in the political power of the military. Nonetheless, both Kérékou and his military officers eventually accepted the popular legitimacy of the national conference and embraced its timetable for the introduction of multiparty politics to Benin.[26]

Co-opted Transitions

A third scenario occurs when leaders are able to **co-opt the transition process** and maintain themselves in power despite the holding of relatively free and fair elections. The co-optation of the democratic process usually follows three major steps.[27] First, unlike the successful cases of transition by national conference, the president under this scenario is acutely aware of the precarious nature of his political rule and acts in a quick, albeit relatively peaceful, manner to preempt the democratization forces. The usual course of action is to quickly accede to opposition demands to dismantle the single-party system, and to legalize all opposition parties within a new multiparty framework. Second, rather than giving the new opposition parties time to organize, and therefore present a viable and competitive alternative to the voters, "snap" elections (often to be held within months) are announced by the ruling party. In this case, the ruling party, which usually still commands a formidable organizational structure and supporters within every region of the country, advocates for the proliferation of numerous new parties so as to divide the opposition vote. Finally, during the period immediately preceding the elections, the ruling party uses its monopoly of the government-controlled print, radio, and television media to dominate the political debate. The net result is a "peaceful," albeit tainted, victory by the ruling president and party.

Multiparty elections held in Côte d'Ivoire in October 1990 offer a classic example of a ruling party's ability to peacefully co-opt the democratization process.[28] Considered by many analysts to be a "master-tactician," President Félix Houphouët-Boigny "completely outmaneuvered" his country's prodemocracy movement by "promptly legalizing all political parties, and acceding to their fullest demands — open presidential and legislative elections — rushing the democratic transformation before opposition leaders could expand or redefine their demands, sharpen their tactics, or properly organize for electoral contests."[29] "When some requested a delay (so they could get organized) this was rejected on the grounds of *their own* recent demonstrations for instant national elections," explains Samuel Decalo, a noted observer of the democratization process in Africa. "Election funds were allocated to all parties so they could not claim being at a disadvantage (some parties took the funds and withdrew from the elections!), and the outcome was never in doubt."[30] Deep divisions within an unprepared opposition and government control of all the major media outlets not only ensured Houphouët-Boigny's victory in presidential elections, with approximately 81 percent of the popular vote, but his ruling party, the Parti Démocratique de la Côte d'Ivoire-Rassemblement Démocratique Africain (PDCI-RDA, Democratic Party of Côte d'Ivoire–African Democratic Assembly), won 163 out of a total of 175 seats in the National Assembly. In short, Houphouët-Boigny's foresight and ability to act quickly and decisively enabled him to peacefully co-opt the democratization process under the guise of free, but ultimately unfair, multiparty elections that left the opposition forces with little alternative but to accept the results and set their sights on future electoral contests.

Guided Democratization

Unlike the process of co-optation, in which leaders are forced to quickly take action, the model of **guided democratization** is one in which an authoritarian regime that is nonetheless committed to democratization maintains tight control over the transition process. The hallmark of this model is an extremely powerful and usually very charismatic leader who, due to the lack of any major competing centers of power, is capable of slowly instituting **democratization from above** according to his own timetable and preferences.

The Ghanaian military regime of Flt. Lt. Jerry Rawlings provides a clear-cut example of the process of guided democratization.[31] Assuming power in a military coup d'état in June 1979, Rawlings led the Ghanaian Armed Forces back to the barracks in September 1979 after Dr. Hilla Limann was elected president in democratic elections. However, political corruption, economic stagnation, and popular discontent with the Limann regime prompted Rawlings to once again assume the leadership of Ghana in a coup in December 1981. Rather than returning to the barracks for a second time, Rawlings remained in power at the head of the Provisional National Defense Council (PNDC), a military-based revolutionary organ that outlawed opposition political parties and implemented its vision to economically restructure the country. The unchallenged status of the PNDC would only be altered in 1992 — nearly eleven years after assuming power — when Rawlings decided that Ghana was ready for another attempt at multiparty democracy.

Rawlings oversaw a deliberately slow and measured liberalization of the Ghanaian political system that ultimately included the writing of a new constitution, the legalization of opposition political parties, the emergence of a private press, and the creation of independent national human rights organizations.[32] In multiparty presidential elections held in November 1992, a combination of popular support within the rural areas, careful planning, and strong control exerted by the ruling PNDC led to a Rawlings victory with 58.3 percent of the popular vote. Claiming that Rawlings and the PNDC had exerted "excessive control" over an inherently flawed election process, opposition leaders boycotted the legislative elections held one month later, thereby ensuring a sweep of the National Legislature by pro-Rawlings parties.[33] Despite the fact that electoral irregularities, most notably flawed voter registration lists reportedly favoring the incumbent government, marred the democratization process, Rawlings nonetheless emerged from the 1992 elections firmly in control of the Ghanaian political system. As was the case with other military leaders intent on promoting guided democracy from above, however, Rawlings's "toughest test" was that of "shedding the image of the radical military dictator and becoming a democratic constitutional ruler able to create a climate of tolerance."[34]

Authoritarian Reaction

In contrast to the previous examples of democratization, **authoritarian reaction** entails high levels of state-sponsored violence against proponents of democracy, in order to preserve the status quo. In this case, the incumbent leader conducts elections that are neither free nor fair, with the intent of stealing votes. The promotion of ethnic fighting in order to divide the opposition and intimidate the general population is often one of the hallmarks of this model. After "winning" the election, the leader subsequently seeks to silence the opposition through such varied means as imprisonment, exile, and, in extreme cases, execution.

BOX 12.2
ASSESSING THE SPREAD OF DEMOCRACY IN AFRICA

A confidence in the inevitable spread of multiparty democracy is one of the bedrock principles of the liberal intellectual tradition (see Chapter 2). The dramatic expansion of African transitions to democracy in the aftermath of the end of the Cold War has strengthened the liberal position and has fostered a series of efforts by foreign policy think tanks and research institutes to measure the strength of this democratization trend.

The Comparative Survey on Freedom annually published by Freedom House, a conservative think tank located in Washington, D.C., constitutes one of the most widely cited measurement projects. The survey uses a seven-point scale ("1" being the highest and "7" being the lowest) to assess two dimensions of freedom: **political rights**, such as the ability to form political organizations free from government intrusion; and **civil liberties**, such as freedom of speech and assembly. The two scores are combined to create a **freedom index**, ranging from the highest combined positive rating of "2" to the highest combined negative rating of "14." Countries are then grouped into three categories: (1) *democratic:* high degree of freedom (2-5 points); (2) *partially democratic:* medium degree of freedom (6–10 points); (3) *undemocratic:* low degree of freedom (11–14 points).

According to the 1998 Freedom House survey, 17 percent (nine countries) of Africa's political systems are democratic, whereas 45 percent (twenty-four countries) are partially democratic and 38 percent (twenty countries) are undemocratic (see Map 12.1). When compared to earlier surveys, the 1998 survey clearly suggests that democracy has made significant strides in Africa since the fall of the Berlin Wall in 1989. In 1988, for example, only 4 percent (two countries) of Africa's political systems were democratic, whereas 31 percent (sixteen countries) were partially democratic and 65 percent (thirty-three countries) were undemocratic.

MAP 12.1   Strength of Democracy

Statistics are drawn from Freedom House, *Freedom in the World: The Annual Survey of Political Rights and Civil Liberties* (Washington: Freedom House, published annually). Contact Freedom House at <fh3@ingress.com> or <http://www.freedomhouse.org>. See also Raymond Duncan Gastil, "The Comparative Survey of Freedom: Experiences and Suggestions," in Alex Inkeles, ed., *On Measuring Democracy: Its Consequences and Concomitants* (New Brunswick: Transaction, 1991), pp. 21–46.

The example of Cameroon demonstrates the extent to which incumbent leaders are willing to maintain themselves in office through the use of authoritarian tactics.[35] In October 1992, President Paul Biya and his ruling Cameroon People's Democratic Movement (CPDM) declared victory in the country's first multiparty presidential elections with 39.9 percent of the popular vote. During the two years preceding the elections, human rights groups estimate that at least four hundred people associated with the democratization movement were killed by the Biya regime, and the elections themselves were fraught with gross violations of human rights and electoral procedures. "Widespread irregularities during the election period, on election day, and in the tabulation of results seriously calls into question, for any fair observer, the validity of the outcome," explained a report of the U.S. National Democratic Institute for International Affairs (NDI), one of the foreign groups that monitored the elections. "It would not be an exaggeration to suggest that this election system was designed to fail."[36]

Biya's self-proclaimed victory in the elections was followed by a wave of repression and arrests directed against opposition elites. For example, John Fru Ndi, the leader of the Social Democratic Front (SDF) who took second place in the presidential elections with 35.9 percent of the popular vote, was placed under house arrest with 135 of his supporters. Another two hundred opposition figures were also jailed, and a state of emergency was declared in the province of Western Cameroon. "The brutality of the forces of law and order, particularly during arrests, is very alarming," explained Solomon Nfor Gwei, the chairman of Cameroon's National Commission for Human Rights and Freedom. "Many detainees are continuously being subjected to psychological and physical torture, some of whom we saw in great pain, with swollen limbs and genitals, blisters and deep wounds and cracks on skulls."[37] In this and other cases, the facade of victory actually encourages authoritarian leaders to unleash waves of repression designed to maintain the status quo at any cost.

Civil War and Contested Sovereignty

At worst, the authoritarian response of the incumbent leader can lead to civil war and the complete breakdown of the state. The result is a state of **contested sovereignty**, in which no one group is capable of asserting its authority over the entire territory or constructing a government considered to be legitimate, either domestically or internationally.

This extreme scenario was characteristic of the bloody clan warfare that erupted in Somalia after Somali dictator Mohammed Siad Barre was overthrown by a coalition of guerrilla forces in January 1991. Rather than abide by an October 2, 1990, accord in which the major guerrilla groups agreed to decide the shape of a post-Siad political system, the United Somali Congress (USC), by virtue of its control of the capital, unilaterally named a Hawiye clan member, Ali Mahdi Mohammed, president of the country. This move heightened the already tense relations between the Isaak-dominated Somali National Movement (SNM), the Hawiye-dominated USC, and the Ogadeni-dominated Somali Patriotic Movement (SPM), as well as relations among scores of other, less-organized clan groupings.[38]

In an action based on a strongly held Isaak belief that the north would continue to be victimized by a southern-dominated government, the SNM announced on May 17, 1991, that the former British Somaliland territory was seceding from the 1960 union to become the Somaliland Republic. This event was followed by the intensification of clan conflict in the southern portion of the country between the USC and the SPM, which, in turn, was exacerbated by a regrouping of Siad's Darod clan groupings under the military banner of the Somali National Front (SNF). Moreover, a brutal intraclan power struggle erupted in Mogadishu between USC forces loyal to interim President Mahdi (a member of the Abgal subclan of the Hawiye) and those led by General Mohamed Farah Aidid (a member of the Habar Gedir subclan of the Hawiye). In short, once the common political enemy no longer existed, traditional clan differences, worsened by the dictatorial divide-and-rule practices of the Siad years, led to an intensification of clan conflict and famine throughout southern and central Somalia.

As it became increasingly clear that the United Nations Security Council was incapable of managing intensifying levels of clan conflict and famine, President George Bush announced in a live television address to the American public on December 4, 1992, that U.S. troops would be deployed in Somalia to "create a secure environment" for the distribution of famine-relief aid. Five days later the first contingent of U.S. troops, led by three teams of Navy SEALs (Sea-Air-Land Commandos), landed on the beaches of Mogadishu and secured the airport and the port. The U.S. military landing, designated "Operation Restore Hope," was carried out under the auspices of a UN Security Council resolution sanctioning foreign intervention. In the weeks that followed, 38,000 troops from twenty countries (including approximately 24,000 U.S. military personnel) occupied various cities and towns throughout central and southern Somalia, and began the task of opening food supply routes, as well as creating distribution networks.[39]

Despite the withdrawal of U.S. troops in May 1994 and the withdrawal of all remaining UN troops in May 1995, a permanent political solution to the Somali crisis as of 1999 has yet to be found. Southern clans refuse to accept the self-proclaimed independence of the northern-based Somaliland Republic, which remains unrecognized by any other country in the world. In the southern and central portions of the country, a tentative cease-fire has only succeeded in recognizing the political-military supremacy of existing clan leaders in their individual regions. Although the famine of 1991–92 has not recurred, thousands of Somalis have died in the periodic intensification of clan-based conflict. The primary problem remains the lack of a centralized Somali state capable of exerting authority over the entire Somali nation. Conflict is sure to continue as long as the Somali nation remains divided among dozens of clan-dominated fiefdoms.

Democratic Consolidation or Decay?

The future prospect of the third wave of African democratization has fostered both optimism and pessimism. Optimism was initially generated by a host of early successes, such as the national conference experiment in Benin.[40] This third wave culminated in what numerous observers have referred to as the

South African "miracle": the emergence of Nelson Mandela as the first democratically elected leader of South Africa.[41] Pessimism has been increasingly generated by the simple reality that several transitions to democracy have resulted in **democratic decay**, often ending in military coups d'état and a return to authoritarianism.[42] In the case of Niger, for example, Colonel Ibrahim Maïnassara Baré achieved the dubious honor of leading the first successful coup d'état against a democratically elected government in francophone West Africa since the beginning of the third wave of democratization. In a throwback to an earlier era of authoritarian rule and highly questionable democratic practices, Colonel Baré announced that there would be multiparty elections in 1996, presented himself as the "civilian" candidate of the ruling party, and subsequently won what international observers agreed to be a grossly flawed electoral contest. Less than three years later in 1999, Baré was assassinated in a military coup d'état and replaced by Commander Daouda Malam Wanke. Needless to say, Wanke's promise of holding free and fair democratic elections in 1999 has been greeted warily by the general population.

Even in those cases marked by a successful transition to more democratic forms of governance, newly elected leaders are confronted with the long-term challenge of ensuring the **consolidation** (institutionalization) of democratic practices in political systems still marked by democratic fragility.[43] "The frequency of democratic breakdowns in this century — and the difficulties of consolidating new democracies — must give serious pause to those who would argue . . . for the inevitability of global democracy," explains Larry Diamond, a senior research fellow at the Hoover Institution.[44] "As a result, those concerned about how countries can move 'beyond authoritarianism and totalitarianism' must also ponder the conditions that permit such movement to endure. . . . To rid a country of an authoritarian regime or dictator is not necessarily to move it fundamentally beyond authoritarianism."[45]

One means for assessing the consolidation of democracy is to examine the evolution of political rights enjoyed by African populations, including the ability to form political organizations free from government intrusion; the meaningful representation of ethnic, racial, religious, and other minority groups in the political process; and the right to choose national and local political leaders through free and fair competitive elections. Although individual countries will obviously vary, the African continent as a whole has benefited from the steadily rising protection of political rights since 1989 (see Figure 12.1). It is important to note, however, that the establishment of a multiparty political system — the political right most often cited by Western observers as the linchpin of democratic practice — can actually undermine the process of democratic consolidation, especially when electoral arrangements make it difficult, if not impossible, for the opposition party to emerge victorious in national elections.

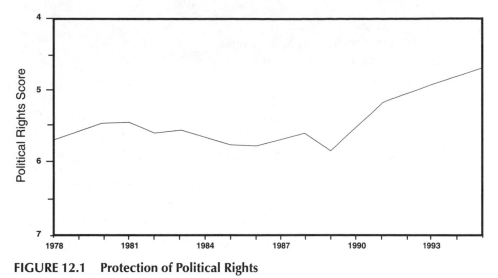

FIGURE 12.1   Protection of Political Rights

Source: Statistics are drawn from Freedom House, *Freedom in the World: The Annual Survey of Political Rights and Civil Liberties* (Washington: Freedom House, annual editions, 1978–1997). See Box 12.2 for a complete discussion of scores.

Botswana is often heralded as a model for more recently emerging democracies because it is Africa's oldest surviving multiparty democracy, in which free and fair elections have been held on a regular basis since independence in 1966.[46] A close examination of legislative election results has nonetheless prompted some critics to characterize Botswana as a *de facto* single-party system (see Table 12.1).[47] Despite the proliferation of political parties, ranging from the labor-oriented Botswana Labour Party (BLP) to the socialist-inspired Botswana National Front (BNF), the ruling Botswana Democratic Party (BDP) consistently won no less than 77 percent of all seats in seven legislative elections that were held between 1965 and 1989.[48] Although the 1994 election results suggested a potential shift toward a two-party system dominated by the BDP and the BNF (the latter of which enjoyed its best showing during the independence era by winning a record thirteen seats [33 percent of the total]), the BDP nonetheless has been able to maintain its political monopoly in large part due to a political system that heavily favors the incumbent president and his ruling party.[49]

It is precisely for this reason that some proponents of democratization argue that the true test of Africa's newly established democratic systems is their ability to foster and survive the **alternation of power** between rival political parties. Benin stands out as the best example of a newly established, multiparty democracy that has successfully weathered an alternation of power through the ballot box. The net political outcome of the 1990 national conference was the 1991 holding of "founding elections," in which a technocrat,

TABLE 12.1

Legislative Election Results in Botswana (parties winning at least one seat)

	1965	1969	1974	1979	1984	1989	1994
BDP	28 (90)	24 (77)	27 (84)	29 (91)	29 (85)	31 (91)	27 (68)
BNF	— (—)	3 (10)	2 (6)	2 (6)	4 (12)	3 (9)	13 (32)
BPP	3 (10)	3 (10)	2 (6)	1 (3)	1 (3)	0 (0)	0 (0)
BIP	0 (0)	1 (3)	1 (3)	0 (0)	0 (0)	0 (0)	0 (0)
	31 (100)	31 (100)	32 (100)	32 (100)	34 (100)	34 (100)	40 (100)

BDP = Botswana Democratic Party
BNF = Botswana National Front
BPP = Botswana People's Party
BIP = Botswana Independent Party

Sources: Statistics are drawn from Botswana Government, *Report to Minister of Public Service and Information on the General Election* (various years, including 1979, 1984, 1989, and 1994); and James H. Polhemus, "Botswana Votes: Parties and Elections: An African Democracy," *The Journal of Modern African Studies* 21, no. 3 (1983):397–430. See also Andreas Danevad, "Responsiveness in Botswana Politics: Do Elections Matter?" *The Journal of Modern African Studies* 33, no. 3 (1995):381–402.

Nicéphore Soglo, was elected president. Mathieu Kérékou, the former Marxist dictator, graciously accepted defeat and retired from the political system, only to return five years later as the leading opposition candidate in the 1996 presidential elections. With Soglo's reelection campaign severely hampered by the poor performance of the national economy and public perceptions of his disregard for the average citizen, Kérékou overcame the political odds and emerged victorious in the presidential elections. Dubbed the "chameleon" by friends and enemies alike — a reference to his changing political views — Kérékou's return to office served as a powerful example of the further consolidation of democratic practices on the African continent.

A second means for assessing the consolidation of democracy is to determine the nature and depth of civil liberties enjoyed by African populations, including the right to freedom of speech and assembly; access to vigorous, independent media; constitutional guarantees of due process by independent judiciaries; freedom of religion and worship; and the general protection of individual rights regardless of one's ethnicity, race, religious creed, or gender. Although individual cases vary, the African continent as a whole has enjoyed the steadily rising protection of civil liberties since 1989 (see Figure 12.2). It is precisely for this reason, argue optimists of Africa's democratic prospects, that one can speak of the gradual strengthening of a **democratic culture** that increasingly will become self-sustaining.

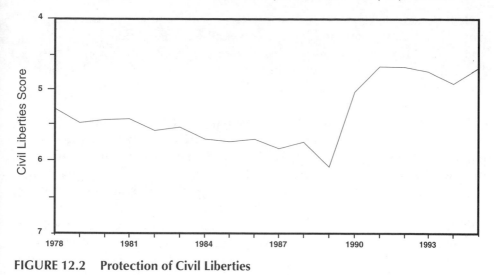

FIGURE 12.2   Protection of Civil Liberties

Source: Statistics are drawn from Freedom House, *Freedom in the World: The Annual Survey of Political Rights and Civil Liberties* (Washington: Freedom House, annual editions, 1978–1997). See Box 12.2 for a complete discussion of scores.

The caution one must nonetheless exercise when assessing the consolidation of newly formed democracies is clearly demonstrated by events in Zambia, a country that in 1991 made a successful transition from a single-party system, headed by President Kenneth Kaunda, to a multiparty political system under the leadership of President Frederick Chiluba of the Movement for Multiparty Democracy (MMD) party.[50] Eighteen months after achieving victory, Chiluba reinstated a "state of emergency" that had existed throughout Kaunda's rule, and arrested and detained without charges at least fourteen members of the official opposition, the United National Independence Party (UNIP). Critics of the government's actions drew parallels between Kaunda's use of states of emergency during the 1970s and the 1980s to silence political opponents and Chiluba's desire to curb rising criticism of his regime's inability to resolve Zambia's pressing economic problems. Most important, critics noted that the domination of Zambia's parliament by Chiluba's ruling MMD party (125 out of 150 seats) called into question the independence of the legislature from the executive, especially after Chiluba was successful in acquiring legislative approval for his harsh measures.[51]

An important aspect of Chiluba's political predicament is the *economic* dimension of the democratization process. Similar to leaders who took office beginning in the 1950s, Chiluba and the other newly elected democratic leaders of the 1990s are confronted with unrealistic popular expectations that the fruits of democratization, especially higher wages and better living conditions, will be widely and quickly shared after the holding of multiparty elections. Indeed, a significant portion of the Zambian people believed a multiparty system would somehow serve as a panacea for the country's economic problems. However, the combination of the overall weakness of the Zambian state and the constraints imposed on executive action by even the minimal checks-and-balances of the democratic system have led to little success within the economic realm, followed by growing public weariness and disenchantment with Chiluba's administration.

Chiluba's declining popularity has again presented the same authoritarian-democratic paradox confronted by the first generation of African leaders during the 1950s. Although largely socialized and trained within an authoritarian tradition, as were his predecessors, Chiluba is expected to abide by the "rules of the game" of Zambia's multiparty political system. Strict adherence to those rules, however, threatened to seal Chiluba's political fate in the 1996 presidential elections, especially after former president Kaunda accepted opposition backing and announced his entry into the race. As a result, Chiluba oversaw the ratification of two constitutional amendments that harkened back to the authoritarian excesses of his predecessor and threatened to undermine the very democratic political system he sought to create. The first required that the parents of any presidential candidate be Zambians by birth. The second limited any presidential candidate to two terms of office. Since Kaunda's parents were born in neighboring Malawi, and he had ruled Zambia for a total of twenty-seven years (1964–1991), he was forced to withdraw from the race. Chiluba's political maneuvering removed the only serious challenge to his rule, and ensured his reelection.[52]

Whether Africa's third wave of democratization will result in further democratic consolidation or democratic decay will largely depend on how the new generation of democratically elected elites responds to the authoritarian-democratic paradox. Will they graciously accept defeat and join the ranks of the **loyal opposition**, as was the case in Soglo's defeat in the 1996 Beninois presidential elections, or will they increasingly turn to a variety of authoritarian tactics to maintain themselves in power, as Chiluba's manipulation of the 1996 Zambian presidential elections illustrates? Indeed, the response of the first generation of African leaders to this authoritarian-democratic paradox in the 1950s ushered in nearly four decades of single-party rule. The ways in which Africa's newly elected democratic leaders resolve these paradoxes during the decade of the 1990s and beyond potentially portend the creation of new forms of political rule, destined to last well into the beginning of the twenty-first century.

Key Terms

third wave of democratization
Africa's second independence
Africa's second liberation
authoritarian-democratic paradox

systems of checks-and-balances
Westminster model
Elysée model
single-party political systems

consensus building
vanguard role
nonparty system
movement democracy
mass participatory democracy
multiparty competition
founding elections
national conference
co-opt the transition process
guided democratization
democratization from above

authoritarian reaction
political rights
civil liberties
freedom index
contested sovereignty
democratic decay
consolidation
alternation of power
democratic culture
loyal opposition

For Further Reading

Ake, Claude. *Democracy and Development in Africa*. Washington: Brookings Institution, 1996.

Bratton, Michael, and Nicolas van de Walle. *Democratic Transitions in Africa: Regime Transitions in Comparative Perspective*. Cambridge: Cambridge University Press, 1997.

Clark, John F., and David Gardinier, eds. *Political Reform in Francophone Africa*. Boulder: Westview, 1997.

Chole, Eshetu, and Jibrin Ibrahim, eds. *Democratisation Processes in Africa: Problems and Prospects*. Dakar: CODESRIA, 1995.

Decalo, Samuel. *The Stable Minority: Civilian Rule in Africa*. Gainesville: Florida Academic, 1997.

Hyden, Goran, and Michael Bratton, eds. *Governance and Politics in Africa*. Boulder: Lynne Rienner, 1992.

Joseph, Richard, ed. *The Democratic Challenge in Africa*. Atlanta: The Carter Center, 1994.

Krieger, Winfried Jung Silke, ed. *Culture and Democracy in Africa South of the Sahara*. Mainz, Germany: V. Hase and Koehler Verlag, 1994.

Mamdani, Mahmood, and Ernest Wamba-dia-Wamba, eds. *African Studies in Social Movements and Democracy*. Dakar: CODESRIA, 1995.

Ottaway, Marina. *Africa's New Leaders: Democracy or State Reconstruction?* Washington: Carnegie Endowment for International Peace, 1999.

Sandbrook, Richard. *The Politics of Africa's Economic Recovery*. Cambridge: Cambridge University Press, 1993.

Schaffer, Frederic C. *Democracy in Transition: Understanding Politics in an Unfamiliar Culture*. Ithaca: Cornell University Press, 1998.

Sisk, Timothy D., and Andrew Reynolds, eds. *Elections and Conflict Management in Africa*. Washington: United States Institute of Peace, 1998.

Widner, Jennifer A. *Economic Change and Political Liberalization in Sub-Saharan Africa*. Baltimore: Johns Hopkins University Press, 1994.

Wiseman, John A., ed. *Democracy and Political Change in Sub-Saharan Africa*. New York: Routledge, 1995.

Notes

1. See Samuel P. Huntington, *The Third Wave: Democratization in the Late Twentieth Century* (Oklahoma: University of Oklahoma Press, 1991).
2. For an introduction to this vast literature, see Michael Bratton and Nicolas van de Walle, *Democratic Experiments in Africa: Regime Transitions in Comparative Perspective* (Cambridge: Cambridge University Press, 1997). See also Rob Buijtenhuijs and Céline Thiriot. *Democratization in Sub-Saharan Africa, 1992–1995: An Overview of the Literature* (Leiden: African Studies Centre, 1995).
3. For example, see Donald Rothchild, "On the Application of the Westminster Model to Ghana," *Centennial Review* 4, no. 4 (Fall 1960); and Barry Munslow, "Why Has the Westminster Model Failed in Africa?" *Parliamentary Affairs* 36 (1983):218–28.
4. See Robert H. Jackson and Carl G. Rosberg, *Personal Rule in Black Africa* (Berkeley: University of California Press, 1982).
5. For a good overview, see Ruth Berins Collier, *Regimes in Tropical Africa: Changing Forms of Supremacy, 1945–75* (Berkeley: University of California Press, 1982).
6. For an early analysis, see Martin Kilson, "Authoritarian and Single-Party Tendencies in African Politics," *World Politics* 25, no. 2 (1963):262–94. See also Lanciné Sylla, *Tribalisme et Parti Unique en Afrique Noire* (Paris: Presses de la Fondation Nationale des Sciences Politiques, 1977).
7. For a good overview, see J. Gus Liebenow, *African Politics: Crises and Challenges* (Bloomington: Indiana University Press, 1986), pp. 225–29.
8. For a critique, see John Lonsdale, "African Pasts in African Futures," *Canadian Journal of African Studies* 23, no. 1 (1989):126–46.
9. *Ibid.*, p. 226.
10. See Julius Nyerere, *Freedom and Socialism: Uhuru and Ujamaa* (Dar es Salaam: Oxford University Press, 1968).
11. Liebenow, *African Politics*, p. 225.
12. *Ibid.*, pp. 228–29.
13. For example, compare the assessments provided by Peter Anyang' Nyong'o, "Africa: The Failure of One-Party Rule," *Journal of Democracy* 3, no. 1 (1992):90–96; and Samuel Decalo, "The Process, Prospects and Constraints of Democratization in Africa," *African Affairs* 91 (1992):7–35.
14. For example, see Douglas Anglin, "Southern African Responses to Eastern European Developments," *The Journal of Modern African Studies* 28, no. 3 (1990):431–55.
15. Quoted in Bratton and van de Walle, *Democratic Experiments in Africa*, pp. 105-6.
16. *Ibid.*, p. 3.

17. Jennifer A. Widner, *Economic Change and Political Liberalization in Sub-Saharan Africa* (Baltimore: Johns Hopkins University Press, 1994).
18. See Guy Martin, "Preface: Democratic Transition in Africa," *Issue: A Quarterly Journal of Opinion* 21, no. 1–2 (1993):6-7.
19. For the most comprehensive analysis, see Bratton and van de Walle, *Democratic Experiments in Africa*.
20. Bratton and van de Walle, *Democratic Experiments in Africa*, p. 198.
21. See Nelson Mandela, *Long Walk to Freedom: The Autobiography of Nelson Mandela* (Boston: Little, Brown, 1995), pp. 619–20.
22. For an overview, see Pearl Robinson, "The National Conference Phenomenon in Francophone Africa," *Comparative Studies in Society and History* 36 (1994):575–610. See also John F. Clark and David Gardinier, eds., *Political Reform in Francophone Africa* (Boulder: Westview, 1997).
23. See Martin, "Preface: Democratic Transition in Africa," p. 6.
24. For discussion, see Jacques Mariel Nzouankeu, "The Role of the National Conference in the Transition to Democracy in Africa: The Cases of Benin and Mali," *Issue* 21, no. 1–2 (1993):44–50; and John R. Heilbrunn, "Social Origins of National Conferences in Benin and Togo," *The Journal of Modern African Studies* 31, no. 2 (1993):277–99.
25. Nzouankeu, "The Role of the National Conference," p. 45.
26. *Ibid.*
27. *Ibid.*
28. For a summary, see Jennifer A. Widner, "The 1990 Elections in Côte d'Ivoire," *Issue* 201 (1991):31–40. See also Yves Fauré, "Democracy and Realism: Reflections on the Case of Côte d'Ivoire," *Africa: Journal of the International African Institute* 63, no. 3 (1993):313–29.
29. Decalo, "The Process, Prospects and Constraints," p. 27.
30. *Ibid.*
31. See Naomi Chazan, "Planning Democracy in Africa: A Comparative Perspective on Nigeria and Ghana," *Policy Sciences* 22 (1989):325–57.
32. See Ruby Ofori, "Ghana: The Elections Controversy," *Africa Report* 38, no. 4 (July-August 1993):33–35.
33. Richard Joseph, "Ghana: A Winning Formula," *Africa Report* 38, no. 1 (January–February 1993):45–46.
34. Ofori, "Ghana: The Elections Controversy," p. 35.
35. For discussion, see Mark Hubbard, "Cameroon: A Flawed Victory," *Africa Report* 38, no. 1 (January–February 1993):41–44.
36. Quoted in *ibid.*, p. 42.
37. Quoted in *ibid.*
38. For an overview of the origins and evolution of these guerrilla groups, see Daniel Compagnon, "The Somali Opposition Fronts: Some Comments and Questions," *Horn of Africa* 13, no. 1–2 (1990).
39. See Walter Clarke and Jeffrey Herbst, eds., *Learning from Somalia: The Lessons of Armed Humanitarian Intervention* (Boulder: Westview, 1997). See

also John L. Hirsch and Robert B. Oakley, *Somalia and Operation Restore Hope: Reflections on Peacemaking and Peacekeeping* (Washington: The United States Institute for Peace, 1995).

40. See Richard Joseph, "Africa: The Rebirth of Political Freedom," *Journal of Democracy* 2 (1992):11–25. In a later article, however, Joseph became more pessimistic. See Joseph, "Africa, 1990–1997: From *Abertura* to Closure," *Journal of Democracy* 9, no. 2 (1998):3–17. For a more recent positive analysis, see E. Gyimah-Boadi, "The Rebirth of African Liberalism," *Journal of Democracy* 9, no. 2 (1998):18–31.

41. See Michael Bratton, "After Mandela's Miracle in South Africa," *Current History* 97, no. 619 (May 1998):214–19.

42. For example, see René Lemarchand, "Africa's Troubled Transitions," *Journal of Democracy* 3, no. 4 (October 1992):98–109.

43. See Richard Sandbrook, "Transitions Without Consolidation: Democratization in Six African Cases," *Third World Quarterly* 17, no. 1 (1996):69–87.

44. Larry Diamond, "Beyond Authoritarianism and Totalitarianism: Strategies for Democratization," *The Washington Quarterly* (Winter 1989):142.

45. *Ibid.*

46. See John A. Wiseman, "Multi-Partyism in Africa: The Case of Botswana," *African Affairs* 76, no. 302 (1977):70–79. See also John Holm and Patrick Molutsi, eds., *Democracy in Botswana* (Gaborone: Macmillan Botswana, 1989).

47. See Roger Charlton, "The Politics of Elections in Botswana," *Africa: Journal of the International African Institute* 63, no. 3 (1993):330–71.

48. Other parties include the Botswana Independence Party (BIP), the Botswana People's Party (BPP), and the Botswana Progressive Union (BPU).

49. Other factors favoring the incumbent include a "weak" civil society and government domination of the media. See Patrick P. Molutsi and John D. Holm, "Developing Democracy When Civil Society Is Weak: The Case of Botswana," *African Affairs* 89, no. 356 (1990):323–40; and James J. Zaffiro, "The Press and Political Opposition in an African Democracy: The Case of Botswana," *The Journal of Commonwealth and Comparative Politics* 27, no. 1 (1989): 51–73. •

50. For an overview, see Eric Bjornlund, Michael Bratton and Clark Gibson, "Observing Multiparty Elections in Africa: Lessons from Zambia," *African Affairs* 91 (1992):405–31.

51. See Melinda Ham, "Zambia: History Repeats Itself," *Africa Report* 38, no. 3 (May–June 1993):13–16.

52. Bratton and van de Walle, *Democratic Experiments in Africa*, pp. 233, 260.

13

Foreign Policy Making and the Pursuit of Pan-Africanism

Reverend Leon Sullivan, founder of the African/African-American Summit, speaking at the second summit held in Libreville, Gabon, May 24–28, 1993.

SENEGALESE FOREIGN MINISTER Doudou Thiam wrote one of the first scholarly books on African foreign policy at the beginning of the contemporary independence era.[1] He called for policymakers of the newly independent African countries to rally around the foreign policy goals of pan-Africanism and African cultural consciousness, while avoiding involvement in the "intense ideological conflict" between the United States and the former Soviet Union.[2] Thiam's book was published in 1963, a noteworthy year in that it coincided with the launching of the Organization of African Unity (OAU): the first intergovernmental organization comprised of all independent African states and designed to promote the **pan-African ideal** of African political cooperation. Later years have witnessed the emergence and rapid expansion of a wide range of experiments in regional economic integration, designed to promote the economic dimension of the pan-African ideal. In the aftermath of the Cold War, renewed discussions over the viability of creating an African Defense Force signaled a new determination on the part of African leaders to promote the military dimension of pan-Africanism. After briefly setting out the foreign policy–making context, the majority of this chapter is devoted to exploring the nature and evolution of these experiments in pan-Africanism.

Understanding the Foreign Policy–Making Context

A strong sense of the interconnectedness between domestic and foreign policies has always been a mark of great diplomats throughout the world. In the 1960s, Senegalese Foreign Minister Thiam eloquently argued that any attempt at disengaging foreign and domestic policies was simply a matter of "practical convenience," with each constituting "two scales in the same balance, two aspects of the same indivisible reality."[3] More than twenty-five years later, Ousmane Tanor Dieng, one of the most senior political advisors to Senegalese President Abdou Diouf, cited the momentous changes occurring in the international system as a result of the Cold War's end and reaffirmed the importance of understanding the interplay between domestic and international factors in foreign policy.[4] As a result, any understanding of African support for the cherished foreign policy goal of promoting the pan-African ideal ultimately must begin with an understanding of the wide variety of governmental and nongovernmental actors that contribute to the formulation and implementation of African foreign policy.[5] An in-depth analysis of the Senegalese foreign policy establishment clearly demonstrates the diversity of elements involved in the foreign policy decision-making process.[6]

President and Bureaucracies of the Executive Branch

Like many other African constitutions, the Senegalese constitution embodies the widely shared belief that foreign policy constitutes the *domaine réservé* (privileged realm) of the president. Specifically drawing upon the highly centralized *Elysée* model of France's Fifth Republic, the Senegalese president is granted a wide array of foreign policy prerogatives under the Senegalese constitution: he is recognized as the commander in chief of the Armed Forces (Article 39); empowered to name Senegalese diplomats abroad and accredit those from foreign countries (Article 40); and authorized to negotiate, ratify, and approve international agreements (Article 75), except in certain specified realms, such as peace treaties and agreements with international organizations, which require ratification by the National Assembly (Article 76).[7] As is the case with its counterparts throughout the African continent, any analysis of Senegalese foreign policy therefore must begin with the personal beliefs and idiosyncrasies of that country's presidents: Léopold Sédar Senghor (1960–80) and Abdou Diouf (1981–present).

Each African head of state is usually complemented by an officially designated vice president or prime minister who occupies the second most influential position in the policy-making establishment. In the case of Senegal, the constitution stipulates that the president is to appoint a prime minister to manage the day-to-day functioning of the government. Unlike his counterparts in other African political systems, the Senegalese prime minister is not beholden to the National Assembly. However, the prime minister maintains a Diplomatic Cabinet under the guidance of a diplomatic advisor, and therefore plays an influential role in the foreign policy–making process.

The current Senegalese political system is significantly different from that of the early 1960s, when the Office of the President and the Office of the Prime Minister were constitutionally independent of each other. During this period, an intensifying power struggle between President Senghor and Prime Minister Mamadou Dia led to the revision of the constitution in 1963 to create a system based on presidential dominance. The current prime minister, Habib Thiam, has longstanding professional and personal links with President Diouf, and his office works closely with the Office of the President and the foreign affairs bureaucracies in the pursuit of Senegalese foreign policy goals.[8]

The Ministry of Foreign Affairs is usually the largest and most active of the foreign affairs bureaucracies within African policy-making establishments, taking responsibility for much of the day-to-day administration of foreign relations.[9] Depending on his personality and bureaucratic skills, the Minister of Foreign Affairs is therefore potentially a key player within the policy-making network. Direct access to the president, combined with links to the far-reaching foreign affairs bureaucracy, provide the minister with important bureaucratic tools to set the foreign policy agenda.[10] In the case of Senegal, for example, former Minister of Foreign Affairs Ibrahima Fall was the driving force behind the Diouf administration's adoption of a more "progressive" stance toward regional African issues, such as the decision to recognize the Marxist regime of Angola, headed by José Eduardo dos Santos.[11] Moustapha Niasse, serving as the current Minister of Foreign Affairs, carries these bureaucratic tools as well.

The Ministry of Defense is another foreign affairs bureaucracy that has played an extremely influential role in African foreign policies. In some cases, this bureaucracy has initiated military coups d'état, which in turn have led to the establishment of military-dominated regimes on the African continent (see Chapter 11). In some cases, the transition to a civilian democracy has been accompanied by policies designed to decrease both the size of the military establishment and its involvement in governmental affairs, including in the realm of foreign policy. In South Africa during the 1980s, for example, the military strongly argued in favor of the Afrikaner regime's decision to undertake destabilization policies against its immediate neighbors.[12] In the wake of the country's first democratic elections in 1994, therefore, the new government headed by Nelson Mandela pledged to restore greater government control over a military force that had become too dominant in both domestic and foreign policies.[13]

In the case of Senegal, strong adherence to the republican ideal of civilian control of the military has not prevented military leaders from playing important behind-the-scenes roles in shaping Senegal's political history.[14] During the 1963 constitutional crisis between President Senghor and Prime Minister Mamadou Dia, pro-Senghor military forces prevailed over those preferring to depose the president. More recently, Army Chief of Staff General Taverez Da Souza was removed from office in 1988, amid charges that he had convened meetings with other high-ranking officers to discuss the potential necessity of military intervention to end the political disturbances following the 1988 presidential elections.

The Senegalese Ministry of Defense is a powerful bureaucratic actor that increased its influence during the 1980s and the 1990s, due to Senegal's internal and external security problems.[15] Military officers have called for the strengthening of the armed forces (most notably the purchase of helicopters) to seek a military solution to the intermittent guerrilla war in the Casamance region of southern Senegal. Furthermore, they have strongly argued in favor of "hot pursuit" operations against neighboring countries (e.g., The Gambia and Guinea-Bissau), which have been accused of providing sanctuary to the guerrillas and inadequately controlling their national territories.[16] Overall, the military has played an influential role in Senegalese foreign policy throughout the Diouf administration, ranging from Senegal's involvement in a number of peace-keeping operations, such as the Cease-Fire Monitoring Group (ECOMOG) in Liberia during the 1980s that was sponsored by the Economic Community of West African States (ECOWAS), to President Diouf's decision to use military force in 1981 to restore President Daouda Diawara to power in The Gambia and in 1998 to maintain President João Bernardo Vieira in power in Guinea-Bissau.[17]

Role of National Legislatures in Foreign Policy

The legislative branch of government has also played an increasingly influential role in African foreign policies.[18] It has served as a vocal arena of national debate, particularly in countries such as Benin that significantly liberalized their political systems during the 1990s. The primary reason behind this newfound legislative role is the creation of democratic political systems that embody the concept of separation of powers between the various branches of government.[19] A question that requires further research is whether the newly empowered legislatures will largely restrict themselves to the national arena, calling to mind the old maxim that "politics stops at the water's edge," or if they will continue to have a growing voice within the realm of foreign affairs.

Beginning in the 1980s, the Senegalese National Assembly emerged as an increasingly vocal arena of national debate. Largely reduced to the role of a "rubber stamp" institution during the Senghor years (there was no opposition voice between 1964 and 1978), the National Assembly increasingly has questioned government policies since the lifting of multiparty restrictions in 1981, most notably in the aftermath of the 1993 legislative elections, in which candidates from five opposition parties won a total of thirty-six seats in the 120-seat National Assembly. The most important foreign affairs components of the National Assembly include the Committee on Foreign Affairs and over twenty Friendship Groups that promote formal and informal contacts between Senegalese representatives and their counterparts in foreign countries.

The willingness of Senegalese representatives to challenge the Executive Branch's foreign policy remains relatively lukewarm, however, and when it does occur it is largely restricted to issues related to the Senegalese economy, such as the domestic costs and impacts of foreign-sponsored structural adjustment programs. Furthermore, the National Assembly must cope with a weak constitutional role relative to that of the Executive Branch, as well as an ongoing negative public image as constituting nothing more than *applaudisseurs* (applauders of government policies). The National Assembly's role in foreign affairs is also seriously hampered by the lack of economic resources, most notably the lack of a sufficient budget that would allow committees and representatives to hire staffs and independently conduct research and fact-finding missions. "If we want the National Assembly to truly play its constitutionally mandated role," explains Representative Sémou Pathé Guèye, a member of the opposition *Parti de l'Indépendance et du Travail* (PIT, Independence and Workers Party), "we must put an end to the disastrous conditions under which Representatives work."[20] As further lamented by Iba Der Thiam, the head of the *Jappoo* (Wolof for "union") party alliance, representatives do not even enjoy individual offices in which to work and privately receive members of their constituencies.[21]

Foreign Policy Impact of Nongovernmental Actors

The formulation and implementation of African foreign policies are also influenced by a wide variety of nongovernmental actors. The print and broadcast media, for example, have flourished in the liberal political environment associated with transitions to democracy during the 1990s.[22] In the case of Senegal, the reporting of the daily government newspaper, *Le Soleil,* is now challenged by the publication of two privately funded daily newspapers, *Le Sud* and *Wal Fadjri,* as well as by a host of sporadically published newspapers, such as *Le Témoin* and *Démocraties.*[23] These private newspapers play an important agenda-setting role and, at the very least, offer a more critical perspective of day-to-day issues in foreign policy. For example, the German government's March 1996 decision to include Senegal in the list of nondemocratic countries for which requests for political asylum would be routinely considered was picked up by the press and turned into a public debate, prompting Minister of Communication Serigne Diop to hold a widely reported special meeting with the German Ambassador to Senegal.[24]

BOX 13.1
AFRICAN/AFRICAN-AMERICAN SUMMIT

A crucial element of the pan-African ideal is the creation of global links between the African continent and peoples of African descent in other regions of the world diaspora. The **African/African-American Summit** captures the essence of this global vision, by seeking to promote closer ties between the fifty-three countries of the African continent and the African-American community that comprises approximately 13 percent of the U.S. population. Although the idea of fostering links between Africa and the African-American community enjoys a rich intellectual history, the actual idea for a summit came to fruition under the leadership of Reverend Leon Sullivan. Originally conceived by Sullivan as a vehicle for strengthening cultural links, the African/African-American Summit has evolved into a burgeoning forum for enhancing international trade and investment.

The inaugural summit was held in Abidjan, Côte d'Ivoire (1991), followed by summits in Libreville, Gabon (1993), and Dakar, Senegal (1995). One of the most noteworthy components of the Dakar meeting was the organizing of an "American Day": a series of workshops and presentations held by numerous U.S. government officials who are responsible for promoting U.S.-African trade and investment. The primary theme of the presentations by U.S. government officials was "building bridges to commercial partnerships." A special emphasis was placed on explaining the "nuts and bolts" of promoting trade and investment, including the proper agencies and individuals to contact, the legal statutes and regulations governing economic partnerships, and sources of financial support and loan guarantees. The most popular U.S. government speaker was Secretary of Commerce Ronald H. Brown, who zealously promoted U.S. trade and investment in Africa prior to his tragic death in 1995.

The fourth African/African-American Summit was held in Harare, Zimbabwe, in 1997. The meeting was attended by approximately three thousand participants, including African heads of state from Botswana, Ethiopia, Senegal, Swaziland, and Uganda, as well as notable African-American politicians, such as two-time presidential candidate Reverend Jesse Jackson, David Dinkins (former Mayor of New York City), Marion Barry (Mayor of Washington, D.C.), and Coretta Scott King, the widow of Martin Luther King, Jr. The official U.S. government delegation was led by Secretary of Transportation Rodney Slater, and was joined by Jack Kemp. The trade and investment exhibition of the summit was dedicated to the memory of Secretary of Commerce Ron Brown, whose early efforts helped to focus the Clinton administration on the importance of trade with Africa.

The personal impact of this meeting was summed up by Leonard Bennet, an African-American attorney participating in the 1997 African/African-American Summit: "We go back [to the United States] with a very positive image of Africa and the fact that we have blacks running their own countries is truly reflective of what we as blacks can achieve. We go back a changed people."

African/African-American Summits

1st   Abidjan, Côte d'Ivoire (April 17–19, 1991)

2nd   Libreville, Gabon (May 24–28, 1993)

3rd   Dakar, Senegal (May 1–6, 1995)

4th   Harare, Zimbabwe (July 22–25, 1997)

5th   Accra, Ghana (scheduled for May 15–22, 1999)

Discussion draws on releases provided by the Summit Office of Rev. Leon H. Sullivan, Phoenix, Arizona, and the author's attendance at the third African/African-American Summit in Dakar, Senegal.

The growing communities of Africans living and working outside of Africa are also influential in the foreign policies of their countries of origin. The seriousness with which the Senegalese government treats nearly 500,000 Senegalese living and working abroad (one of every sixteen citizens) is aptly demonstrated by the June 1993 decision to rename the Ministry of Foreign Affairs the Ministry of Foreign Affairs and of Senegalese Abroad.[25] When one examines the growing Senegalese inclination toward warmer relations with the United States during the 1980s and the 1990s, one is left wondering to what degree this has been influenced by the large numbers of Senegalese who sought their fortunes in the United States and are now capable of mobilizing financial resources for a variety of business undertakings in their country of birth. Indeed, in 1996 the Senegalese government aided in the creation of an investment consortium of Senegalese living in the United States, as a means for attracting greater investment into Senegal and promoting expanding trade links between the two countries.

Public opinion has also exerted an influential, albeit intermittent, influence in African foreign policies. As in other African countries, the strengthening of the democratization process portends greater popular input into the policy-making process, as the policies of a new generation of African leaders are increasingly held accountable to public opinion. In the case of Senegal, it has been argued that public opinion, inflamed by radio broadcasts by *Radio France Internationale,* was the primary factor that led to bloody clashes between Senegal and Mauritania in 1989.[26] Despite the fact that this conflict was neither desired nor promoted by President Diouf of Senegal or President Ould Taya of Mauritania, both of these leaders, despite their best efforts to contain public passions, were confronted by violent clashes that spiraled out of control. In a sense, both leaders, as well as the foreign policies of their respective countries, became "prisoners" of public opinion.[27]

Finally, one must also take into account the impact of religious groups and leaders on African foreign policies.[28] In the case of Senegal, religious leaders known as marabouts have historically been an integral part of the domestic political system, and play both informal and formal roles in the making of foreign policy.[29] For example, the marabouts played a critical informal role in reducing tensions between Senegal and Mauritania in the aftermath of the 1989 border conflict, by undertaking an unofficial form of shuttle diplomacy across the river that separates the two countries. In a formal sense, one of President Diouf's closest advisors is Moustaffa Cisse, a marabout who served as the Senegalese ambassador to Egypt and to Saudi Arabia.

The power of the marabouts is derivative of the population's belief in the spiritual powers of their personal religious guides. The marabouts enjoy almost complete financial autonomy from state control due to a highly complex system of alms collection by *taalibe* (disciples) who, depending on the charisma and power of individual marabouts, are capable of channeling enormous amounts of money into a designated cause. The marabouts therefore are capable of mobilizing potent protest to undesired foreign policies and supporting others with little fear of state retribution. A dramatic case in point occurred in the mid-1980s, when the Diouf administration was forced to withdraw an invitation to Pope John Paul II to visit the country due to the threats of leading marabouts to call upon their *taalibe* to occupy the runways at the international airport. Although the Pope was subsequently reinvited and visited Senegal several years later in 1991, to the wide acclaim of both Muslims and Christians, the marabouts had clearly served notice that sensitive issues had to be raised with them in advance if the Diouf administration wished to avoid embarrassing public confrontations. In short, a complete understanding of the formulation and implementation of Senegal's foreign policy, as well as that of other African countries with sizeable Muslim populations, must account for the role of religion.

Pan-Africanism and the Organization of African Unity

Inspired by the anticolonial activities of peoples of African descent living in North America and the West Indies during the nineteenth and twentieth centuries, African nationalists sought to promote a unified African front against colonial rule. What subsequently became known as the pan-African ideal was most forcefully enunciated for the first time at the 1945 meeting of the Pan-African Congress held in Manchester, England. At the conference, participants adopted a "Declaration to the Colonial Peoples" that affirmed the "rights" of all colonized peoples to be "free from foreign imperialist control, whether political or economic," and "to elect their own governments, without restrictions from foreign powers."[30] In a separate "Declaration to the Colonial Powers," participants further underscored that if the colonial powers were "still determined to rule mankind by force, then Africans, as a last resort, may have to appeal to force in the effort to achieve freedom."[31]

The pan-African ideal gained momentum as a result of the first wave of independence during the 1950s. In an opening address to the first gathering of independent African nations on African soil, held in 1958 in Accra, Ghana, President Kwame Nkrumah proclaimed: "Never before has it been possible for so representative a gathering of African Freedom Fighters to assemble in a free independent African state for the purpose of planning for a final assault upon imperialism and colonialism."[32] According to Nkrumah, the realization of the pan-African ideal required a commitment between African leaders and their peoples to guide their countries through four stages: (1) "the attainment of freedom and independence"; (2) "the consolidation of that independence and freedom"; (3) "the creation of unity and community between the African states"; and (4) "the economic and social reconstruction of Africa."[33]

Despite overwhelming agreement among African leaders that pan-Africanism constituted a worthy foreign policy goal, sharp disagreement existed over the proper path to ensure such unity. One group of primarily francophone countries known as the **Brazzaville Group** (named after the capital of Congo-Brazzaville), sought a minimalist approach: the coordination of national economic policies through standard diplomatic practices. Little consideration was given to the possibility of creating continent-wide institutions. In sharp contrast, Nkrumah and other leaders, who belonged to what became known as the **Casablanca Group** (named after the Moroccan city), argued instead that the success of pan-Africanism required a *political union* of all independent African countries, patterned after the federal model of the United States of

America. In speech after speech, Nkrumah promoted two key themes that became the hallmark of this international vision: "Africa must unite!" and "Seek ye first the political kingdom!"[34]

A third group of African leaders, who belonged to what became known as the **Monrovia Group** (named after the capital of Liberia), rejected the idea of political union as both undesirable and unfeasible, primarily due to the assumption that African leaders would jealously guard their countries' new-found independence. They nonetheless sought a greater degree of cooperation than that espoused by the Brazzaville Group. Led by Alhaji Abubakar Tafawa Belewa, the Prime Minister of Nigeria, the Monrovia group called for the creation of a *looser organization* of African states. According to this vision, African countries would guard their independence but promote growing cooperation and the harmonization of policies in a variety of functional areas, most notably economic, scientific, educational, and social development. An important component of the Monrovia Group approach was a desire to create continent-wide institutions that would oversee and strengthen policy harmonization.

On May 25, 1963, thirty-one African heads of state largely embraced the Monrovia vision by launching the **Organization of African Unity** (OAU), the first pan-African, intergovernmental organization of independent African countries based on African soil. The OAU is headquartered in Addis Ababa, Ethiopia, and is headed by a secretary general elected by member states. All major decisions and resolutions are formally discussed at the annual Assembly of Heads of State and Government after the biannual meetings of the Council of Ministers. The **sovereign equality** of all member states is an important guiding principle of the organization and significantly differs from the **Great Power domination** of the United Nations, given the special power conferred upon the five permanent members of the UN Security Council: Britain, China, France, Russia, and the United States.

Although the creation and continued vitality of the OAU have been described as a "victory for pan-Africanism,"[35] both critics and sympathetic observers have questioned the organization's ability to play an effective role in African politics and international relations. In a special issue of the *Nigerian Journal of International Affairs*, which assessed the OAU's continued relevance on the "Silver Jubilee" (twenty-five-year) anniversary of the organization's creation, one Nigerian scholar expressed "sadness" over the fact that, despite the best of intentions, the OAU had failed to live up to the expectations of its original framers.[36] The OAU's effectiveness can be tentatively assessed by exploring several elements of the OAU Charter.

Inviolability of Inherited Frontiers

The most important theme of the OAU Charter is support for the territorial integrity of frontiers inherited from the colonial era. Due to the multiethnic nature of most African countries, African leaders remain fearful that changing even one boundary will open a Pandora's box of ethnically based secessionist movements and lead to the further **Balkanization** of the African continent into ever smaller economic and political units.

In the case of the Nigerian civil war (1967–70), for example, the OAU not only refused to sanction the provision of aid to Biafra, the secessionist southeast portion of the country, but voted a series of resolutions that underscored official support for the Nigerian federal government.[37] This decision was particularly upsetting to international human rights activists, as well as several African countries aiding the secessionist government, because the military-dominated Nigerian government was using very effective starvation methods designed to bring the Biafrans — government and general population alike — to their knees.[38]

As ethnic tensions and separatist movements intensify in the post–Cold War era, African leaders remain firmly committed to maintaining borders inherited from the colonial era. Although the OAU recognized the sovereignty of Eritrea in 1993, after a UN-sponsored referendum in that country resulted in overwhelming popular support for independence, African leaders subsequently noted that this process did not call into question the hallowed concept of the inviolability of frontiers. Unlike the majority of African countries, Eritrea was federated to Ethiopia after independence from colonial rule, and therefore enjoyed the legal right to withdraw from that voluntary union. However, in similar cases of voluntary federation that have unraveled in the post–Cold War era, such as northern Somalia's 1991 unilateral declaration of independence as the Somaliland Republic, as well as other cases where a disgruntled region, such as the southern Sudan, has affirmed the right of self-determination, the OAU continues to reaffirm the concept of territorial integrity.

Noninterference in Domestic Affairs

The second most important guiding principle of the OAU Charter is noninterference in the internal affairs of member states. In the early years of the organization, African leaders debated whether to allow military leaders who had illegally deposed their civilian counterparts to maintain their OAU seats. This debate was resolved in favor of recognizing whatever group controlled the reins of power within a particular country.[39] More significant was the silence among African leaders concerning human rights abuses in OAU member states. "Increased repression, denial of political choice, restrictions on the freedom of association, and like events occurred, with rare murmurs of dissent," explains Claude Welch, Jr., a specialist of human rights in Africa. "The OAU seemed to function as a club of presidents, engaged in a tacit policy of not inquiring into each other's practices."[40] During the 1970s, for example, Ugandan dictator Idi Amin was elected OAU chair despite his personal involvement in "politically sanctioned repression and murders" in Uganda.[41]

Although still highly reluctant to criticize their counterparts, African leaders are nonetheless beginning to accept a growing role for the OAU in addressing human rights abuses. In 1981, the annual Assembly of Heads of State and

Government held in Banjul, Gambia, adopted the **African Charter on Human and People's Rights** (popularly referred to as the **Banjul Charter**). This human rights code officially went into effect in October 1986, and has served as the guiding principle for a variety of human rights groups that emerged during the 1980s.[42] In addition to encompassing **first generation rights** (civil and political liberties) usually associated with the Western world, and **second generation rights** (economic and social rights) usually associated with the socialist world, the Banjul Charter has been described as "breaking some new ground" through the adoption of **third generation rights** intended to protect the rights of individual peoples or ethnic groups.[43]

Despite the ratification of the Banjul Charter, however, the OAU's response to events in Nigeria during 1995 demonstrates the continued difficulty of translating human rights rhetoric into policy action. In response to disturbances among the Ogoni ethnic group in southeastern Nigeria, which began in 1990 over control of that region's vast oil resources, Nigeria's military regime unleashed a brutal campaign of suppression that included the November 1995 execution of Nobel Peace Prize candidate Ken Saro-Wiwa and eight other Ogoni activists on trumped-up murder charges.[44] Although OAU Secretary General Salim Ahmed Salim expressed "disappointment" over the fact that the Nigerian generals failed to "respond positively" to OAU appeals for clemency, the organization did not adopt concrete, comprehensive measures to punish or to internationally isolate the Nigerian regime.[45]

Peaceful Settlement of Disputes

The peaceful settlement of all disputes by negotiation, mediation, conciliation, or arbitration constitutes a third guiding principle of the OAU. Yet strict adherence to the first two principles — support for territorial integrity and noninterference in internal affairs — historically has impeded the OAU's ability to mediate either internal conflicts or those between two or more member states. In the case of the 1967–70 Nigerian civil war, automatic support for the territorial integrity of Nigeria seriously called into doubt (at least from the view of the secessionist Igbos) the OAU's ability to serve as an impartial negotiator. It is for this reason that the OAU Commission of Mediation, Arbitration and Conciliation was "stillborn,"[46] and the majority of African-initiated arbitration efforts have been carried out on an ad hoc basis by African presidents. For example, Djiboutian President Hassan Gouled Aptidon utilized his country's stature as the headquarters for the Intergovernmental Authority on Drought and Development (IGADD) to mediate the conflict between Ethiopia and Somalia. According to I. William Zartman, a specialist of conflict resolution, such efforts have led to success in only 33 percent of roughly twenty-four cases, and this success was often only temporary in nature as warring parties returned to the battlefield.[47]

The ability to dispatch peace-keeping or peace-making forces once a conflict has broken out is a critical aspect of conflict resolution. The OAU Founding Fathers attempted to prepare for this eventuality by planning the creation of an African High Command: a multinational military force comprised of military contingents from OAU member states. The African High Command never made it beyond the planning stage, however, leading once again to a variety of ad hoc measures. In 1981, the OAU sponsored the creation of a short-term, all-African military force designed to resolve an expanding civil war in Chad.[48] Comprised of approximately 4,800 troops from the Democratic Republic of the Congo (Congo-Kinshasa), Nigeria, and Senegal, the OAU force "failed to achieve any concrete solution" due to financial, logistical, and political difficulties, and within a few months was "forced to withdraw."[49]

The most notable outcome of the lack of OAU coordination in the military realm has been a variety of military interventions by individual countries and intergovernmental organizations. Four sets of actors have periodically intervened in African conflicts: (1) the *United Nations*, as demonstrated by the Security Council's 1991 decision to sponsor a series of U.S.-led military operations in Somalia, usually referred to as "Operation Restore Hope"; (2) *African regional organizations*, such as the decision of the Economic Community of West African States (ECOWAS) to sponsor a series of Nigerian-led military operations in Liberia; (3) *Foreign Powers*, most notably the former Soviet Union, the United States, and France; and (4) *African Powers*, as demonstrated by Nigeria's 1997 dispatch of troops to neighboring Sierra Leone to restore a civilian government to power. From the perspective of pan-Africanists, these four types of intervention are ultimately undesirable: rather than representing the consensus opinion of OAU member states, such interventions theoretically are driven by the self-interests of the intervening actor or actors.

Two developments underscore the OAU's desire to take a more proactive role in African conflicts in the post–Cold War era. In 1993, the OAU Assembly of Heads of State and Government adopted a resolution creating the Mechanism for Conflict Prevention, Management and Resolution: a formal consultative process ideally designed to prevent the outbreak and further spread of conflicts on the African continent.[50] The inspiration for this consultative process was a forward-thinking document, "Towards a Conference on Security, Stability, Development and Cooperation in Africa," popularly referred to as the **Kampala Document**, which was the result of a 1991 conference convened by former Nigerian President Olusegun Obasanjo.

The most important development of the post–Cold War era is a new African consensus on the necessity of creating a multinational **African Defense Force**, capable of responding militarily to African crises. In May 1997, African leaders agreed that such a force should be comprised of existing military units of contributing OAU member states, and that these units would be equipped with the aid of foreign powers, most notably the United States and France. The African Defense Force would remain under the operational command of the OAU. Unresolved issues include which countries should be eligible to contribute forces (e.g., should involvement only be limited to democratic countries?) and

BOX 13.2

OAU SUMMIT OF HEADS OF STATE AND GOVERNMENT

The **OAU Summit of Heads of State and Government** is one of the most important annual events of the African diplomatic calendar. The summit serves as a unique diplomatic meeting ground that provides African leaders with an important regional forum for engaging in debate and promoting African views on a variety of international issues.

One of the most significant ongoing debates revolves around two decisions taken at the nineteenth Annual OAU Summit in 1983: (1) recognition of the sovereign independence of the former Spanish Sahara as the Saharan Arab Democratic Republic (SADR); and (2) admission of the SADR as a full voting member of the OAU. The response of Moroccan King Hassan II, whose country claims the territory, was to withdraw his country from the OAU in 1983. The debate over the SADR has contributed to a rising anglophone-francophone rift within the OAU, as demonstrated by the fact that the majority of anglophone member-states recognizes the SADR, whereas the francophone member-states are increasingly sympathetic to Moroccan claims of sovereignty.

Host Countries and Chairpersons of OAU Summits

Founding Summit: Addis Ababa, Ethiopia (1963)
Emperor Haile Selassie (Ethiopia)

1st Cairo, Egypt (July 21–24, 1964)
Gamal Abdel Nasser (Egypt)

2nd Accra, Ghana (October 21–25, 1965)
Kwame Nkrumah (Ghana)

3rd Addis Ababa, Ethiopia (November 5–9, 1966)
Emperor Haile Selassie (Ethiopia)

4th Kinshasa, Congo-Kinshasa (September 11–14, 1967)
Mobutu Sese Seko (Congo-Kinshasa)

5th Algiers, Algeria (September 13–16, 1968)
Houari Boumedienne (Algeria)

6th Addis Ababa, Ethiopia (September 6–10, 1969)
Ahmadou Ahidjo (Cameroon)

7th Addis Ababa, Ethiopia (September 1–5, 1970)
Kenneth Kaunda (Zambia)

8th Addis Ababa, Ethiopia (June 21–23, 1971)
Moktar Ould Daddah (Mauritania)

9th Rabat, Morocco (June 12–15, 1972)
King Hassan II (Morocco)

10th   Addis Ababa, Ethiopia (May 23–25, 1973)
        Yakabu Gowan (Nigeria)

11th   Mogadishu, Somalia (June 12–15, 1975)
        Mohammed Siad Barre (Somalia)

12th   Kampala, Uganda (July 28–August 1, 1975)
        Idi Amin (Uganda)

13th   Port Louis, Mauritius (July 2–5, 1977)
        Seewoosagur Ramgoolam (Mauritius)

14th   Libreville, Gabon (July 2–5, 1977)
        Omar Bongo (Gabon)

15th   Khartoum, Sudan (July 18–21, 1978)
        Gaafar Mohammed Numeiri (Sudan)

16th   Monrovia, Liberia (July 17–21, 1979)
        William Tolbert (Liberia)

17th   Freetown, Sierra Leone (July 1–4, 1980)
        Siaka Stevens (Sierra Leone)

18th   Nairobi, Kenya (July 24–28, 1981)
        Daniel arap Moi (Kenya)

19th   Tripoli, Libya (1982) — cancelled due to boycott

19th   Addis Ababa, Ethiopia (June 8–11, 1983)
        Mengistu Haile Marian (Ethiopia)

20th   Addis Ababa, Ethiopia (November 12–15, 1984)
        Julius Nyerere (Tanzania)

21st   Addis Ababa, Ethiopia (July 18–20, 1985)
        Abdou Diouf (Senegal)

22nd   Addis Ababa, Ethiopia (July 28–30, 1986)
        Sassou Nguesso (Congo-Brazzaville)

23rd   Addis Ababa, Ethiopia (July 27–30, 1987)
        Kenneth Kaunda (Zambia)

24th   Addis Ababa, Ethiopia (May 24–28, 1988)
        Moussa Traoré (Mali)

25th   Addis Ababa, Ethiopia (July 24–26, 1989)
        Hosni Moubarak (Egypt)

26th   Addis Ababa, Ethiopia (July 9–11, 1990)
        Yoweri Museveni (Uganda)

27th   Abuja, Nigeria (June 3–5, 1991)
        Ibrahim Babangida (Nigeria)

28th   Dakar, Senegal (June 29–July 1, 1992)
        Abdou Diouf (Senegal)

29th   Cairo, Egypt (June 28–29, 1993)
       Hosni Mubarak (Egypt)

30th   Tunis, Tunisia (June 13–15, 1994)
       Zine El-Abidine Ben Ali (Tunisia)

31st   Addis Ababa, Ethiopia (June 26–28, 1995)
       Meles Zenawi (Ethiopia)

32nd   Yaounde, Cameroon (July 8–10, 1996)
       Paul Biya (Cameroon)

33rd   Harare, Zimbabwe (June 2–4, 1997)
       Robert Mugabe (Zimbabwe)

34th   Ouagadougou, Burkina Faso (June 8–10, 1998)
       Blaise Compaoré (Burkina Faso)

what type of decision-making body should be capable of authorizing when and where to intervene (e.g., should intervention be based on the consensus of all OAU member-states or should a smaller body of representative members be responsible?). Discussions concerning the African Defense Force nonetheless remain at an exploratory stage, and the Mechanism for Conflict Prevention, Management and Resolution has yet to be tested in regard to a specific African conflict.

Opposition to Colonialism and White Minority Rule

The final and most successful principle embodied within the OAU Charter is the unswerving opposition to colonialism and white minority rule. Principally concerned with the past existence of minority white-ruled regimes in Zimbabwe, Namibia, South Africa, and the former Portuguese territories of Angola, Mozambique, Guinea-Bissau, and Sao Tome and Principe, the OAU established a Liberation Committee based in Dar es Salaam, Tanzania, to aid liberation movements with both economic and military assistance.[51] Although disagreements often arose over which tactics would best ensure transitions to majority-ruled governments (e.g., should one support "dialogue" with a white regime or fund a guerrilla insurgency?), every OAU member expressed public opposition to the continued existence of minority white-ruled regimes. The work of the Liberation Committee largely came to an end in 1994, when South Africa made the transition to a multiracial, multiparty democracy.

Regional Economic Cooperation and Integration

Inspired by the success of the European Union and encouraged by the UN-sponsored **Economic Commission for Africa** (ECA), based in Addis Ababa, Ethiopia, African leaders have sought to create regional entities capable of promoting regional cooperation and integration. This vision of African international relations was best outlined by the OAU's publication in 1981 of a document: *Lagos Plan of Action for the Economic Development of Africa, 1980–2000*, which proposed the establishment of an **African Economic Community** (AEC) that would be based on an **African Common Market** (ACM).[52] The guiding logic of the *Lagos Plan of Action* is that the creation of intergovernmental economic organizations in each of Africa's five major regions — North, East, West, Southern, and Central Africa — is the best means for ensuring the ultimate creation of a continent-wide AEC. Treaty discussions were launched at the Twenty-Seventh Annual Meeting of the OAU Heads of State and Government, held in 1991 in Abuja, Nigeria, and a treaty was signed in 1994. The thirty-third OAU summit, held in 1997 in Harare, Zimbabwe, also served as the first summit of the AEC.

The flourishing of experiments in regional cooperation and integration throughout the contemporary independence era demonstrates the firm commitment of African leaders to the economic dimension of the pan-African ideal. By the end of the 1980s, it was estimated that at least 160 intergovernmental economic groupings existed on the African continent, with thirty-two such organizations in West Africa alone.[53] Among the most notable and far-reaching economic groupings in each of Africa's major regions (including dates of launching) are the Economic Community of West African States (ECOWAS, 1975); the Union of the Arab Maghreb (UAM in North Africa, 1989); the Southern African Development Community (SADC, 1980); the Economic Community of Central African States (ECCAS, 1983); and the Intergovernmental Authority on Drought and Development (IGADD) in Northeast Africa (1986). These regional organizations are complemented by a few larger groupings, such as the Lomé Convention, which promotes preferential trade links between the European Union and dozens of countries from Africa, the Caribbean, and the Pacific.

African leaders offer several rationales for seeking regional cooperation and integration. The simplest reason is the firm belief that there is strength in numbers. In order to effectively compete within an increasingly competitive international economic system, dominated by economic superpowers (e.g., the United States and Japan) and powerful regional economic entities (e.g., the European Union), African countries must band together and pool their respective resources. Second, African leaders desire to promote self-sustaining economic development and particularly the industrialization of the African continent. Struggling with the reality that many of their countries are economically impoverished and lack the tools for the creation of advanced industries, African leaders believe that they can build upon the individual strengths of their neighbors to forge integrated and self-sustaining regional economies.

Most important, regional economic schemes are perceived as the best means for creating self-reliant development, thereby reducing and eventually ridding the African continent of the ties of dependency inherited from the colonial era.[54] For example, African leaders are rightfully concerned that national control over the evolution of their respective economies is constrained by Africa's trade dependency on Europe, at the expense of intraregional trade links with African countries. It is for this reason that the primary objective of early regional economic schemes was to promote intraregional trade with neighbors who theoretically share a common set of development objectives — either due to special geographic features, historical ties, or a shared religion, such as Islam in North Africa.[55] By strengthening these ties with like-minded neighbors, a stronger African economic entity is expected to emerge that will be capable of reducing foreign influence and strengthening Africa's collective ability to bargain with non-African powers on a more equal basis.

Early optimism began to wane in the aftermath of the launching of several regional integration efforts, which included the creation of supranational authorities and formal economic unions designed to promote intraregional trade and investment. In the case of the East African Community (EAC), the 1967 decision of Kenya, Tanzania, and Uganda to create a common market with common services, coordinated by a supranational governing body, collapsed less then ten years later, and was followed in 1978–79 by Tanzania's military intervention in Uganda to overthrow the dictatorial regime of Idi Amin. As explained by Olatunde Ojo, a specialist of regional cooperation and integration in Africa, several factors that contributed to the EAC's decline clarify why other similar efforts, from the 1960s to the 1980s, either failed or demonstrated minimal progress.[56]

An initial problem was the polarization of national development and the perception of unequal gains.[57] As typically occurred in other cases in Africa where the creation of a common market served as the cornerstone of the regional grouping, the most industrialized country (Kenya) usually reaped the benefits of economic integration at the expense of its partners (Uganda and Tanzania). For example, Kenya's share of intracommunity trade increased from 63 percent in 1968 to 77 percent in 1974, whereas Uganda's share decreased from 26 to 6 percent during the same period. In addition, despite the fashioning of a common policy toward the establishment of new operations by multinational corporations (MNCs), the majority of these firms decided to locate their bases of operations in Kenya due to its more advanced economy and workforce, as well as its extensive infrastructural network of roads, railroads, ports, and airports.

The EAC also foundered due to the inadequacy of compensatory and corrective measures.[58] In every integration scheme, some countries inevitably benefit more than others. As a result, policymakers can implement measures, such as the creation of regional development banks or the disproportionate sharing of customs revenue, to correct the imbalance and compensate those countries expected to lose out in the short term. In the case of the EAC, a regional development bank was created to disburse funds in the following manner to the three members: Kenya (22 percent), Tanzania (38 percent), and Uganda (40 percent). However, in this and other cases of integration in Africa, even the richest members are usually incapable of subsidizing bank operations. The actual finances provided to the most needy members therefore never even begin to approach true development needs or completely compensate for losses incurred.

A third stumbling block to successful regional integration of the EAC was ideological differences and the rise of economic nationalism.[59] Simply put, ideological differences often ensure a radically different approach to development projects, which in turn can significantly hinder regional integration (see Chapter 8). In the case of Kenya, a pro-West capitalist regime was very open to private enterprise and foreign investment, particularly the opening of local offices of MNCs. The socialist-oriented regime of Tanzania, however, opted for a self-help strategy known as *ujamaa* (the Kiswahili word for brotherhood), which not only denounced private enterprise as exploitative, but also restricted the flow of foreign investment, and strongly controlled the MNCs. When combined with the growing public perception of unequal gains between the two countries, these ideological differences led to often acrimonious public debate between President Jomo Kenyatta of Kenya and President Julius Nyerere of Tanzania, and to the rise of economic nationalism in both countries.

A final element that contributed to the EAC's decline was the impact of foreign influences.[60] Whereas Kenya developed close relationships with the Western bloc nations (e.g., the United States and Great Britain), Tanzania pursued close links with the socialist bloc (particularly the People's Republic of China), and Uganda sought links with the former Soviet Union and the Arab world. These links ensured that the EAC became embroiled in the Cold War rivalry of the 1960s and the 1970s, and contributed to the creation of an outwardly directed "strategic image," which prompted EAC member states to look "outward" toward their foreign patrons rather than "inward" toward their natural regional partners.

Beginning in the 1980s, the failure and stagnation of classic integration schemes prompted African leaders to undertake looser forms of regional **economic cooperation** in a variety of functionally specific areas, such as transportation infrastructure (e.g., regional rail links), energy (e.g., hydroelectric projects on common rivers), and telecommunications.[61] The logic behind pursuing this form of regionalism is that it does not require the creation of supranational authorities, nor does it require policymakers to sacrifice national control over the sensitive areas of foreign trade and investment. This looser form of economic cooperation is gathering strength in the post–Cold War era, particularly as democratically elected elites increasingly assume power and seek to promote cooperation with other democracies within their regions.

The 1992 transformation of the Southern African Development Coordination Conference (SADCC) into the Southern African Development Community (SADC) provides a good example of this growing trend in African regional relations. Originally conceived as a vehicle for reducing the economic dependence of the Frontline States on South Africa during the apartheid era, the newly reformed SADC now counts South Africa among its members, and is seeking to enhance traditional cooperation in a variety of functional realms, most notably transportation.[62] The new SADC stands poised at "the threshold of a new era," according to a report recently published by the African Development Bank in conjunction with the World Bank and the Development Bank of South Africa.[63] "Although its effects and the inequities it has embedded will linger for a long time to come, the demise of apartheid opens up prospects unimaginable even a few years ago," explains the report. "New opportunities have emerged in every sector of economic activity for expanded trade and mutually beneficial exchanges of all kinds among the countries of southern Africa."[64]

Several factors are essential to understanding the optimism surrounding SADC's newfound status as a model for economic cooperation in Africa, particularly in terms of reducing Southern Africa's dependence on foreign economic interests and creating the basis for self-sustaining development in the post–Cold War era.[65] First, the inclusion of a highly industrialized South Africa provides SADC with an engine for economic growth that will potentially reinvigorate the entire region. In this regard, South Africa may play a leadership role similar to that enjoyed by Germany in the European Union, the United States in NAFTA, and, to a lesser degree, Nigeria in ECOWAS. The vast majority of SADC members (seven out of ten) also share a common British colonial heritage. Although a shared colonial past is not a precondition for effective regional cooperation, it nonetheless facilitates such technical matters as which language should serve as the official language of communication (in the case of both SADC and the EAC, English).

A third facilitating factor is the decline in ideological differences between SADC member states that accompanied the end of the Cold War. Whereas Angola, Mozambique, and Zimbabwe have discarded in varying degrees their adherence to Marxist principles of development, South Africa has officially renounced its apartheid system and Tanzania and Zambia have dismantled significant portions of their formerly socialist economies. In essence, there exists a growing consensus among SADC member states that effective regional economic cooperation must be based on a shared commitment to some variant of the liberal capitalist model of development (see Chapter 8).

SADC's greatest strength is a regional commitment to conflict resolution and to the promotion of shared democratic values.[66] Except for the case of Angola, the Cold War's end and the rise of democratization movements have led to the end of civil wars and the holding of democratic elections throughout the SADC countries of Southern Africa. One of the most important lessons of regional integration theory, which draws upon the success of the European Union, is that the existence of elites with a shared commitment to democracy is the foundation of long-term economic cooperation and development. It is for this reason that the 1992 Windhoek Treaty (named after the capital of Namibia), which consecrated the launching of SADC, underscored the political dimension of regional relationships and its critical role in the continued expansion of economic cooperation.[67] The leaderships of SADC member states recognize that the fruits of pan-Africanism can only be achieved by the settlement of civil war and the promotion of democracy in Angola and other countries throughout the African continent. As a result, conflict resolution remains an important cornerstone of the pan-African ideal at the beginning of the twenty-first century.

Key Terms

pan-African ideal
African/African-American Summit
Brazzaville Group
Casablanca Group
Monrovia Group
Organization of African Unity (OAU)
sovereign equality
Great Power domination
Balkanization
African Charter on Human and
    People's Rights
Banjul Charter

first generation rights
second generation rights
third generation rights
Kampala Document
African Defense Force
OAU Summit of Heads of State and
    Government
Economic Commission for Africa
    (ECA)
African Economic Community (AEC)
African Common Market (ACM)
economic cooperation

For Further Reading

Aluko, Olajide, ed. *The Foreign Policies of African States*. London: Hodder and Stoughton, 1977.

Aly, Ahmad A. H. M. *Economic Cooperation in Africa: In Search of Direction*. Boulder: Lynne Rienner, 1994.

Amate, C. O. C. *Inside the OAU: Pan-Africanism in Practice*. New York: St. Martin's, 1986.

El-Ayouty, Yassin, ed. *The Organization of African Unity after Thirty Years*. New York: Praeger, 1994.

Khadiagala, Gilbert M. *Allies in Adversity: The Frontline States in Southern African Security, 1975–1993*. Athens: Ohio University Press, 1994.

Lavergne, Real, ed. *Regional Integration and Cooperation in West Africa: A Multidimensional Perspective*. Trenton: Africa World, 1997.

Martin, Guy. "African Regional Cooperation and Integration: Achievements, Problems and Prospects." In Ann Seidman and Frederick Anang, eds., *Twenty-First Century Africa: Towards A New Vision of Self-Sustainable Development*. Trenton: Africa World, 1992 (pp. 69–100).

Ojo, Olatunde. "Regional Co-operation and Integration." In Olatunde Ojo, D. K. Orwa, and C. M. B. Utete, *African International Relations*. London: Longman, 1985 (pp. 142–83).

Olusanya, G. O. "Reflections on the First Twenty-Five Years of the Organization of African Unity." *Nigerian Journal of International Affairs* 14, no. 1 (1988):67–72.

Onwuka, Ralph I, and Amadu Sesay, eds. *The Future of Regionalism in Africa.* New York: St. Martin's, 1985.

Oyejide, Ademola, and Ibrahim Elbadawi and Paul Collier, eds. *Regional Integration and Trade Liberalization in Sub-Saharan Africa.* New York: St. Martin's, 1997.

Shaw, Timothy M., and Olajide Aluko, eds. *The Political Economy of African Foreign Policy.* New York: St. Martin's, 1984.

Shivji, Issa G. *The Concept of Human Rights in Africa.* Dakar: CODESRIA, 1989.

Wright, Stephen., ed. *African Foreign Policies.* Boulder: Westview, 1998.

Zartman, I. William., ed. *Traditional Cures for Modern Conflicts: African Conflict "Medicine".* Boulder: Lynne Rienner, 1999.

Notes

1. Doudou Thiam, *La Politique Étrangère des États Africains: Ses Fondements Idéologiques, Sa Réalité Présente, Ses Perspectives d'Avenir* (Paris: Presses Universitaires de France, 1963).
2. *Ibid,* pp. 2, 116.
3. Thiam, *La Politique Étrangère,* p. xi.
4. Ousmane Tanor Dieng, "Exposé sur la Politique Extérieure du Sénégal," speech delivered on September 15, 1989, to a meeting of members of the ruling Socialist Party (text provided by the Ministry of Foreign Affairs).
5. For a general introduction to the African foreign policy literature, see Stephen Wright, ed., *African Foreign Policies* (Boulder: Westview, 1998); Vernon McKay, ed., *African Diplomacy: Studies in the Determinants of Foreign Policy* (New York: Praeger, 1966); Kenneth Ingham, ed., *The Foreign Relations of African States* (London: Butterworth, 1974); Olajide Aluko, ed., *The Foreign Policies of African States* (London: Hodder and Stoughton, 1977); and Timothy M. Shaw and Olajide Aluko, eds., *The Political Economy of African Foreign Policy* (New York: St. Martin's, 1984).
6. For an introduction to this literature, see W. A. E. Skurnik, *The Foreign Policy of Senegal* (Evanston: Northwestern University Press, 1972). See also Momar-Coumba Diop, ed., *Le Sénégal et Ses Voisins* (Dakar: Sociétés-Espaces-Temps, 1994); and Peter J. Schraeder (with Nefertiti Gaye), "Senegal's Foreign Policy: Challenges of Democratization and Marginalization," *African Affairs* 96 (1997):485–508.
7. See Cheikh Tidiane Thiam, *Droit Public du Sénégal (vol. 1): L'État et le Citoyen* (Dakar: Les Editions du CREDILA, 1993).
8. See Badara Diouf, "Le Nouveau Gouvernement: Un Nouveau Challenge pour Habib Thiam," *Le Soleil* (March 16, 1994): 8.

9. See Maurice A. East, "Foreign Policy-Making in Small States: Some Theoretical Observations Based on a Study of the Uganda Ministry of Foreign Affairs," *Policy Sciences* 4, no. 4 (1973):491–508. See also O. O. Fafowora, "The Role of the Ministry of External Affairs in the Formulation of Nigerian Foreign Policy: Personal Reminiscences," *Quarterly Journal of Administration* 18, no. 3–4 (1983–84):92–110.

10. Elhadj Mbodj, "Senegal's Foreign Policy." Typed notes of a presentation made at the University of Wisconsin, Madison (no date).

11. *Ibid.*

12. See Kenneth W. Grundy, *The Militarization of South African Politics* (Bloomington: Indiana University Press, 1986).

13. See Nelson Mandela, "South Africa's Future Foreign Policy," *Foreign Affairs* 72, no. 5 (1993):86–97. See also Neta Crawford, "South Africa's New Foreign and Military Policy: Opportunities and Constraints," *Africa Today* 43, no. 1–2 (1995):88–121.

14. See Momar Coumba Diop and Moussa Paye, "Armée et Pouvoir au Sénégal." Paper presented at a CODESRIA-sponsored seminar on "Military and Militarism in Africa," Accra, Ghana, April 21–23, 1993, pp. 8-9.

15. *Ibid.* See also Abdoulaye Ndiaye, "Généraux Civils," *Jeune Afrique* no. 1934 (February 3-9, 1998), pp. 44–45.

16. Personal interviews at Senegal's Ministry of Defense, spring 1996.

17. For an excellent overview, see Robert A. Mortimer, "Senegal's Role in Ecomog: The Francophone Dimension in the Liberian Crisis," *Journal of Modern African Studies* 34, no. 2 (1996):293–306.

18. For a historical overview, see Victor T. Le Vine, "Parliaments in Francophone Africa: Some Lessons from the Decolonization Process," in Joel Smith and Lloyd D. Musolf, eds., *Legislatures in Development: Dynamics of Change in New and Old States* (Durham: Duke University Press, 1979), pp. 125–54.

19. For example, see Philip W. Alderfer, "Legislators' Attitudes in a New Democracy: The Zambian Experience." Paper presented at the thirty-eighth annual meeting of the African Studies Association, Orlando, Florida, November 3–6, 1995.

20. Quoted in Papa Mor Sylla, "Le Travail des Députés: Entre les Séances-Marathon et le Repos Prolongé," *Le Soleil* (July 27, 1995): 5.

21. *Ibid.*

22. See Louise M. Bourgaulf, *Mass Media in Sub-Saharan Africa* (Bloomington: Indiana University Press, 1995).

23. See Abdou Latif Coulibaly, "Rôle de la Presse dans la Sauvegarde et la Consolidation de la Démocratie au Sénégal," *Afrique Espoir* no. 12 (December 1994):15–19.

24. See the series of articles and op-ed pieces in *Le Soleil, Le Sud*, and *Wal Fadjri* during the week of March 11–18, 1996.

25. Joel Millman, *The Other Americans: How Immigrants Renew Our Country, Our Economy, and Our Values* (New York: Viking, 1997), p. 198.

26. See Ron Parker, "The Senegal-Mauritania Conflict of 1989: A Fragile Equilibrium," *The Journal of Modern African Studies* 29, no. 1 (1991):155–71; and Anthony G. Pazzanita, "Mauritania's Foreign Policy: The Search for Protection," *The Journal of Modern African Studies* 30, no. 2 (1992):281–304.

27. It has also been argued that negative public reactions to the deaths of Senegalese peacekeepers taking part in ECOMOG operations in Liberia played a significant role in President Diouf's decision to withdraw these troops in 1993. Mortimer, "Senegal's Role in Ecomog," p. 300.

28. For example, see Sulayman Nyang, "The Islamic Factor in Libya's Africa Policy," *Africa and the World* 1, no. 2 (1988):13–23.

29. See Leonardo A. Villalón, *Islamic Society and State Power in Senegal: Disciples and Citizens in Fatick* (Cambridge: Cambridge University Press, 1995).

30. Adekunle Ajala, "Background to the Establishment, Nature and Structure of the Organization of African Unity," *Nigerian Journal of International Affairs* 14, no. 1 (1988):36.

31. *Ibid.*

32. Quoted in *ibid.*, p. 39.

33. *Ibid.*, p. 30.

34. See David Rooney, *Kwame Nkrumah: The Political Kingdom in the Third World* (New York: St. Martin's, 1980).

35. G. O. Olusanya, "Reflections on the First Twenty-Five Years of the Organization of African Unity," *Nigerian Journal of International Affairs* 14, no. 1 (1988):67.

36. *Ibid.*, p. 80.

37. Bukar Bukarambe, "Regional Order and Local Disorder: The OAU and Civil Wars in Africa," *Nigerian Journal of International Relations* 14, no. 1 (1988):98.

38. For example, see John J. Stremlau, *The International Politics of the Nigerian Civil War, 1967–1970* (Princeton: Princeton University Press, 1977).

39. R. A. Akindele, "The Organization of African Unity: Four Grand Debates among African Leaders Revisited," *Nigerian Journal of International Affairs* 14, no. 1 (1988):82–85.

40. Claude E. Welch, Jr., "The Organization of African Unity and the Promotion of Human Rights," *The Journal of Modern African Studies* 29, no. 4 (1991): 537.

41. *Ibid.*, p. 538.

42. *Ibid.*

43. *Ibid.*, pp. 538–39.

44. See Eghosa E. Osaghae, "The Ogoni Uprising: Oil Politics, Minority Agitation and the Future of the Nigerian State," *African Affairs* 94, no. 376 (1995): 325–44.

45. Quoted in Howard W. French, "Nigeria Comes On Too Strong." *New York Times* (November 19, 1995): E3.

46. I. William Zartman, "Inter-African Negotiation," in John W. Harbeson and Donald Rothchild, eds., *Africa in World Politics: Post-Cold War Challenges* (Boulder: Westview, 1995), pp. 209–33.

47. I. William Zartman, ed., *Collapsed States: The Disintegration and Restoration of Legitimate Authority* (Boulder: Lynne Rienner, 1995), p. 241.

48. See I. William Zartman and Samuel Amoo, "Mediation by Regional Organizations: The OAU in Chad," in Jacob Bercovitch and Jeffrey Rubin, eds., *Mediation in International Relations* (New York: St. Martin's, 1992).

49. Ibrahim A. Gambari, "The Role of Foreign Intervention in African Reconstruction," in I. William Zartman, ed. *Collapsed States: The Disintegration and Restoration of Legitimate Authority* (Boulder: Lynne Rienner, 1995), p. 229.

50. Zartman, *Collapsed States*, p. 243.

51. R. A. Akindele, "The Organization of African Unity and Conflict Situation in Southern Africa," *Nigerian Journal of International Affairs* 14, no. 1 (1988):124–54.

52. Guy Martin, "African Regional Cooperation and Integration: Achievements, Problems and Prospects," in Ann Seidman and Frederick Anang, eds., *Twenty-First Century Africa: Towards A New Vision of Self-Sustainable Development* (Trenton: Africa World, 1992), p. 70.

53. *Ibid.*, p. 73.

54. See S. K. B. Asante (with David Chanaiwa), "Pan-Africanism and Regional Integration," in Ali A. Mazrui, ed. *General History of Africa* (vol. 8): *Africa since 1935* (Paris: UNESCO, 1993), pp. 724–43.

55. See Kenneth Grundy, "The Impact of Region on Contemporary African Politics," in Gwendolen M. Carter and Patrick O'Meara, eds., *African Independence: The First Twenty-Five Years* (Bloomington: Indiana University Press, 1985), pp. 97–125.

56. Olatunde Ojo, "Regional Co-operation and Integration," in Olatunde Ojo, D. K. Orwa, and C. M. B. Utete, *African International Relations* (London: Longman, 1985), pp. 142–83. See also Christian P. Potholm and Richard A. Fredland, eds., *Integration and Disintegration in East Africa* (Lanham: University Press of America, 1980); and Arthur Hazlewood, *Economic Integration: The East African Experience* (London: Heinemann, 1975).

57. Olatunde Ojo, "Regional Co-operation and Integration," pp. 159–61.

58. *Ibid.*, pp. 161–66.

59. *Ibid.*, pp. 166–69.

60. *Ibid.*, pp. 169–71.

61. Ahmad A. H. M. Aly, *Economic Cooperation in Africa: In Search of Direction* (Boulder: Lynne Rienner, 1994).

62. These countries include Angola, Botswana, Lesotho, Malawi, Mozambique, Swaziland, Tanzania, Zambia, and Zimbabwe. For an analysis of their evolving interaction, see Gilbert M. Khadiagala, *Allies in Adversity: The Frontline*

States in Southern African Security, 1975–1993 (Athens: Ohio University Press, 1994).

63. Colleen Lowe Morna, "Southern Africa: New Era of Cooperation," *Africa Report* 40, no. 3 (1995):65.

64. *Ibid.*

65. For example, see Jesmond Blumenfeld, *Economic Interdependence in Southern Africa: From Conflict to Cooperation?* (New York: St. Martin's, 1992). For a more recent analysis, see Richard Gibb, "Southern African in Transition: Prospects and Problems Facing Regional Integration," *The Journal of Modern African Studies* 36, no. 2 (1998):287–306.

66. Thomas Ohlson and Stephen John Stedman (with Robert Davies), *The New Is Not Yet Born: Conflict Resolution in Southern Africa* (Washington: Brookings Institution, 1994).

67. The treaty states that Southern African leaders "must find a more abiding basis for continuing political solidarity and cooperation, in order to guarantee mutual peace and security in the region; and to free resources from military to productive development activities." *Ibid.*

14

Africa in World Politics

President Jerry Rawlings (Ghana), President Bill Clinton, and First Lady Hillary Rodham Clinton draped in locally produced kente cloth in Accra, Ghana, during the first stop of President Clinton's six-country presidential visit to Africa in 1998.

THREE INTERNATIONAL EVENTS dramatically influenced the evolution of African politics and society during the twentieth century. The extended global conflict of World War II (1935–45) heralded the decline of Europe as the most powerful region of the world and the emergence of African nationalist movements intent upon achieving independence from colonial rule. The outbreak and intensification of the **Cold War** (1947–89) transformed the newly independent African countries into proxy battlefields between the unparalleled superpowers of the post–World War II era: the United States and the former Soviet Union. African conflicts often having little (if anything) to do with the ideological concerns of communism or capitalism threatened to become East-West flashpoints in the face of growing U.S.-Soviet involvement. A third watershed event, the fall of the Berlin Wall in 1989, signaled the end of the Cold War but not the end of international rivalry in Africa. The ideologically based Cold War between the United States and the former Soviet Union has been replaced by a **Cold Peace,** in which the major northern industrialized democracies struggle for economic supremacy in the highly competitive economic environment of the 1990s.[1] This chapter is devoted to exploring the involvement of a host of international actors in African politics and society from the Cold War to the Cold Peace.

Role of Foreign Powers

Many important policies affecting the future of African politics and society are decided in Paris, Washington, Berlin, and Tokyo: the capitals of the four **Great Powers** that remain heavily involved throughout Africa at the beginning of the twenty-first century.[2] France maintains the most extensive political-military and economic relationships with African countries, most notably in **francophone Africa**, those former French and Belgian colonies where, among a variety of factors, French serves as an "official language of administration and education."[3] The United States often became the most influential political-military actor in the nonfrancophone portions of the African continent during the Cold War era, and increasingly has sought to promote economic links in the post-Cold War era.[4] Japan and Germany emerged during the 1980s as extremely involved economic actors, and have achieved the status of the second or third most important sources of economic aid or trade for individual African countries (often behind the leading roles of France and the United States).[5]

Britain's official interest in maintaining privileged colonial ties, once rivaled only by that of France, dramatically waned during the Cold War except in the case of South Africa.[6] Economic decline forced British policymakers to make difficult decisions as to where increasingly limited economic resources would contribute the most to British foreign policy interests, ultimately leading to the downgrading of British ties with the majority of its former colonies. Britain's most noteworthy ongoing involvement with its former African colonies takes place within the context of the **Commonwealth of Nations,** a loose association of former British colonies that holds an annual summit meeting of heads of state.[7]

Other, traditionally less powerful colonial powers, such as Spain, were never important diplomatic players due to the lack of extensive colonial holdings.[8] Weaker colonial powers demonstrated only sporadic interest in their former colonies during times of crisis, such as Belgium in Central Africa and Italy in the Horn of Africa.[9] Portugal, however, has exhibited a renewed interest in strengthening cultural ties with its former colonies and played an important role in promoting the resolution of civil wars in Angola and Mozambique during the 1990s.[10]

Despite extensive involvement during the Cold War era, the former **communist bloc** countries have drastically reduced their political-military and economic presence on the African continent. The preoccupation of Russian leaders with the economic and political restructuring of the former Soviet Union has precluded any meaningful diplomatic role in Africa.[11] The one notable vestige of the previously active foreign policy of the People's Republic of China (PRC) is an ongoing diplomatic battle with Taiwan as to which capital — Beijing or Taipei — is recognized by African governments as the official seat of the Chinese government.[12] Other communist bloc countries that once enjoyed privileged relations with the African continent either completely disappeared (e.g., the former East Germany, which now constitutes part of a reunified Germany),[13] or became marginalized (e.g., Cuba) due to their pariah status within the international system and a drastic reduction in aid formerly provided by their socialist patrons.[14]

A variety of **middle powers** plays varying roles on the African continent. Canada and the Nordic countries, most notably Sweden, demonstrate a strong humanitarian interest, particularly concerning famine relief in the Horn of Africa and Southern Africa.[15] During the height of the Arab-Israeli conflict, Israel pursued an aggressive policy that exchanged Israeli technical aid for diplomatic recognition of the state of Israel.[16] Other Middle Eastern powers, such as Saudi Arabia, pursue religiously based policies regarding the predominantly Muslim states of North and Northeast Africa.[17] Iran in particular seeks to foster links with Islamist regimes and movements in the Sudan, Egypt, and Algeria. India and Brazil lead their respective regions in seeking to expand economic relations with the African continent.[18]

Cooperation and Conflict during the Cold War

As the nationalist urges of independence movements swept the countries of Africa during the 1950s, marking the beginning of the end of European colonialism, two U.S. politicians of widely divergent political perspectives underscored the necessity of rethinking U.S. foreign policy toward Africa. "For too many years," Vice President Richard M. Nixon noted in 1957, after returning from a twenty-two-day tour of the continent, "Africa in the minds of many

Americans has been regarded as a remote and mysterious continent which was the special province of big game hunters, explorers and motion picture makers."[19] Recognizing the importance of an emerging Africa in the international scene — especially within the context of the East-West struggle — Nixon recommended that President Dwight D. Eisenhower authorize the creation of a separate Bureau of African Affairs within the State Department, an idea that reached fruition in 1958.

Also in 1957, Senator John F. Kennedy criticized what he perceived as Washington's inability to come to grips with the question of colonialism and the growing forces of nationalism in Africa.[20] Kennedy later warned that the "only real question is whether these new nations [of Africa] will look West or East — to Moscow or to Washington — for sympathy, help, and guidance in their effort to recapitulate, in a few decades, the entire history of modern Europe and America." In order to blunt what he perceived as the steady decline of U.S. prestige in Africa as a result of growing communist bloc influence, Kennedy concluded that the U.S. government "must embark on a bold and imaginative new program for the development of Africa."[21]

Despite their partisan rivalries, both Nixon and Kennedy shared Cold War beliefs that sought to enlist African leaders on the side of the United States in an emerging East-West rivalry with the communist bloc countries. The policymakers of Charles de Gaulle's France, Mao Zedong's China, and Nikita Khrushchev's Soviet Union shared Washington's perception of Africa's importance in the emerging Cold War environment of the 1950s. As a result, they were equally fervent in the pursuit of African allies, contributing to Africa's emergence as an arena of Great Power competition. Several themes reflective of this competition during the Cold War era are nicely illustrated by an analysis of the specific involvement of the United States and France in francophone Africa.

Complementary Interests among the Western Great Powers

American and French foreign policies toward francophone Africa were driven by different sets of motivating factors during the Cold War era. American policymakers were principally guided by the ideological interest of containing the former Soviet Union and its communist allies.[22] A variety of presidential doctrines, beginning with the Truman Doctrine in 1947 and culminating in the Reagan Doctrine of the 1980s, declared Washington's self-appointed right to intervene against communist advances throughout the world, including in francophone Africa. As a result, pro-West administrations, such as Senegal under President Abdou Diouf, were treated as potential American allies deserving of foreign aid, whereas Marxist administrations, such as Madagascar under Didier Ratsiraka, were isolated. American policymakers also sought special relationships with strategically important regional actors, such as Morocco in North Africa, Ethiopia in the Horn of Africa, and South Africa in Southern Africa, that offered special military access rights or maintained important U.S. technical facilities (e.g., telecommunications stations) deemed critical to containment policies in Africa.[23]

French policymakers sought first and foremost to consolidate and promote the *rayonnement* (spread) of the most notable aspects of French culture, including the French language and intellectual traditions.[24] Also referred to as the promotion of *la francophonie* (a greater French-speaking community), this policy is best represented by the biannual Franco–African summit attended by the leaders of France and francophone Africa (see Box 14.1). Economic interests were perceived by French policymakers as both parallel and integral to the promotion of French culture, as witnessed by the organization of thirteen former French colonies and Equatorial Guinea in the **franc zone**. Created in 1947, the franc zone constitutes a supranational financial system in which France serves as the central bank, and a common currency, the *Communauté Financière Africaine* (CFA) franc, is tied to the French franc and guaranteed by the French treasury. By wedding its fiscal policy to the franc zone, France has sought to preserve monetary stability and French influence throughout francophone Africa.[25]

As long as the United States and France were pursuing fundamentally different but complementary foreign policy interests, francophone Africa remained the chief beneficiary of a **complementary Cold War regime** in which U.S.-French relations tended to be balanced, cooperative, and predictable.[26] Regardless of whether France was led by the conservative partisans of Charles de Gaulle or the socialists of François Mitterrand, French policymakers predictably claimed that historical links and geographical proximity justified placing francophone Africa within France's sphere of influence. The implicit assumption of what is referred to as the French version of the Monroe Doctrine is that francophone Africa constituted France's *domaine réservé* (natural preserve) or *chasse gardée* (private hunting ground), and therefore remained "off-limits" to other great powers, regardless of whether they were friends like the United States and the other northern industrialized democracies, or enemies such as the former Soviet Union and other "radical" powers.[27]

During the Cold War, this conception of francophone Africa was wholeheartedly accepted and even encouraged by American policymakers. The White House in particular expected France and the other European allies to take the lead in their former colonial territories. As succinctly stated by George Ball, undersecretary of state in the Kennedy administration, the United States recognized Africa as a "special European responsibility," just as European nations were expected to recognize "our [U.S.] responsibility in Latin America."[28] According to American policymakers, France emerged as the only European power with both the long-term political will and the requisite military force capable of thwarting communist powers from exploiting instability. Much to the chagrin of French policymakers, this perception led some analysts to refer to France as Washington's de facto *gendarme* (policeman) in francophone Africa.[29]

Africa as a Proxy Battlefield for East-West Conflict

A second major trend of the Cold War era was the emergence of the African continent as a battlefield for proxy wars, as both the Western and communist blocs became militarily involved in regional conflicts.[30] In almost every case, regional conflict was exacerbated by one superpower's reaction to the other's involvement in a particular crisis situation. Soviet involvement, as well as its mere threat, was enough to capture the attention of Western (especially American) policymakers and often provoke an escalation of the conflict. Western intervention in the Democratic Republic of the Congo (Congo-Kinshasa) during 1978 provides an illustrative case.

On May 13, 1978, Assistant Secretary of State for African Affairs Richard Moose awoke to a phone call informing him that, on the night before, the Front de Libération Nationale du Congo (FLNC, Front for the National Liberation of the Congo) had mounted its second invasion of Congo-Kinshasa in little over a year. In just four days, the FLNC was able to capture the mining center of Kolwezi, the capital of Congo-Kinshasa's Shaba province and the source of nearly 75 percent of the country's export earnings. With the safety of U.S. and European citizens potentially at risk and the pro-West Mobutu Sese Seko facing a serious threat to his rule, the White House received requests from the French and Belgian governments to take part in a joint military operation that would include military engagements with the FLNC. The so-called Shaba II crisis quickly became the focus of the Carter administration, due to its origins in Marxist-ruled Angola and the possibility that the insurgents were being accompanied by Cuban advisors and troops.

President Carter adopted the consensus opinion of his senior national security advisors to take part in a joint military operation. The U.S. role included the provision of transport and logistical support for French and Belgian paratroopers. In a total of thirty-eight flight missions, U.S. planes transported approximately 2,500 French and Belgian troops and accompanying munitions and transport vehicles to the staging area of Kamina, for an eventual assault of four hundred French paratroopers on the primary objective of Kolwezi. Although the French forces were successful in establishing control over Kolwezi and routing the remainder of FLNC forces in Shaba, one hundred Europeans lost their lives.[31]

The Cold War rhetoric of senior U.S. policymakers clearly underscored the East-West dimension of this crisis. In an opening statement at a press conference on May 25, 1978, less than two weeks after the beginning of the Shaba II invasion, Carter sternly remarked that the Cuban leader Fidel Castro bore a "heavy responsibility" for the "deadly attack" that was launched from Angolan territory.[32] This tough talk was reinforced by even stronger Cold War rhetoric by National Security Advisor Zbigniew Brzezinski. In a May 28 television appearance on "Meet the Press," Brzezinski claimed that the invasion had been launched with Moscow's blessing and charged the Soviets with a "shortsighted attempt to exploit global difficulties."[33] The Carter administration was beginning to appear weak and confused in the face of Soviet-Cuban advances in Africa. Not only were more than twenty thousand Cuban troops stationed in Angola, but the Soviets and the Cubans had massively and decisively intervened on the side of Marxist Ethiopia in that country's 1977–78 war with Somalia — leaving behind nearly fifteen thousand Cuban troops and Soviet advisors. Already under fire from conservative congressional critics for advancing a Strategic Arms Limitation Talks (SALT) treaty with the Soviet Union, a low-key response to the Shaba II invasion would have left Carter open to charges of being "soft" on communism, potentially damaging the chances for ratification of the treaty in the Senate. According to Assistant Secretary of State for African Affairs Richard Moose, the primary objective of Carter's White House advisors during Shaba II was to show how "tough" and "decisive" the president could be when it came to communism.[34]

Indiscriminate Support for Allies

American and French foreign policies toward francophone Africa were also complementary in terms of what one scholar has referred to as their "creative ambiguity" concerning the normative goal of promoting democracy.[35] In the case of France, one can argue that French policymakers sought to spread French culture with the same ideological fervor with which American policymakers sought to prevent the spread of communism. Consequently, when francophone countries renounced their special relationship with France, as Guinea did in 1958 when it voted against the creation of a revised French community of states, French retribution was swift: all aid to Guinea was abruptly cut off by an angry de Gaulle. But as long as these countries maintained strong support for *la francophonie* and close ties with France, even authoritarian leaders were unlikely to find themselves under heavy pressure from Paris to democratize. For example, when asked why France did not militarily intervene when David Dacko, the democratically elected president of the Central African Republic, was overthrown in a military coup d'état in 1966, Jacques Foccart, the architect of French foreign policy under de Gaulle, replied that the new leader, Jean-Bedel Bokassa, "after all was a very pro-French military man."[36]

Contradictions were also evident in Washington's advocacy for democracy in Africa and U.S. national security interests. Whenever the ideal of democracy clashed with the national security objective of containing communism, containment often prevailed at the expense of democracy. It is for this reason that a succession of both Democratic and Republican administrations were willing to downplay the internal shortcomings of a variety of U.S. allies, such as Ethiopia's Haile Selassie, Somalia's Siad Barre, Congo-Kinshasa's Mobutu Sese Seko, and a host of Afrikaner regimes in South Africa, in favor of their strong support for U.S. anticommunist policies.[37] Even the Carter administration's human rights program, which questioned the wisdom of identifying the United

---

BOX 14.1

FRANCO-AFRICAN SUMMITS AND
SUPPORT FOR *LA FRANCOPHONIE*

France's determination to preserve and strengthen *la francophonie* is best demonstrated by the biannual **Franco-African summit** attended by the presidents of France and francophone Africa. These summits have been described as the centerpiece of franco-African cultural relations, primarily because they are perceived as "family reunions" designed to strengthen already close personal relationships between the French president and his African counterparts. The careful nurturing of close, high-level personal ties is the cornerstone of each gathering, and is equally important as regards the day-to-day decision making related to French foreign policy toward Africa. Although the worldwide **Francophone summit**, the seventh of which was held in Vietnam in 1997, also serves as a meeting ground of French and African heads of state, it does not serve as intimate a role as the Franco-African summit due to the attendance of powerful francophone states, most notably Canada and to a lesser degree Belgium, that are perceived by France as cultural rivals.

Franco-African Summits

1st   Paris, France (November 13, 1973)

2nd Bangui, Central African Republic (March 5, 1975)

3rd   Paris, France (May 10–11, 1976)

4th   Dakar, Senegal (April 20–21, 1977)

5th   Paris, France (May 22–23, 1978)

6th   Kigali, Rwanda (May 21–22, 1979)

7th   Nice, France (May 8–10, 1980)

8th   Paris, France (November 3–4, 1981)

9th   Kinshasa, Democratic Republic of the Congo (October 8–9, 1982)

10th Vittel, France (October 3–4, 1983)

11th Bujumbura, Burundi (December 11–12, 1984)

12th Paris, France (December 11–13, 1985)

13th Lome, Togo (November 14–15, 1986)

14th Antibes, France (December 10–12, 1987)

15th Casablanca, Morocco (December 14–16, 1988)

16th La Baule, France (June 19–21, 1990)

17th Libreville, Gabon (October 5–7, 1992)

18th   Biarritz, France (November 7–9, 1994)

19th   Ouagadougou, Burkina Faso (December 4–6, 1996)

20th   Paris, France (November 27–28, 1998)

Quotations are from Guy Martin, "Continuity and Change in Franco-African Relations," *The Journal of Modern African Studies* 33, no. 1 (1995):1–20.

States with inherently unstable dictatorships, was compromised by strategic exceptions. When the pursuit of human rights clashed with perceived national security interests, especially in countries of strategic importance, such as Iran, the Philippines, South Korea, and Congo-Kinshasa, national security interests prevailed.[38]

Emergence of the Cold Peace and Economic Competition

The end of the Cold War transformed the international order and set the stage for dramatic changes in Great Power involvement in Africa. The most notable immediate change was that one superpower, the Soviet Union, ceased to exist, and its successor state, the Russian Republic, was too preoccupied with the economic and political restructuring of its domestic system to play any sort of meaningful role on the African continent. Equally important, Germany and Japan had overcome the defeat of World War II to join the United States and France as the most influential Great Powers on the African continent. However, expectations of Great Power cooperation in the post–Cold War era have been dampened by the emergence of a Cold Peace, in which the northern industrialized democracies compete for markets and influence throughout the African continent. Four specific themes reflective of this emerging Cold Peace are once again nicely illuminated by focusing on American and French involvement in francophone Africa.

Transformation of Foreign Policy Interests

The fall of the Berlin Wall marked the beginning of the end of the complementary Cold War regime among the Western democracies and its gradual replacement with a new competitive international environment, in which Great Power policies increasingly are being driven by the same factor: *economic self-interest*. In the case of France, policymakers were confronted by an intensifying economic crisis on the African continent that created rising pressures for change within the carefully crafted web of economic ties that bound the French economy to those of francophone Africa.[39] With many of their clients on the verge of financial bankruptcy, French policymakers initially decided to undertake an economic bailout that entailed massive increases in foreign aid. French aid to francophone Africa increased from the already substantial level of $3.7 billion in 1980–82 to $8.2 billion in 1990–92 — a nearly 120 percent increase during a ten-year period. Once it became clear that the short-term bailouts were insufficient and that projected aid levels were beyond France's fiscal capabilities, French policymakers took the extraordinary step in January 1994 of devaluing the CFA franc by 50 percent. The decision sent shock-waves throughout the CFA franc zone, which had never before suffered a devaluation. Most important, the devaluation signaled that France's commitment to the cultural imperative of *la francophonie* no longer took precedence over the pursuit of economic self-interest in an increasingly competitive, post–Cold War environment.

In the case of the United States, the end of the Cold War fostered the decline of ideologically based policies in favor of the pursuit of trade and investment. In 1996, the Clinton administration unveiled America's first formal trade policy for aggressively pursuing new markets throughout Africa, including in francophone Africa.[40] This report led to the creation of an interagency Africa Trade and Development Coordinating Group, which is jointly chaired by the National Economic Council (NEC) and the National Security Council (NSC). The launching of the Clinton administration's long-awaited trade policy was a significant departure from the Cold War deference to European economic interests in their former colonies. This policy was preceded by the launching in 1992 of a series of highly publicized speeches rejecting Washington's past support for France's privileged role in francophone Africa in favor of a more aggressive approach to promoting U.S. trade and investment. "The African market is open to everyone," explained former Assistant Secretary of State for African Affairs Herman Cohen in a 1995 speech in Libreville, Gabon, explicitly designed to denounce the concept of a *chasse gardée*. "We must accept free and fair competition, equality between all actors." The most noteworthy example of the administration's determination to highlight and advance expanding U.S. economic interests on the African continent was President Clinton's decision to make a twelve-day presidential trip to Africa in 1998, which included stops in Botswana, Ghana, Rwanda, Senegal, South Africa, and Uganda. For the first time in U.S. history, a sitting U.S. president had led an extended diplomatic mission to Africa, intent on improving U.S.-African ties and promoting U.S. trade and investment on the African continent.[41]

Rising Economic Competition among the Great Powers

The transformation of foreign policy interests in the post-Cold War era has contributed to the rise of Great Power economic competition throughout Africa, particularly in the highly lucrative petroleum, telecommunications, and transport industries. In the eyes of French policymakers, the penetration of American and other Western companies constitutes "at best an intrusion" and "at worst an aggression" into France's *chasse gardée*. The seriousness with which this issue is treated at the highest levels of the French policy-making establishment was demonstrated by the public admission of Minister of Cooperation Michel Roussin that a series of meetings had been held on how best to "defend" French interests, including those within the economic realm, against those of the United States.[42]

Intense competition between the government of Congo-Brazzaville, Elf-Aquitaine (the French oil corporation), and Occidental Petroleum Corporation (Oxy), a United States–based oil company, is an excellent example of the potential future stakes involved in rising U.S.-French economic competition.[43] Desperately in need of nearly $200 million in order to pay government salaries prior to the holding of legislative elections, newly elected President Pascal Lissouba "naturally turned for help to Elf-Aquitaine (which controls 80 percent of the country's oil production)."[44] When its French manager refused to approve either a $300 million loan or "a request for a $300 million mortgage on the future production of three promising new offshore oil deposits," Lissouba initiated secret negotiations with the United States–based Oxy. An agreement was signed, but ultimately renounced eight months later by the Lissouba administration due to "intense French pressure."[45]

The very public war of words between the U.S. State Department and the French Ministry of Cooperation reached a feverish pitch during the fall of 1996, and demonstrated how economic competition had spilled over into the political realm. Minister of Cooperation Jacques Godfrain chided Secretary of State Warren Christopher for his decision to make his first (and last) official visit to Africa approximately four years after assuming office, and literally weeks before the U.S. presidential elections of November 1996. Christopher responded to the perceived diplomatic slight by demanding an official apology. When none was forthcoming, he publicly criticized French policy: "All nations must cooperate, not compete, if we are going to make a positive difference in Africa's future," explained Christopher. "The time has passed when Africa could be carved into spheres of influence, or when outside powers could view whole groups of states as their private domain."[46] Not to be outdone, Godfrain responded in kind: "If I were a political or electoral counselor to President Bill Clinton, I would advise him to worry more about helping African development after the elections."[47]

The diplomatic war of words also had important ramifications within international organizations, as witnessed by U.S.-French competition in 1996 over the future leadership of the United Nations. The Chirac administration led a losing battle to reelect Secretary-General Boutros Boutros-Ghali for a second term of office. The Clinton administration had vowed early on to utilize its veto right to block Boutros-Ghali's candidacy, and did so at a November 19 meeting of the Security Council. The Chirac administration responded by threatening to veto any candidate from a nonfrancophone country, and strongly promoted the candidacy of Amara Essy, Côte d'Ivoire's foreign minister. In the end, Kofi Annan, a native English speaker from Ghana who was perceived among French policymakers as the "American candidate," was chosen

by the Security Council on December 13, 1996. The most plausible explana-
tion as to why the Chirac administration ultimately backed away from its earlier support of Essy was the loss of support among francophone African
leaders who ultimately rallied around Annan's candidacy. When confronted
with the possibility that an extended stalemate between the United States and
France might lead to the selection of a non-African Secretary-General, the
francophone African leaders placed their common heritage as Africans before
their more select common attachment to *la francophonie*.

Rhetoric versus Reality in Support for Democratization

The emergence of economic competition during the Cold Peace has affected
Great Power support for democratization. The end of the Cold War raised
expectations that the Western democracies would promote democracy and
human rights as the cornerstones of a new democratic international order that
would be consistently applied to all regions of the world, including in francophone Africa. Scholars, activists, and policymakers in both the United States
and France increasingly coalesced around the Wilsonian concept of making
political democratization a precondition for the improvement of economic
and political relations with Paris and Washington. However, the simultaneous
emergence of pro-democracy movements throughout francophone Africa
threatened the very essence of France's carefully crafted francophone network:
the potential replacement of staunchly pro-French, undemocratic leaders
with opposition candidates less enamored with France and more sympathetic
to seeking closer ties with other northern industrialized democracies (see
Chapter 11).[48]

To the surprise of many, President François Mitterrand initially embraced
these democratization movements in a much-quoted speech at the 1990
Franco-African summit held in La Baule, France, and warned his counterparts
in francophone Africa that future French aid would be contingent on their
willingness to promote true democratic change. What became known as the *la
Baule Doctrine* suggested that the promotion of democracy would become the
new hallmark of French foreign policy in francophone Africa. The bold
rhetoric of democratization was nonetheless forestalled by the reality of ongoing foreign aid programs designed to keep pro-French leaders in power.[49] In
the case of Cameroon, French aid to the authoritarian regime of President Paul
Biya expanded from $159 million in 1990 to $436 million in 1992, the year of
the country's first multiparty presidential elections. The primary reason for the
dramatic increase in French aid was to ensure Biya's victory, especially as the
most popular opposition candidate was John Fru Ndi, an anglophone politician perceived as a threat to French interests in Cameroon. Any misunder-
standings generated by earlier French rhetoric were resolved at the 1992
Franco-African summit held in Libreville, Gabon. At this meeting, French
Prime Minister Pierre Bérégovoy privately stated that when confronted with
the potentially conflicting goals of promoting democracy, ensuring develop-

ment, and maintaining security, the leaders of francophone Africa were expected to adopt the following order of priorities: above all, security, followed by development and, finally, democratization.[50]

The election of Jacques Chirac as president of France in May 1995 coincided with an increasingly turbulent period in French foreign policy.[51] The growing contradictions in France's democratization policies were demonstrated by the Chirac administration's response to a February 1996 coup d'état in Niger, the first against a democratically elected government in France's former colonies since the beginning of the democratization process in 1990. Despite a commitment in 1995 by Minister of Cooperation Jacques Godfrain that France would intervene to reinstate a democratically elected government if a defense treaty had been signed with that country, France refused to intervene in Niger and ultimately decided to work with the military regime headed by Colonel Ibrahim Maïnassara Baré.[52] Not surprisingly, the democratically elected francophone neighbors of Niger were worried by French inaction. In a throwback to an earlier era of authoritarian rule and highly questionable democratic practices, Colonel Baré announced that there would be multiparty elections in 1996, presented himself as the candidate of the ruling party, and subsequently "won" inherently flawed elections to the congratulatory toasts of local French diplomats.

American diplomats have typically been more vocal than their French counterparts in their support for democratization throughout francophone Africa. This vocal stance is not due to a greater American commitment to promoting democracy in Africa, relative to that espoused by France and the other industrialized democracies. In fact, there is abundant evidence of ongoing contradictions between Washington's pro-democracy rhetoric and its foreign policy actions. For example, punitive measures designed to enforce pro-democracy rhetoric are at best unevenly applied depending on the perceived importance of the African country. Although the Clinton administration was quick to enforce comprehensive economic sanctions against the ministate of The Gambia when that country's military took power in a coup d'état in 1994, it refused to do so against the military dictatorship of Nigeria, an important source of American oil, prior to the holding of democratic elections in 1999.

The unusually vocal stance of American diplomats in francophone Africa primarily stems from a self-interested calculation that the United States has little to lose and everything to gain by excoriating pro-French leaders who impede the transition to a new political order.[53] The logic of diplomatic competition at the local level is based on perceptions of the democratization process as a "zero-sum game:" one person's gain is another's loss. From the perspective of local U.S. ambassadors, for example, promoting multiparty democracy is a low-cost strategy with potentially high returns — namely, the replacement of pro-French elites with new leaders potentially more sensitive to U.S. interests. From the perspective of local French ambassadors, the reverse holds true, which explains why French policymakers tend to emerge as protectors of the status quo. In the case of Benin, Nicéphore Soglo's victory in the 1991 presidential elections led to the formation of a regime more interested in promoting closer ties with the United States. Critics of French policies argue that local French diplomats provided significant support to Soglo's predecessor, Mathieu Kérékou, who emerged victorious in the 1996 presidential elections and subsequently installed a regime that in many respects represented a return to the status quo. In short, an important dimension of the Cold Peace is Great Power pursuit of the favor of emerging African elites, with often dire consequences for the consolidation of democracy in Africa.

Reassessments of Unilateral Intervention

The emergence of new security challenges, such as the growing numbers of **collapsed states**[54] beset by ethnic, religious, and political rivalries, has fostered renewed international debate over the desirability of foreign intervention in Africa, and has contributed to rising U.S.-French tensions. The American response to these security challenges was sharply influenced by the series of United States–led military interventions in Somalia under the auspices of the UN, which is referred to as Operation Restore Hope.[55] A turning point occurred on October 3-4, 1993, when eighteen U.S. soldiers were killed and seventy-eight others were wounded in a fierce battle in Mogadishu, Somalia. With the Cable News Network (CNN) providing almost instantaneous transmission to audiences in the United States and abroad, the victorious Somali forces not only paraded a captured American helicopter pilot, Corporal William Durant, through the streets of Mogadishu, but also dragged the naked corpse of an American soldier past mobs of Somali citizens who vented their anger by spitting on, stoning, and kicking the body. These dual media images triggered a firestorm of public debate that ultimately forced President Clinton to withdraw American forces from Somalia.

The lessons "learned" from the American military experience motivated a May 1994 policy directive, Presidential Decision Directive 25 (PDD-25), which outlined fairly restrictive conditions that had to be met before the United States would agree to any further UN-sponsored military operations, regardless of whether American troops took part. Among the most important conditions relevant to America's experience in Somalia was the prior "consent of the [warring] parties" before any forces are deployed.[56] The simple message of PDD-25 was that the United States "cannot resolve the conflicts of the world but does not believe that the United Nations is capable of making and keeping peace, particularly when hostilities among parties still exist."[57]

The most important result of PDD-25, which in essence rejected any future American involvement in UN-sponsored peace-making operations designed to militarily impose peace among warring parties, was an extremely cautious approach to ethnically and religiously based conflicts in Africa and elsewhere abroad. In the case of Rwanda, extremists among the Hutu ethnic group unleashed a reign of terror against the Tutsi minority, as well as against Hutu deemed sympathetic to the plight of the Tutsi, that according to a UN report issued in December 1994, had resulted in the execution of between 500,000 and 1,000,000 unarmed civilians. Fearful of being drawn into "another Somalia," the Clinton administration not only initially blocked the dispatch of 5,500 troops requested by Secretary-General Boutros-Ghali, but instructed administration spokespersons to avoid labeling the unfolding ethnic conflict as "genocide," lest such a label further inflame American public sympathy and demand American intervention as was the case in Somalia.[58]

The experience in Somalia also significantly affected the Clinton administration's approach to conflict resolution in Africa and abroad.[59] Entering office at a period in which internal civil conflicts were multiplying throughout the African continent, the Clinton administration was expected to formulate and adopt a comprehensive policy of conflict resolution that went beyond the sporadic policies of previous administrations. However, the Clinton administration was initially split between two currents of thought on conflict resolution. The first emphasized the classic belief that African issues unnecessarily distract the administration and potentially plunge the White House into unwanted domestic political controversies. According to this viewpoint, American involvement, even in terms of conflict resolution, should be limited in order to avoid entanglement in "future Somalias."[60]

A second, more activist approach to conflict resolution was also derivative of the Somali experience, but underscored the massive costs associated with Operation Restore Hope that could have been avoided by earlier, preventive action. "The choice is not between intervening or not intervening," explained one policymaker in the Clinton administration. "It is between getting involved early and doing it at a cheaper cost, or being forced to intervene in a massive, more costly way later."[61] As witnessed by the Clinton administration's cautious approach to the initial stages of the Rwandan conflict, the events of October 1993 in Somalia clearly strengthened the position of those warning against getting too closely involved in "intractable" conflicts in Africa.

Unlike the United States, France took the lead in undertaking a series of military interventions in Rwanda between 1990 and 1994.[62] The Mitterrand administration's decision to intervene was the manifestation of the long-term French goal of integrating the former Belgian colonies of the Great Lakes region into the French sphere of influence. Mitterrand's military interventions also fostered one of the rare examples of popular outrage in France regarding policy toward francophone Africa, especially when it was learned that the Mitterrand administration had provided the authoritarian Rwandan regime of Major General Juvénal Habyarimana with over $160 million in economic aid and an untold amount of military aid from 1990 to 1994 — essentially contributing to the genocide that unfolded in 1994.

France's attempt to rationalize military intervention in Rwanda as a humanitarian response to local suffering was dubious at best. In reality, the Mitterrand administration's actions were aimed at stemming the invasion and steady advance beginning in October 1990 by the Rwandan Patriotic Front (RPF), a guerrilla army supported by Uganda and perceived by French policymakers as hostile to France and "under Anglo–Saxon influence."[63] From the perspective of most French policymakers, the RPF's military victory in 1994 constituted the first time that a francophone country had "fallen" to Anglo-Saxon influence. Some policymakers even perceived Rwanda as the beginning of a series of regional "dominos" that eventually could lead to Anglo-Saxon domination of portions of Central Africa to the "detriment" of France and *la francophonie*.[64] According to this culturally inspired theory, Central Africa could become a "Trojan horse" projecting Anglo-Saxon influence throughout the remainder of francophone Africa.

The dilemmas associated with French military intervention were demonstrated by the Chirac administration's response to the expansion of the regional crisis in the Great Lakes region, particularly the emergence and spread of a guerrilla insurgency in eastern Congo-Kinshasa in 1997. French policymakers perceived the Great Lakes crisis in francophone-anglophone terms: the guerrilla insurgency in eastern Congo-Kinshasa was led by Laurent-Désiré Kabila, who in turn was strongly supported by and allied with the Rwandan government of Paul Kagame and the Ugandan government of Yoweri Museveni.[65] As a result, the French considered Kabila's guerrilla movement to be under Anglo-Saxon influence, and therefore hostile to France. The worst-case scenario envisioned by French policymakers occurred when Kabila's guerrilla army overthrew the Mobutu regime in May 1997, and installed a new government with Kabila as president that was strongly allied with Rwanda and Uganda, which in turn were closely allied with the United States. According to this vision, Kabila's emergence as the president of Congo-Kinshasa not only constituted a clear victory for Anglo-Saxon influence at the expense of *la francophonie,* but also raised the possibility that Congo-Kinshasa might serve

---

BOX 14.2

JAPANESE NEOMERCANTILISM IN AFRICA

Japan has traditionally pursued a **neomercantilist** foreign policy toward Africa that underscores the overriding importance of securing economic self-interest *(kokueki)* relative to other foreign policy goals, including the promotion of socioeconomic development and democratization in the target country. A rising economic superpower with the world's second largest gross national product (GNP), Japan also earned the distinction of being the first Great Power of the post–World War II era to reconstitute national security in largely economic terms.

The hallmark of Japanese neomercantilism has been the vigorous use of an increasingly generous foreign aid budget to penetrate foreign economic markets and promote Japanese trade and investment. As a result, Japanese foreign aid has been overwhelmingly targeted toward four categories of countries: (1) important sources of raw materials vital to Japanese industry, such as copper in Zambia, uranium in Niger, and chromium in Madagascar; (2) potential future sources of such raw materials, including chromium in the Sudan and oil in Gabon; (3) major sources of highly valued Japanese foodstuffs, such as fish products from Senegal; or (4) major economic markets capable of absorbing Japanese exports, such as Kenya and Nigeria.

The pursuit of a neomercantilist foreign policy ensured that Japan was well positioned to take advantage of the end of the Cold War. Unlike the Americans and the French, who continue to struggle with evolving policies in light of altered foreign policy interests in the post–Cold War era, Japanese policymakers simply reinforced already existing policies. Indeed, a purely economic policy that is both ideologically and culturally blind — the essence of the so-called Japanese model — is ideally suited for the increasingly competitive economic environment of the post–Cold War era.

A close partnership between government and big business *(kanzai ittaishugi)* is an essential ingredient of Japan's economic success in Africa. All Japanese government agencies, most notably the Ministry of Finance, the Ministry of International Trade and Industry (MITI), and the Japanese International Cooperation Agency (JICA), operate from the assumption that big business and diplomacy are both complementary and mutually reinforcing. They therefore highlight the importance of working closely with the Japanese business community *(zaikai)* to promote Japanese trade and investment in Africa. Even in the Ministry of Foreign Affairs, the Japanese bureaucracy most inclined to argue the political ramifications of a given policy, career diplomats accept and promote the economic imperatives of international diplomacy.

The close partnership between government and big business is further facilitated by a wide variety of ancillary groups and organizations. The Japan External Trade Organization (JETRO) maintains offices in the capitals of several strategically located countries — Algeria, Côte d'Ivoire, Egypt, Kenya, Nigeria, South Africa, Tanzania, and Zimbabwe — that represent the most important economies on the African continent. The Japan Overseas Cooperation Volunteers (JOCV) program, the Japanese equivalent of the U.S. Peace Corps, sends abroad more than one thousand Japanese volunteers on an annual basis, with approximately 25–30 percent being sent to serve in African countries. Japanese policymakers and corporate leaders have also formed numerous "private" committees, such as the Africa Society of Japan and the Keidanren Committee on Sub-Saharan Africa, that guide official government policy. The Keidanren Committee has been especially effective in that it includes the leadership of dozens of the most influential Japanese corporations.

Discussion draws on Jun Morikawa, *Japan and Africa: Big Business and Diplomacy* (Trenton: Africa World, 1997); and William R. Nester, *Japan and the Third World: Patterns, Power, Prospects* (New York: St. Martin's, 1992).

as a potential springboard for the further spread of Anglo-Saxon influence throughout francophone Africa.

The Chirac administration's attempt to play a more proactive role in the Great Lakes region was restrained by a variety of factors. First, the lack of interest among the other Great Powers, especially the United States, stymied French proposals to create a UN-sponsored, multilateral military force to be dispatched to eastern Congo-Kinshasa, ostensibly to protect refugees from Burundi and Rwanda but in reality designed to strengthen the Mobutu regime. Second, the option of unilateral French intervention was out of the question due to the publicly stated promise of the Rwandan government and Kabila's guerrilla forces to militarily engage French forces. Unlike earlier French military interventions in Rwanda, French military forces would have been confronted by battle-hardened militaries capable of inflicting heavy casualties. Even if the Chirac administration had been willing to accept the public uproar that would have accompanied French casualties in any unilateral military intervention, the French military was incapable of independently moving and sustaining the large numbers of troops and military equipment necessary for a long-term engagement in such a vast military theater. In short, French military action in the largest country of francophone Africa was essentially vetoed by a combination of local and international forces — regardless of French policy preferences.

Involvement in the United Nations

African leaders consider membership in the United Nations and its related agencies to be one of the most important elements of African international relations. In addition to serving as a concrete symbol of African independence, UN membership historically has provided African leaders with an important international forum for promoting African views on a variety of international issues, such as unequivocal support for complete decolonization, opposition to apartheid in South Africa, the promotion of socioeconomic development, and the need for disarmament and attention to regional security. Most important, the UN provides a unique forum for diplomatic negotiations. Financially unable to maintain embassies throughout the world, let alone throughout the African continent, African diplomats take advantage of the fact that almost all countries maintain a permanent mission in New York to carry out the day-to-day business of diplomacy.[66]

In an era when it has become fashionable for U.S. citizens and policymakers to criticize the UN as providing few if any tangible benefits to U.S. foreign policy, it is important to recognize that UN agencies often play substantial administrative and developmental roles in many African countries. In several African capital cities, there are a variety of UN offices whose budgets and staffs sometimes approach those of their counterparts within the host government. In Dakar, Senegal, offices represent a variety of UN agencies, including the United Nations Development Programme (UNDP), the United Nations International Children's Emergency Fund (UNICEF), the United Nations High Commissioner for Refugees (UNHCR), the World Health Organization (WHO), the International Labour Organisation (ILO), and the United Nations Educational, Scientific, and Cultural Organization (UNESCO). Capturing the sentiment of African policymakers during the 1960s, a Senegalese diplomat noted that "these agencies were perceived as critical to the fulfillment of African development goals during the initial independence era, and provided a source of hope especially for those African countries lacking both the resources and the expertise to implement the studies and programs pursued by each of these agencies."[67]

In the aftermath of the Cold War, however, a highly vocal segment of African leaders and intellectuals is often apt to associate the UN with foreign intervention and the imposition of Western values. This perception is due to the replacement of the classic international norms of sovereignty and nonintervention in the affairs of UN member-states with a new set of norms that focus on human rights protection and humanitarian intervention, particularly to save refugees and other peoples threatened by civil conflict and starvation.[68] As aptly noted by former UN Secretary General Boutros-Ghali, "the time of absolute and exclusive sovereignty . . . has passed; its theory was never matched by reality."[69]

The series of UN-sponsored military interventions in Somalia from 1992 to 1995 serves as one of the most notable examples of the UN's increasingly interventionist role in African politics and society. At its height, the UN military operation included over 38,000 troops from twenty countries, and led to the effective occupation of southern and central Somalia. The intervention was launched in the absence of any official invitation from a legal Somali authority (which, in any case, did not exist), and in direct opposition to heavily armed militia groups who shared a historical mistrust of UN intentions and operations dating back to the colonial era.[70] From the perspective of the UN, the collapse of the Somali state and the intensification of a brutal civil war demanded UN intervention; the conflict was not only spilling over into the neighboring territories of Kenya, Ethiopia, and Djibouti, but had contributed to the creation of a humanitarian crisis in which approximately 330,000 Somalis were at "imminent risk of death."[71] According to this logic, the UN could justify international intervention, even in the absence of an official invitation by a legally constituted authority, on the grounds of "abatement" of a threat to international peace.[72]

The Somali case is part of a growing international trend of prompting even internationally recognized governments to accept UN-sponsored humanitarian intervention.[73] In the case of the Sudan, for example, a combination of civil war and drought-induced famine, which led to the deaths of over 500,000 civilians since 1986, prompted the United Nations Office of Emergency Operations in Africa (OEOA) to undertake a humanitarian intervention in 1989 known as Operation Lifeline Sudan.[74] Constituting one of the largest peacetime humanitarian interventions ever undertaken in UN history, Operation Lifeline Sudan was made possible only by mounting international pressure on the Sudanese regime to recognize the scope of the problem and to accept UN-sponsored intervention. Ultimate acceptance, however, did not ensure ultimate happiness on the part of the Sudanese regime. "Even when the initial issues of involvement are resolved, relations between the donors and the recipient country or population are never entirely harmonious," explains a group of specialists on conflict resolution, led by Francis M. Deng, a Sudanese national who served as Special Representative of the United Nations Secretary General for Internally Displaced Persons. "The dichotomy expressed between 'us' and 'them' becomes inevitable as the nationals feel their pride injured by their own failure and dependency, while the donors and relief workers resent the lack of gratitude and appreciation."[75]

Influence of International Financial Institutions

African perceptions of eroding sovereignty have been reinforced by the rising influence of international financial institutions in African economies. By the beginning of the 1980s, African leaders were struggling to respond to the effects of a continent-wide economic crisis. A combination of internal economic decline and mounting international debt was compounded by the "crisis of the state": the existence of bloated, corrupt, and inefficient government bureaucracies increasingly incapable of responding to the day-to-day needs of their respective populations (see Chapter 10). In order to obtain necessary international capital, most African leaders had little choice but to turn to two international financial institutions: the International Monetary Fund (IMF), which issues short-term stabilization loans to ensure economic solvency; and the World Bank, which issues long-term loans to promote economic development. Unlike typical loans that simply require the recipient to make regular scheduled payments over a specific period of time, those of the IMF and the World Bank have included a series of **conditionalities** designed to restructure African economies and political systems in the image of the northern industrialized democracies.[76]

The emergence of **economic conditionalities** was signaled by the 1981 publication of a World Bank study, *Accelerated Development in Sub-Saharan Africa: An Agenda for Action*. The major conclusion of this report was that misguided decisions of the first generation of African leaders were responsible for the mounting economic crisis of the 1980s. In order to resolve this crisis, the World Bank and the IMF proposed the linking of all future flows of Western financial capital to the willingness of African leaders to sign and implement **structural adjustment programs** (SAPs): economic blueprints designed to radically restructure African economies. Four sets of private sector reforms are characteristic of SAPs: (1) the termination of food subsidies that kept food prices artificially low, effectively discouraging farmers from planting food crops; (2) the devaluation of national currencies to stimulate exports and the domestic production of manufactured products; (3) the trimming of government bureaucracies; and (4) the privatization of parastatals (state-owned corporations). In short, the SAPs embodied the liberal economic consensus of the northern industrialized democracies that Africa's future economic success depended on the pursuit of an export-oriented strategy of economic growth that systematically dismantled all forms of governmental intervention in national economies.[77]

A second World Bank report published in 1989, *Sub-Saharan Africa: From Crisis to Sustainable Growth: A Long-Term Perspective Study,* heralded the emergence of **political conditionalities** in IMF and World Bank–sponsored SAPs. In addition to claiming that African countries following IMF and World Bank economic prescriptions were performing better than those that were not, the 1989 report went beyond previous studies by underscoring that the success of economic reforms was dependent on the promotion of **good governance**. Theoretically inclusive of all types of political systems, the concept of good governance in reality constituted the politically correct term for the establishment of multiparty democratic political systems similar to those in the northern industrialized democracies. The IMF and the World Bank had affirmed that all future flows of Western financial capital were contingent on the willingness of African leaders to promote the democratization of their respective political systems.

The economic and political conditionalities imposed by the IMF and the World Bank were often challenged by African policymakers and academics. During the 1980s, the SAPs were criticized due to their complete disregard for the political dilemmas confronted by African leaders.[78] IMF and World Bank economists failed (and even refused) to take into consideration that the cutting off of government subsidies of food — one of the previously cited four pillars of private sector reform always included in SAPs — could lead to often violent urban riots. In the case of the Sudan, for example, the launching of a SAP in 1985 sparked an urban insurrection that contributed to the overthrow of the regime of Gaafar Mohammed Nimeiri.[79] The implementation of the three remaining pillars of private sector reform also entailed serious political risks, due to their tendency to reinforce short-term economic hardships. The devaluation of the national currency meant an immediate decline in the already marginal buying power of the average citizen, and the trimming of government bureaucracies and the privatization of parastatals triggered significant increases in already high levels of national unemployment. In retrospect, the lack of political sensitivity was due to the fact that the SAPs were usually formulated by international economists with little (if any) political training or firsthand knowledge of the individual African countries their programs were supposed to serve.

The SAPs of the 1990s were also strongly challenged by African policymakers and academics despite the fact that both the IMF and the World Bank had undertaken serious efforts to assess, and when possible incorporate, African sentiments into policy-planning documents. Africans were particularly critical of the consensus of IMF and World Bank economists that economic and political conditionalities were mutually reinforcing, and therefore could be pursued simultaneously.[80] As demonstrated by Africa's experiments with democratization after the fall of the Berlin Wall in 1989, the creation of democratic political systems complete with institutional checks-and-balances has hindered the implementation of SAPs (see Chapter 12). Indeed, democratically elected African presidents and congressional representatives are hesitant to enact legislation that will place significant economic burdens on already impoverished populations — essentially committing political suicide in favor of their political opponents.

An important element of African critiques of SAPs involves the applicability of the so-called **Asian model of development**: rapid export-oriented growth that led to the economic success of the "Asian tigers" of Hong Kong, South Korea, Singapore, and Taiwan.[81] The example of South Korea is especially noteworthy. Success in this case was largely due to authoritarian policies that directly contradict the political conditionalities imposed on African leaders. In South Korea, a military leadership intent upon ending corruption and promoting economic development illegally took power in a 1961 military coup d'état and significantly curtailed political pluralism and participation.[82] The implications of this "lesson" (i.e., that the successful implementation of highly unpopular SAPs requires an enlightened form of authoritarianism) were reinforced by Ghana's implementation of SAPs during the 1980s under the authoritarian leadership of Flt. Lt. Jerry Rawlings. Often cited by IMF and World Bank studies as a "model" for other African countries, the Rawlings regime was able to impose draconian SAP policies due to its iron-fisted control over the political system. The authoritarian nature of the Rawlings regime enabled it to impose SAPs that discriminated against the urban population, particularly workers, while preventing the strikes and urban unrest that derailed similar programs in other African countries.[83]

African leaders have sought to curb the impact of economic and political conditionalities by formulating alternative frameworks for development. One of the earliest and most controversial attempts was the adoption of the **Lagos Plan of Action** (LPA) at the 1980 OAU Assembly of Heads of State and Government held in Freetown, Sierra Leone. The LPA was not taken seriously in international financial circles, due to its contradictory assumption that Western governments and financial institutions would finance the pursuit of self-reliant economic development designed to delink the African continent from the international economic system. In 1989, the Economic Commission for Africa (ECA) published a document, *African Alternative Framework to Structural Adjustment Programmes for Socio-Economic Recovery and Transformation (AAF-SAP)*, that drew at least the grudging acceptance of IMF and World Bank economists. Acknowledging that African leaders were partially responsible for Africa's economic crisis, and that some form of economic restructuring was necessary, the 1989 report nonetheless castigated the IMF and World Bank for ignoring the social and political impacts of SAPs. The report specifically called upon international donor agencies to promote **structural adjustment with a human face**: to plan for and respond to the short-term negative social impacts (e.g., rising unemployment) that inevitably accompany the good-faith efforts on the part of African leaders to implement SAPs.

The end of the Cold War has had a dramatic effect on the role of conditionalities in African economic relations. The terms of the debate have shifted away from such Cold War–inspired questions as whether Marxism or an African variant of socialism is favorable to capitalism, or whether single-party or multiparty regimes can better promote the welfare of their respective peoples. Instead, the IMF and the World Bank now consider how to best facilitate the creation of capitalist, multiparty political systems throughout Africa. The confidence of international financial institutions was demonstrated in 1994 by the publication of two World Bank reports: *Adjustment in Africa: Reforms, Results, and the Road Ahead,* and *Adjustment in Africa: Lessons from Country Case Studies.* Both reports assert that SAPs are "working," and that one has only to examine the in-depth analyses of individual cases to understand the validity of IMF and World Bank claims in this area. Toward this end, these reports offer rhetorical support to African demands for structural adjustment with a human face. However, the primary thrust of both documents is that the future provision of financial resources depends on the willingness of African leaders to maintain reform efforts designed to create free market economies and multiparty political systems.

The critical dilemma confronting Africa's newly elected democratic leaders is the extent to which they will attempt to work with international financial institutions. If they wholeheartedly embrace SAPs for the future economic health of their societies, they are bound to alienate important political actors within their political systems and therefore run the risk of losing subsequent democratic elections. In the case of Benin, for example, the democratically elected government of Nicéphore Soglo was rejected in the 1996 presidential elections after only one term of office, at least partially as a result of his administration's strong support for externally inspired SAPs. In contrast, if democratically elected African leaders refuse to embrace SAPs, they run the risk of losing access to international capital and contributing to the further decline of their economies. Cautiously optimistic interpretations suggest that reform-minded African leaders and external supporters of change must adopt "realistic, hardheaded" analyses of Africa's economic plight that avoid both the Afro-pessimism of critics of change and the overly optimistic "cheerleading" stance of those who believe that change can be implemented quickly, smoothly, and relatively free of pain.[84] Although even the best-intentioned and most reform-minded African leaders may find themselves "hemmed in" by a variety of international constraints that restrict policy choices, they are nonetheless capable of pursuing paths that may lead to economic success over the long term.[85]

Key Terms

Cold War
Cold Peace
Great Powers
francophone Africa
Commonwealth of Nations
communist bloc
middle powers
la francophonie
franc zone
complementary Cold War regime
domaine réservé
chasse gardée
Franco-African summit

Francophone summit
la Baule Doctrine
collapsed states
neomercantilist
conditionalities
economic conditionalities
structural adjustment programs (SAPs)
political conditionalities
good governance
Asian model of development
Lagos Plan of Action
structural adjustment with a
  human face

For Further Reading

Akinrinade, Sola, and Amadu Sesay, eds. *Africa in the Post–Cold War International System*. London: Cassell Academic, 1998.

Brune, Stefan, and Joachim Betz and Winrich Kuhne, eds. *Africa and Europe: Relations of Two Continents in Transition*. Munster and Hamburg: Lit Verlag, 1994.

Callaghy, Thomas M., and John Ravenhill, eds. *Hemmed In: Responses to Africa's Economic Decline*. New York: Columbia University Press, 1993.

Clapham, Christopher. *Africa and the International System: The Politics of State Survival*. Cambridge: Cambridge University Press, 1996.

Decalo, Samuel. *Israel and Africa: Forty Years, 1956–1996*. Gainesville: Florida Academic, 1997.

DeLancey, Mark W., and William Cyrus Reed, Rebecca Spyke, and Peter Steen. *African International Relations: An Annotated Bibliography* (2nd ed.). Boulder: Westview, 1997.

Deng, Francis M., Sadikiel Kimaro, Terrence Lyons, Donald Rothchild, and I. William Zartman. *Sovereignty as Responsibility: Conflict Management in Africa*. Washington: Brookings Institution, 1996.

Harbeson, John W., and Donald Rothchild, eds. *Africa in World Politics: Post–Cold War Challenges* (2nd ed.). Boulder: Westview, 1995.

Laïdi, Zaki. *The Superpowers and Africa: The Constraints of a Rivalry 1960–1990*. Chicago: University of Chicago Press, 1990.

Mkandawire, Thandika, and Adebayo Olukoshi, eds. *Between Liberalisation and Oppression: The Politics of Structural Adjustment in Africa*. Dakar: CODESRIA, 1995.

Morikawa, Jun. *Japan and Africa: Big Business and Diplomacy*. Trenton: Africa World, 1997.

Patman, Robert G. *The Soviet Union and the Horn of Africa: The Diplomacy of Intervention and Disengagement*. Cambridge: Cambridge University Press, 1990.

Prendergast, John. *Frontline Diplomacy: Humanitarian Aid and Conflict in Africa*. Boulder: Lynne Rienner, 1996.

Schraeder, Peter J. *United States Foreign Policy toward Africa: Incrementalism, Crisis and Change*. Cambridge: Cambridge University Press, 1994.

Snow, Phillip. *The Star Raft: China's Encounter with Africa*. New York: Weidenfeld and Nicolson, 1988.

Notes

1. See Jeffrey E. Garten, *A Cold Peace: America, Japan, Germany, and the Struggle for Supremacy* (New York: The Twentieth Century Fund, 1993).
2. See Waldemar Nielson, *The Great Powers and Africa* (New York: Praeger, 1969). For an analysis of the 1980s, see Olajide Aluko, ed., *Africa and the Great Powers in the 1980s* (Lanham: University Press of America, 1987). See also Richard J. Payne, *The Nonsuperpowers and South Africa: Implications for U.S. Policy* (Bloomington: Indiana University Press, 1990).
3. See Guy Martin, "Francophone Africa in the Context of Franco-African Relations," in John W. Harbeson and Donald Rothchild, eds., *Africa in World Politics*, 2nd ed. (Boulder: Westview, 1995).
4. See Peter J. Schraeder, *Incrementalism, Crisis and Change: United States Foreign Policy toward Africa* (Cambridge: Cambridge University Press, 1994).
5. For Germany, see Rolf Hofmeier, "German-African Relations: Present and Future," in Stefan Brune, Joachim Betz, and Winrich Kuhne, eds., *Africa and Europe: Relations of Two Continents in Transition* (Munster and Hamburg: Lit Verlag, 1994), pp. 71–86; and Brigitte Schulz and William Hansen, "Aid or Imperialism? West Germany in Sub-Saharan Africa," *The Journal of Modern African Studies* 22, no. 2 (1984):287–313. For Japan, see William R. Nester, *Japan and the Third World: Patterns, Power, Prospects* (New York: St. Martin's, 1992).
6. See Yusuf Bangura, *Britain and Commonwealth Africa: The Politics of Economic Relations, 1951–75* (Manchester: Manchester University Press, 1983). See also David Styan, "Does Britain Have an Africa Policy?" *L'Afrique Politique* (1996):261–86.
7. At the annual meeting held October 24–27, 1998 in Edinburgh, Britain, for example, African countries comprised 35 percent (eighteen) of all attendee nations (total of fifty-one).
8. See Phillip C. Naylor, "Spain and France and the Decolonization of Western Sahara: Parity and Paradox, 1975–87," *Africa Today* 34, no. 3 (1987):7–16. See also Aaron Segal, "Spain and Africa: The Continuing Problem of Ceuta

and Melilla," in Colin Legum and Marion E. Doro, eds., *Africa Contemporary Record: Annual Survey and Documents 1987–88,* vol. 20 (New York: Africana, 1989), pp. A71–A77.

9. See Maria Cristina Ercolessi, "Italy's Policy in Sub-Saharan Africa," in Stefan Brune, Joachim Betz, and Winrich Kuhne, eds., *Africa and Europe: Relations of Two Continents in Transition* (Munster and Hamburg: Lit Verlag, 1994), pp. 87–108.

10. See Norman MacQueen, "Portugal and Africa: The Politics of Re-Engagement," *The Journal of Modern African Studies* 23, no. 1 (1985):31–51.

11. See Robert G. Patman, *The Soviet Union and the Horn of Africa: The Diplomacy of Intervention and Disengagement* (Cambridge: Cambridge University Press, 1990).

12. See Bruce D. Larkin, *China and Africa, 1949–1970: The Foreign Policy of the People's Republic of China* (Berkeley: University of California Press, 1971); and Philip Snow, *The Star Raft: China's Encounter with Africa* (Ithaca: Cornell University Press, 1986). See also Yan Xuetong, "Sino-African Relations in the 1990s," *CSIS Africa Notes* 84 (1988):1–5; and S. Chan, "China's Foreign Policy and Africa: The Rise and Fall of China's Three Worlds Theory," *Round Table* 296 (1985):376–84.

13. See Gareth M. Winrow, *The Foreign Policy of the GDR in Africa* (Cambridge: Cambridge University Press, 1990).

14. See Carmelo Mesa-Lago and June S. Beikin, eds., *Cuba in Africa* (Pittsburgh: University of Pittsburgh, 1982).

15. See Olav Stokke, ed., *Western Middle Powers and Global Poverty: The Determinants of the Aid Policies of Canada, Denmark, the Netherlands, Norway, and Sweden* (Uppsala: Scandinavian Institute of African Studies, 1989).

16. See Joel Peters, *Israel and Africa: The Problematic Friendship* (New York: St. Martin's, 1992). See also Samuel Decalo, *Israel and Africa: Forty Years, 1956–1996* (Gainesville: Florida Academic, 1997).

17. See John Creed and Ken Menkhaus, "The Rise of Saudi Regional Power and the Foreign Policies of Northeast African States," *Northeast African Studies* 8, no. 2 (1986):1–22.

18. For Brazil, see P. D. Collins, "Brazil in Africa: Perspectives on Economic Cooperation among Developing Countries," *Development Policy Review* 3, no. 1 (1985):21–48. For India, see Ajay K. Dubey, *Indo-African Relations in the Post-Nehru Era (1965–1985)* (Delhi: Kalinga, 1990). See also S. S. Karnik, "India-Africa Economic Relations: A Select Bibliography," *Africa Quarterly* 25, no. 3–4 (1988):63–110.

19. Richard M. Nixon, "The Emergence of Africa, Report to President Eisenhower by Vice President Nixon," *Department of State Bulletin* 36, no. 930 (April 22, 1957):640.

20. John F. Kennedy, "The Challenge of Imperialism: Algeria," in Theodore C. Sorensen, *"Let the Word Go Forth": The Speeches, Statements, and Writings of John F. Kennedy* (New York: Delacorte, 1988), pp. 331–37.

21. John F. Kennedy, "The New Nations of Africa," in Theodore C. Sorensen, *"Let the Word Go Forth,"* pp. 365, 368.

22. See Charles W. Kegley, Jr., and Eugene R. Wittkopf, *American Foreign Policy: Pattern and Process* (New York: St. Martin's, 1992); and John Spanier and Steven W. Hook, *American Foreign Policy since World War II,* 13th ed. (Washington: Congressional Quarterly, 1995).

23. For example, see Jeffrey A. Lefebvre, *Arms for the Horn: U.S. Security Policy in Ethiopia and Somalia 1953–1991* (Pittsburgh: University of Pittsburgh Press, 1991).

24. Edward A. Kolodziej, *French Foreign Policy under DeGaulle and Pompidou: The Politics of Grandeur* (Ithaca: Cornell University Press, 1974).

25. Olivier Vallée, *Le Prix de l'Argent CFA: Heurs et Malheurs de la Zone Franc* (Paris: Karthala, 1989).

26. For discussions of the foreign aid regime of the Cold War and its aftermath, see Steven W. Hook, *National Interest and Foreign Aid* (Boulder: Lynne Rienner, 1995); and Steven W. Hook, ed., *Foreign Aid toward the Millennium* (Boulder: Lynne Rienner, 1996).

27. Martin, "Continuity and Change," 1995.

28. George Ball, *The Disciples of Power* (Boston: Little, Brown, 1968).

29. See James O. Goldsborough, "Dateline Paris: Africa's Policeman," *Foreign Policy* 33 (Winter 1978–79): 174–90. For a sympathetic analysis of France's role, see Pierre Lellouche and Dominique Moisi, "French Policy in Africa: A Lonely Battle against Destabilization," *International Security* 3, no. 4 (1979):108–33.

30. See Zaki Laïdi, *The Superpowers and Africa: The Constraints of a Rivalry 1960–1990* (Chicago: University of Chicago Press, 1990); and Arthur L. Gavshon, *Crisis in Africa: Battleground of East and West* (Boulder: Westview, 1984).

31. See U.S. House of Representatives, Committee on International Relations, Subcommittee on International Security and Scientific Affairs, *Congressional Oversight of War Powers Compliance: Zaire Airlift,* Hearing, August 10, 1978, 95th Congress, 2nd Session (Washington: Government Printing Office, 1978).

32. See "News Conferences, May 4 and 25 (Excerpts)," *Department of State Bulletin* 78, no. 2016 (July 1978):18.

33. See "Meet the Press," *Department of State Bulletin* 78, no. 2016 (July 1978):26.

34. Personal interview with Moose, June 26, 1989.

35. See Guy Martin, "Continuity and Change in Franco-African Relations," in John W. Harbeson and Donald Rothchild, eds., *Africa in World Politics* (Boulder: Westview, 1995).

36. Foccart, *Foccart Parle,* 1995, p. 287.

37. Michael Clough, *U.S. Policy toward Africa and the End of the Cold War* (New York: Council on Foreign Relations, 1994), pp. 76–100.

38. For an overview of U.S. containment policies, see F. Ugboaja Ohaegbulam, "Containment in Africa: From Truman to Reagan," *TransAfrica Forum* 6, no. 1 (Fall 1988): 7–34.

39. For a discussion of these trends, see Richard Sandbrook, *The Politics of Africa's Economic Recovery* (Cambridge: Cambridge University Press, 1993); and Thomas M. Callaghy and John Ravenhill, eds., *Hemmed In: Responses to Africa's Economic Decline* (New York: Columbia University Press, 1993).

40. Department of Commerce, "A Comprehensive Trade and Development Policy for the Countries of Africa. A Report Submitted by the President of the United States to the Congress," February 1996.

41. The only exceptions to this trend include President Bush's one-day visit to Somalia in 1993 while in transit to the Middle East and President Carter's March 29–April 2, 1978 visit to Nigeria in 1977.

42. Antoine Glaser and Stephen Smith, *L'Afrique sans Africains: Le Rêve Blanc du Continent Noir* (Paris: Editions Stock, 1994).

43. Martin, "Francophone Africa," 1995, pp. 180–81.

44. *Ibid.*, p. 180.

45. *Ibid.*, p. 181.

46. Howard W. French, "France Refuses to Apologize to U.S. for Africa Comments," *New York Times* (October 18, 1996): A5.

47. *Ibid.*

48. For an overview, see John F. Clark and David E. Gardinier, eds., *Political Reform in Francophone Africa* (Boulder: Westview, 1997)

49. See Agir Ici et Survie, *La France à Biarritz: Mise en Examen de la Politique Française* (Paris: Karthala, 1995). See also Jean-François Bayart, *La Politique Africaine de François Mitterrand* (Paris: Karthala, 1984).

50. Glaser and Smith, *L'Afrique sans Africains*, 1994, p. 102.

51. See Roland Marchal, "La France en quête d'une politique Africaine?" *Politique Etrangère* no. 4 (Winter 1995–96):903–16.

52. See Howard W. French, "France's Army Keeps Grip in African Ex-Colonies," *New York Times* (May 22, 1996): A3.

53. Personal interview.

54. See I. William Zartman, ed., *Collapsed States: The Disintegration and Restoration of Legitimate Authority* (Boulder: Lynne Rienner, 1995).

55. See Walter Clarke and Jeffrey Herbst, eds., *Learning from Somalia: The Lessons of Armed Humanitarian Intervention* (Boulder: Westview, 1997). See also John L. Hirsch and Robert B. Oakley, *Somalia and Operation Restore Hope: Reflections on Peacemaking and Peacekeeping* (Washington: The United States Institute for Peace, 1995).

56. See Thomas L. Friedman, "U.S. Pays Dearly for an Education in Somalia," *New York Times* (October 10, 1993): sec. 4, p. 1.

57. *Ibid.*

58. Douglas Jehl, "Officials Told to Avoid Calling Rwanda Killings 'Genocide'," *New York Times* (June 10, 1994): A8.

59. For a general overview, see David R. Smock and Chester A. Crocker, eds., *African Conflict Resolution: The U.S. Role in Peacemaking* (Washington: United States Institute of Peace, 1996).

60. See Cason and Martin, "Clinton and Africa," 1993, p. 2.

61. *Ibid.*

62. See Gérard Prunier, *The Rwanda Crisis: History of a Genocide* (New York: Columbia University Press, 1995).

63. Stephen Smith, "France-Rwanda: Lévirat Colonial et Abandon dans la Région des Grands Lacs," in André Guichaoua, ed., *Les Crises Politiques au Burundi et Rwanda (1993–1994): Analyses, Faits et Documents* (Paris: Karthala, 1995), p. 452.

64. Glaser and Smith, pp. 182–85.

65. See Gérard Prunier, "The Great Lakes Crisis," *Current History* 96, no. 610 (1997):1–7.

66. K. Mathews, "The African Group at the UN as an Instrument of African Diplomacy," *Nigerian Journal of International Affairs* 14, no. 1 (1988):226–58.

67. Personal interview, Dakar, Senegal, January 1995.

68. Francis M. Deng et. al, *Sovereignty As Responsibility: Conflict Management in Africa* (Washington: Brookings Institution, 1996), p. 5.

69. Boutros Boutros-Ghali, *An Agenda for Peace: Preventive Diplomacy, Peace-Making, and Peace-Keeping* (New York: United Nations, 1992), p. 9.

70. Somali distrust of the UN stems from the 1950 decision of that international body to support the reimposition of Italian colonial rule over what is currently known as the Republic of Somalia. See John L. Hirsch and Robert B. Oakley, *Somalia and Operation Restore Hope: Reflections on Peacemaking and Peacekeeping* (Washington: United States Institute for Peace, 1995).

71. Terrence Lyons and Ahmed I. Samatar, *Somalia: State Collapse, Multilateral Intervention, and Strategies for Political Reconstruction* (Washington: Brookings Institution, 1995), p. 24.

72. Christopher C. Joyner, "International Law," in Peter J. Schraeder, ed., *Intervention into the 1990s: U.S. Foreign Policy in the Third World* (Boulder: Lynne Rienner, 1995), pp. 229–46.

73. Francis M. Deng, *Protecting the Dispossessed: A Challenge for the International Community* (Washington: Brookings Institution, 1993).

74. Francis M. Deng and Larry Minear, *The Challenges of Famine Relief: Emergency Operations in the Sudan* (Washington: Brookings Institution, 1992).

75. Deng et. al, *Sovereignty as Responsibility*, p. 11.

76. For an excellent overview, see Thomas M. Callaghy and John Ravenhill, eds., *Hemmed In: Responses to Africa's Economic Decline* (New York: Columbia University Press, 1993).

77. Stephen K. Commins, ed., *Africa's Development Challenges and the World Bank: Hard Questions, Costly Choices* (Boulder: Lynne Rienner, 1988); and Bonnie K. Campbell and John Loxley, eds., *Structural Adjustment in Africa* (New York: St. Martin's, 1989).

78. See Jennifer A. Widner, ed., *Economic Change and Political Liberalization in Sub-Saharan Africa* (Baltimore: Johns Hopkins University Press, 1994).

79. See Ernest Harsch, "After Adjustment," *Africa Report* (May–June 1989):48.

80. See Richard Sandbrook, *The Politics of Africa's Economic Recovery* (Cambridge: Cambridge University Press, 1993).

81. World Bank, *The East Asian Miracle: Economic Growth and Public Policy* (Washington: World Bank, 1993).

82. See Thomas M. Callaghy and John Ravenhill, "If Korea Can Do It, Why Not Africa? Or: Limited Current Relevance But Possible Future Model," in Callaghy and Ravenhill, *Hemmed In*, p. 546.

83. See Jeffrey Herbst, *The Politics of Reform in Ghana, 1982–1991* (Berkeley: University of California Press, 1993).

84. Callaghy and Ravenhill, *Hemmed In*.

85. *Ibid.*

APPENDIX 1

List of Acronyms

Acronym	Definition
AAAA	American African Affairs Association (U.S.)
AAF-SAP	African Alternative Framework to Structural Adjustment Programmes for Socio-Economic Recovery and Transformation
AAI	African-American Institute (U.S.)
AAPS	African Association of Political Science
ACAS	Association of Concerned Africa Scholars (U.S.)
ACM	African Common Market
AEC	African Economic Community
AEF	*Afrique Equatoriale Française* (French Equatorial Africa)
AFDL	*Alliance des Forces Démocratiques pour la Libération* (Alliance of Democratic Forces for Liberation) (Democratic Republic of the Congo)
AHD	African Historical Dictionaries series (U.S.)
AHSA	African Heritage Studies Association (U.S.)
AOF	*Afrique Occidentale Française* (French West Africa)
ANC	African National Congress (South Africa)
ANC	*Armée Nationale Congolaise* (Congolese National Army) (Democratic Republic of the Congo)

Acronym	Definition
ASA	African Studies Association (U.S.)
BDF	Botswana Defence Force
BDF	Botswana Democratic Front
BDP	Botswana Democratic Party
BHN	Basic Human Needs
BIP	Botswana Independent Party
BLP	Botswana Labour Party
BNF	Botswana National Front
BPP	Botswana People's Party
BPU	Botswana Progressive Union
CASS	Centre for Advanced Social Science (Nigeria)
CCM	*Chama Cha Mapinduzi* (Revolutionary Party) (Tanzania)
CELZA	*Cultures et Elevages du Zaire* (Farms and Ranches of Zaire) (Democratic Republic of the Congo)
CERDET	Center for Study and Research on Democracy in the Third World (Senegal)
CFA	*Communauté Financière Africaine* (African Financial Community)
CIA	Central Intelligence Agency (U.S.)
CIES	Council for the International Exchange of Scholars (U.S.)
CITES	Convention on International Trade in Endangered Species
CODESRIA	Council for the Development of Social Science Research in Africa (Senegal)
COSATU	Confederation of South African Trade Unions
CPDM	Cameroon People's Democratic Movement
CND	*Centre National de Documentation* (National Documentation Center) (Democratic Republic of the Congo)
CNN	Cable News Network (U.S.)
DIA	Defense Intelligence Agency (U.S.)
DOM-TOM	*Départements d'Outre Mer-Territoires d'Outre-Mer* (Overseas Departments and Territories) (France)

Acronym	Definition
DSP	*Division Spéciale Présidentielle* (Special Presidential Division) (Democratic Republic of the Congo)
EAC	East African Community
ECA	Economic Commission for Africa
ECCAS	Economic Community of Central African States
ECOMOG	ECOWAS Monitoring Group (Liberia)
ECOWAS	Economic Community of West African States
ELF	Eritrean Liberation Front
EPLF	Eritrean People's Liberation Front
EPRDF	Ethiopian People's Revolutionary Democratic Front
FAZ	*Forces Armées Zairoises* (Zairian Armed Forces) (Democratic Republic of the Congo)
FDLD	*Front Démocratique pour la Libération de Djibouti* (Democratic Front for the Liberation of Djibouti)
FEPACI	*Fédération Panafricaine des Cinéastes* (Pan-African Film-Makers Federation) (Burkina Faso)
FESPACO	*Festival Panafricain du Cinéma de Ouagadougou* (Pan-African Film Festival of Ouagadougou) (Burkina Faso)
FLNC	*Front de Libération Nationale du Congo* (National Front for the Liberation of the Congo) (Democratic Republic of the Congo)
FNLA	*Frente Nacional de Libertação de Angola* (Front for the National Liberation of Angola)
FPR	*Front Patriotique Rwandais* (Rwandan Patriotic Front)
FRELIMO	*Frente de Libertação de Moçambique* (Front for the Liberation of Mozambique)
FRUD	*Front pour la Restauration de la Démocratie* (Front for the Restoration of Democracy) (Djibouti)
GDP	gross domestic product
GEAR	Growth, Employment, and Redistribution (South Africa)
GECAMINES	*Général des Carrières et des Mines* (General of Quarries and Mines) (Democratic Republic of the Congo)
GECOMIN	*Générale Congolaise des Minérais* (Congolese General of Minerals) (Democratic Republic of the Congo)

Acronym	Definition
GNP	gross national product
IFP	Inkatha Freedom Party (South Africa)
IGADD	Intergovernmental Authority on Drought and Development
IGNU	Interim Government of National Unity (Liberia)
ILO	International Labour Organisation
IMF	International Monetary Fund
ISA	International Studies Association
JETRO	Japan External Trade Organization
JICA	Japanese International Cooperation Agency
JMPR	*Jeunesse du Mouvement Populaire de la Revolution* (Youth of the Popular Movement of the Revolution) (Democratic Republic of the Congo)
JOCV	Japan Overseas Cooperation Volunteers
KANU	Kenya African National Union
LPA	Lagos Plan of Action
LPAI	*Ligue Populaire Africaine pour l'Indépendance* (African Popular League for Independence) (Djibouti)
MITI	Ministry of International Trade and Industry (Japan)
MMD	Movement for Multiparty Democracy (Zambia)
MNCs	multinational corporations
MPL	*Mouvement Populaire de Libération* (Popular Movement of Liberation) (Djibouti)
MPLA	*Movimento Popular de Libertação de Angola* (Popular Movement for the Liberation of Angola)
MPR	*Mouvement Populaire de la Révolution* (Popular Movement of the Revolution) (Democratic Republic of the Congo)
MTTs	mobile training teams (U.S.)
NAFTA	North American Free Trade Agreement
NCA	Nations of Contemporary Africa series (U.S.)
NCNC	National Council of Nigeria and the Cameroons
NCNC	National Council of Nigerian Citizens
NDI	National Democratic Institute for International Affairs (U.S.)

Acronym	Definition
NEC	National Economic Council (U.S.)
NMW	Nations of the Modern World series (U.S.)
NP	National Party (South Africa)
NPC	Northern Peoples' Congress (Nigeria)
NPFL	National Patriotic Front of Liberia
NPP	New Patriotic Party (Liberia)
NRA	National Resistance Army (Uganda)
NRM	National Resistance Movement (Uganda)
NSC	National Security Council (U.S.)
NSEP	National Security Education Program (U.S.)
NSF	National Science Foundation (U.S.)
NUEW	National Union of Eritrean Women
OAU	Organization of African Unity
OEOA	United Nations Office of Emergency Operations in Africa
OLF	Oromo Liberation Front (Ethiopia)
OPEC	Organization of Petroleum Exporting Countries
PAC	Pan African Congress (South Africa)
PAIGC	*Partido Africano da Indepêndencia da Guiné e Cabo Verde* (Independence African Party of Guinea and Cape Verde)
PDCI-RDA	*Parti Démocratique de la Côte d'Ivoire–Rassemblement Démocratique pour l'Assemblée* (Democratic Party of Côte d'Ivoire–African Democratic Assembly)
PDD-25	Presidential Decision Directive 25 (U.S.)
PIT	*Parti de l'Indépendance et du Travail* (Independence and Workers Party) Senegal
PMAC	Provisional Military Administrative Council (Ethiopia)
PNDC	Provisional National Defense Council (Ghana)
POW	Prisoner of War
PPD	*Parti Populaire Djiboutien* (Djiboutian Popular Party)
PRC	People's Redemption Council (Liberia)
PRC	People's Republic of China
RAINBOW	Research, Action, and Information Network for Bodily Integrity of Women

Acronym	Definition
RPF	Rwandan Patriotic Front
RPP	*Rassemblement Populaire pour le Progrès* (Popular Assembly for Progress) (Djibouti)
SACP	South African Communist Party
SADC	Southern African Development Community
SADCC	Southern African Development Coordination Conference
SADF	South African Defense Force
SADR	Saharan Arab Democratic Republic
SALT	Strategic Arms Limitation Talks
SANDF	South African National Defence Force
SAPs	structural adjustment programs
SDF	Social Democratic Front (Cameroon)
SEALs	Sea-Air-Land Commandos (U.S.)
SNF	Somali National Front
SNM	Somali National Movement
SOZACOM	*Société Zairoise pour la Commercialisation des Minéraux* (Zairian Company for the Commercialization of Minerals) (Democratic Republic of the Congo)
SPM	Somali Patriotic Movement
SRC	Supreme Revolutionary Council (Somalia)
SSRC	Social Science Research Council (U.S.)
SWAPO	South West Africa People's Organization (Namibia)
TANZAM	Tanzanian-Zambian Railroad
TPLF	Tigrean People's Liberation Front (Ethiopia)
UAM	Union of the Arab Maghreb
UDI	Unilateral Declaration of Independence (Zimbabwe)
UDPS	*Union pour la Démocratie et le Progrès Social* (Union for Democracy and Social Progress) (Democratic Republic of the Congo)
UGEC	*Union Générale des Etudiants Congolais* (General Union of Congolese Students) (Democratic Republic of the Congo)
ULIMO	United Liberation Movement of Liberia
UN	United Nations

Acronym	Definition
UNAZA	*Université Nationale du Zaire* (National University of Zaire) (Democratic Republic of the Congo)
UNDP	United Nations Development Programme
UNESCO	United Nations Educational, Scientific, and Cultural Organization
UNI	*Union Nationale de l'Indépendance* (National Union for Independence) (Djibouti)
UNICEF	United Nations International Children's Emergency Fund
UNIP	United National Independence Party (Zambia)
UNITA	*União Nacional para a Independência Total de Angola* (National Union for the Total Independence of Angola)
UNHCR	United Nations High Commissioner for Refugees
UNTC	*Union Nationale des Travailleurs Congolais* (National Union of Congolese Workers) (Democratic Republic of the Congo)
UPC	*Union des Populations du Cameroun* (Union of the Populations of Cameroon)
UPEZA	*Union Progressiste des Etudiants Zairois* (Progressive Union of Zairian Students) (Democratic Republic of the Congo)
USAID	United States Agency for International Development
USC	United Somali Congress
USIA	United States Information Agency
USOR	*Union Sacrée de l'Opposition Radicale* (Sacred Union of Radical Opposition) (Democratic Republic of the Congo)
WBS	World Bibliographical Series
WHO	World Health Organization
WIGMO	Western International Ground Maintenance Organization
WPE	Workers Party of Ethiopia
WSLF	Western Somali Liberation Front
ZANU	Zimbabwe African Nationalist Union
ZAPU	Zimbabwe African People's Union

APPENDIX 2

Country Name Changes in Africa during the Contemporary Independence Era

Original Name	Current Name/Disposition
Basutoland	Lesotho
Bechuanaland	Botswana
Belgian Congo	Democratic Republic of the Congo (often referred to as Congo-Kinshasa)
Biafra	Secessionist portion of southeastern Nigeria that declared independence in 1967. A three-year civil war (1967–70) ended in defeat and reincorporation into Nigeria.
British Somaliland	Former British colony that five days after independence in 1960 voluntarily federated with Italian Somaliland to form the Republic of Somalia.
British Togoland	Ghana
Central African Empire	Central African Republic
Dahomey	Benin
French Congo	Congo (often referred to as Congo-Brazzaville)
French Equatorial Africa (AEF)	French colonial unit that included Cameroon, Central African Republic, Chad, Congo (Brazzaville), and Gabon.
French Somali Coast	Djibouti
French Somaliland	Djibouti

Original Name	Current Name/Disposition
French Soudan	Mali
French Territory of Afars and Issas	Djibouti
French West Africa (AOF)	French colonial unit that included Benin, Burkina Faso, Côte d'Ivoire, Guinea, Mali, Mauritania, Niger, and Senegal.
German East Africa	Tanzania
Gold Coast	Ghana
Italian Somaliland	Former Italian colony that after independence in 1960 voluntarily federated with British Somaliland to form the Republic of Somalia.
Ivory Coast	Côte d'Ivoire
Kamerun	Cameroon
Katanga	Secessionist province of southeastern Democratic Republic of the Congo that declared its independence in 1960. Secession was ultimately rejected after a Katangese leader, Moise Tshombe, was named prime minister of the Democratic Republic of the Congo. Also known as Shaba province.
Malagasy Republic	Madagascar
Mali Federation	Short-lived (three-month) federation of two former French colonies that subsequently declared independence in 1961 as the countries of Senegal and Mali.
Northern Cameroons	Northern portion of a British trusteeship territory that opted through a United Nations–sponsored plebiscite in 1961 to federate with Nigeria.
Northern Rhodesia	Zambia
Nyasaland	Malawi
Oubangui Chari	Central African Republic
Portuguese Guinea	Guinea-Bissau
Rhodesia	Zimbabwe
Ruanda-Urundi	Former Belgian trusteeship territory that achieved independence in 1961 as two separate countries: Burundi and Rwanda.

Original Name	Current Name/Disposition
Saharan Arab Democratic Republic (SADR)	Former Spanish territory annexed by Morocco and Mauritania that has declared its independence. Mauritania renounced any claims to its portion, which was annexed by Morocco. The SADR was granted "observer status" by the Organization of African Unity (OAU).
Senegambia	Unsuccessful federation (1981–89) of two independent countries (Senegal and The Gambia) that reverted back to their separate, independent status in 1989.
Shaba	See Katanga
Somaliland Republic	Former British Somaliland territory that seceded from the Republic of Somaliland in 1991. As of 1999, no country has recognized Somaliland's independence.
South West Africa	Namibia
Southern Cameroons	Southern portion of a British trusteeship territory that opted through a United Nations–sponsored plebiscite in 1961 to federate with Cameroon.
Southern Rhodesia	Zimbabwe
Spanish Guinea	Equatorial Guinea
Spanish Sahara	See Saharan Arab Democratic Republic (SADR)
Tanganyika	Tanzania
Togoland	Togo
United Arab Republic	Unsuccessful federation of Egypt and Syria (1958–61).
Upper Volta	Burkina Faso
Western Sahara	See Saharan Arab Democratic Republic (SADR)
Zaire	Democratic Republic of the Congo
Zanzibar	Former British colony that federated with Tanzania in 1964.

APPENDIX 3

Political Leadership in Africa during the Contemporary Independence Era

Country	Political Leadership	
ALGERIA	1962–65	Ahmed Ben Bella
(Algiers)	1965–78	Col. Houari Boumedienne
	1978–79	Rabah Bitat
	1979–92	Col. Benjedid Chadli Benjedid
	1992	Mohammed Boudiaf
	1992–94	Ali Kafi
	1994–99	Gen. Liamine Zeroual
	1999–	Abdelaziz Bouteflika
ANGOLA	1975–79	Antonio Agostinho Neto
(Luanda)	1979-	José Eduardo dos Santos
BENIN	1960–63	Hubert Coutoucou Maga
(Porto-Novo)	1963–64	Lt. Col. Christophe Soglo
	1964–65	Sourou-Migan Apithy
	1965	Tahirou Congacou
	1965–67	Gen. Christophe Soglo
	1967–68	Lt. Col. Alphonse Amadou Alley
	1968–69	Émile-Derlin Zinsou
	1969–70	Lt. Col. Paul Émile de Souza
	1970–72	Hubert C. Maga
	1972	Justin Ahomadegbé
	1972–91	Col. Mathieu Kérékou
	1991–96	Nicéphore Soglo
	1996-	Mathieu Kérékou

Country		Political Leadership
BOTSWANA	1966–80	Sir Seretse Khama
(Gaborone)	1980–97	Quett Ketumile J. Masire
	1997–	Festu Mogae
BURKINA FASO	1960–66	Maurice Yaméogo
(Ouagadougou)	1966–80	Lt. Col. Sangoulé Lamizana
	1980–82	Col. Sayé Zerbo
	1982–83	Maj. Jean Baptiste Ouedraogo
	1983–87	Capt. Thomas Sankara
	1987–	Capt. Blaise Compaoré
BURUNDI	1962–66	King Mwami Mwambutsa IV
(Bujumbura)	1966	King Mwami Ntare V
	1966–76	Capt. Michel Micombero
	1976–87	Col. Jean-Baptiste Bagaza
	1987–93	Maj. Pierre Buyoya
	1993	Melchior Ndadaye
	1993–94	Sylvie Kinigi
	1994	Cyprien Ntaryamira
	1994–96	Sylvestre Ntibantunganya
	1996–	Maj. Pierre Buyoya
CAMEROON	1960–82	Ahmadou Ahidjo
(Yaounde)	1982–	Paul Biya
CAPE VERDE	1975–81	Aristides Pereira
(Praia)	1991–	Antònio Mascarenhas Monteiro
CENTRAL	1960–66	David Dacko
AFRICAN	1966–79	Col. Jean-Bédel Bokassa
REPUBLIC	1979–81	David Dacko
(Bangui)	1981–93	Gen. André Kolingba
	1993–	Ange-Félix Patassé
CHAD	1962–75	Ngarta (François) Tombalbaye
(Ndjamena)	1975–79	Gen. Félix Malloum
	1979	Lol Mahamat Chaoua
	1979–82	Goukouni Oueddei
	1982–90	Hissène Habré
	1990–	Col. Idriss Déby
COMOROS	1975	Ahmed Abdullah Abderemane
(Moroni)	1975–76	Prince Said Mohammed Jaffar
	1975–78	Ali Soilih
	1978–89	Ahmed Abdallah Abderemane
	1989	Bob Denard
	1989–96	Said Mohamed Djohar

Country	Political Leadership	
COMOROS (Moroni) *continued*	1996–99 1999 1999–	Mohamad Taki Abdulkarim Tadjiddine Ben Said Massonde Col. Azaly Assoumani
CONGO (Brazzaville)	1960–63 1963–68 1968–77 1977–79 1979–91 1991–92 1992–97 1997–	Abbé Fulbert Youlou Alphonse Massamba-Débat Capt. Marien Ngouabi Col. Joachim Yhombi-Opango Col. Dénis Sassou-Nguesso André Milongo Pascal Lissouba Gen. Dénis Sassou-Nguesso
COTE D'IVOIRE (Abidjan)	1960–93 1993–	Félix Houphouët-Boigny Henri Konan Bédié
DEMOCRATIC REPUBLIC OF THE CONGO (Kinshasa)	1960 1960–61 1961 1961–64 1964–65 (from 1960–65, 1965–97 1997–	Patrice Lumumba Col. Mobutu Sese Seko (formerly Joseph Désiré Mobutu) Joseph Ileo Cyrille Adoula Moise Tshombe Joseph Kasavubu served as president) Gen. Mobutu Sese Seko Laurent-Désiré Kabila
DJIBOUTI (Djibouti City)	1977–99 1999	Hassan Gouled Aptidon Ismael Omar Guelleh
EGYPT (Cairo)	1922–52 1952–54 1954–70 1970–81 1981–	King Farouk Gen. Muhammad Neguib Col. Gamal Abdel Nasser Col. Anwar Sadat Lt. Gen. Hosni Mubarak
EQUATORIAL GUINEA (Malabo)	1968–79 1979–	Francisco Macías Nguema Lt. Col. Teodoro Obiango Nguema Mbasogo
ERITREA (Asmara)	1993–	Issaias Afwerki
ETHIOPIA (Addis Ababa)	1270–85 1285–94 1294–99 1299–1314 1314–44	Yekuno Amlak Saloman I Bahr Asgad; Senfa Asgad; Hezba Ared; Kedma Asgad; Zhin Asgad Wedem Ared Amda Seyon I

Country	Political Leadership	
ETHIOPIA	1344–72	Newaya Krestos
(Addis Ababa)	1372–82	Newaya Maryam
continued	1382–1413	Dauti (David) I
	1413–14	Tewodos (Theodore) I
	1414–29	Yeskaq
	1429–34	Endreyas; Takla Maryam; Sarwa Iyasus; Amda Iyasus
	1434–68	Zara Yakob
	1468–78	Baeda Maryam
	1478–94	Eskender
	1494	Amda Seyon II
	1494–1508	Naod
	1508–40	Lebna Dengel (Dauti II)
	1540–59	Galawdewos (Claudius)
	1559–63	Minas
	1563–97	Sarsa Dengel
	1597–1603	Yaqob (I)
	1603–4	Za Dengel
	1604–7	Yaqob (II)
	1607–32	Susneyos
	1632–67	Fasiladas
	1667–82	Yohannes I
	1682–1706	Isayu I
	1706–8	Takla Haymanot
	1708–11	Tewoflos
	1711–16	Yostos
	1716–21	Dauti III
	1721–30	Bakaffa (Asma Giorgis)
	1730–55	Iyasu II (with Menetewab as regentess)
	1755–69	Iyoas I
	1769–1855	"Era of the princes" in which at least eighteen men held the title of emperor in as many as thirty different periods.[1]
	1855–68	Tewodros (Theodore) II
	1868–72	Takla Giorgis II
	1872–89	Yohannes (John) IV
	1889–1913	Menelik II
	1914–16	Iyasu V (Lij Iyasu)
	1916–30	Zauditu (Empress)
	1930–74	Emperor Haile Selassie
	1974	Lt. Gen. Aman Andom
	1974–77	Brig. Gen. Teferi Banti

Country		Political Leadership
ETHIOPIA	1977–91	Maj. Mengistu Haile Mariam
(Addis Ababa)	1991–95	Meles Zenawi
continued	1995–	Ngasso Gidada
GABON	1961–67	Léon M'Ba
(Libreville)	1967–	Omar Bongo
THE GAMBIA	1965–94	Dawda Kairaba Jawara
(Banjul)	1994–	Capt. Yahya A. J. J. Jammeh
GHANA	1957–66	Kwame Nkrumah
(Accra)	1966–69	Lt. Gen. Joseph A. Ankrah
	1969	Brig. Gen. Akwasi O. Afrifa
	1969–72	Kofi A. Busia
	1972–78	Lt. Col. Ignatius K. Acheampong
	1978–79	Lt. Gen. Frederick Akuffo
	1979	Flt. Lt. Jerry Rawlings
	1979–81	Dr. Hilla Limann
	1981–	Flt. Lt. Jerry Rawlings
GUINEA	1958–84	Ahmed Sékou Touré
(Conakry)	1984–	Col. Lansana Conté
GUINEA-BISSAU	1974–80	Luíz De Almeida Cabral
(Bissau)	1980–99	Gen. João Bernardo Vieira
	1999–	Malam Bacai Sanha
KENYA	1963–78	Jomo Kenyatta
(Nairobi)	1978–	Daniel arap Moi
LESOTHO	1966–70	King Motlotlehi Moshoeshoe II
(Maseru)	1970–86	Chief Leabua Jonathan
	1986–91	Maj. Gen. Justin Lekhanya
	1991–93	Col. Elias P. Ramaema
	1993–95	Ntsu Mokhehle
	1995–96	King Moshoeshoe II
	1996–	King Letsie III
LIBERIA	1848–56	Joseph J. Roberts I
(Monrovia)	1856–64	Stephen A. Benson
	1864–68	Daniel B. Warner
	1868–70	James S. Payne I
	1870–71	Edward J. Roye
	1871–72	James S. Smith
	1872–76	Joseph J. Roberts II
	1876–78	James S. Payne II
	1878–83	Anthony W. Gardiner
	1883–84	Alfred F. Russell
	1884–92	Hilary R. W. Johnson

Country	Political Leadership	
LIBERIA	1892–96	Joseph J. Cheeseman
(Monrovia)	1896–00	William D. Coleman
continued	1900–04	Garretson W. Gibson
	1904–12	Arthur Barclay
	1912–20	Daniel E. Howard
	1920–30	Charles D. B. King
	1930–44	Edwin J. Barclay
	1944–71	William V. S. Tubman
	1971–80	William R. Tolbert
	1980–90	Samuel K. Doe
	1990–94	Amos Sawyer
	1994–95	David D. Kpormakor
	1995–96	Wilton Sankawulo
	1996–97	Ruth Sando Perry
	1997–	Charles Taylor
LIBYA	1951–69	King Idris
(Tripoli)	1969–	Col. Muammar Mohammed Qaddafi
MADAGASCAR	1960–72	Philibert Tsiranana
(Antananarivo)	1972–75	Gen. Gabriel Ramanantstoa
	1975	Col. Richard Ratsimandrava
	1975	Gen. Gilles Andriamahazo
	1975–93	Lt. Comdr. Didier Ratsiraka
	1993–96	Albert Zafy
	1996–97	Norbert Ratsirahonana
	1997–	Albert Zafy
MALAWI	1964–94	Hastings Kamuzu Banda
(Lilongwe)	1994–	Bakili Muluzi
MALI	1960–68	Modibo Keita
(Bamako)	1968–91	Lt. Moussa Traoré
	1991–92	Lt. Col. Amadou Toumani Touré
	1992–	Alpha Oumar Konaré
MAURITANIA	1960–78	Moktar Ould Daddah
(Nouakchott)	1978–79	Lt. Col. Mustapha Ould Mohammed Salek
	1979	Lt. Col. Ahmed Ould Bouceif
	1979	Lt. Col. Mohammed Khouna Haidalla
	1979–80	Lt. Col. Mohammed Mahmoud Ould Louly
	1980–84	Lt. Col. Mohammed Khouna Haidalla
	1984–	Col. Maaouya Ould Sid'Ahmed Taya
MAURITIUS	1968–82	Seewoosagur Ramgoolam
(Port Louis)	1982–95	Aneerood Jugnauth
	1995–	Navin Ramgoolam

Country	Political Leadership	
MOROCCO	1956–61	King Mohammed V
(Rabat)	1961–	King Hassan II
MOZAMBIQUE	1975–86	Samora Moisés Machel
(Maputo)	1986–	Joaquim Alberto Chissano
NAMIBIA	1990–	Sam Shafiishuna Nujoma
(Windhoek)		
NIGER	1960–74	Hamani Diori
(Niamey)	1974–87	Lt. Col. Seyni Kountché
	1987–91	Col. Ali Saïbou
	1991–93	Amadou Cheiffou
	1993–96	Mahamane Ousmane
	1996-99	Col. Ibrahim Mainassara Baré
	1999–	Commander Daouda Malam Wanke
NIGERIA	1960–66	Alhaji Abubakar Tafawa Belewa
(Abuja)	1966	Gen. Johnson Aguiyi-Ironsi
	1966–75	Lt. Col. Yakabu Gowon
	1975–76	Brig. Gen. Murtala Mohammed
	1976–79	Lt. Gen. Olusegun Obasanjo
	1979–83	Alhaji Shehu Shagari
	1983–85	Maj. Gen. Mohammed Buhari
	1985–93	Maj. Gen. Ibrahim Babangida
	1993	Chief Ernest Adegunle Shonekan
	1993–98	Gen. Sani Abacha
	1998–99	Gen. Abdulsalami Abubakar
	1999–	Olusegun Obasanjo
RWANDA	1962–73	Grégoire Kayibanda
(Kigali)	1973–94	Maj. Gen. Juvénal Habyarimana
	1994	Dr. Théodore Sindikubgabo
	1994–	Pasteur Bizimungu (although Maj. Gen. Paul Kagame holds actual power)
SAO TOME	1975–91	Manuel Pinto da Costa
& PRINCIPE	1991–	Miguel Trovoada
(Sao Tome)		
SENEGAL	1960–80	Léopold Sédar Senghor
(Dakar)	1981–	Abdou Diouf
SEYCHELLES	1976–77	James R. Mancham
(Victoria)	1977–	France Albert René
SIERRA LEONE	1961–64	Milton Margai
(Freetown)	1964–67	Albert Margai
	1967–68	Lt. Col. Andrew Juxon-Smith

Country	Political Leadership	
SIERRA LEONE	1968–85	Siaka Stevens
(Freetown)	1985–92	Maj. Gen. Joseph Saidu Momoh
continued	1992–96	Capt. Valentine E. M. Strasser
	1996	Brig. Gen. Julius Maada Bio
	1996–97	Ahmad Tejan Kabbah
	1997–98	Lt. Col. Johnny Paul Koromah
	1998–	Ahmad Tejan Kabbah
SOMALIA	1960–67	Aden Abdullah Osman Daar
(Mogadishu)	1967–69	Abdirashid Ali Sharmarke
	1969–91	Maj. Gen. Mohamed Siad Barre
	1991–	No central government; territories controlled by individual clan leaders.
SOUTH AFRICA	1994–99	Nelson M. Mandela
(Pretoria)	1999	Thabo Mbeki
SUDAN	1956	Ismail al-Azhari
(Khartoum)	1956–58	Abdullah Khalil
	1958–64	Lt. Gen. Ibrahim Abboud
	1964–65	Sir el-Khatim el-Khalifah
	1965–66	Muhammed Ahmad Mahgoub
	1966–67	Sayed Sadiq el-Mahdi
	1967–69	Muhammed Ahmad Mahgoub
	1969	Abubakr Awadallah
	1969–85	Col. Gaafar Mohammed Nimeiri
	1985–86	Lt. Gen. Abdel Rahman Swar al Dahab
	1986–89	Ahmed Ali el-Mirghani
	1989–	Lt. Gen. Omar Hassan Ahmad al-Bashir
SWAZILAND	1968–82	King Sobhuza II
(Mbabane)	1982–83	Dzeliwe Shongwe
	1983–86	Ntombi Thawala
	1986–	King Mswati III
TANZANIA	1962–85	Julius Nyerere
(Dodoma)	1985–95	Ali Hassan Mwinyi
	1995–	Benjamin Mkapa
TOGO	1960–63	Sylvanus Olympio
(Lome)	1963–67	Nicholas Grunitzky
	1967	Col. Kleber Dadjo
	1967–	Gen. Gnassingbé Eyadéma
TUNISIA	1956–87	Habib Bourguiba
(Tunis)	1987–	Zine El-Abidine Ben Ali

Country	Political Leadership	
UGANDA	1962–71	Apollo Milton Obote
(Kampala)	1971–79	Maj. Gen. Idi Amin
	1979	Yusuf Lule
	1979–80	Godfrey Binaisa
	1980	Paulo Mwanga
	1980–85	Apollo Milton Obote
	1985–86	Lt. Gen. Tito Okello
	1986–	Yoweri Museveni
ZAMBIA	1964–91	Kenneth D. Kaunda
(Lusaka)	1991–	Frederick Chiluba
ZIMBABWE	1980–	Robert Mugabe
(Harare)		

Sources: See Harvey Glickman, ed., *Political Leaders of Contemporary Africa South of the Sahara: A Biographical Dictionary* (Westport: Greenwood, 1992); April A. Gordon and Donald L. Gordon, eds., *Understanding Contemporary Africa,* 2nd ed. (Boulder: Lynne Rienner, 1996); Robert H. Jackson and Carl G. Rosberg, *Personal Rule in Black Africa: Prince, Autocrat, Prophet, Tyrant* (Berkeley: University of California Press, 1982); Mark R. Lipschutz and R. Kent Rasmussen, *Dictionary of African Historical Biography,* 2nd ed. (Berkeley: University of California Press, 1987); and Alan Rake, *Who's Who in Africa: Leaders for the 1990s* (Lanham: Scarecrow, 1992).

Note

1.   Mark R. Lipschutz and R. Kent Rasmussen, *Dictionary of African Historical Biography,* 2nd ed. (Berkeley: University of California Press, 1987), p. 65.

INDEX